TRANSFORMED!

BECOMING
THE EXTRAORDINARY MASTERPIECE
GOD CREATED YOU TO BE

BY
RICHARD FLEW

Richard Flew, Eagles Wings Publishing
Seymours House, Sunnyside Road North
Weston-super-Mare
North Somerset
BS23 3PZ
https://transformationandgrowth.org/

TRANSFORMED!
Richard Flew – 1st edition.
All rights reserved.
EAGLES-WINGS-PUBLISHING
ISBN-13: 978-1-7384938-0-7

CONTENTS

ACKNOWLEDGEMENTS

Thank you to all who unwittingly helped in the creation and development of TRANSFORMED!

To my wife, Audrey, who has put up with me for nearly 50 years. We created a marriage that thrived and lasted.

To our talented and hard-working offspring:

Rachel, David and Peter.

All now in the fullness of their lives and careers, themselves transforming and growing.

My special thanks to the many authors who unknowingly contributed to TRANSFORMED! I am particularly indebted to:

Professor Robert E Quinn; *Margaret Elliott Tracy Collegiate Emeritus Professor in Business Administration; Emeritus Professor of Management and Organisations, University of Michigan.* The core concepts of positive organisations, leadership, and the response of individuals leading change and making a difference are his and his alone. I have noted the idea of the Fundamental State of Leadership and his books, particularly:

Building the Bridge as You Walk on It: A Guide for Leading Change, 1st ed (San Francisco: Jossey-Bass, 2004)[1], and:

The Positive Organization: Breaking Free from Conventional Cultures, Constraints, and Beliefs.[2] Berrett-Koehler Publishers.

"Building The Bridge As You Walk On It" is a key concept throughout TRANSFORMED!

John C. Maxwell; *Pastor, Leadership Expert, Speaker and Author.* Most of the thinking and actions in TRANSFORMED! belong to him, and these are acknowledged here. TRANSFORMED! would not exist in this form without his leadership, wisdom and direction. His many leadership books have been a constant source of inspired action. His citations are numerous and bear testimony to his beneficial influence.

Both the above inspiring leaders have provided an underpinning foundation of spiritual, practical knowledge and understanding over the last decade. I avidly read and digested all the wisdom and direction for personal application in them, along with over two hundred other books.

---

[1] Robert E. Quinn, *Building the Bridge as You Walk on It: A Guide for Leading Change*, 1st ed (San Francisco: Jossey-Bass, 2004).

[2] Robert E. Quinn, *The Positive Organization: Breaking Free from Conventional Cultures, Constraints, and Beliefs*, First Edition (Oakland: Berrett-Koehler Publishers, Inc, 2015).

UNDERSTANDING THE LAYOUT OF THIS HANDBOOK

Whether you use this as a hand-book to help gain insight for transformation and growth or as a workbook, using the steps to climb, please apply it to yourself as you see fit. Listed below are essential Key Helps for the notation and intentionally designed layout as you read:

Custom Symbol Bullet Points Explanation For Use:
- Important List Point
- ❖ Fundamentally Important Reflection Point
- ➢ Breakout Action Point
- ✓ Masterpiece Living Point

Certain Important Words are Capitalised for Understanding
The purpose is that they relate to you, the reader, especially and mentally noted as you read past them. For Example:

❖ **Your Life under God has Unlimited Potential To Become One of The Greatest Stories Ever Told!**

Firstly – this is a Fundamentally Important Reflection Point.
Secondly – it has "Capitalised Words that Relate Specifically to You" as an individual, where you are right now. They are highlighted by capitalisation to indicate to you that the word capitalised is for you specifically. In novels and everyday reading, obviously, they should not be written in this way. These books are different and require a different approach. They are designed:

Book 1 *TRANSFORMED!* – for your Transformation and Growth.
Book 2 *CONNECTED!* – for your Connection with God, your Inspiration, your Response.
Book 3 *FULFILLED!* – ultimately your Action to Fulfilment.

I accept this may not be conventional and may seem strange at first reading. But nothing in our written language conveys the sense of individual-directed meaning, inspiration, response and action that this technique allows. As you read, your mind will separate instinctively, usually capitalised words such as titles, names, and proper nouns. The rest is for your personalised understanding and action.

Custom Lists Explanation For Use:

Making the Shift to Thinking Differently is *TRANSFORMED!* I have written some long lists as part of this book. The lists are intended to help you understand the "Big-Picture" aspects of this book. They are not designed for prose reading. Instead, they are designed for the effects, as shown below:

- ❖ **Big-picture Grasping, God-honouring and Understanding His Thinking Lists.**
    - ❖ Enabling "seeing the whole of the concept lists" with a starting title.
    - ❖ Allowing an eye-scanning overview at a glance.

- ❖ **With bold text chunks as handles to doors that open to greater focus on a vital area.**
    - ❖ Each list point is an individual world of deep personal reflection.
    - ❖ Each list point is foundational to understanding.

- ❖ **Each list point is vital to your transformation and growth action "Mindset".**
    - ❖ Each list point, if genuinely accepted, will act to propel you forwards every day.
    - ❖ You can Choose to Live on the Other Side of Yes! or not.

- ❖ **All are Choices.**

As the short list above demonstrates, they are designed for big-picture-grasping, whole-concept visualisation, and overall picture scanning, giving you distinct worlds of personal reflection. The bold text chunks are door handles to hold and open, with offset sub-points that are no less important but offset to allow individual reflection and understanding. If I had continued the prose in this manner, these vital concepts would have been lost in the dense wording and sentences.

PREFACE

Why Was TRANSFORMED! Written?

Ephesians 2:10 NLT: "For we are God's masterpiece. He has created us anew in Christ Jesus, so we can do the good things he planned for us long ago."

Romans 12:1-2 NIV: "Therefore, I urge you, brothers and sisters, in view of God's mercy, to offer your bodies as a living sacrifice, holy and pleasing to God – this is your true and proper worship. Do not conform to the pattern of this world, but be transformed by the renewing of your mind. Then you will be able to test and approve what God's will is – his good, pleasing and perfect will."

~~~

Has anyone ever told you that you are God's Unique Masterpiece? That you were created utterly unique in all time and eternity? Wholly unique in the gifts, talents, and Potential that God placed in you before you were born? No?

Well, now is the time to understand and accept these profound truths! It started for me with a growing conviction that I was "not where I am meant to be in life". Furthermore that there were more talents and Potential inside me than I had ever realised. I had not the least suspicion of my abilities. Then came the stunning lesson from scripture, God's Word, that as a unique human being, I already had placed within me unique unlimited Potential and Purpose that was crying out to be unlocked and used to make a difference for others in this world.

I wrote this book with a background of experience of nearly seven decades of life – with all its ups and downs. I wrote it because although many, many other books by brilliant and experienced highly educated people did exist, this one did not!

It is written with a backdrop of five decades of faith in Christ, albeit much of it lukewarm, lacking in understanding, and dangerously accepting the culture of my times. Our perceptions can be cruel deceivers and crushers of Potential. Our cultures can and almost always imprison human Potential unless it is deliberately supportive of your endeavours.

This book is written with the enlightening words from Romans 12, vv1-2 above. These verses helped to wake me from complacency, mediocrity and the fatal acceptance that "this is all that there is to this life". It is written with the delightful and life-changing understanding that there is more Potential in you and me than we can ever think possible, the unlimited Potential of the hidden, unique and special gifts God placed in us at birth.

If you have a history (and most of us do have that sort of history) of the experience of hurt, feelings of inadequacy, failure at many levels, and low self-esteem, and if you have the smallest suspicion that you are "not where you are meant to be", then welcome because *TRANSFORMED!* was written for You! It is not written from a position of extensive leadership experience, ordained ministry management, or understanding of traditional theology but written from the profound depths of my own spiritual experience.

Oddly, and yet significantly, I have no experience whatsoever of traditional qualifications to write this book. What I have been given is a burning desire within me to unlock God's Potential and Purpose already existing within every one of Us. A burning birthed in the failure, injustice, inadequacy and hurts of the past, but also birthed in the brilliant writing in Romans 12, vv1-2 that transformation is possible, transformation is necessary, and transformation is God's Purpose for both you and me.

It is written from the realisation that God created me uniquely for Himself and that transformation and growth are what He intends, His abundance and surplus are available, and growth is the vehicle He plans to use to bring us closer to Him.

It is written with the profound belief that we are created to learn and grow to do what we may not have done before and that this transformation and growth is healthy and normal. You see, like many who will read this book:

I needed simplicity of understanding,

I needed a map for the higher path ahead and, crucially,

I needed a set of steps to walk one at a time.

I needed the simplicity of Awaken, Unlock, Act to grasp in three words what *TRANSFORMED!* is all about.

But be warned, this journey never ends, and it is all uphill.

I also needed a breath-taking vista of the destination, a long-term focus for this journey. I needed that vision to undertake this journey. But it is more than that: I am called to take this journey because I was created for this, and this is God's Purpose and Destiny for me.

God created us with unique, Unlimited Potential, with talent and abilities to be discovered and used. He created us with His gifts already placed within us at birth for His Glory and the Good of Others. He created us for a close relationship with Him. He created us with His Purpose and Destiny within us:

❖ Destiny for me is – *both Now and Our Destination*! Not just tomorrow, not only in the future, not just at some vague, unknowable time beyond our comprehension, not just beyond our lifetime, not just a beguiling nostalgia, not just a distant, misty shore far away;

❖ Destiny for me is – right here and now, literally this present *moment*, in my relationship with the Living God, the God and Father of Our Lord Jesus Christ;

❖ Destiny, for me, is – the *immanent* Presence of God. He is my Destination;[3]

❖ Destiny for me is, as described in Jeremiah 29:11 NIV, *"For I know the plans I have for you," declares the Lord, "plans to prosper you and not to harm you, plans to give you hope and a future";*

❖ Destiny for me is – *knowing* why God created me and what He created me for.

These, indeed, are the truths of God's Destiny for you and me. Superficially, they read as happy and blessed thoughts but do not underestimate God's Word. They are the most serious declaration of intent for every individual on this earth who seeks God with all their heart and is wholeheartedly committed to Him. Brilliantly, the scriptures tell for all who will believe by seeking His Forgiveness through Faith in Jesus Christ:

❖ The Lord *deliberately* forgets my past;

❖ The Lord *is* my present;

❖ The Lord *plans* my future;

❖ His Destiny for me is *Himself;*

❖ Nothing less.

❖ This is Your Destiny if You Choose.

~~~

---

[3] Immanent is the "indwelling" of God in ourselves.

THIS EXPLANATION IS WRITTEN FOR YOU

(copied from TRANSFORMED!)

Now, remembering what you have just read above, I hope that may have induced positive, uplifting, energising, and transformative thoughts within you. If you can, use them positively to be the force for God that He intends them to be, for He is the God of Abundance and Surplus.

But I realise that many of us may be far from this and much less positive. You may be pushing through the fog of current bad experiences, failure, and less-than-good feelings about the present.

Can I suggest you try this: channel and funnel your real pain from your past and present – all your imagined failure, all your imagined inadequacy, into a secure storage area within your mind. This might take some practice to achieve. I funnel mine into a hidden locker called "negative influences and hurtful comments" (disregarding them and refusing to respond), and I chain them up and store them in their secure storage, ready to be brought out and used for God's Higher Purpose. They will be used to motivate me, to refresh my Calling and for me to write as if my life was at stake for those who will yet break out and transform and grow!

So, for you, just as you are in your present state, whatever that might be, I will:

✓ Write for those unable to articulate their heart's yearnings.

✓ Write for those in their own prisons but who somehow miraculously found this book – it is for you, your unleashing, your unlocking, and the discovery of Your Purpose under God.

✓ Write for those in prison, that they may unlock themselves to be freer than their captors.

✓ Write for those feeling dispossessed from life in heart and mind.

✓ Write for those who feel their lives are pointless.

✓ Write for those who feel their lives have no meaning.

✓ Write for those people who are disregarded and wasted in their work.

✓ Write for those who are bullied and harassed, and made to feel as nothing by those who are transactional, using them for their own purposes only.

✓ Write for those who have no voice, but whose voice can and must be heard, because they will be strengthened to break out even while in their intolerable situation.

✓ Write for those crying out to be led for their lives to have meaning and to make a difference.

✓ Write for those who have unused, unique, unlimited Potential within them, and who cry out to be released to make a difference – this book is for you.

✓ Write for those who long and yearn to have their unique, unlimited potential unlocked and released to the world as God always intended.

4

✓ Write for those whose years the locusts have laid waste.

✓ Write so those wasted years may be offered back to God.

✓ Write to enable those who passed through their pain and those wasted times to offer those years back to God because He brought them through to Himself.

✓ Write for those who mourn their unfulfilled lives, that they may Awaken for the God of Abundance Who Created Them for Himself.

✓ Write for those who mourn their unfulfilled lives that they may Unlock their Unique, Unlimited Potential for God, and discover God's Calling for their lives.

✓ Write for those who mourn their unfulfilled lives, that they may Act *to lead Others to Live their fulfilled lives Fully.*

✓ Write for the captives to be set free to serve the Living God as He intended.

✓ Write to help those who read this to be Transformed and Grow to Become the People God Always Created Them to Be.

✓ Write to help those who read this to Unlock their Unique Unlimited Potential and Discover their Purpose and the Purpose for which God Created them.

✓ Write to help those who read this book to Awaken, Unlock, and Act so that Others will Understand and respond as they will to the God Who Created them.

✓ Write so that Others will Fulfil God's Purposes in the days that He gave them on this earth.

And the memories? The hateful comments? The bullying and negative experiences and those toxic thoughts that haunted me? Ah! Yes, all those past thoughts that I chained up – they will all be brought out from their secure storage.

They will not be unused; the pain and the wasted years will not have been in vain.

They will all be burnt in the fire of my awakening, my unlocking, and my actioning, and used to feed the flames of my wholehearted Commitment to my Creator God and His People.

And then I will write as if my life and the Lives of Others (you particularly) depended on it. I will write so that Others, being valued and having value added to them at birth, can also be Transformed and Grow, becoming the people God always created them to be and know the closeness of their Creator and His Son, Jesus Christ.

You see, I realised I had a choice to make. Either to stay where I was – post-trauma – or to Awaken, Unlock and Act, Choosing to Make a Difference for God where I was, with what I had, in the time that I had, with the life I was given.

Only I could make that Choice. You must decide for Yourself.

It is about courage and the freedom to decide – the courage to break out every day for God and the freedom to choose to make a difference for His Glory.

Thus was *TRANSFORMED!* conceived, and born.

Welcome to *TRANSFORMED!*

The exclamation mark is intentional
because this is God's Perfect Plan for Us both
as His Extraordinary Created Masterpieces.

❖   You are Created and Called by God as His
Extraordinary Masterpiece for Himself and Others!
(This is Your "WHO?" And "WHY?"
What Might Be Your Response Now That You Know That Truth?)

❖   You are Created and Called by God to "LIVE"
an Extraordinary LIFE, Your Best Life,
of Transformation and Growth!
(But it is Your Choice – Don't waste Opportunities
for Your Transformation and Growth.)

❖   You are Created by God a Completely
Unique Human Being in all History, Time, and Eternity!
(No one can take that away from You except You.)

❖   You are Destined by God to "LIVE" an
Extraordinary LIFE, Your Best Life, of Significance and Purpose!
(No one can take Your Place,
Replace or Stop You from Fulfilling Your Purpose,
except for Your Choice Not to.)

❖   *You are Designed by God to "LIVE" an Extraordinary LIFE, Your*
Best Life, with Mindsets
of Intentionality, Growth, Significance,
Potential, Meaning and Abundance!
(No one ever wanted anything less!)

❖   You are Designed by God to "LIVE" an Extraordinary LIFE, Your
Best Life of Greatness for God and Others!
(This is absolutely true, and it is not about You, but about Others.)

❖ **You are Designed by God to "LIVE" an Extraordinary LIFE, His Planned Best Life for You of God's Transcendent Higher Purpose!**
(Discover that Unique Authentic Higher Purpose for Yourself.)

❖ **Your Life under God has Unlimited Potential To Become One of The Greatest Stories Ever Told!**
(Don't waste it Because Only You can Write it.)

❖ **You are Created and Called by God as His Extraordinary Masterpiece to Live a Life of Greatness for Himself and Others!**
(You cannot stay where You think you are; You need to start on the road to where You are Meant to Be.)

~ ~ ~

It will require All Your Strength, Your Mind, Your Heart, Your Focus, Your Unlimited Potential, Your Commitment, Your Contribution, Your Action, Your Service and Your Sacrifice both for God Who Created You and for Others.

If You can understand and accept these truths, then the only question worth asking is, "What might be Your Unlimited Potential?" And then, "What might be Your Unlimited Potential to Grow for God and Your Unlimited Potential to Grow and Impact Others?" And then again, "If God created me as His Extraordinary Masterpiece, am I not destined to be His Masterpiece for Him and also for Others?"

Ultimately, we must all answer the question: "Am I fulfilling God's Purposes for Myself, Living a Life of Greatness for Him and for Others in My Generation?"

I can affirm that God intends you to be His Extraordinary Masterpiece. I sincerely hope that *TRANSFORMED!* will challenge you as you have never been challenged before to become the unique person God created you to be and live your Best Life of God's Transcendent Higher Purpose.

Welcome to* TRANSFORMED! *and Start the Daily Breakout to Become the Extraordinary Masterpiece God Created You to Be. For His Glory and Others.

> **A Handbook for Your Transformation and Growth**
> *(as God intended for your life)*
>> **A Handbook for the Totally Committed**
>> *(however inadequate or broken you may feel!)*
>> **A Handbook for Wholehearted Action**
>> *(wherever you are starting from)*
>> **A Handbook for Greatness for God**
> *(the seeds of greatness for God are already within you)*
>> **With Potential, Purpose and Passion**
>> *(your life that truly matters)*
>> **Called For God's Higher Purpose**
>> *(your life of contribution)*
>> **To Live for His Glory**
>> *(your life of intentionality)*
>> **To Make A Difference For Others**

~~~

Growing To Become The
Extraordinary Masterpiece God Created You To Be
Unlocking The Unlimited Potential You Never Imagined You Had
Climbing To Where You Are Meant To Be
With Total Commitment to God
Intentionally Living Your
Best Life For Him
And For Others
Every Day

~~~

God's Transcendent Higher Purpose is that we should be Transformed!
TRANSFORMED! *is God's Higher Purpose for Us.*
It is Overwhelming and Unending;
It is Life-Affirming, and it is God's Perfect Plan for You.
It is Our Best Life of God's Higher Purpose Enabling,
Starting with Ourselves, Then the Unlocking and Releasing of Others.
All for the praise of His Glory.

INTRODUCTION
A Handbook for Action

TRANSFORMED! – THE DREAM
This is My Dream to develop God-Created Significance in Others:
That every Living Person on this planet, through Faith in Jesus Christ,
would be Enabled to Realise, Be Transformed, Unlocking their God-
Created Potential in Themselves and Others and Take their God-enabled
Opportunities to Grow, Living their Best Lives to Become the
Extraordinary Masterpieces God Actually
Planned and Created Them to Be:

- ➢ *To Unlock their Unique Unlimited Potential.*
- ➢ *To Grow their Seeds of Greatness for God.*
- ➢ *To Discover their God-Given Purpose.*
- ➢ *To Live out God's Transcendent Higher Purpose.*
- ➢ *Living a Life of Intentionality for God.*
- ➢ *Living a Life of Significance for God.*
- ➢ *Living a Life of Contribution for God.*
- ➢ *Living a Life that Matters for God.*
- ➢ *Living a Life to Make a Difference For Others.*

~~~

A dream full of Hope, Potential, Purpose,
Possibilities, Vision, and Destiny.

~~~

For God, People Matter.
I want to help readers to understand this fact
and then see themselves Unlocked and Unleashed
to go and do something about it. For Others.

Why TRANSFORMED!?

TRANSFORMED! is written for people like you. It is written for people who may not yet exist, by which I mean that you may have yet to discover that God created you to be His transformed and growing people, just like His Son, Jesus Christ. It is written for people like you who continually ask the question: "There must be more to life than this?" Whatever you imagine your "this" to be. It is written for someone like you who has always wanted to live a life of Significance that Matters. It is written for someone like you who yearns to be valued, who longs to live a life of contribution, who feels you have so much more to give than even you suspect, but for some reason, has never been offered those opportunities. Hopefully, the preface stimulated your thinking that there is, and always was, planned to be more to life than the mediocrity our contemporary culture imposes on us. You are not alone! Over 50 years ago, as a young man, I felt like you and asked the same question. I have belatedly realised we all have that in-built desire to matter and live meaningful lives, to live Our Best Lives. God created us as individuals to share those desires: they are essential and good desires.

But one of the most fundamental discoveries I have also made is that God created us to live Our Best Life at His Transcendent Higher Level – the life He always planned for you to live. Now, this is not what you might imagine at first sight. Immediately, you may think of hierarchy, spiritual maturity (whatever that might mean), one-upmanship, being better than others, competing with others for scarce resources and so on. It is not. It is primarily about personal transformation and growth. One of the most profound statements I have discovered recently is the following quotation.[4]

> *Dr. Stephen Covey wrote in his final book,*
> *The Eighth Habit (I paraphrase):*
> *"Those who develop a vision of great things, who suspect there may be more to themselves than they realised, who take the initiative and tap in to higher motivations, these people find and use their voice, and choose to influence and inspire others to do the same.*
> *It is the birth right of the human family."*

These extraordinary comments touched a chord in my heart in a way that few

---

[4] Covey, pp. 27–28.

passages of text have ever managed. I hope it does for you as well and that it kick-starts the questioning and seeking process that will see you set free to be transformed to become the person you were created, designed and meant to be. A person full of Hope, Growth, Potential, Purpose, Fulfilment, Connecting with Others, and yes, Happiness. Dr Covey's comment about "suspecting there may be more to ourselves than we realise" is a key to our understanding of the Unlimited Potential that lies within every human being. Besides, there is another vitally important facet of growth that is part and parcel of this bigger jigsaw. It was something that, although I thought necessary, I could not 'see' because of my slow thinking, something that is common to us all. That facet is real growth, **Personal Growth**, Intentional Personal Growth, and undertaken at such a level and reality that it may have escaped you in the past and even now may be unknown. Dr Covey spoke of "initiative, higher motivations, greatness, contribution, influence and potential". All remarkable and essential Growth concepts that you will discover for yourself later.

> *"You have the fingerprints of God all over you."*
> *Joel Osteen, Next Level Thinking*

(The above quotation cited in the footnote below.[5])

Growing to Live Your Best Life and Become the Extraordinary Masterpiece You Were Created to Be by God is all about Your Story, Your Awakening, Your Potential, Your Purpose, Your Calling, and Your Destiny for God and Others. It is an Astounding and Extraordinary story if You Choose. So, I excitedly invite you to Choose and Start Your Journey of Transformation.

The foundation of *TRANSFORMED!* is that we are not where we are meant to be. If we are not where we are meant to be, then, despite being blindingly obvious, we are not where we are meant to be. If true for you and me, the implications of that statement are utterly earth-shattering, life-shaking, culture-overturning, and potentially mind-transforming as we reflect on those implications. We are not talking about careers, jobs, or money (or lack of it), but about the "huge elephant in the room" of "Why?" we are here, "Who created us and Why?"

God created you and me to live Our Best Lives as His Extraordinary Masterpieces for His Higher Purpose. His Higher Purpose is not creating just a

---

[5] Joel Osteen, *Next Level Thinking: 10 Powerful Thoughts for a Successful and Abundant Life,* First edition (New York: FaithWords, 2018), p. 37.

freedom from life or difficulties but a *freedom to* be fully engaged in something greater than ourselves. Indeed, others have added that with that freedom, there comes an *obligation* to. Freedom to *Love Him with all our heart,* freedom to *Live a Life of Connection with Him* and freedom to live a *Life of Contribution for Others* through the example of the servant leadership of Christ. Therefore, the correct assumption is that unless we have discovered God's purposes for us and are intentionally living to be Transformed and Growing, then that is why we are not where we are meant to be, and not being transformed or growing, just living a life of mediocrity. But if you and I know we are <u>not</u> where we are meant to be, we can very quickly start the total transformation and journey to where we <u>are</u> meant to be. That is our Daily choice, the road to Greatness and Significance for God.

For most of us, modern life is simply a constant game of distraction by all that we experience (desperately seeking the *freedom from*) until we fall exhausted by our efforts into bed. We repeat the same stupid process the next day. We live on the false assumption that everything is 'fine' (with never enough time to stop and ask big, awkward questions about why we are here, who created us and what we are designed to do!) and 'fine' simply because it is 'normal' and no one has encouraged us to think differently.

Until now.

However, it won't be easy.

And this situation is the default one by which we live. So that's all there is, isn't there? That's it? We live to, at best, acquire and survive? That's all we have to get out of bed for?

As a young man, I vividly remember one day thinking out loud, "There must be more to life than this?"

Or is there another, better, overwhelmingly simple, and yet brilliantly wonderful way? Well, there is! This book attempts to blow open the secret that Jesus Christ intended, but unfortunately, it has been hidden by the traditional church for nearly two millennia. I kid you not! Until now.

You see, Friends, we have a Daily Choice of personal agency to make. Only you can make that choice. A Daily Choice either to step out in a God-honouring direction as we unlock our unlimited Potential, discover our Purpose, unlock Potential in others, and fulfil our Destiny. Or, we can choose to stay where we are and remain inward-focussed, irrelevant, purposeless, confined by our culture and constrained by our mediocrity-based status quo.

> *"Everyone chooses one of two roads in life:*
> *The old and the young, the rich and the poor, men and women alike.*
> *One is the broad, well-travelled road to mediocrity, the other the*
> *road to greatness and meaning. The range of possibilities that exists*
> *within each of these two destinations is as wide as the diversity of*
> *gifts and personalities in the human family. But the contrast*
> *between the two destinations is as night is to the day. The path to*
> *mediocrity straitjackets human potential. The path to greatness*
> *unleashes and realizes human potential."*
> *Dr. Stephen Covey, The Eighth Habit*

(Above quotation cited in footnote below.[6])

Dr Covey's quote states that you can choose the "normal" life of mediocrity and stay as you are, or you can choose to live a "life of greatness and contribution."

His earlier use of the term "voice" is essential to understand. He means your "Unique Personal Significance". This choice of road is achievable through a Mindset of daily growth. This growth inspires a lifetime of uplifting transformation to become the Extraordinary Masterpiece God created you to be. And this is what the apostle Paul refers to in Romans ch.12, vv1-2,

Romans 12:1-2 NIV, "Therefore, I urge you, brothers and sisters, in view of God's mercy, to offer your bodies as a living sacrifice, holy and pleasing to God – this is your true and proper worship. Do not conform to the pattern of this world, but be transformed by the renewing of your mind. Then you will be able to test and approve what God's will is – his good, pleasing and perfect will."

It is all about being set free by believing God's Truths in Scripture and spoken by Jesus Christ so that we *can* be set free. Set free by believing His Word, putting our faith in Christ, and starting the transformation process to become the new person God calls us to be. Transformation and Growth are central to all this. This is our "Why?" I seek to induce in the reader the need to "Breakout" to Awake, to Unlock, and to Act. The need to Breakout from imprisoning culture, thinking and actions. It needs long-term commitment and intentionality, a simple methodology that works for each of us. A "Breakout" from "where we are", growing to "where we are meant to be", "Growing to Become the Extraordinary Masterpiece God Created Us To Be".

---

[6] Covey, pp. 27–28.

> *"Within every individual there is potential*
> *that will never be discovered outside God's purpose."*
> **Erwin McManus**

(Above quotation cited in footnote below. [7])

Don't Take My Word for It!

St. Paul also wrote about these truths in his letter to the Ephesians 2:10 NIV, "For we are God's handiwork, created in Christ Jesus to do good works, which God prepared in advance for us to do." And all while growing to live our Best Lives and become the extraordinary masterpieces God created us to be.

As Dr Carol Dweck wrote in her brilliant and mind-blowing book, *Mindset: Changing the Way You Think to Fulfil Your Potential:* "the growth Mindset lets people—even those who are targets of negative labels—use and develop their minds fully. Their heads are not filled with limiting thoughts, a fragile sense of belonging, and a belief that other people can define them." [8]

Dr Dweck continues:

For thirty years, my research has shown that the view you adopt for yourself profoundly affects the way you lead your life. It can determine whether you become the person you want to be and whether you accomplish the things you value. How does this happen? How can a simple belief have the power to transform your psychology and, as a result, your life? Believing that your qualities are carved in stone—the fixed Mindset—creates an urgency to prove yourself over and over. If you have only a certain amount of intelligence, a certain personality, and a certain moral character— well, then you'd better prove that you have a healthy dose of them. It simply wouldn't do to look or feel deficient in these most basic characteristics.

There's another Mindset in which these traits are not simply a hand you're dealt and have to live with, always trying to convince yourself and others that you have a royal flush when you're secretly worried it's a pair of tens. In this Mindset, the hand you're dealt is just the starting point for development. This Growth Mindset is based on the belief that your basic qualities are things you can cultivate through your efforts, your strategies, and help from others. Although people may differ in every which way—in

[7] Erwin Raphael McManus, *Seizing Your Divine Moment: Dare to Live a Life of Adventure* (Nashville, Tenn: Thomas Nelson Publishers, 2002), pt. 3193.
[8] Carol S Dweck, *Mindset: Changing the Way You Think to Fulfil Your Potential*, 2017, p. 80.

their initial talents and aptitudes, interests, or temperaments—everyone can change and grow through application and experience.

The passion for stretching yourself and sticking to it, even (or especially) when it's not going well, is the hallmark of the Growth Mindset. This is the Mindset that allows people to thrive during some of the most challenging times in their lives. [9]

Extensive quotes but essential in kick-starting our minds to start out on the road to "where we are meant to be".

What *TRANSFORMED!* seeks to achieve is inspire, challenge and direct you to action in order to help you break out to become transformed as God always intended, to give you a route map forward from now, to provide you with some handles to grip on to, a runway for you to take off. These are founded on God's truths and seek to launch us all beyond escape velocity to God's Transcendent Higher Purpose. The pursuit and meaning of every human being on this planet is about Higher Purpose, living a life of significance that matters. For those who have faith in God through Jesus Christ, this means God's Higher Purpose for them: its realisation, its discovery, its Potential, its capacity, its results. Everything else is a sideshow and a distraction from our Higher Purpose.

The burning question is, therefore, "How are you and me to transform our lives so that we can live our Best Lives and achieve God's Higher Purpose for our lives?" Or even simpler, "How do We Grow to Become the Masterpiece God Created Us to Be?" Well, read on!

Someone has said, "We are all born geniuses – but by the time we are adults, 99.99% of us are de-geniused." Becoming an "adult" must only be our starting point for continuous adult transformation and growth. Therefore, this is not the normal point at which we should stop, but the gateway to the real life of transformation and growth we are created for.

Remember the dream at the beginning? Unlocking Potential in Others? Now, hold that dream in your mind, my dear reader, as you start unlocking Potential in yourself, beginning the inspired breakout to transformation. You are on the cusp of your extraordinary transformation to whom God intends you to become. You can remind yourself of the following:

- ❖ I am Created and Called by God to Breakout, Daily, to a Life of Higher Purpose, to Live MY Best Life for Others
- ❖ I am Created and Called by God to Love Him with all My Heart and Others, as myself
- ❖ I am Created and Called by God to Grow the Seeds of Greatness already within me

---

[9] Dweck, pp. 6-7.

❖ I am Created and Called by God to Make a Difference for Others
❖ I am Created and Called by God to Live a Life that Truly Matters for Others
❖ I am Created and Called by God to Live a Life of Intentionality for Others
❖ I am Created and Called by God to Live a Life of Significance for Others
❖ I am Created and Called by God to Live a Life of Contribution for Others
❖ I am Created and Called by God to Seize Opportunities to Value Others
❖ I am Created and Called by God to Fulfil and stretch out my Potential for Others
❖ I am Created and Called by God to Live with a New Mindset of Transformation and Growth, Daily
❖ I am Created and Called by God to Understand His Purposes
❖ I am Created and Called by God to Be fully Engaged For, and Continually Renewed in Him for Others
❖ I am Created and Created and Called by God to, Daily, be Renewed and Transformed for Others
❖ I am Created and Called Simply to Make a Difference for Others

This is not about me, and although we are focussed on You right now, it is not about You per se, but about our Fulfilled Lives of God's Transcendent Higher Purpose, making the Daily Decision to Breakout For Others. What We Are All Called to "Do" is "To Be Transformed" and Awaken! Choosing Daily to Intentionally Breakout! This is the Process, "By The Renewing of Your Minds", Romans 12:2 NIV, "Do not conform to the pattern of this world, but be transformed by the renewing of your mind. Then you will be able to test and approve what God's will is – his good, pleasing and perfect will."

Despite the imperfect manifestations of Christian actions, thought, and beliefs over two millennia, God's Word, the Bible, has not changed. God's Word will never change. William Tyndale was not wrong in attempting his translations, and millions who have read the scriptures have benefited both in temporal and eternal senses, myself amongst them.

For me, after fifty years of "Churchianity" (interestingly, my auto word replacement presciently suggested "church inanity"!), what has become clear to me is that we cannot go on as we are. We have reached and gone past years ago the point of irrelevance to post-Christian Western society. The Reformation was the most momentous time of change in the two millennia since the time of Christ. But now, as then, a time of overwhelming change for the better is necessary. This is the Transformation. Your Transformation!

It is a time when new generations will break out from current religious thinking and cultures that have clearly run their course and are no longer relevant. Rather like the causes and effects of the Reformation's biblical impacts, what is needed is a new return to scriptural truths that will galvanise and transform our thinking literally back to the thoughts, intentions, and actions of Christ. This can only be rediscovered as we become like Him in our entire thinking and actions. This is why I describe the challenges before us as Breakouts. Because there is work to be done, Potential to be unlocked, Purpose to be discovered, and only the committed will win through to take their prize.

50 (Daily) BREAKOUTS! – The Start!

➢ **Breakout! to be Inspired!**
  ➢ Breakout! from Where You Think Are
  ➢ Breakout! to understand Who Created You
  ➢ Breakout! to understand Why You Are Created
  ➢ Breakout! to understand Who You Are Created To Be
  ➢ Breakout! to understand You are God's Extraordinary Masterpiece

➢ **Breakout! to Where You Are Meant To Be**
  ➢ Breakout! from Your False Assumptions
  ➢ Breakout! to Awaken!
  ➢ Breakout! to Challenge those False Assumptions
  ➢ Breakout! to break free from your current thinking
  ➢ Breakout! from your narrative of failure Mindset
  ➢ Breakout! from your narrative of inadequacy Mindset
  ➢ Breakout! from your narrative of unworthiness Mindset
  ➢ Breakout! from your narrative of pointlessness Mindset
  ➢ Breakout! to Focussed Thinking
  ➢ Breakout! to Full Awareness through Critical Thinking

➢ **Breakout! to Live Your Best Life**
  ➢ Breakout! to Full Commitment to God
  ➢ Breakout! to God's Calling for You
  ➢ Breakout! to a Life of Contribution
  ➢ Breakout! to a Life that Matters

➢ **Breakout! to Your Transformation and Growth**
  ➢ Breakout! to Intentionality and Integrity Living to Make a Difference
  ➢ Breakout! to Significance and Meaning Living to Make a Difference
  ➢ Breakout! to Anticipation and Urgency Living to Make a Difference
  ➢ Breakout! to Abundance and Surplus Living to Make a Difference
  ➢ Breakout! to Focus and Commitment Living to Make a Difference
  ➢ Breakout! to Action and Opportunities Living to Make a Difference

➢ **Breakout! to AWAKE! To LIVE Your Best Life for God**
  ➢ Breakout! to Awareness of Your Best Life

➢ Breakout! to Develop Your Life

➢ Breakout! to Think over Your Best Life

➢ **Breakout! to UNLOCK! Potential for Your Best Life for God**

  ➢ Breakout! to God's Calling Mindset

  ➢ Breakout! to Breakout to Live Your Best Life Mindset

  ➢ Breakout! to Grow Your Best Life Mindset

➢ **Breakout! to ACT! Contributing For Others to Live Their Best Lives**

  ➢ Breakout! to Engage Others in their Best Lives Mindset

  ➢ Breakout! to Lead Others to their Best Lives Mindset

  ➢ Breakout! to Rally Others to their Best Lives Mindset

  ➢ Breakout! to Legacy Others to their Best Life Legacy Mindset

  ➢ Breakout! to the fundamental state of leadership [10] for God

➢ **Breakout! to live the other side of "Yes!"**

  ➢ Breakout! to Break Through!

  ➢ Breakout! to a renewed focus on God

  ➢ Breakout! to a renewed seeking of God

  ➢ Breakout! to a greater desiring of God

  ➢ Breakout! to greater uplift and direction of heart and life, Daily

  ➢ Breakout! to greater hopefulness and Purpose of heart and life, Daily

These Breakouts will enable You to Break Through to become the Extraordinary Masterpiece God created you to be; Breaking free from what you think you know, your self-limiting "certainties"; Breaking free from your culture, which is "metaphorically killing/inhibiting/preventing" you from reaching your Potential; And stopping you from becoming the person God always planned for you to be.

As I read the scriptures about Jesus Christ, I cannot but see Him seeking to break through His Disciples' fixed Mindsets and encourage them through faith in Him to Make a Difference in Others. He is setting them free not only <u>from</u> their separation from God by faith in Him but free <u>to be reconnected truly</u> with their Creator, Who only ever wanted to be fully connected with them and through them to Others. This indeed is Your Breakout that God intends You to Undertake, <u>A Breakout! Only You Can Undertake.</u>

  ➢ A Breakout! by Awaking, Unlocking and Acting

---

[10] Ryan Quinn and Robert Quinn, *Lift, 2ⁿᵈ Edition*, 2015.

> ➤ A Breakout! that Expects Your Wholehearted Commitment to God
> ➤ A Breakout! that will only Succeed by Building the Bridge as You Walk on it

It's all about HOPE that today and tomorrow will be better through transformation and growth. And it's all about your CHOICE and the discovery that you will become what you CHOOSE.

TRANSFORMED! is all about Hope, Choice, Unlimited Unlocked Potential, Higher Purpose, Living a Life of Significance and Making a Difference. The outline of the process is:
> ➤ Wake up - Being Awake
> ➤ Switch On - Being Switched On
> ➤ Unlock - Unlocking Potential
> ➤ Breakout - Preparing for Opportunities
> ➤ Act - Seizing Opportunities

This is the Releasing/Unleashing Cycle that many/most of us need to go through every morning/day (but this is OK) to get to the point where we can then act: Intentionally, Anticipating and Planning to Contribute, Planning acts of Significance for Others, to make a Difference for Others today. Because we only have Today.

Decades of status quo Mindsets have so deadened our thinking and effectively disabled our God-given capabilities that we need, at least in the short term, a methodology for quick success that will encourage us onwards. That's also OK. Because being awake, switched on, unlocked, breaking out, and acting will, with practice, become the "new/originally intended normal". This will enable intentionality, anticipating and planning to be significant for others, becoming central to all that we think, all that we are, and all that God always intended us to be.

In his recently published book, *The Economics of Higher Purpose*, Professor Bob Quinn states: "Leadership requires you to adopt the positive Mindset and have the ability to imagine and create what may be outside the current culture. When you find an authentic higher purpose, you acquire new feelings and thoughts. When you articulate and embrace a higher purpose, you enter a new life path."[11]

This is vital to understand. Because where you are going, no one has ever

---

[11] Robert E Quinn and Anjan V Thakor, *The Economics of Higher Purpose: Eight Counterintuitive Steps for Creating a Purpose-Driven Organization*, 2019, pt. 633.

been before, no one else can, and no one knows the path, simply because your extraordinary uniqueness as created by God is just that – unique. But you are already stepping outside your birth culture, armed only with a growing conviction that you are "not where you are meant to be". You are starting to understand what others cannot and may never understand. You are creating a new culture with new mindsets that God always planned for you to reach, enjoy and Live Your Best Life, fulfil His purposes, and impact Others uniquely.

A NOTE ABOUT CONTENTS

A Positive Path To Opportunities, Possibilities And Progress

The heart of *TRANSFORMED!* is to embrace God in your present, Daily, Today, and every day, to Live Your Best Life of God's Higher Purpose. It is about being transformed by the renewal of your minds and empowered with inner strength through His Spirit. It is about being made complete with all the fullness of life and power that comes from God, that God always planned for you to have. Jesus Christ is God's Extraordinary Masterpiece, and is our example. We are designed and created to become like Him and Grow To Become The Extraordinary Masterpiece God Created Us To Be.

You are of Extraordinary Value to the One Who Created You. God has already placed within you Your Unique Personal Significance abilities and capacities that we can describe as your Greatness. All it needs is to be drawn out from within you, where it has been hidden since birth.

TRANSFORMED! is that process – the discovery of Potential, Purpose and Destiny, creating Hope that tomorrow can be better through Intentional Transformation and Growth. The contents of Your Best Life of God's Higher Purpose are deliberately multi-layered and multi-directional. They are described as being "dynamic", as steps, Mindsets, levels, callings, decisions, breakouts, thinkings, keys, commitments, directions, dynamic actions, and essentials or simple understandable chapter headings that encourage a linear pathway solely for clarity of thought. I have also introduced concepts of flight in a metaphor for the three primary levels or sections. Starting notably with intensive pilot training and preparations, secondly, pre-flight checks and testing of upgraded avionics, then, thirdly, the notion of take-off to high-altitude supersonic flight being the desired result, "Where We Are Meant To Be". Which is where God always Planned For You To Be!

None of this just happens. A God-focussed-thinking heart and mind becoming saturated with Scripture are prerequisite foundations. You don't have to try to be perfect or show off with hyper-spiritual language. You don't need to be ordained or a cleric or in any position of leadership. A heart open to God's leading, the humility and desperation to learn, the understanding that you are not where you are meant to be, and a personal sense of urgency are all that is required of you.

Wholehearted, focussed Commitment, Intentionality, Unlocking Potential, Discovering Purpose, and a deep desire to Contribute and Make a Difference for

Others, every day will characterise your life from now on if You Choose. Ideally, you need to transform your Mindsets with all of these Steps directing you all at the same time! Please focus on what works better for you as you choose to intentionally transform your thinking from where you are, Growing To Live Your Best Life of God's Higher Purpose and transforming that life to reach "Where You Are Meant To Be". To fulfil God's Purposes in Our Generation.

Wholehearted Commitment is everywhere in *TRANSFORMED!* Its importance cannot be understated, and the following may be helpful:

- ❖ **Wholehearted Commitment is achieved and experienced when we are committed to our Purpose.**
- ❖ **We are Wholeheartedly Committed when we are Fully Aligned with our Purpose.**
- ❖ **Wholehearted Commitment ensues from Alignment with Our Purpose.**
- ❖ **"When we Commit to a Purpose" is firstly about Alignment with that Purpose, then effortlessly riding the wave of Commitment that ensues.**

Merriam-Webster defines Dynamic as used here and in Contents both:

- *as an adjective, dynamic, marked by usually continuous and productive activity or change*
- *and as a noun, dynamic, an underlying force or cause of change and growth.*[12]

---

[12] 'Merriam-Webster.Com', *Merriam-Webster* <https://www.merriam-webster.com/dictionary/dynamic>

LEVEL 1

BE INSPIRED TO AWAKE!

Level 1 – "Intensive Pilot Training and Preparation" towards God's Best Life for You – AWAKE! To Your "Why?"

❖ **Breakout to Your Calling!** – With The Extraordinary Dynamic* *Awareness* to *Awaken! Daily*

❖ **Your Key Thinking:** Awaken! to Breakout and Challenge All Your Assumptions

❖ **Your Key Commitments to Dynamic Action 1** – *Focussing and Thinking Intentionally, Daily,* on the right things

➤ **Step 1 – AWAKEN – To Your Best Life of God's Higher Purpose:** This is the start of the transformation. Awake and Understand to Create the Desire and Intentionality to Change with Awareness by Challenging the Assumptions of Your Birth Culture with Critical Thinking, Creating a Sense of Urgency.

➤ **Step 2 – To Awareness! Of Your Best Life of God's Higher Purpose:** This step is both the foundation and creator of the hope that tomorrow will be better, being the driver of the enlarged vision that enables forward movement to success. Create the Understanding and Awareness of God's Abundance as His Masterpieces to Seek His Highest Calling.

➤ **Step 3 – To Develop! Your Best Life of God's Higher Purpose:** is the real choice to begin. Create the Character and Integrity to Endure, Moving from Knowing to Learning, from Using to Investing, and Making the Most of What God has Already Given You. Grow the seeds of greatness.

➤ **Step 4 – To Think! Over Your Best Life of God's Higher Purpose:** is the mortar that cements together all these Level One foundations. Create the Capacity, Commitment and Anticipation to Think Differently, Moving to Next-Level Thinking by Asking the Right Questions.

Step 1

Awaken! To Your Best Life

High Road of God's Destiny/Soul Trek (Anon)

Where We Are Meant to Be
cannot be reached from
"Here, the Land of Wrong Assumptions".
You cannot stay "Here" because You will miss Your Destiny;
But the deep chasm between you and your goal cannot be crossed.
Now, be under no illusion; this is the most difficult
and yet the greatest journey you can ever choose to undertake.

If You Choose,
You must make the choice to travel towards and start from the
"Land of Extraordinary Awareness for God";
There is no easy shortcut;
Only from thence can you even Begin on the Uphill Path that leads
On through the "Land of Focussed Intentionality for God";
Then, further on and up through the
"Living Forest of the Majestic Oaks of Righteousness
and Greatness for God"
and "cresting the eagle-viewed sunlit high uplands" To Reach "There",
The Extraordinary Land of "Where We Are Meant to Be",
The Promised Land of God's Purposes,
Potential, Possibilities and Opportunities,
The Land of God's Abundance and Surplus,
Growing to Become the Extraordinary Masterpiece God
Created You to Be.

And when you get "There" you will find God has
already gone ahead, His Holy Spirit Calling You
Ever Onward and Upward
and is Expectantly Waiting for You as You Delight in Him,
Fully Committed To Fulfil His Purposes In Your Generation,
Because You Live the Other Side of Yes!

~~~

"He gives power to the weak and strength to the powerless;
Even youths will become tired and weak,
And young men will fall in exhaustion;
But those who trust in the Lord will find new strength.
They will soar high on wings like eagles;
They will run and not grow weary,
They will walk and not faint."
Isaiah 40:29-31 NLT

~~~

❖ **Key Purpose: This is the start of the transformation – the Breakout.** Awake and Understand. Create the Desire and Intentionality to Change to Awareness by Challenging the Assumptions of Your Birth Culture with Critical Thinking, Creating a Sense of Urgency.

❖ **Key Learning (Always Facing the Unknown without Fear):** You are at point zero. Everything from here on up is intentional. You will be asked to choose to Awaken and to what. The 50 Compelling Reasons (Yes, there are that many!) to Live Your Best Life will inspire you. Embrace Transformation and Growth. Much is new to you and probably overwhelming.

❖ **Key Action (Building The Bridge As You Walk On It):** Don't give in, dig in, then move out, then Wake up and Walk Through The Gates of Your Cultural Prison. This is *TRANSFORMED!* boot camp. Only those who are Fully Understanding and Fully Committed will get through to the next step.

It's early morning.
The last darkness of the night retreats as the sun rises.
And the alarm clock's insistent raucous noise assails the slumbering brain as we sleep, and all at once, we are assaulted in all our senses to a vague awareness that someone or something needs, nay insists upon our attention, to act! ...But what? How? Why? What day is it? What time is it? Where am I? Who am I?!

Breakfast? Or Breakout! – To Your Best Life?

The cessation of the noise as we hit the silence button momentarily relieves the clamour, but then new feelings arise as the mind surfaces from sleep... to semi-conscious awareness, to "Oh My Goodness", look at the time, we have overslept! The tyranny of the urgent explodes all over our minds as we grapple with and then grasp the implications of whatever our waking reality hits us with.

Oh, dear!

Responsibilities!

Things we would rather not do!

Yes, we have been sleeping, but now we must arise and act, for the day stretches before us, a day of decision-making, of action, of activity. Just deciding what clothes to wear is almost too much at this time of the morning, but decide we must! For many of us, waking = chaos = frantic catching of public transport or driving = going to work = another day of working in a workplace that neither satisfies nor fulfils but frustrates and depletes us daily, and if only we can reach Friday, or the next day off, or the next shift break, we can regroup our mind and hearts ready to be mentally battered again.

For others, we may not be able to work, either through ill-health or disability, or because we are rejected by others or even by ourselves, or voluntarily retired. All may be induced with feelings of the pointlessness of life, the repeated actions of yesterday that create a daily downward spiral of mental decline that is only interrupted by food, drink, or drugs.

> *Some awake to an alarm clock.*
> *Some Awake To Their Calling.*
> *(Anon.)*

Whatever your time of life, whatever your state of mind, whatever your age, *TRANSFORMED!* is your alarm clock! We all generally awaken to another day of "average", or even worse, "mediocrity", certainly less than what we could be, so we imagine. Work that is often demeaning, depleting, suffocating and dehumanising.

Most of us awaken to another day of potential-sapping and purpose-sapping "normal":

- Normality that assumes hierarchy in every area of life
- Normality that assumes switching people's creativity off every day
- Normality that defines people by colour, creed, beliefs, or orientation

- Normality that lives without thinking the thinkable and without seeing the seeable
- Normality that is "reacting to life"
- Normality that fails to appreciate every human being as being created in the image of God
- Normality that fails to value every human being as having unique personal significance
- Normality that assumes scarcity and depletion
- Normality that assumes problem-solving rather than Purpose-Seeking

Fortunately, incredibly, wonderfully, God has provided another path. You see, we have a choice. Not any old choice. Not just a simple choice to move or eat. But you can make this life-giving, life-directing, life-lifting, destiny-defining fundamental Choice; You Can Rewrite the Script...

50 Remarkable and Compelling Reasons for Your Best Life

- ❖ How many do we need?
- ❖ What does a Best Life look like?
- ❖ What might my Best Life look like?
- ❖ What does God's Best Life for you and me look like?
- ❖ What does He intend for each life He has created?
- ❖ So many questions!

OK, let's just stop, relax, refresh. Gather thoughts and Focus.

Romans 12:1-2 NIV:
"Therefore, I urge you, brothers and sisters, in view of God's mercy, to offer your bodies as a living sacrifice, holy and pleasing to God – this is your true and proper worship. Do not conform to the pattern of this world, but be transformed by the renewing of your mind. Then you will be able to test and approve what God's will is - his good, pleasing and perfect will."

I intend to introduce you to the fundamental basis behind *TRANSFORMED!* You see, you and I are created for a reason. God's Best Life for You is an Intentional Life that Loves Him with all Your heart, soul, strength and mind and is focussed on Purpose and action for others, valuing and adding value to them.

The choice to Lead and Live Your Best Life is just that, Your Choice. It is primarily the choice to self-lead, not out of selfishness, but the necessity to undertake that first and then lead others to the same.

- ✓ **It is your Best Life like Jesus Christ for God and for Others!**
  - ✓ It is your Best Life of Unlocked Dynamic Potential and Discovered Purpose for God and for Others!
  - ✓ It is your Extraordinary, Focussed, Best Life, Determined and Intentional Life for God and Others!
  - ✓ It is your Extraordinary Masterpiece, Best Life of Contribution for God and for Others!
  - ✓ It is your Extraordinary Best Life Mindset of God's Abundance Life!
  - ✓ It is your Extraordinary Best Life of Unique Personal Significance!
  - ✓ It is your Extraordinary Best Life on God's Higher Level of Living!
  - ✓ It is your Best Life with an Abundance and Surplus Mindset!
- ✓ **It is your Best Life that desires to Matter for God and Others!**
  - ✓ It is your Best Life that desires to Make a Difference for God and Others!
  - ✓ It is your Best Life of The Extraordinary Awareness to Awaken!
  - ✓ It is your Best Life of Awareness to Seek His Highest Calling!
  - ✓ It is your Best Life of Development, Creating the Character and Integrity to Endure!
  - ✓ It is your Best Life of Thinking and Creating the capacity, Commitment and anticipation to think differently!
  - ✓ It is your Best Life of The Extraordinary Decision to Unlock!
- ✓ **It is your Best Life of Breakout to your Highest Calling for God's Higher Purpose!**
  - ✓ It is your Best Life of Growing and creating Mindsets for Growth, Connection and Contribution!
  - ✓ It is your Best Life of Engagement, Creating Enrolled hearts that are Fully Engaged and Continually Renewed!
  - ✓ It is your Best Life of The Extraordinary Transformation to Act!
  - ✓ It is your Best Life of Leadership to lead yourself and Others to God's Higher Purpose!
  - ✓ It is your Best Life of Rallying to Continue for God in the Service of Something Greater than Yourself!
  - ✓ It is your Best Life of Legacy, Changing the Future so that lives are changed just as God intended them to be!
- ✓ **It is your Best Life of Transformation and Growing Living!**
  - ✓ It is your Best Life of Intentionality and Integrity Living!
  - ✓ It is your Best Life of Significance and Meaning Living!
  - ✓ It is your Best Life of Anticipation and Urgency Living!

- ✓ It is your Best Life of Abundance and Surplus Living!
- ✓ It is your Best Life of Focus and Commitment Living!
- ✓ It is your Best Life of Action and Opportunity Living!
- ✓ It is your Best Life of Significance for God and for Others!
- ✓ **It is your Best Life of Purpose and Hope!**
  - ✓ It is your Best Life of Intentionality!
  - ✓ It is your Best Life of Intentional Choice!
  - ✓ It is your Best Life of Discovered Potential!
  - ✓ It is your Best Life of Potential without Limits!
  - ✓ It is your Transformational Best Life for the individual!
  - ✓ It is your Transformational Best Life for all Others they come in contact with!
- ✓ **It is your Best Life designed and "hard-wired" to lead lives for Purpose and Destiny!**
  - ✓ It is your Best Life, hard-wired to understand God's purposes!
  - ✓ It is your Best Life, hard-wired to discover, develop and deploy your God-designed potential!
  - ✓ It is your Best Life, hard-wired to matter, to be loved, to belong, to be seen, heard and valued!
  - ✓ It is your Best Life, hard-wired to be inspired, to be engaged!
  - ✓ It is your Best Life, hard-wired to be authentic and to make a difference for others!
  - ✓ It is your Best Life hard-wired through personal responsibility before God to lead purposeful, intentional, meaningful, fulfilled, and wholehearted lives!
  - ✓ It is your Best Life, hard-wired to lead lives that are courageous, compassionate, and committed!
  - ✓ It is your Best Life, hard-wired with empathy, patience, and humility with authentic vulnerability!
  - ✓ It is your Best Life, hard-wired for connection, giving Purpose and meaning to our lives!
  - ✓ It is your Best Life, hard-wired for lives that are passionate, significant and consequential!
  - ✓ It is your Best Life, hard-wired for contribution to God and for Others!
  - ✓ It is your Best Life, hard-wired to carry out His plans for us that He planned before time began, to do great things for God!
  - ✓ It is the Best Life you are Meant to Live, Living and Growing Where You are Meant To Be!

The results are that Your Life can be:

➤ The Best Life you are Meant to Live, Living and Growing Where You are Meant To Be.

➤ The Best Life that Jesus Lived and showed by example.

➤ The Best Life that Jesus talked about and promised.

➤ The Best Life God created you to LIVE.

If this ridiculously long list is what constitutes a Best Life, what else do you need to understand that we really are "not where we are meant to be"? In fact, we are so far off course that we could well be in another universe. And hence, our chapter heading takes on a significance that is nothing short of astounding. In other words:

> *God intends Your Best Life to be an Extraordinary Dynamic Life transformed by the renewal of our minds and Lived for Him and for Others.*
> *Few have asked and less have answered these questions since the days of early Christianity.*
> *Certainly I had not conceived them when I started to write TRANSFORMED!*
> *All I had was some very basic assumptions about higher purpose, leadership and making a difference for God.*
> *So, again, What is God's Best Life for you?*
> *What is God's Best Life for me?*
> *It is our Best life, Our Extraordinary Masterpiece Life.*

Very few of us awaken to fulfil our Potential, discover our Purpose and move to another level daily, even if we are aware of this. I certainly was not aware that I carried Potential around inside me, unseen and unrecognised! Still less was I cognisant of Purpose, and the understanding of a Calling was utterly beyond me. Until recently.

The Awakening to our Calling is also the wake-up call to the Breakout that we must undertake if we are to fulfil our God-given Potential. And Breakout is fundamental to the thinking that must underpin every part of our being, *Breakout* as a Choice, Daily, and *Breakout* as a Clear Pathway in our Journey to the "Land of Extraordinary Awareness".

The gates opening to the light, as shown on the cover of this book, are an unmistakable metaphor, not as a Groundhog Day event, but as the deliberately aware choice to both open and pass through them and past those confining gates however ornate they might look or even how comforting they may seem when shut at night. They must be passed through both Daily and Continually as we travel the uphill path to "Where We are Meant To Be".

Before Why? Who Created You for Your Best Life?

We cannot even begin to understand "where we are" without first asking the question, "*WHO?*" This is asking the Creator Question, and without asking the Creator Question and receiving the answer, we can never possibly hope to ask fully and then fully understand our "Why?" or our "How?", or our "What?"

For me, the "Who?" question is best summed up by scripture in the book of Jeremiah, Ch. 29, verses 11-13, AMP: "For I know the thoughts and plans that I have for you, says the Lord, thoughts and plans for welfare and peace and not for evil, to give you hope in your final outcome. Then you will call upon Me, and you will come and pray to Me, and I will hear and heed you. Then you will seek Me, inquire for, and require Me [as a vital necessity] and find Me when you search for Me with all your heart."

God's intended life for you and I is
nothing short of extraordinary.
It is utterly unique to you and I, and no one else can live it.
Nothing ordinary or normal in it and a million miles away
from everything we "know" and accept as "living".
Being brutally honest, everything we have come to accept as
life is second best mediocrity dressed up as living.
Talk about the living dead?
Sadly, we are living it!
Normal life!

God's intended life that is really Life is
Transforming through Growth and thus:
Growing to Become the Extraordinary Masterpiece
God Created You to Be.

So, we have a deliberate, intentional and focussed God who designs, who plans, who executes those deliberate, intentional, designs and plans, and the pinnacle, the priority, the focus of all this is people. His creation. And here, God states with breathtaking simplicity, "Pray to me, seek me, and I guarantee and ensure you will find me."

In Christ, we find defining all He did on this earth those same aspects just stated. Deliberate, intentional, focussed, with design, planning, acting with absolute integrity to connect with people and then connect those people to Himself and His Father. Everything else was a sideshow.

Like His Son Jesus, God's Masterpiece People are designed and called to live extraordinary, courageous, wholehearted, unlimited lives of masterpiece thinking and action daily, every day of their lives. As Paul writes in Ephesians 2:10 NLT: "For we are God's Masterpiece. He has created us anew in Christ Jesus, so we can do the good things he planned for us long ago." Like Christ, these people, as Paul also writes in Romans 12:2 NIV, "Do not conform to the pattern of this world, but be transformed by the renewing of your mind. Then you will be able to test and approve what God's will is – His good, pleasing and perfect will."

➤ These people choose to love and commit themselves daily to God through Christ;

➤ They are His people who are Committed to their own Transformation and Growth;

➤ They Commit to Growing Others in like manner;

➤ They live the Transformation and Growth Mindset;

➤ They are living the life of Contribution God created them to live;

➤ They are aware that God has a Destiny for them, and here is the essential core:

➤ They are "doing the good things He planned for us long ago."

God's Masterpiece People, as a result of Transformation and Growth, are Intentionally Different; they are Intentionally, Extraordinarily Self-aware; they realise who created them; they realise why God placed them on this earth, and they realise what their Purpose is. They think differently, and they are focussed with positive thinking on acting differently by growing and lifting others as God designed and intended us to do. In short, they are extraordinary people modelling their lives on the real Life that Christ promised.

They understand one of the greatest yet most misunderstood and ignored truths of scripture that they are created and called by God as His Masterpieces for Others. Masterpiece thinkers are intentionally transforming and growing their minds continually and living for others, as Paul wrote in Romans ch.12, vv1-2 and

Ephesians ch.2, v10. They intentionally live with the transformation and growth Mindsets below. They anticipate doing for others the good things God planned for them long ago, a cause larger and other than themselves; they anticipate being fully engaged and able to undertake proving His good and perfect will; they anticipate God showing up in their lives and making all the difference.

They Choose to live as God's Masterpiece, thinking for others today. They understand the Potential within them is unlimited. They live with Purpose. Every day is started with the deliberate Choice and Commitment to Live for God. They Choose to Live, Daily, the Extraordinary Transformational Leadership Masterpiece of Jesus' Life that He modelled as He grew others. They Choose to Contribute, Daily, for Others.

If you and I have realised through faith in Christ that we are individually created and called by God, then we should be encouraged that this is not a competition between individuals, who traditionally have been "taught" by "dress-coded clergy" – those who unintentionally gave the impression of greater "understanding/holiness/closeness to God/further on the road" style of living, which we could never attain. It is very, very fortunate that this writer cannot and will not attempt that.

What I can and will do is encourage you personally and individually by stating and affirming your value, your status, and your potential relationship with God, who created you in the first place. Now, before critics shoot me down with well-meaning accusations of the continuing cultural drift towards self-centred, isolating living through social media, which is true, may I remind us all of Dr Rick Warren's First Things First statement from his best-selling book, *The Purpose Driven Life*: "You were made by God and for God—and until you understand that, life will never make sense."[13]

"The greatest tragedy is not death, but life without purpose."[14] He helpfully goes further, writing about Purpose. "Knowing your Purpose motivates your life. Purpose always produces passion. Nothing energises like a clear purpose."[15]

Because you and I are individually created by God, it follows that understanding this, and doing something about it, is incredibly important. Also, understanding that it is not for our benefit primarily but for Others completes the "Big Picture". And that implied sense of interconnectedness is a recurring theme in the New Testament.

The four Gospels of Christ's Life clearly show all the extraordinary human facets above that He displayed and consistently lived out. His life epitomised

---

[13] Rick Warren, *The Purpose Driven Life: What on Earth Am I Here For?*: Zondervan, 2012), p. 22.
[14] Warren, *The Purpose Driven Life*, p.34.
[15] Warren, *The Purpose Driven Life*, p. 36.

these deliberate life actions. These are the essential mind of Christ, the "Core" of His life and what propelled, motivated, sustained and made Him as God's Son Masterpiece, the intentional, significant, anticipating, abundant, and focussed man of action for His Father and Others that He was. We are created and called by Him to literally live His Life that is real life. The Potential within you and me to live this "ALIVE" Life is unlimited. But it only happens with Daily Consecration, Daily Dedication, Daily Commitment, and the Deliberate Choice to Connect with our Creator, who alone Created us to be "ALIVE" with the Choice to "ACT". We need to wake up because there is no time to lose.

We need the clarity of Paul's letter to the Ephesians ch. 2, v. 8, where he writes with profound simplicity that we are saved by grace through faith, that is, your salvation and mine do not originate or proceed from within ourselves, but "it is the gift of God". First "Who?", then "Why?"

> *Make Today the Best Day of Your Life*
> *Make this year the Best Year of Your Life*
> *Make the rest of your Life your Best Life for God.*

We are Not Where We are "Meant to Be"

But Why is this?
And if we are living lives less than what we could be,
Who are we meant to be?
Where are we meant to be?
Where are we designed to reach?
Why are we like we are?
Are we destined from birth to live lacklustre lives of only survival if we are lucky?
We can ask these questions because, in most people, there is this unarticulated, unspoken need to matter and make a difference. We are not "Where We are Meant to Be".
Why do we yearn for what we cannot see?
Why are we not where we are meant to be? Possible answers:

- Status Quo
- Education failures
- Culture pressures

What has prevented us? Possible answers:

36

- We accepted what was told to us
- We have conformed
- We Are Asleep whilst pretending to live

What change must be undertaken?

- Start practising being Awake!
- Grow to Become the Extraordinary Masterpiece God Created You to Be
- (Remembering it's not about You, but for Him and for Others)

At what Higher Level must we be thinking, acting, living and serving?

What is God's Higher Purpose for us?

What does "Where We Are Meant to Be" look like?

How do its citizens act? How do they think? What are their relationships based on?

Can we ever reach "Where We are Meant to Be"? Now, that is significant! Yes, it is God's Higher Level. A clue is found in Paul's letter to the church at Ephesus:

Ephesians 4:1 NIV: "As a prisoner for the Lord, then, I urge you to live a life worthy of the calling you have received".

So, someone has called us and the most crucial aspect to understand is that you and I *are* called. Our "Calling" is personal, specific and unique in object, character, and origin. God calls in the sense of a whole life call. And so this sense of being called lives gives us a clue to the land of "Where We are Meant to Be". You see, at the simplest level, being "called" by another person, say, a family member or a neighbour, in the regular connectivity of life, represents the interaction between two people. Each is known by the other. "Where We Are Meant to Be" can be understood not so much as a place but as a relationship. Therefore, it is not a destination to be reached but an ideal held and followed. And in the context of being "Called" by God, we are offered the opportunity to respond and walk closer or reject and turn away to separation. As human beings, being relational is a fundamental underpinning of our lives. There is nothing painfully greater than a relationship that has been sundered, especially unintentionally. So, we are Called to Reconnect To and Relate with God, Who created us in the first place.

God's Higher Purpose

50 Remarkable and Compelling aspects of God's Higher Purpose within an individual:

- ❖ **God's Higher Purpose exists in every human being but awaits discovery.**
  - ❖ God's Higher Purpose unleashes our God-created, Unique Personal Significance.
  - ❖ God's Higher Purpose enables us to live lives of fulfilled Purpose released to the world.
  - ❖ God's Higher Purpose enables us to live lives for Potential, Purpose, Passion and Destiny.
  - ❖ God's Higher Purpose is not imposed.
  - ❖ God's Higher Purpose is not a slogan or a quotation.
  - ❖ God's Higher Purpose can only be discovered.

- ❖ **God's Higher Purpose chooses us.**
  - ❖ God's Higher Purpose cannot be discovered by conventional transactional thinking.
  - ❖ God's Higher Purpose desires the fullest contribution.
  - ❖ God's Higher Purpose demands total Commitment and must be acted upon.
  - ❖ God's Higher Purpose inspires your unlimited Potential.
  - ❖ God's Higher Purpose elicits your Unlimited Potential.
  - ❖ God's Higher Purpose transcends the individual.
  - ❖ God's Higher Purpose gives back more than it receives.

- ❖ **God's Higher Purpose fully engages and continually renews.**
  - ❖ God's Higher Purpose co-creates the emerging future of alternative possibilities.
  - ❖ God's Higher Purpose is unique to the individual.
  - ❖ God's Higher Purpose is unique to an organisation of individuals.
  - ❖ God's Higher Purpose transcends the ego.
  - ❖ God's Higher Purpose involves others.
  - ❖ God's Higher Purpose enables us to be authentic and to make a difference for others.
  - ❖ God's Higher Purpose is a journey, not a destination.

- ❖ **God's Higher Purpose involves everyone.**
  - ❖ God's Higher Purpose focuses on the common good.
  - ❖ God's Higher Purpose asks people to imagine a better future.
  - ❖ God's Higher Purpose is the arbiter of (defines) direction and decisions.
  - ❖ God's Higher Purpose draws out a Best Life.
  - ❖ God's Higher Purpose does not exist in conventional thinking.

- ❖ God's Higher Purpose is focussed on valuing others.
- ❖ God's Higher Purpose is Focussed on adding value to others.

❖ **God's Higher Purpose encourages Transformation and Growth.**
- ❖ God's Higher Purpose encourages Intentionality and Integrity.
- ❖ God's Higher Purpose encourages Significance and Meaning Living.
- ❖ God's Higher Purpose encourages Anticipation and Urgency Living.
- ❖ God's Higher Purpose encourages Focus and Commitment Living.
- ❖ God's Higher Purpose encourages Action and Opportunity Living.
- ❖ God's Higher Purpose indicates that tomorrow can be better.
- ❖ God's Higher Purpose indicates a better collective future.
- ❖ God's Higher Purpose values purpose before profit.
- ❖ God's Higher Purpose must be continually clarified.
- ❖ God's Higher Purpose enables positive cultures to emerge.

❖ **God's Higher Purpose enables us to discover, develop and deploy our God-designed Potential.**
- ❖ God's Higher Purpose enables us to live lives of profound Purpose and meaning.
- ❖ God's Higher Purpose enables us to live lives that are courageous, compassionate and committed.
- ❖ God's Higher Purpose enables us to lead purposeful, intentional, meaningful, fulfilled, wholehearted and unlimited lives.

❖ **God's Higher Purpose enables us to live lives that are passionate, significant and consequential.**
- ❖ God's Higher Purpose enables us to live lives using God's extraordinary birth gifts – unique Potential, Capacities, Capabilities, Talents, and Vision that are summed up in unlimited Potential and Unique Purpose found in our hearts, minds and spirits.
- ❖ God's Higher Purpose enables lives of Empathy, Patience, and Humility underpinned with Authentic Vulnerability.
- ❖ God's Higher Purpose unleashes our Potential for Greatness for Others, the Greatness described by Christ.

> ➢ *God has a Perfect Plan for You if You will accept it!*
> ➢ *It is all Good News!*
> ➢ *He Created You in Accordance with His Plan for Himself and Other People*
> ➢ *Yes, it is true that the World is a mess (in general) and that Your Life May Be a Mess, You May Feel Worthless and You May be Far From God*
> ➢ *But as You Seek Him, He Promises to Reveal Himself to You!*
> ➢ *He Plans to Transform You Through Faith in Christ*
> ➢ *That Transformation involves You "Becoming the Masterpiece God Created You to Be!"*
> ➢ *God has His Unique Higher Purpose just for You*
> ➢ *Now is the time to Start, Understanding Where You are Meant to Be*
> ➢ *You Cannot stay Where You Are, but must walk The Uphill Path of God's Transformation for You.*
> ➢ *So Don't Waste the Completely Unique Life Given You By God!*
> ➢ *Seek Him with All Your Heart and Daily Commit Yourself to Him!*
> ➢ *Start Intentional Growth by Unlocking Your God-Potential, Discovering His Purposes for You*
> ➢ *Simply Ask God, by Seeking and Knocking at His Door and He Will Answer Your Asking, Seeking and Knocking!*
> ➢ *Love Him with all Your Heart, Mind, Soul, and Strength*

God's Higher Purpose is the domain of God's Extraordinary Masterpiece People. In reading and actioning "Transformed!" we are reaching and stretching from our God-gifted potential starting point, and for most of us, that is simply "Where we are" to become all that we are "Meant" to be. Now, if this all sounds to the average human being like "airy-fairy gobbledegook", you are both entirely correct and also entirely wrong, all at the same time. Please stay with me on this; "all" will become clear.

This is The Good News of the Gospel of Jesus Christ simply laid out and not the tedious sin management charade we were led to believe Christianity was all about. It is not, and I am not joking.

"What's Right?" – Questions To Consider

I have adapted questions posed by Kurt Wright from his book *Breaking the Rules.* His essential starting point instead of "What's wrong?" is simply to ask, "What's right?"

- The initial question is simply, "What's right?" or "What's working?"
- Next, "What makes it right?" or "Why does it work?"
- Third, "What would be ideally right?" or "What would work ideally?"
- Fourth, "What's not yet quite right?"
- Last, "What resources can I find to make it right?" [16]

Or from a God-centred point of view:

➢ **What do I know is already right?**
The agenda-setting question.
(What do we know of God's plans for us?)

➢ **What is it that makes it right?**
The energy-generating question.
(Why did God plan all this in this way?)

➢ **What would be ideally right?**
The vision-building question.
(What is His Purpose, and what are we to become?)

➢ **What's not yet quite right?**
The gap-defining question.
(Where are we on this continuum?)

➢ **What resources can I find to make it right?**
The action-engaging question.
(What must we do to start {again} on the journey?)

---

[16] Kurt Wright, *Breaking The Rules: Accessing Your Inner Wisdom*, 3rd printing 2015, pt. 645.

Embrace Transformation and Growth

But a word of warning. You see, God asks us to be Transformed by the Renewal of Our Minds. This means "Change!" Everywhere in scripture, He is always on the go, and what is He doing? Every famous biblical person is in the process of improvement and change. Many refused to accept God's better ways for them and suffered as a result.

And not any old meaningless, pointless change. "Growing to Become the Extraordinary Masterpiece God Created You to Be" is essential for you and me. It may be painful for some, especially if they cannot see, understand or even contemplate the essence of the change that God has planned for them. That is why the title is not "Changing to Become..." but "Growing to Become...". Growth is *essential* if you and I are to, well, Grow! From Birth, we grow, and it is ordinary, unnoticed and crucial. We subconsciously embrace it because it is so normal.

But why is it that often the adult who grew automatically as a child develops a distinct lack of flexibility in the one area of our being, our minds, that will constrain, limit and deplete us if not exercised, challenged and encouraged to stay supple and responsive, and improved? As long as we cling to the notion of change = pain, we will never become the people God planned us to be – His Masterpiece People. The social behaviour known as loss-avoidance syndrome is where, at its simplest level, people prefer the known to the unknown, and their minds convince them that this is the safest route for living because the known = comfort = no pain, or so their thinking assumes. Wrong assumptions can destroy or severely limit people.

So, in calling us to be TRANSFORMED! God is encouraging transformation and renewal through growth (continuing change), which is essential and awesome. Now, awesome is not a word I would ever ordinarily use, but in the context of this book's title, creating Extraordinary Masterpieces, then Awesome seems restrained! Change = Growth = Essential = Where We are Meant to Be = Awesome!

Don't become like the person who, having faithfully washed up by hand in a church kitchen for years, suddenly could not cope with a machine dishwasher simply because it was an overwhelming change, and they excused themselves from their former faithful work. They could not see the benefits it would bring, not least of which was raised standards of cleanliness for the items just washed and the removal of the uncleanliness of damp, reused drying cloths that were irregularly replaced. They could not see the benefits but also actively ruled themselves out of the benefits as they resisted the change. Status Quo living effectively equates to the acceptance of mediocrity and always results in a "less than life" that accepts lack of fulfilment or any substantial progress and improvement as the way life was meant to be. Wake up, folks, don't accept that lie!

Transformation and Growth are what we are created for. In fact, as we shall see later, Growth = the Life You are Created for, not based on some unnamed fear that lurks ready to pounce. Later in the book, we will extend this to Abundance and Surplus thinking compared to Depletion and Scarcity thinking. The world in which we Live accepts by default that Scarcity is the default. It underpins everything we believe or do, and it leads us wrongly to accept underachieving as normality. We are not where we are meant to be.

Wake Up And Walk Through the Gates of Your Cultural Prison

Even for believers in Christ, Culture Prisoners in a Cultural Prison is where we all are at most stages of our lives. Christ shows us in His life what He did with His cultural prison. And like any prison, whether physical or mental, we were never designed to be there. At some point in our lives, we must wake up to escape and:

➢ Stop conforming to the pattern of this world but be transformed by the renewing of your mind, then you will be able to test and approve God's purpose for you. (Romans ch. 12, v. 2)

➢ Wake up! Get up! Step-up! Call upon the Lord God Daily!

➢ Break-out of the culture (every day) that is holding you down and back!

➢ Break-in to unleash the potential God has created in you and discover his purposes for you!

➢ Don't look back! Don't focus on past losses. Focus on what God created you for!

➢ You can stop the cycle of depletion and scarcity thinking by which your culture is continually "killing" you!

➢ You and I are designed to be equipped, deployed and destined for God's greatness already placed within us!

➢ You and I are created extraordinary people by God to enjoy living the life for his glory that God always planned for us to Live!

➢ You can wake up and realise your status in Christ!

➢ Move your focus from doing church and attending, to being the Church of Christ and transforming through growing!

➢ You can focus on and choose to become that person God always planned for you to be!

It is all Your Choice...!

Jeremiah 33:3 NIV:

"Call to me, and I will answer you and tell you great and unsearchable things you do not know."

Romans 12:2 NLT:

"Don't copy the behaviour and customs of this world, but let God transform you into a new person by changing the way you think. Then you will learn to know God's will for you, which is good and pleasing and perfect."

Jeremiah 29:11-13 NIV:

"For I know the plans I have for you," declares the Lord, "plans to prosper you and not to harm you, plans to give you hope and a future. Then you will call on me and come and pray to me, and I will listen to you. You will seek me and find me when you seek me with all your heart."

Waking up in the morning, for most people, is a conscious act. For many, it can be hard. God has called us, those who have put their faith in Christ, to be transformed, to break out and break free from the constraints, rules, assumptions and all the other false cultural norms that detain us, in order to become the individuals and people God always created and planned for us to be.

> *'We are all prisoners. We are confined within our "thought walls." We each have a set of beliefs we have accumulated from experience. We refer to these beliefs or assumptions as "the conventional Mindset."'*
> *The Economics of Higher Purpose,*
> *Professors Quinn and Thakor.*

(Above quotation cited below. [17])

Breaking free from the tyranny of natural assumptions and rules that we make and are imposed on us, especially in churches, must be daily. These are the assumptions that often have bound us by personal history or cultural acceptance.

Use Transformational Enquiry and Questioning. Give yourself and others permission to ask transforming questions of yourselves and God. Of course, seek answers in scripture. That goes without saying and is a prerequisite. To commence our journey, we may start with a vitally important question. Where is God taking me/you? That is an assumption and an entirely correct growth

---

[17] Robert E Quinn and Thakor, pt. 1360.

assumption. But it has enormous implications.

List the categories of assumptions. Group them together. Where you or I may now be is like facing a long, high, impenetrable wall, as if we are in prison, the prison of wrong assumptions. It may be the prison of wrong assumptions that we have about ourselves. It may be the prison of wrong assumptions that others have held about us and that we have subconsciously absorbed so that they are now self-fulfilling prophecies.

And what God calls us to, is to grow and develop in Christ and walk through that wall of illusory assumptions that we have allowed our lives to be bound by. The wall of unhelpful and probably false assumptions is just that. Incidentally, I awoke one morning to realise that I had walked through, or in reality, awoken on the other side and, looking around me, found, to my great surprise, that the wall was an illusion. It did not actually exist, but it used to feel like that.

How can it possibly be that we can be held for decades by our false assumptions, even as Christians in churches and deny ourselves or be denied by others in clergy leadership positions the life God always planned for us to live? The perfect analogy is that we are/have been/will continue to be like the turkeys pecking the ground by the runway, never realising we were meant to take off and fly. No disrespect to turkeys intended, but God in Christ always planned for you and me to live the lives He gives us, a life that is really Life at His Higher Level, and to soar on eagle wings close to Him.

God created us for His purposes, His vision and His destiny; for consecration and dedication with courage, connection and commitment to Him; to lead lives that are wholly for Him. They are to be lives dedicated to God. They are to be lives of wholehearted connection with God. We are created to be inspired and transformed, not fearful. Christ restores us in Himself to God.

- ❖ But do not get caught by the illusion of understanding!
- ❖ Beware of success and the illusions it creates!
- ❖ Grow your growth Mindset. Use everything and every opportunity as a learning/growing experience. Nothing needs to be wasted!
- ❖ Observe, learn, and improve!

This is what Christ was teaching His disciples, and collective learning is key to Christ's Church. It was so when He walked this earth. Paul assumes it. We must relearn it. We must relearn being a learning-growing-action church as Christ instructed Peter. The "Feed my sheep" in John ch.21, vv15-17 is "grow my people by helping them grow themselves" in modern parlance.

Is it possible that Christ was teaching the emergence of collective intelligence leading to emergence and self-organisation, an emergent process, with experiential learning? Moving from conventional thinking to transformative thinking and deep learning is hard. What is needed is a total challenge and change of deeply held assumptions that are wrong and an illusion.

TRANSFORMED! cannot be understood from a perspective of knowledge, intelligence or understanding but from the closeness of the relationship with God that we aspire to. Never forget we are as close to God as we wish to be.

Transformed!

Means To Intentionally

Breakout every Day, Today.

Breakout to Extraordinary Awareness

Breakout to Unlock Extraordinary Potential

Breakout to Extraordinary Action

These are the reasons we put our feet

On the floor as we get out of bed.

~~~

As You Awake to Breakout

Your Priorities are Re-established Every Day

You Awake to Grow Every Day

Your Commitment Recommences Every Day

Your Potential is drawn from within You Every Day

Your Fulfilled Purpose is Recommenced Every Day

God Awakes You to Growth, Commitment,

Potential and Purpose for Him Every Day

And God Honours Those Who Honour Him Every Day.

Today

Conclusions for Step 1

AWAKEN! To Your Best Life

Key Thought – Wake up and Walk Through The Walls of Your Cultural Prison

If you have read this far, please be encouraged. It may be that you know this better than the way it is written here in this book. Please remember this is written for people who are grappling and possibly struggling with these new concepts, new breakout, new awareness, and new challenges, and they have never been challenged to change or transform themselves in their lives. This is a hard, relentless, but nevertheless transformative life change that is both essential and doable. But it is not easy. Nothing in life that is worthwhile or essential is easy.

Some may have given up before the end of this first chapter – Awaken! To Your Best Life. But Awakening is non-negotiable. Without this transformational start, understanding your "Who?" and your "Why?", you will be unable to make the essential move forwards and progress through to the Transformation and Growth God created you for. It is also vital to understand that this process of transformation and growth is not a linear progression. Much of this is essential to tackle and take place all at once!

Okay, let's reflect on where we are, having reached the end of this first step. Congratulations on having got this far! In a very real sense, Level 1 and this first step is the most significant step to get up and over since this is the first real cliff to climb. The transformation of thinking from traditional, inward-focussed, mediocrity-accepting normal life, together with your own religious culture, is enormous, overwhelming and quite possibly mentally chaotic.

It is especially chaotic because you are being asked to let go of all the assumptions that have underpinned your life to this point in time, assumptions that you grew up with and assumptions you have unquestioningly accepted.

I have introduced new concepts, new truths, new thinking, and all this may be uncomfortable. Any change in the assumptions that we have based our lives on up to this point will be hard, strange, and yet, hopefully, exciting in a new way that requires deep learning and deep thinking. The new concept of sustained internal growth that you will feel will, I believe, be tangible, worthwhile and fulfilling. You will know you are growing because you will feel it! The corollary is also true – if you cannot feel improvement, transformation and growth, then it is not happening.

To recap, you have been introduced to the sub-headings of:
- ➤ **Breakfast? Or Breakout! – To Your Best Life?**
- ➤ **50 Remarkable and Compelling Reasons for Your Best Life**
- ➤ **Before "Why?" Who Created You for Your Best Life?**
- ➤ **We are Not Where We are "Meant to Be"**
- ➤ **God's Higher Purpose**
- ➤ **Questions To Consider**
- ➤ **Embrace Transformation and Growth**
- ➤ **Wake Up And Walk Through the Gates of Your Cultural Prison**

I have listed them here with the symbol of Breakout Action Points and not just sub-headings. Each one is meaningful and relevant. This is daunting stuff to consider, and I feel almost overwhelmed having written it! But it is also foundational. We cannot attempt to transform and grow without having first climbed and overcome the cliffs of these basic concepts. As Americans would write, this is Transformation 101.

And all of the above should be set against the overall concept of "Next Level Thinking". There is nothing special in "Next Level Thinking" that we cannot benefit from enormously. Where You and I were raised thinking that "where we were" was constant, that the lives we were living were just "normal", and accepting the mediocrity that we are starting to understand was not "where we are meant to be", these assumptions need to be blown apart and replaced. Transformation and Growth must become your new normal, uplifting, motivating, exciting and defining. The old assumptions will not be of any use where you are going.

The thinking that you will always be where you are and that you cannot change/improve/transform to become the person you were always designed to be is wrong. In truth, it was more than that – it was a self-induced, self-taught, self-deluding, self-accepted lie. Now for some positive thinking actions. They are deliberately non-academic and straightforward. By all means, take a pen and write some thoughts down on paper. The simple act of writing will cause significant improvements in understanding since, as you write, you will find yourself disciplined in that writing and then returning to improve the first draft. You may not understand the concepts thoroughly, but I believe everyone can write down how they "felt" upon reading. You may wish to look back and highlight sections that touched chords in your heart. That is important.

I suggest you simply reread the sub-headings listed above. Do an internal assessment and ask yourself the following questions and directions:

1. What new insights have I learned?
2. How does it make me feel just reading those headings?
3. Choose the ones that stand out in meaning to you.
4. Think about why you feel they are important.
5. What choices might you need to make right now?
6. Think about how you can start the transformation you wish to see?

Review the last three sub-headings of **Questions To Consider, Embrace Transformation and Growth, Wake Up And Walk Through the Gates of Your Cultural Prison.** Over the next three days, pick one aspect from each that resonates with you and take decisive action.

I can affirm to you that this can be the start of momentous, meaningful, wonderful, life-changing and potentially world-changing thinking and actions beyond your current conception and experience. And it starts and grows with the "Next Level Thinking" and actions you are already considering and may be excited by subconsciously. To that next step, we now turn.

Step 2

To Awareness! Of Your Best Life

You and I are Created and Called for God's Higher Purpose, Our Best Life, which is for our Salvation, Transformation and Personal Growth to reach towards our Potential for God through Redemption in Christ, meaning:
Re-Creation in Christ,
Renewal in Christ,
Restoration in Christ,
Re-Direction in Christ;
For His Purpose, Vision, and Destiny, and through Personal Transformation and Growth with Joyful Discipline, reaching our Fullest Potential, for Lifting Others Intentionally with us, to Fulfil God's Purposes in our Generation, and to be Filled to the Measure of all the Fullness of God in Jesus Christ.

Therefore, I Freely Choose to Love, Worship and Adore You Intentionally, Lord God, Today. I Choose this day to Contribute by Living a Life of Total Commitment, Ongoing Transformation, Personal Growth, and an Intentional Life of Significance to Influence, Lift and Inspire
Others to be the same in Jesus Christ.

~~~

Romans 12:2 AMP: "Do not be conformed to this world (this age), (fashioned after and adapted to its external, superficial customs), but be transformed (changed) by the (entire) renewal of your mind (by its new ideals and its new attitude), so that you may prove (for yourselves) what is the good and acceptable and perfect will of God, even the thing which is good and acceptable and perfect
(in His sight for you)".

~~~

❖ **Key Purpose: This step is both the foundation and creator of the hope that tomorrow will be better, being the driver of the enlarged vision that enables forward movement to success. Create the Understanding and Awareness of God's Abundance as His Masterpieces to Seek His Highest Calling.**

❖ **Key Learning (Always Facing the Unknown without Fear):** The first step is always the hardest and highest. Congratulations on persevering. None of this is easy. It takes time to allow new thinking to flood your mind. For many who, like me, are older when we got to this point, it can take possibly a decade or more to replace old Mindsets with Transformation and Growth Mindsets.

And walking out of your cultural prison is probably the toughest thing you can accomplish. Well done! But the battle has yet to begin in earnest!

❖ **Key Actions (Building The Bridge As You Walk On It):** We now turn to Awareness – Greater Awareness. Redemption is central. You will see how you are "hard-wired" as a human being for "We are designed and hard-wired to lead lives for potential, purpose, passion and destiny", along with many other aspects that you may have wondered where they came from. Understanding and living the life God always planned for us to live fills me with hope – I hope it does you. Finally, you will discover as you take action that vulnerability is key to our understanding of both ourselves and God.

Ultimate Purpose – the 7 Higher Purposes of God

Discovering God's Higher Purpose for yourself; Living at God's Higher Level. God created us uniquely for His purposes, His vision and His destiny; for consecration and dedication with courage, connection and commitment to Him; to lead lives that are courageous and consequential for Him; to lead lives that fulfil His purposes for us.

✓ They are to be lives dedicated to God.
✓ They are to be lives of wholehearted connection with God.
✓ We are created to be inspired and transformed, not fearful, as Christ restores us in Himself to God, and we are to discover our identity in Him.

Our Lord, Jesus Christ, was the most aware, awakened, and discerning person ever. He correctly understood everyone, everything, every culture; He perfectly understood the past, the present, the future; He challenged everyone to be transformed, to be born again; He encouraged everyone to discover, use and fulfil all of God's plans and purpose through their talent and potential. One testified of Christ, "No man ever spoke like this man". Wow!

Start with Jesus's Life of Leadership: how He lived and the life He invites us all to live. He discovers His Higher Purpose at around the age of ten, and He lives for that Higher Purpose, He loves for that Higher Purpose, He leads for that Higher Purpose, He Prays for that Higher Purpose, and He dies for that Higher Purpose.

And the only question here is, "What was it that He had discovered?" It was that He, Jesus, was The Christ, and His Purpose was to recreate and connect people back to God. Purpose is absolutely central to that profoundly simple core aspect, the truth that "People Matter". We are destined to become conformed to the image of His Son. Romans 8:29. In Christ, we were created by God for His

Purpose. His Higher Purpose. There is no other reason to exist. Jesus as Creator exemplified all of these "Higher Purposes", and it is God's perfect plan for His People:

❖ God's Higher Purpose 1. *You are Chosen, Created and Called by God for His Purpose, to live for His Glory: You are uniquely created and called by God because of His eternal love for you, and Foreknown, Predestined, Called, Justified, Glorified, and Redeemed, so to be Conformed to the exact image of Christ, our hearts and minds illuminated with the light of the knowledge of God's glory displayed in the face of Christ, personally connected to Him in worship, all in Christ, for His Purpose, which is to lead lives of holiness with Him forever. Romans: 8, 28-29; Ephesians 1; 2 Corinthians 4, v6.*

❖ God's Higher Purpose 2. *Your Destiny for Transformation in Christ is His Purpose: God's plans and designs for you are personal faith in Christ, restoration in Christ, transformation in Christ and eternal perfection, yes, in Christ. Ephesians 2:10.*

❖ God's Higher Purpose 3. *You are Designed by God for His Purpose: We have God-designed aspects in every human being as we live and connect with others with His Mindsets: We are designed and "hard-wired" to lead lives for purpose and destiny; hard-wired to understand God's purposes; hard-wired to discover, develop and deploy your God-designed potential; hard-wired to matter, to be loved, to belong, to be seen, heard and valued; hard-wired to be inspired, to be engaged; hard-wired to be authentic, and to make a difference for others; hard-wired through personal responsibility before God to lead purposeful, intentional, meaningful, fulfilled, and wholehearted lives; hard-wired to lead lives that are courageous, compassionate, and committed; hard-wired with empathy, patience, and humility with authentic vulnerability; hard-wired to contribute; hard-wired for connection giving purpose and meaning to our lives; hard-wired for lives that are passionate, significant and consequential; hard-wired for lives of contribution for God and for Others; hard-wired for lives of greatness for God; hard-wired to carry out His plans for us that He planned before time began, to do great things for God. Ephesians 2, 10.*

❖ God's Higher Purpose 4. *Your Wholehearted living is His Purpose: We are to live our lives focussed on and sincerely connected with Him through worship and a unique relationship with Him, seeking Him wholeheartedly: We are to discover His unique purpose(s) for us individually, through conscious consecration, decisive dedication, wholehearted courageous commitment, considered contribution, enjoying lives of His surplus and abundance, not the world's scarcity and depletion, and purposefully engaged in something bigger than ourselves, to dare greatly for Him. Psalm 32: 8.*

❖ God's Higher Purpose 5. *Your Connection with Himself and Others is His Purpose: We are planned, created, and activated through faith in Christ to connect and synchronise with God, Christ His Son, Christ's Church, and every other human being on this planet authentically with love, respect and compassion through shared purpose, shared vision, shared knowledge and mutual respect without judgement. As we come to faith, discovering our purpose(s) in Christ, we embrace His priorities and seek to act always in ways consonant with those priorities. Through connection with God, we are to be actively transformed, growing and maturing continuously in Him. Ephesians 2: 4-5.*

❖ God's Higher Purpose 6. *Your Growing others is His Purpose: We are created to lead other people to discover and fulfil God's created purpose(s) for them; individual and community transformation is His purpose; we are to ensure they belong, that they matter and that they matter in God's bigger picture; we are created to help other people grow, to contribute without seeking for reward, to make others great first, which is the truest act of friendship and sincerest exhibition of unadulterated love; to intentionally connect with, listen to, challenge and impact the behaviours and culture of individuals and the community around us; we are created to leave this world a better place than when we entered it. Colossians 3: 12-17.*

❖ God's Higher Purpose 7. *Like Christ, your Servant Leadership and Legacy are His Purpose: Being leaders for God is a choice, not a position. We are all planned to be leaders like Jesus whose sole purpose is to help other people connect firstly, with God in Christ, and secondly, with their God-given purpose individually and corporately; to make sure they matter and feel valued; to inspire them to become what they are meant to be; to unlock, unleash and nurture God-given potential in others with a Mindset of growth; to help them discover and release their gifts, talents, along with their unrealised unlimited potential, purpose and possibilities; to contribute by leading people to a better place; and lastly, but no less importantly, to ensure the baton is passed on and a God-honouring legacy ensues.*

Welcome to God's Higher Purpose life that you were created for by Him in Christ. Christ discovers His Higher Purpose, He lives for that Higher Purpose, He loves for that Higher Purpose, He leads for that Higher Purpose, He Prays for that Higher Purpose, and He dies for that Higher Purpose. It is called Transformational Servant Leadership, and it is God's Higher Purpose for you. Live like Christ, Love like Christ, and Lead like Christ.

Starting Awareness for Your Best Life

"When you believe in abundance, you believe there are enough of God's blessings—

enough fulfilment, enough opportunity, enough happiness, and enough love—out there
for everyone. I encourage you to take that point of view because it opens you up to other
people. If you tend to think of the world as a place of scarce resources and limited
opportunities, then you'll see fellow travellers as threats who'll take what is out there
and leave nothing for you.
Competition can be healthy because it motivates you,
and you will always find others who want what you want.
With an abundance mentality, you believe there are rewards enough for everyone,
so competition is more about striving to do your best
and encouraging others to do the same."
Nick Vujicic.[18]

~~~

"If you want to expand your capacity, and therefore your life, you need to be willing to take greater risks. You need to be willing to stand alone. You need to gather the courage to do what others might not do—not just for the sake of doing something bold and risky, but because you can see the potential reward."[19]

"We were talking about adding value to people, and he (interviewer) said, 'John, you've built your reputation on the foundation of being passionate about adding value to people. How have you kept your passion hot and your energy up for forty-five years?' I couldn't wait to answer his question because we were talking about my passion, my life. The reasons I stay excited about it are simple:

- I value people.
- I believe people can improve their lives.
- I am improving mine so I can give more.
- I know how to help people improve their lives.
- I see results in the many people I have helped."[20]

"To be significant, all you have to do is make a difference with others wherever you are, with whatever you have, day by day."[21]

---

[18] Nick Vujicic, *Life without Limits: Inspiration for a Ridiculously Good Life* (New York: Doubleday, 2010), pp. 175–76 <http://ebook.yourcloudlibrary.com/library/BCPL-document_id-f1yg9> [accessed 22 May 2020].

[19] John C. Maxwell, *No Limits: Blow the Cap off Your Capacity*, First Edition (New York: Center Street, 2017), Anais Nin quoted, p. 263.

[20] John C. Maxwell, *No Limits*, pp. 307–8.

[21] John C. Maxwell, *Intentional Living: Choosing a Life That Matters*, First edition (New York: Center Street, 2015), p. 3.

"Are you living on the other side of, Yes!?"

"Bruce Barton said, 'Nothing splendid has ever been achieved except by those who dared believe that something inside them was superior to circumstances.'" [22]

All quotes from John C. Maxwell.

~~~

I choose to be a Transformational and Inspirational Leader by writing for Others and for God. It is my Choice, my Purpose, my Calling, my Destiny and my Legacy. I believe I am called to do this. My life experiences and opportunities allowed by God demand nothing less. I wonder if you are thinking of making choices that reflect entirely who you are, your experiences and your potential for a Higher Purpose, also?

> *"We are not human beings having a spiritual experience; we are spiritual beings having a human experience."*
> *(attributed to Pierre Teilhard de Chardin)*

(Quote above not cited – this attribution has not been proven.)

If this is true, then we must seek to answer the questions:
- ❖ *Who created us?*
- ❖ *Who are we?*
- ❖ *Why are we here?*
- ❖ *Where do we come from?*
- ❖ *What is our purpose?*
- ❖ *What is our calling?*
- ❖ *Why?*

This is my "Why?":

God created me for this purpose: living a life that matters with the Mindsets of Intentionality, Growth and Significance to Inspire others to find their Purpose,

---

[22] John C. Maxwell, *No Limits*, p. 264.

Unlocking and Unleashing their Potential, just "Lifting the Lid off People".

I profoundly believe that only God in Christ speaking to us through the centuries in Scripture can answer those deep questions that we may never have asked ourselves before. Deep within every one of us is a desperate need to matter, to belong, to be recognised. Deep and often unarticulated.

Now, none of the following is easy. If it were, it would have been done centuries ago. But I want you to be encouraged because this is entirely within your capabilities. A life of unlimited potential and purpose awaits you if you choose because it is already within you. It is simply a choice, your choice to make a start on this road. Beyond making the initial choice to transform, the start of this journey is to challenge your "conventional Mindset": accept the fact that you are almost inevitably confined within your "thought walls". We all are confined to a greater or lesser extent by our self-imposed mental limitations. Convention and culture constrain and straightjacket everyone. The quote below helpfully sheds light on the problem:

"It isn't that they cannot find the solution. It is that they cannot see the problem" – G. K. Chesterton.[23]

But first, a question that was posed to a class of students recently:

"When does the future determine the present?"[24]

The silence that follows that question is used by its questioner, Bob Quinn, to elicit a personal response in his lectures. Bob is very grandfatherly in speaking to these students (as he is in age and fact). Hold that question aside for a minute.

But I will also ask us a question that, like the one above, causes us to ponder to the depths of our souls even if there is no ready answer. And it is simply this:

"What is Your Potential?"

"Excuse me!?" you say.

I understand the "Uh?!" feeling.

Okay, if you are not sure of my meaning, how about considering this: "What is the limit of your Potential?" Of course, stating the question in this way seems, on the face of it, ridiculous, simply because Potential, by its very nature, is untested, unstated and unknown. It is unlimited and cannot be limited in you.

So, What is Your Potential:......?

I wonder what your thoughts are right now. Are there glimpses of past good

---

[23] 'G.K. Chesterton Quotes (Author of Orthodoxy) (Page 2 of 96)' <https://www.goodreads.com/author/quotes/7014283.G_K_Chesterton?page=2> [accessed 29 May 2020].

[24] 'When Does Future Determine the Present?', *Robert E. Quinn* <https://robertequinn.com/uncategorized/when-does-future-determine-the-present/> [accessed 21 May 2020].

and bad experiences flashing through your mind in quick succession? Are there "seeds" of possibilities and thoughts jumping around, all seemingly disconnected? Is there overload going on in your mind?

"When does the future determine the present?" and "What is your Potential?" These questions can appear to us as a car crash. Unanticipated and causing mental shock simply because the implications are disconcerting and new.

Professor Quinn's answer to his perplexed, brain-crashing question of "When does the future determine the present?" is simply this: "When we Commit to a Purpose".[25] OK, now, say it out loud slowly, as Professor Quinn does…

Both questions have profoundly influenced me in a positive way. It was like waking up from a dreamy sleep to realise that I had "potential". Although having not done very well in Physics at school, I do remember some sort of electrical connection! But seriously, I figured, if there is potential in me, which has lain undiscovered, redundant and not even suspected for years, I can wake up, I can be aware. There also crept into my mind the thought that the future could and must impact our present if our minds (once awake) rise to the challenge of discovering a Purpose to which we can be Committed.

Suddenly, those bright twin lights, Potential and Purpose, jolted me from my default thinking, "Life is what happens to me", and a great dawning of new awareness flooded over me, releasing me from the limitations of past academic failure, the deeply hurtful opinions of others, even my religious past, and then there came an extraordinary explosion of relief and joy that my past need not define my future or destiny. That, indeed, I could discover my Purpose to which I could be Committed.

> *Dr. Stephen Covey wrote in his book,* **The Eighth Habit:**
> *"Deep within each one of us there is an inner longing to live a life of greatness and contribution,*
> *to really matter, to really make a difference.*
> *We may doubt ourselves and our ability to do so,*
> *but I want you to know of my deep conviction*
> *that you can live such a life.*
> *You have the potential within you. We all do.*
> *It is the birth-right of the human family."*

---

[25] 'When Does Future Determine the Present?', *Robert E. Quinn*
<https://robertequinn.com/uncategorized/when-does-future-determine-the-present/>
[accessed 21 May 2020].

(Quote above cited below). [26]

Can I tell you that Dr Covey's truly extraordinary comments above touched a chord in my heart that few have ever managed. I hope they do for you as well, and that it kick-starts the questioning and seeking process that will set you free to be transformed, to become the person you were created, designed and meant to be: a person full of hope, growth, unlimited potential, purpose, fulfilment, and yes, happiness. That awesome comment about "suspecting there may be more to themselves than they realised" is a key to our understanding, along with another vitally important facet that is part and parcel of this bigger jigsaw. It was something that although I thought important, I could not "see" because of my slowness of thinking, which is common to us all.

We will be looking at Growth later on. Personal Growth. Intentional Personal Growth at such a level and reality that may have escaped you in the past and even now may be unknown. Dr Covey spoke of "initiative, higher motivations, greatness, contribution, influence and potential". All remarkable and essential Growth concepts that you will discover for yourself later.

TRANSFORMING – Growing to Become the Masterpiece You Were Created to Be is all about Your Story, Your Awakening, Your Potential, Your Purpose, Your Calling, and Your Destiny for Others. It is an Astounding and Extraordinary story if You Choose.

➢ Wake up - Being Awake
➢ Switch On - Being Switched On
➢ Unlock - Unlocking Potential
➢ Breakout - Preparing for Opportunities
➢ Act - Seizing Opportunities

This is the Releasing/Unleashing Cycle that many/most of us need to go through every morning/day (but this is OK) in order to get to the point where we can then undertake Intentional, Anticipating and Planning to Contribute, acts of Significance for Others, to make a Difference for Others today. Because we only have Today.

Decades of status quo Mindsets have so deadened our thinking and effectively so disabled our God-given capabilities that we need, at least in the short term, a methodology for quick success that will encourage us onwards. That's also OK. Because being awake, switched on, unlocked, breaking out, and acting will, with practice, become the new/originally intended normal that enables intentionality, anticipating and planning to be significant for others to

---

[26] Covey, p. 28.

be replaced. They must be central to all that we think, all that we are, and all that God always intended us to be.

In his recently published book, *The Economics of Higher Purpose*, Professor Quinn states: "Leadership requires you to adopt the positive Mindset and have the ability to imagine and create what may be outside the current culture."[27]

"When you find an authentic higher purpose, you acquire new feelings and thoughts. When you articulate and embrace a higher purpose, you enter a new life path."[28]

This is vital to understand. Because where you are going, no one has ever been before, and no one knows the path, your path, simply because your uniqueness as created by God is just that – unique. You are already stepping outside your birth culture, armed only with a growing conviction that you are "not where you are meant to be". You are starting to understand what others cannot and may never understand and creating a new culture where God always planned for you to reach, enjoy, fulfil His purposes, and impact others uniquely.

So, I excitedly invite you to Choose and Start Your Journey of Transformation...

Redemption

To be transformed from who you were to who you are to become under God means a total change. As you become aware of the enormity, not only of God's standards but, more importantly, of His purposes, the potential inside you, and best of all, His unlimited possibilities for you, the Lord through His indwelling Holy Spirit will enable you to start this seemingly overwhelming process. He will enable you by awakening, by awareness, by alignment, by engagement, by inviting you to wholeheartedly call on and seek the Lord daily. He will enable you to act with the heart of Christ, with His Greatness, imitating His Wholeheartedness, His Courage, His Compassion, His Commitment and His Focus.

Your very self can now be understood as the unique person God-creating event that it is. Your Identity, who you think you are, will be renewed as you see God's purposes, possibilities, and your potential is drawn out from you. All your past, your experiences, and your difficulties, however overwhelming and desperately bad, will start to be seen in the light of God's plans for you.

In scripture, "blind" Bartimaeus was defined by his blindness. In a sense, that was his badge, his "problem", his "label", his "bondage", his "addiction", and his "abuse". What might be your own label or unhelpful definition? What would you

---

[27] Robert E Quinn and Thakor, pt. 635.
[28] Robert E Quinn and Thakor, pt. 662.

place in here: [***]? What is your situation, your 'hopeless' position, your past identity, which you feel you are or think you are?

For myself, I would place in "[***]" my early academic failures, my 20 years working in a large organisation under the bottom of the "pile", my sense of worthlessness, my lack of achievement, other people's nastiness towards me, past teacher's ill-informed criticism of me etc., etc. Put them all there "[***]". Pile it all up. Insert every disappointment, every failure, every difficulty, every criticism that hurt you and every other pain. These are your past but also your unhealthy, self-imposed identities. They are not God's new identity for you in Christ.

But remember this: Bartimaeus became healed Bartimaeus, seeing Bartimaeus, God-worshipping Bartimaeus. You are not your past. God is your future.

Look at the identity transformation of the Apostle Paul. When he was Saul, he was a murderer and persecutor of the Church of Christ. When God transformed his identity totally, he became Paul, the "least of all the apostles". He was recreated in Christ and given a new identity, new significance, new potential, new purpose, new inspiration, new passion, new conscience, new vision, a new discipline, new focus, and new destiny.

But he had to let go of his old identity. It was not for him any longer. He moved dramatically to God's Higher Level, living for God's Higher Purpose. If anyone had good cause to look back in embarrassment and shame at his old life and believe it disqualified him from his new life, well, God did not tell him because Paul never looked back.

The Heart Of A Created Human Being

"You and I are Individually Created and Called for God's Higher Purpose, which is for our Salvation, Transformation, and Personal Growth to reach towards our Potential for God through Redemption in Christ, meaning:

Re-Creation in Christ,

Renewal in Christ,

Restoration in Christ, and

Re-Direction in Christ;

For His Purpose, Vision, and Destiny, and through Personal Transformation and Growth with Joyful Discipline;

Reaching our Fullest Potential in a Life of Significance and Meaning;

Lifting Others Intentionally with us to Fulfil God's Purposes in our Generation;

To be Filled to the Measure of all the Fullness of God in Jesus Christ. Therefore, I Freely Choose to Love, Worship and Adore You Intentionally, Lord

God, Today. I Choose this day to Contribute by Living a Life of Total Commitment, Ongoing Transformation, Personal Growth, and an Intentional Life of Significance and Meaning to Influence, Lift and Inspire Others to be the same in Jesus Christ. "This is the Jesus Life." R.F.

"Lord, lead me onwards and upwards, towards Yourself and all that you can and would impart to this soul upon whom and in whom You have set Your love. Fulfil your purpose through this soul for Your Glory and the redemption, renewal, redirection, fulfilment and destiny of others in the days that you give me on this earth." R.F.

We are created for Transformational Leadership; everyone is, in the sense that we are created to love God first and then do everything we can, not just to "love" others, but to help transform them to become the people God always planned for them to become. Discovering God's Higher Purpose for yourself; Living at God's Higher Level.

You and I are not a random result of evolution. You and I are Designed by God for His Higher Purpose: You and I are uniquely God's Extraordinary Masterpiece, and we have God-designed "hard-wired" aspects in us and every human being as we connect with others:

- ✓ **We are designed and hard-wired to lead lives for potential, purpose, passion and destiny;**
  - ✓ hard-wired to understand God's Purposes;
  - ✓ hard-wired to live lives for God's Higher Purpose;
  - ✓ hard-wired to discover, develop and deploy our God-designed potential;
  - ✓ hard-wired to live a life of fulfilled purpose released to the world;
  - ✓ hard-wired to love, to love God, and to love others;
- ✓ **hard-wired to matter, to be loved, to belong, to be seen, to be heard, to be valued;**
  - ✓ hard-wired to be inspired, to be active;
  - ✓ hard-wired to be fully engaged and continually renewed;
  - ✓ hard-wired to be authentic;
  - ✓ hard-wired to make a difference for others;
  - ✓ hard-wired through personal responsibility before God to lead purposeful, intentional, meaningful, fulfilled, wholehearted and unlimited lives;
- ✓ **hard-wired to lead lives that are courageous, compassionate, and committed;**
  - ✓ hard-wired for lives of contribution for God and Others;

✓ hard-wired to live lives with empathy, patience, and humility underpinned with authentic vulnerability;

✓ hard-wired for connection, giving purpose and meaning to our lives;

✓ hard-wired for lives that are passionate, significant and consequential;

✓ hard-wired to be connected with God and filled with His Spirit;

✓ hard-wired to love Him with all our hearts, and with all our souls, and with all our strength, and with all our minds;

✓ hard-wired to carry out His plans for us that He planned before time began, to do great things for God. Ephesians: 2, 10 NIV.

Every aspect above is full of purpose, inspiration, connection and passion. The one word you will never read as an aspiration here in this book is "fear". But we almost always live with it in some aspect of our minds. I can most assuredly tell you that God never intended you or me to lead lives based on fear. Yet that is what we precisely do. And we are so often habituated to doing this that we "see" it as normal. It sits quietly in the background, ready to raise its ugly, insidious head and condemn us to live lives based on fear.

Now, this is not the fear of danger near cliff edges, speeding vehicles, or crossing roads. These are the excellent and safe precautions we need to take in life: active, dynamic, risk-assessing precautions. We are not discussing that approach to life. We are unlocking our Creator's intentions. We were never created to live in fear and a "continuous fearful responding to life". We are designed and intended to Choose and, as Professor Quinn urges – commit to a purpose", God's Higher Purpose.

Just contemplating God's Higher Purpose for you and your significance as a created human being changes and renews your mind, feelings, and understanding and sets you on the road to a more profound and fuller experience of your creation, identity significance, potential and purpose. Living in this higher level of consciousness, in turn, will inspire your passion, vision, and focus and then define your destiny. This is the transformation and renewal of mind spoken of by Paul in Romans ch.12, vv1-2. But it is only achieved with intentionality. It does not just happen like a warm feeling washing over you or the emotional inspiration produced by music. This happens when deliberately chosen as a life course to live at a higher level for God.

The eternal questions in the heart of every human being are elementary:

❖ Who am I?

❖ Why do I exist?

❖ What is my purpose?

❖ Why this constant feeling that my life must have meaning and without meaning, it is pointless and without purpose?

There is a simple but infinitely profound answer: Scripture tells us that you are created by God for His eternal purposes. Unless we have a relationship with God, who created us, our lives can never have meaning or significance. Unless we ask God to answer each of us individually the question, "Why did God create me?" we will never know His purposes for us. And the human soul craves meaning since we are created for it.

But further questions arise:

- ❖ Why does God in scripture place His total emphasis on His people?
- ❖ Why did He create us?
- ❖ Why is it so imperative that we reconnect with Him through His Son, Jesus Christ?
- ❖ Why is an individual important to God?
- ❖ Why are you and I so important to God?
- ❖ Why must it be so crucial for you and me to understand, recognise His love for us and do something about it?

Three quotes from Dr Rick Warren, *The Purpose Driven Life*:

It is only in God that we discover our origin, our identity, our meaning, our purpose, our significance, and our destiny. Every other path leads to a dead end."[29]

Neither past nor future generations can serve God's purpose in this generation. Only we can. Like Esther, God created you "for such a time as this." God is still looking for His people to fulfil His purposes and then transform the course of history. The Bible says, "The eyes of the LORD search the whole earth in order to strengthen those whose hearts are fully committed to him." Will you be a person God can use for his purposes? Will you serve God's purpose in your generation?[30]

As D. L. Moody said, "The Bible was not given to increase our knowledge but to change our lives.[31]

~~~

To kick-start our quest for answers, we need to know that God has created twelve fundamental characteristics within every human being, in their heart, mind, soul and body. We need to understand how we are created. What defines us as thinking human beings? It is not how we look, how we walk, how we talk, how we drive a

---

[29] Warren, *The Purpose Driven Life*, p. 22.
[30] Warren, *The Purpose Driven Life*, p. 316.
[31] Warren, *The Purpose Driven Life*, p. 191.

car or what language we speak. What, then, are the fundamental aspects of our self and creation? Here are some of those key aspects.

They were created, present and perfectly expressed in Jesus Christ. They are every person, unique, individually designed aspects of:

- ❖ Creation
- ❖ Identity
- ❖ Potential
- ❖ Purpose
- ❖ Inspiration
- ❖ Passion
- ❖ Vision
- ❖ Intentionality
- ❖ Focus
- ❖ Anticipation
- ❖ Significance
- ❖ Destiny

They made Christ in human terms, how He functioned, how He acted, how He lived, moved, and had His being, and especially they made Him who He was.

"The greatest discovery in human experience is self-discovery, because with it comes an understanding of our origin in the Creator, our inherent value, and how we are to fulfil our leadership purpose. Personal leadership is the divine assignment for which God designed and made you. Your leadership attitude will come alive when you discover and start living according to your true nature." – Myles Munroe has written.

You will discover who you really are by understanding your uniqueness, and the above aspects will help you with that task. They make you who you are. They make you utterly unique, not only on this earth but throughout the universe and for all eternity. He also designed every single human being to live with Wholeheartedness, Courage, Compassion and Commitment if they so wish. We also need to admit the three irreducible needs of every human being: to be loved, to belong and to be connected. We are designed like this, and without recognising and understanding these crucial aspects, we can never be fulfilled. We can never be fulfilled until we discover what God has created on the inside of us, drawing it forth. We can never be fulfilled until we realise the potential that He created in us and every human being, then go forward as God intended to fulfil His purposes in our lifetimes. This is the life that Jesus spoke about, John 10:10 AMPC: "I came that they may have and enjoy life, and have it in abundance (to the full, till it overflows)."

And when all these aspects of a human being are taken as a whole, we realise that scripture is absolutely right when we are told in Ephesians 2:10 NLT: "For we are God's masterpiece. He has created us anew in Christ Jesus, so we can do the good things he planned for us long ago." One of the greatest and most necessary privileges Christians can realise and enjoy is the freedom and ability to choose God in Christ as the one and only Source of all they are.

- ❖ **He created us, you and me, for His Higher Purpose**
  - ❖ He created us with our unique Identity
  - ❖ He created us to become uniquely Significant
  - ❖ He created us with our unique Potential
  - ❖ He created us with our unique Purpose
  - ❖ He created us to be Inspired by Purpose
  - ❖ He created us to be Passionate for Purpose
  - ❖ He created us with Vision and capable of enormous vision
  - ❖ He created us with a Conscience and with Purpose
  - ❖ He created us to be Disciplined on Purpose
  - ❖ He is our Focus forever
  - ❖ He is our Destiny forever
- ❖ **He created you and me for His pleasure and purposes** (the world sees only evolution and humanistic philosophy as the reason and foundation for life. The philosopher Bertrand Russell avowed, "Unless you assume a God, the question of life's purpose is meaningless).[32]
  - ❖ He created our unique Identity since there will never be another you! (The world seeks to destroy our God-given identity.)
  - ❖ He created our Significance (the world ignores at best and rubbishes what God has planned, which is servant leadership significance and significance to impact others positively). Significance yearns to make a difference. "To be significant, all you have to do is make a difference with others wherever you are, with whatever you have, day by day."[33]
  - ❖ He created our Potential (the world would deny and ignore this, but God has placed this within every one of us).
  - ❖ He created our Purpose (the world would limit us to self-interest and seeking to emulate celebrities. God has bigger plans for each of us such that they are beyond our comprehension).

---

[32] 'Reference Request - Source of a Russell Quote about Purpose and Meaninglessness', *Philosophy Stack Exchange*
<https://philosophy.stackexchange.com/questions/64916/source-of-a-russell-quote-about-purpose-and-meaninglessness> [accessed 21 May 2020].
[33] John C. Maxwell, *Intentional Living*, p. 2.

- ❖ **He created us to be Inspired** (the world would replace this with its depleting inward focus, self-obsession, and invidious crushing comparison with others).
  - ❖ He created us to be Passionate (the world would deny and laugh at the passion that ensues from the triple strengths of potential, purpose and inspiration); passion fuels vision.
  - ❖ He created us to be Compassionate (the world would deny and laugh at such apparent foolishness) towards Others.
  - ❖ He is our Vision (the world would limit our vision to a vainglorious, self-promoting, me-first attitude. God's vision for us individually is greater than we can ever imagine).
  - ❖ He created us with a Conscience that powerfully directs when the truth is told.
  - ❖ He enables our Discipline when we cannot help but act in accordance with our purpose.
- ❖ **He is our Focus** (the world hates our focus on our Creator, but scripture consistently confirms that God heeds – by carefully listening to us – and strengthens those who consecrate, dedicate and courageously commit themselves daily to Him).
- ❖ **He is our Destiny** (the world would proudly deny that God exists. We humbly assert He is our inspiration, He is our passion, He is our vision, He is our focus, He is our destiny now and forever).

Not only should God be the focus of our affections, but if we can recognise Him as the true source of who we are, why we are, where we are and where our destiny lies, we will find that choice is the most significant understood choice we can make. In so doing, we reset the course of our future automatically based on our Creator. He is our <u>one</u> and only Source.

> *"Lord God almighty, I recognise You are the Source of all that I am, all that I aspire to and my destiny."*

These are the ideals and what God intended. But humankind's sinful nature and separation from God destroy from birth these ideals. Indeed, the cultures within which we grow and which we inhabit, wherever we live in the world, all prevent these ideals from ever surfacing again. As we grow up, we live with the suspicion that there must be more to our lives than what we have, what we understand and what we experience. It is an unarticulated yearning, longing and seeking for what is the lost connection with our Creator.

But this is no mystical effect that many over the centuries have expressed.

They could only express their hearts through the culture in which they lived. They did not have a language that could speak the truths of scripture because they "saw and experienced" their lives through their limited cultural lens.

Once in half a millennium, someone may come who breaks out of their cloying past and culture. Renewed by their scriptural understanding, they set themselves in a new upward direction. Like King David of the Old Testament, Martin Luther was a man who fulfilled God's purpose in his generation. In England, William Tyndale, through countless hours of lone scholarship, translated the scriptures and produced a body of translation that would become the basis of the majority of the so-called King James Bible. The positive and long-lasting effect of his work of translation has been incalculable.

When we are separated from all that God has for us and would call us to, how does it make us feel? We feel alone, aimless, unfulfilled, purposeless, and defined and limited by others because of comparison with them, their attitudes towards us, along with the catastrophic limitations of our cultures at every level of our experience. And this separation is not only in terms of salvation. It is the very heart of the human condition that limits, depletes and destroys the lives God planned to be great for Him. When these God-created, God-installed characteristics are ignored, suppressed, unused, or undeveloped, the feelings of emptiness, being lost, and purposeless are always a present reality. God never planned it that way, but what He does plan, however, is evident in scripture.

Ephesians 2:10 AMPC:
"For we are God's own handiwork (His workmanship), recreated in Christ Jesus, born anew that we may do those good works which God predestined (planned beforehand) for us taking paths which He prepared ahead of time, that we should walk in them living the good life which He prearranged and made ready for us to live."

1 Peter 2:9 NIV:
"But you are a chosen people, a royal priesthood, a holy nation, God's special possession, that you may declare the praises of him who called you out of darkness into his wonderful light."

What astounding and extraordinary truths from the Master Himself. You and I are the result of His purpose and choice and given a unique position in the mind of God. That purpose cries out for the release of the potential and purpose designed, created and placed in you and me by our Father God. That Mind created us to share His Mind, His Heart, His Plans, His Vision; to see as He sees and to understand as He understands. This is living at an extraordinary, altogether different, higher level of experience, understanding, and consciousness with God Himself. This is God-centredness. We need to realise that where we are is not where God intended us to be, and in that pressing onwards and upwards to God's sunlit uplands, we will find the purpose and fulfilment that He created us to seek.

This is why Jesus exhorts us to become the wide-eyed, open-minded heart of a small child again, as we all were before convention, custom, and the stultifying effects of our cultures created the death of dreams. As we became adults, we were told from every direction that we had to "grow up", which meant acting our lives out of fear, the fear of failure, and the fear of success.

Even as I write, I am conscious of an all-pervading subliminal fear of failure, criticism and rejection. What if my God-created potential, purpose, vision, focus and destiny are merely a mirage? How foolish will I feel if I get all this wrong? Away from me, deadly spirits of melancholy and unnamed fears! I am a unique child and creation of God Himself. My origin, identity, significance, potential, purpose, passion, inspiration, vision, focus and destiny are my Heavenly Father's planned gifts to me. How dare you seek to destroy what Christ Himself created. Away from us, you theologians who created systems of belief to feed your deadly game of one-upmanship. You create knowledge and beliefs, but not wisdom and understanding and hearts consecrated, dedicated and committed to God through activated individual potential and purpose. Like the Pharisees of old, you did not enter the kingdom of heaven yourselves and stopped others also attempting the same.

But scripture clearly states Christ has placed His Spirit within me. Ephesians 2, v10 AMPC tells of us being "recreated in Christ Jesus" in the continuous present tense. He is our origin; He is our identity; He has created significance and potential within us; He is our purpose; He is our vision, and He is our destiny.

Yes, we are redeemed sinners saved by grace. But our church systems and the very creeds we hold never allow us to become all that God in Christ intended. In fact, they actively prevent that because they are focussed on the system and not the people. Some people may be sincerely attracted to liturgy and creeds and prayer book services. But, fundamentally, all this is a smokescreen to continue the traditions of the past. What a tragedy.

The greatest truth for us is that God intends to transform us by being re-created in Jesus Christ, who not only gave everything He had for His Purpose but even now lives within those who trust in Him to enable that transformation to be completed. Our destiny is to be transformed, to unlock and maximise our potential and to discover the purposes that God has created within us. Our purpose is to fulfil His purpose in our generation and to grow and benefit others. We are designed and expected to grow ourselves and "take flight" to soar on eagles wings and seek the face of God.

It is, therefore, not to be wondered why the traditional church continually fails and declines when the chief aim appears to be conformation to their weekly rituals, their creeds, their systems of belief, and their dwindling band of adherents who trudge every week to their inward-focussed clubs of comfort, conformity, and community.

In his letter to the Roman Church in ch.12, v1-2, Paul writes of a very different outcome God has planned for us. He says, "Be transformed by the renewing of your mind." Two simple actions but containing dramatic changes in lives consecrated to Christ. Transformation means overwhelming change. It means breaking with the past. It means breaking from our old selves and cultures, and it means, for some, a difficult transition. The renewing (present continuous) of our minds is likewise not easy. Lord, "transform me to fulfil your purposes in my generation. Enable me to be transformed for the purposed fulfilment of my life for your glory and praise."

> *"You have to want what God wants*
> *in order to receive what he wants to give you."*
> *Erwin McManus, The Last Arrow.*

(Above quotation cited below. [34])

Proverbs 20:5 NIV says, "The purposes of a person's heart are deep waters, but one who has insight draws them out." See also Romans ch.12, v2, which speaks of proving and discovering God's purposes.

We can read much about the inherent human aspects of origin, identity, significance, potential, purpose, inspiration, passion, vision, focus and destiny. The first five are found, created or formed and already within us. The second five flow or rather ensue from the first five and emanate through us. This is all good stuff because they kick start the strategic thinking and breakout that humans need from the mediocre, the status quo, especially in churches, the accepted what is, in order to see and plot the path to what could be. They allow us to be inspired.

Sadly, experience shows us that few people in the traditional church ever start this path of breakout. Most will settle for and metaphorically "fight" for the comfortable, the known, the mediocre, the commonplace, their culture, and their community without ever being able to consider a better way.

---

[34] Erwin Raphael McManus, *The Last Arrow: Save Nothing for the next Life*, First Edition (New York: WaterBrook, 2017), p. 178.

They choose a life of mediocrity, the status quo and the path to slow decline whose gentle downward slope is illusory. They imagine that mediocrity is normal. They have never been led to see and choose what God sees and has planned for them. The default life they choose is tradition, comfort and a life that cannot imagine anything beyond; what a heart-aching tragedy. To live a life that dies full of self and not emptied for God. Full of regrets that they never made a difference for God in their generation as He intended.

All the advances humans have ever made were made by those who dared to think differently, to see and consider new realities that others could not or would refuse to see. Never despise visionaries who dare to dream the 'what if?'... or the 'why not?'

But God has created all this potential within every living being for a higher purpose. His Higher Purpose. He has created our origin, identity, significance, potential, purpose, inspiration, passion, vision, focus and destiny. They are God-created and God-centric aspects. The potential to understand and use these God-created aspects is within every human being. As others have said, "What we are is God's gift to us; what we make of ourselves is our gift to God." So we have a choice to make. We can either choose self-centred lives that are "filled" with aimless distraction. Or we can embrace our God-created lives, listen to Him, read His word in scripture and live them fully engaged and continually renewed in Him.

Jeremiah 29, vv11-14 AMP:
"For I know the plans I have for you," declares the Lord, "plans to prosper you and not to harm you, plans to give you hope and a future. Then you will call on me and come and pray to me, and I will listen to you. You will seek me and find me when you seek me with all your heart. I will be found by you," declares the Lord.

God's purposes in verses 11-12 create our identity and purposes in Him, then allow and create a vision that leads us to His destiny in verses 13-14. Destiny in scripture is a dual destination now and forever. In other words, our destiny both includes us in the now of our lives to fulfil His purposes for Him in our generation and then, more importantly, leads us to complete fulfilment through connection with God in Christ for eternity.

We can never know God's perfect fulfilment for us outside and apart from Him. Colossians 2:9-10 NIV: "For in Christ all the fullness of the Deity lives in bodily form, and in Christ, you have been brought to fullness."

"The strength in VISION is that it INSPIRES, helps you to see your PURPOSE, and it is a catalyst for POWER". – *Vision, Inspiration, Purpose, Power* by Susan G. Smith.[35]

Living The Life God Always Planned For Us To Live

So, in living the life God always planned for us to live:

❖ **Our Creation in Christ, properly understood, should lead to identity and significance.**
  ❖ Our Identity in Christ, properly recognised and understood with potential, should lead to purpose, vision and destiny.
  ❖ Our Significance in Christ, properly recognised, ensures we matter to God.
  ❖ Our Potential created in us by Christ properly recognised and understood should illuminate identity and purpose.
  ❖ Our Purpose designed for us in Christ properly recognised and understood should lead to heart longings that seek God's vision and destiny.
  ❖ Our Inspiration will proceed from the understanding of potential and purpose.
  ❖ Our Passion will be seated in that inspiration and proceed from all our lives for God.
❖ **Our Vision illuminated for us in Christ should lead to engagement and empowerment with God and His destiny for us.**
  ❖ Our Focus centred on God's purposes will draw us ever forward and upward to our Destiny.
  ❖ Our Destiny in Christ now and forever, properly recognised and understood, will lead to greater effectiveness for God and, ultimately, to eternity with Him forever.

All these vital but little recognised or understood aspects are designed by God and placed in those He calls for the praise of His Glory. The traditional church's major problem is that its hierarchy, which never understood these things, created a system of beliefs as the raison d'être for the church. They, thereby, have consistently starved their adherents of the God-created aspects that Christ intended to transform His Church with. This is beyond a tragedy. Jesus spoke of the Pharisees and experts in the law. "Woe to you experts in the law, because you have taken away the key to knowledge. You yourselves have not entered, and you have hindered those who were entering." – Luke 11:52 NIV.

---

[35] Susan G. Smith, *Vision, Inspiration, Purpose, Power - Take Action And Discover Your Personal Keys To Success*, Kindle (HubCap Media; 1 edition (15 April 2013)), pt. 92.

And all these are in the heart of a leader for Christ. As Christ showed, leadership is all about connecting people to their purpose so that they can be great for God through servant leadership. It is about maximising in your people the God-created aspects that they were created for and encouraging them to Wholeheartedness, Consecration, Dedication, Courage, Compassion and Commitment.

2 Chronicles 16:9 AMPC:
"For the eyes of the Lord run to and fro throughout the whole earth to show Himself strong on behalf of those whose hearts are blameless toward Him."

Origin, Identity, Significance, Potential, Purpose, Inspiration, Passion, Vision, Focus, and Destiny are all aspects of your God-created life of Higher Purpose.

- ❖ Creation is where you come from and understanding Who created you.
- ❖ Identity is who you are and the qualities you espouse. Identity is important because it has the triple effect of uniqueness, continuity and affiliation at the same time. God's impact on your identity is critical; otherwise, confusion will reign. This created identity is separate from possible considerations such as cultural, national, professional, ethnic, gender, or religious identity.
- ❖ Significance is vital because you matter, you have a created need to matter, and you matter to God. Who you are is immeasurably more important than what you know.
- ❖ Potential is what God has placed within you from birth. You are created with potential, and this potential is designed to connect with Him and impact others and the world for Him. Yes, you may have particular aptitudes and creativeness. But this potential is at a higher level within you.
- ❖ Purpose is your "WHY?" and God created you for His Purposes. Purpose awaits your discernment and discovery because you are designed this way.
- ❖ Inspiration will catch you unawares and move you like nothing else.
- ❖ Passion is God's gift within you that has unknowingly awaited the discovery of unlocked potential, discovered purpose, and inspiration that you never suspected.
- ❖ Vision, alongside all the others above, is your unique human capacity to "see" what others may not, to "see" what others cannot, to "see" what others may never. "See" why you are created; "see" your picture of the future that creates passion in you. But your God-inspired vision is a precious thing. See it, Guard it, feed it, action it; all for God who places that vision within you.

❖ Focus is knowing where you must go and with courage not accepting failure, looking not backwards, but simply pressing forwards to God's goal, believing in the God of miracles, for whom all things are possible.

❖ Destiny is your future, both in this life and eternally. Amazingly, Psalm 37:38 NIV tells us, "But all sinners will be destroyed; there will be no future for the wicked". No future and no destiny. But also scripture tells us in 1 Corinthians 2:9 KJV, "But as it is written, Eye hath not seen, nor ear heard, neither have entered into the heart of man, the things which God hath prepared for them that love him". Your Destiny is God planned, God defined, God directed, and God completed.

These ten human aspects, which are spiritually discerned, unseen and, for most people, unknown, are all vitally connected within you. They are placed within you by God, your Creator, from birth. They are designed to be what makes you 'you' and who you are meant to be, and what defines you. They underpin your life, your hopes, the way you feel, and maybe what you are just waking up to. These are for all who live as God intended, at His Higher Level, for His Higher Purpose. His Higher Purpose is designed, created and available just for you, the way you are, and the authentic person you could yet become if only you will wake up and start walking into the destiny God has for you right now.

It is indeed unfortunate that for centuries, our religious forbears thought mostly in terms of inescapable human sin and, equally, unattainable holiness. These opposites held people in limbo, almost in suspended animation. Of course, there _was_ separation from God because of our sin, but then also there was <u>life-giving forgiveness and salvation</u> summed up in redemption that is ours through faith in our Saviour, Jesus Christ. These are undoubtedly the underpinning foundations of Christianity, and the atoning sacrifice of Christ for our sins must never be downplayed or forgotten.

But there is an equally important other side to this coin. What did God intend should be the outcome for those who have put their faith in Christ? As assured by the Scriptures, the forgiveness of sins is clearly a significant outcome for those believing in Christ. But it seems that for most of church history, sin and sin management as a means of managing and manipulating believers has been the official outcome. Transformed human beings have mostly not been the focus, nor has it been translated to the primary outcome that Christ intended and Paul experienced and wrote about frequently in the New Testament.

It is clearly shown in scripture that Christ was awakening His disciples' understanding to His Authentic Higher Purpose as He lived among them. And His Purpose? To set them free and with their potential unleashed to become the men and women of His Church, God created them to be.

Your life has been one long cycle of preparation under God's watchful eye. He created you, gave you your identity, and significantly made you in His image. He is preparing you for the release of your Potential for Him and your Discovery of His Purposes and will inspire you with a Passion and Vision to focus on His destiny for you.

Greater Awareness Through Vulnerability and Authenticity

As a Christian, all the above may be true, but without first asking the question, "Who?" we cannot possibly hope to fully ask and then understand, "Why?" For me, the "Who?" question is best summed up by scripture in the book of Jeremiah 29, verses 11-13 AMP: "For I know the thoughts and plans that I have for you, says the Lord, thoughts and plans for welfare and peace and not for evil, to give you hope in your final outcome. Then you will call upon Me, and you will come and pray to Me, and I will hear and heed you. Then you will seek Me, inquire for, and require Me (as a vital necessity) and find Me when you search for Me with all your heart."

So, we have a deliberate, intentional and focussed God who designs, who plans, who executes those deliberate, intentional, designs and plans, and the pinnacle, the priority, the focus of all this is people. His creation. And here, God states with breathtaking simplicity, "Pray to me, seek me, and I guarantee and ensure you will find me."

In Christ, we find defining all He did on this earth, those exact same aspects just stated. Deliberate, intentional, focussed, with design, planning, acting with absolute integrity to connect with people and then connect those people to Himself and His Father. Everything else was a sideshow.

Perhaps we need the clarity of Ephesians 2, v.8, where the apostle Paul writes with profound simplicity that we are saved by grace through faith, that is, your salvation and mine do not originate or proceed from within ourselves, but "it is the gift of God". First, "Who?", then "Why?".

We need to go back to Genesis to understand how God's grace started. Where did the rescue plan commence? We need to understand that to all our theologically correct list of God's attributes should be added "Vulnerability". God, alone, is infinitely vulnerable simply because He made man in His own image. He sent His Son, who became human, and with His humanity came "vulnerability" and the "vulnerability" to die. This is our God who gives Himself and is prepared to die to redeem us. Perhaps the concept of God's "vulnerability" as a theological reality in creating vulnerable people is limiting but enlightening because we are created in His own image. I add this here to show that vulnerability is a human requirement for greater awareness and growth.

It is essential to understand that when Adam and Eve transgressed, God came "looking" for them, and he did not condemn; He did not shout or show anger; He simply asked a question, with tears in His eyes: "Where are you?" A profound question to which He already knew the answer. God, in His infinite love, had started the plan to reconnect with His wayward creation. Only a vulnerable God creates humans with free will, and when they mess it up, He seeks them out, as Jesus did, to reconnect with His created people. Sending His Son is the greatest act of a vulnerable God, who, with those same tear-filled eyes of love, will not let us go. There is found our "Who?" and our "Why?" together.

My "Who?" comes from the simple fact that I have been created on purpose and for His purpose by God in Christ, who intentionally planned, designed me, and created me to live for His Glory. My "Who?" is profoundly influenced by these facts and completed by adding that all this is to conform me to the image of Christ. So only by understanding my Creator's "Who?" and His "Why?" can I possibly start to have any clarity as to my "Who?" and "Why?". So my "Why?" must start with my "Who?". And it must start with absolute clarity in knowing why Christ acted as He did.

Ephesians, again but now chapter 2, v10 AMP: "For we are God's (own) handiwork (His workmanship), recreated in Christ Jesus, (born anew) that we may do those good works which God predestined (planned beforehand) for us (taking paths which He prepared ahead of time), that we should walk in them) living the good life which He prearranged and made ready for us to live). Deliberate, focussed intentionality, with design and planning with perfect execution of His plans."

So, why do we live and act with the language of scarcity and depletion and not that of abundance and surplus because that is God's plan and Higher Purpose for everyone individually? As I look back, I have always been deeply saddened by closed or clearly closing churches. Two of the hardest years of my life came about due to taking the job of a Church Warden. This led to the emergent understanding that all my life has been continuing to this point in time. I started looking back. Two thousand years, to be precise. I discovered that I had to find out why Christ's church is like it is, How it got to this point, and How we will get to where God always planned us to be. What came out of that Awareness quest were more questions:

❖ What is my "Why?", based on my "Who?"? To inspire people to understand and do what God has created them for, called them for and created a future for.

75

- ❖ My "Why?", based on my "Who?", is to start the transformation of the Church of Christ back towards what Christ planned it to be.
- ❖ My "Why?", based on my "Who?", is to get back to the future by understanding what His "Why?", "How?" and "What?" were. Then, rebooting a church with that "Why?", "What?" and "How?" with laser focus and structure.

Conclusions for Step 2

Awareness! Of Your Best Life

Key Thought – Trust God As You Have Never Trusted Before

If you can understand God's creative actions in giving you your Origin, Identity, Significance, Potential, Purpose, Inspiration, Passion, Vision, Focus, and Destiny and accept these with a new greater awareness of God's perfect plans for you, then you are making progress!

Let's reread the sub-headings listed above again. As before, they are listed here with the symbol of Breakout Action Points: read these carefully; they are not just sub-headings.

> ➤ **Ultimate Purpose – the 7 Higher Purposes of God**
> ➤ **Starting Awareness for Your Best Life**
> ➤ **Redemption**
> ➤ **The Heart Of A Created Human Being**
> ➤ **Living The Life God Always Planned For Us To Live**
> ➤ **Greater Awareness Through Vulnerability and Authenticity**

I suggest, again, that you simply reread the sub-headings listed above. Do an internal assessment and ask yourself the following questions and directions:

1. Are you discovering the real purposes of God for your life and starting to understand what he has planned for you?
2. Do you feel more aware of greater things that you have not considered before?
3. Are you feeling the stunning common sense behind the "Hard-Wired" list?
4. Are you able to accept God's creative actions and thinking for you as an individual?
5. Are these truths starting to change your thinking and awareness?
6. Find two choices you need to make right now.
7. Think about how you can enable greater awareness of God.

Step 3

To Develop! Your Best Life

"You are hand-picked by God.
You cannot become or discover all that you are created and meant to be
until you wholeheartedly seek God to discover Him for all that He Is."

If this is true, then we must seek to answer the questions:
Who created us?
Who are we?
Why are we here?
Where do we come from?
What is our purpose?
What is our calling?
Why?

~~~

Our cultures subdue the human spirits God creates through the status quo.
Our Christian Church systems prevent the unlocking of our potential,
they prevent the discovery of purpose, and they halt
the transformation and growth of individuals
who would otherwise grow to become
the Extraordinary People God
created them to be.
Period.

~~~

❖ **Key Purpose: This is the real choice to begin with. Create the Character and Integrity to Endure, Moving from Knowing to Learning, from Using to Investing, and Making the Most of What God has Already Given You. Grow the seeds of Greatness.**

➢ **Key Learning (Always Facing the Unknown without Fear):** We have seen how Awareness is vital to access in your life. As we turn to the Develop step, you will be helped by many smaller steps, and one of the most effective is to "Know Where You Are (and Where You Are Going)", a necessary precursor mini step in your Transformation and Growth. You will be encouraged when you discover the 40 Remarkable and Compelling Daily Commitment Choices, and even more by the 50 Remarkable and

Compelling Reminders of Your Best Life Success (Because Being Wobbly is Normal!)

❖ **Key Actions (Building The Bridge As You Walk On It):** The key Action to undertake for this step is to consciously create a Growth Environment, consciously decide to Live Your Best Life, and consciously Live Intentionally. All Development is all intentional. It won't come knocking on your door asking to be let in. None of this works like that! I may add that it won't just happen by praying for it alone. God honours Commitment and Action. The Bridge Will Build As You Walk On It – guaranteed!

Know Where You Are (and Where You Are Going)

The pursuit and meaning of every human life on this planet is purpose and living a life that matters. For those who have faith in God through Jesus Christ, this means God's Higher Purpose: its realisation, its discovery, its capacity, and its results. Everything else is a sideshow and a distraction from our Higher Purpose. The burning question is, therefore, "How are you and me to transform our lives so that we live and fulfil God's Higher Purpose for our lives?" Other questions may fill our minds, and they are asked at this point in *TRANSFORMED!* By now, you will have the clarity to respond:

❖ Where am I!?
❖ Who am I!?
❖ Why am I here?
❖ And then:
❖ Why do I exist!?
❖ What am I supposed to do?
❖ What is my destiny?

And then again:

❖ How can I make a difference?
❖ How can I live a life that Matters?
❖ How can I live a Significant life?
❖ How can I live a Fulfilled life?
❖ How far can I go?

These are the vital self-evident questions that you may be pondering right now. They almost seem simple, trivial and childish, but without the clarity that attempting to answer those questions will bring, you and I cannot move forward in our quest for understanding and fulfilment, to enable our lives to matter, to live the lives we are created for – our Best Lives.

This book is not about knowledge, IQ, or even life-long experience. It is not about learning or acquiring what others cannot and will never know or live through. It is not about a hierarchy of intelligence, position, or life; it is not a competition against others where only one person wins. I cannot sum it up more succinctly than Dr Brene Brown, in her book *Daring Greatly*, where she writes this: "Who we are matters immeasurably more than what we know or who we want to be."[36]

It is simply all about unlocking the unique unlimited potential that God places inside people when they are created. It is about enabling people to understand that where they are is never where they are meant to be. It is all about intentional personal transformation and growth with continuous improvement. It is all about your unlocked unlimited potential to fulfil your personal purpose. It is all about living lives of significance that matter, lives that make a difference, and that can only come from serving others.

Got it?

Not difficult, is it?

Not "Rocket Science" either.

An analogy with flight is instructive for our goals. One essential understanding is the need to relentlessly match and overcome the gravitational pull of the status quo, your culture and your comfort zone.

To use another analogy, it is uphill all the way.

- ➤ None of *TRANSFORMED!* works without effort
- ➤ None of this happens without intentionality and action
- ➤ None of this commences without the decision to start
- ➤ None of this is initiated without the internal desire to change and unlock your potential
- ➤ None of this is initiated without the internal desire to unlock your potential for others
- ➤ None of this happens unless you get out of your comfort zone and start
- ➤ None of this happens unless you stretch yourself beyond your wildest dreams
- ➤ None of this happens unless you step out of your self-limiting culture
- ➤ None of this happens unless you step up to make a difference

[36] Brené Brown, *Daring Greatly: How the Courage to Be Vulnerable Transforms the Way We Live, Love, Parent and Lead*, 2013, p. 177.

> ➤ None of this happens unless you desire to live a life that matters
> ➤ None of this happens unless you discover your God-created purpose

None of this can happen unless your God-created unlimited potential is awoken, unlocked, unleashed, developed and acted upon to live a life of God-created purpose and destiny.

You see, that quote above, "Who we are matters immeasurably more than what we know or who we want to be"[37] was foremost in the Creator's mind.

Ephesians 1:4 NIV: "For he chose us in him before the creation of the world to be holy and blameless in his sight."

If we have been "chosen to be", I suggest we need to understand this scripture's implications. While I recognise that there are bright spots within the Christian Church and that there are many who, historically and in contemporary society, have worked to bring real spiritual transformation to believers seeking truth, it would be fair also to say the institutional Church has tended to control and suffocate the voices of those most in need of radical inner change.

Sadly, in general, our society, our cultures, our educational systems, our businesses, and even our churches have failed to understand such simple aspects and continue to place their faith in the power-based hierarchy as the only way to conduct life, faith and learning. From the earliest days after the Apostles' deaths, those who had known and been trained by Jesus died, and the Church in Rome became all-powerful. The inevitable choice of their Graeco-Roman traditions infected their thinking, their practice, and their desire for power at the expense of others. They went their own ways to keep themselves in control, and unsurprisingly, this was true even of the Church!

It is not too over the top to confidently state that you and I have been effectively "lied" to for two millennia. Our cultures' systems are fundamentally based as they have been on hierarchy and power domination, with the historic collusion of our forebears and those hierarchies in their own diminishment and disempowerment. This very effectively precluded the possibility of the transformation and growth plans that God intended and showed through His Son, Jesus Christ, when He walked this earth.

We need to see the BIG PICTURE. We need Daily Transformation and Growth to guide understanding here. If we can understand what might yet be, we can gain the clarity to assess where we are. Are you focussed solely on living for yourself, or are you focussed on developing others?

We were never designed to live low-level average or below-average lives. We know or certainly suspect, within ourselves is something greater than we

---

[37] Brown, *Daring Greatly*, p. 177.

can express, perhaps subconscious, unarticulated and suppressed feelings that where we are is not where we could and should be. Our Creator designed us for something greater than we can articulate.

John C. Maxwell, in his book *No Limits*, says: "If you don't have others who believe in you, then let me be the first. I believe in you. And I want the best for you. I want you to believe in yourself. I can loan you my belief, but that only works for a short time. To be successful, you must believe in yourself. You can be successful if others don't believe in you, but you cannot be successful if you don't believe in yourself. And to make a change, you must take action and do the right things that will allow you to possess self-belief."[38]

Nothing could be closer to my heart as I write *TRANSFORMED!* I can affirm that you have everything in you that you need to live a *TRANSFORMED!* Life.

Create a Growth Environment

Only you can create a Growth Environment where one did not exist before. You may move to one, but that is your choice. So the effect is the same because you have woken sufficiently to determine that where you are is "not where you should be" or even where you need to be or stay.

It is ultimately your choice, and this is significant because it is intentional. No one stumbles inadvertently to a place where you can grow, except in rare circumstances. These places need to be created, especially for those who are likely to be living in challenging situations.

In *No Limits*, John C. Maxwell also states that "A Growth Environment" Is a Place Where...
1. *Others Are Ahead of You*
2. *You Are Continually Challenged*
3. *Your Focus Is Forward*
4. *The Atmosphere Is Affirming*
5. *You Are out of Your Comfort Zone*
6. *You Wake Up Excited*
7. *Failure Is Not Your Enemy*
8. *Others Are Growing*
9. *People Desire Change*

---

[38] John C. Maxwell, *No Limits*, p. 36.

10. Growth Is Modelled and Expected [39]

By looking at the above definition of a Growth Environment, we can start to understand where we are. This is vitally important for anyone on the cusp of Wakeup and Breakout from where they are, wherever that may be. Laid out below are the core scriptures for this book:

Ephesians 2:10 NLT:
"For we are God's masterpiece. He has created us anew in Christ Jesus, so we can do the good things he planned for us long ago."

Jeremiah 29:11-14 NIV:
"For I know the plans I have for you," declares the Lord, "plans to prosper you and not to harm you, plans to give you hope and a future. Then you will call on me and come and pray to me, and I will listen to you. You will seek me and find me when you seek me with all your heart. I will be found by you," declares the Lord, "and will bring you back from captivity. I will gather you from all the nations and places where I have banished you," declares the Lord, "and will bring you back to the place from which I carried you into exile."

Here are the first shoots of God's plans for you and me. Here are God's plans for people who start to focus on Him, are wholly committed to Him, and intentionally seek Him with all their hearts. Central to those plans are 12 aspects/concepts of transformation and growth with:

- ❖ potential
- ❖ purpose
- ❖ passion
- ❖ possibility
- ❖ hope
- ❖ inspiration
- ❖ intentionality
- ❖ significance
- ❖ anticipation
- ❖ abundance
- ❖ focus
- ❖ action
- ❖ vision
- ❖ destiny

---

[39] John C. Maxwell, *No Limits*, pp. 281–89.

All are ensuing in response to individual transformation and growth as a stream gushes from a mountainside. None of this can be "learnt" from a book. It can only be realised and discovered daily through Intentional Transformation and Growth.

This is *TRANSFORMED!*, the inner workings. It is also the outworking of the Higher 7 Purposes of God for you and me that we showed in Step 2. They were uniquely created, present and perfectly expressed in Jesus Christ. They are the "every person", unique, individually created 12 aspects of the following:

This is God's created plan for you and me. Through Creation and our God-given Identity, we are God's Masterpieces.

This is God's intended extraordinary unlimited life for us and the seedbed of Greatness for Others. This is the Identity of Masterpiece People and how they Live. They Live Lives of Transformation and Growth with Mindsets of:

- ❖ Intentionality
- ❖ Significance
- ❖ Anticipation
- ❖ Abundance
- ❖ Focus
- ❖ Action

These are the six results of God's unlimited intentions through us for others – this is "our voice" – Our Unique Personal Significance.

God's Masterpiece People Live Lives that have:

- ❖ Potential
- ❖ Purpose
- ❖ Passion
- ❖ Vision
- ❖ Inspiration
- ❖ Destiny

They made Christ in human terms who He was, how He functioned, how He acted, how He lived, moved, and had His being, and especially they made Him who He was towards others. These are the human aspects of the Life of Christ laid out to give us a better understanding and, through that, to commit ourselves to walk this "Highway".

These are the biblical Eight foundational "Highway" truths of Christ's life with priceless questions (they are the "Highway" He chose to walk – He calls us to follow likewise).

Living Your Best Life

We are all called not only for the above and understanding our Purpose but also to Intentionally Live a Life of Significance. A Life that recognises God's Abundance and Surplus, Living a Life of Anticipation and that we choose with the focus to impact/lift/add value/make a difference/lead in the lives of others today by seizing opportunities as we look for them.

What do we want to say? What results do we want to achieve?
Focus on the outcomes and the results you want to achieve.
What results do we want to create?
My single focus is to unlock and unleash potential in others, especially in churches that are failing. As John C. Maxwell describes it, he "loves to lift the lid off others!" Just five words: take the lid off people!

- Purposeful Engagement
- Belief
- Commitment
- Connection

It is all about People and their growth.

> *"There is a raw self within each of us, too, that is our seed of destiny. Like acorns, we are oaks-in-waiting, raw potential waiting to find our calling. At the core of our destiny lies the necessity of choice, the potential to choose to become something that has never existed before. When we fail to express our embedded gifts, we starve our seed of destiny... A calling is the urge to give our gifts away."*
> **Richard Lieder**

(Quote above cited below. [40])

Because this is what it is all about: Growing transformed people who transform themselves, transform their future, and change their Destiny, Change the Future and help others do the same. Keep that single focus, and don't dissipate it by making it complicated or confusing your priorities with multiple focuses. Create a Compelling Vision. Create a Purpose that Matters with Focus and Execution through a Growth Mindset and a Growth Environment.

"If you want to make a difference, do it now! To be significant, all you have

---

[40] Richard Leider, 'Is Leading Your Calling?', *Leader to Leader*, 2004.31 (2004), 36–40.

to do is make a difference with others wherever you are, with whatever you have, day by day."[41] – John C. Maxwell

TRANSFORMED Keywords: Growth, Potential, Purpose, Personal Transformation, Significance, Anticipation, Intentionality, Intentional living, Abundance and Surplus, Inspire Others to act, Unlocking and Unleashing Unlimited Potential, Transformational Leadership, Focus, Wholeheartedness, Meaning, Proactive, Living Lives that Matter, Consequential, Fulfilling God's Purposes, Awareness, Wake Up, Breakout, Create Positive Culture, Best Life, Higher Purpose.

All wonderfully uplifting, motivating, and inspiring words that will help you understand and define Your Best Life, which, as we know, is absolutely unique. No one else can live it or fulfil it. It is just for you, and your best life will be unlike everyone else's, so a comparison is pointless.

My Best Life statement goes as follows (but please don't follow it – create your own!):

"We are created and called for God's Higher Purpose, which is for our Transformation through Redemption in Christ meaning Recreation in Christ, Renewal in Christ, Restoration in Christ, and Redirection in Christ for His Purpose, Vision, Fulfilment and Destiny, through personal growth. We are created to reach our fullest potential, lift others intentionally with us, fulfil God's Transcendent Higher Purpose in our generation, and be filled to the measure of all the fullness of God in Jesus Christ. I choose this day to contribute by living an intentional life of significance to influence, lift and inspire others to be the same in Jesus Christ."

We need to wake out from the default lives we live, and thinking that this is life, so that we are then enabled to live the real life, what Jesus called "life that is truly life" – significance through intentionally growing others first. We need to stop living lives that are "normal". We need to break out of the cultural prison we inhabit, which treats Christianity as merely an optional 'add-on', and instead realise that God created you and me intentionally for His Higher Purpose.

Traditional churches have made this almost impossible because we have had indelibly marked in our minds that "church" is a building where we go to repeat the same events every Sunday, being "taught" by dress-coded clergy, seated in rows in front of them. Everything, from the design and layout of the building, the format of the "service", and the religious culture-based language used throughout the service – in the hymns and prayers, is all about clergy control and the Mindsets of scarcity and depletion. Truly, it was the same in Jesus's

---

[41] John C. Maxwell, *Intentional Living*, p. 2.

times. But, putting it in the vernacular, He "was having none of it".

The Church system of gathering in a building to "worship", to "ask forgiveness for our sins", to "pray" using the language of scarcity with an abundant God, to "pray" for "good results" and "safety" for people and situations is a scandalous indictment of our failure to understand and act properly upon clear scripture exhortations and teaching.

Fundamentally, if you and I have not connected and recommitted to our Abundant God the moment we awaken every morning, we have lost before we start the day. Worship, Consecration, Dedication and Total Commitment are when we wake up and lie down, not primarily when we "attend" a "worshipping" service.

But we are called to live renewed lives with renewed hearts and minds as Romans 12:1-2 NIV clearly states: "Therefore, I urge you, brothers and sisters, in view of God's mercy, to offer your bodies as a living sacrifice, holy and pleasing to God – this is your true and proper worship. Do not conform to the pattern of this world, but be transformed by the renewing of your mind. Then you will be able to test and approve what God's will is – his good, pleasing and perfect will."

Upon what must the renewed mind be based? There can only be one answer: the mind of Christ. He acted with intentionality, purpose, and vision to unequivocally separate himself from the dress-coded clergy and their thinking of His day to build Transformational Leaders who would take His Gospel to the ends of the earth, starting with those right in front of Him!

He was not primarily "building a community"; He was "building individuals". When you try to "build community", the focus is on "community" for its own sake, whatever that may be and with its own limiting culture. All traditional communities have hierarchy and leaders. The very nature of a community is that the members subordinate themselves to the culture. They can never be more than the culture or even its leader. It completely misunderstands and ignores the focus of Christ. When you build individuals one at a time to Live their Best Lives, the process is anticipatory, assuming their value and significance. This can only be through Transformational Servant Leadership. The focus is on transforming people whose focus is on transforming others through the unlocked and unleashed unlimited potential already within them. Thus, a God-focussed community of individuals ensues, but it is not an envisaged end.

Yes, salvation through faith is essential, but the result was always planned to be people transformed deliberately through their Potential, Value and Significance, helping others to be similarly transformed: essentially a vitally cascading growth system. Something much greater, more vital and profoundly dynamic ensues from Transformational Leadership than "community". Community always subjugates its inmates to its culture. Community always focuses on its leader. Crucially, it can never be better than its leader. It can only be limited. Every God-created person has unlimited potential. Culture and Community will always conspire to deny that potential the light of day. Transformational Leadership sets people free to "fly" and become the individuals God always planned for them to become for Him.

Have you not noticed Christ was never "at the front" but always "in the midst", transforming those deeply connected with Him one moment, one day at a time? His message, along with His messianic destiny, was to make utterly clear that after loving His Father God with all our hearts, souls, strength and mind, our focus and priority is to love others. When clarified with His directions for being great through being a servant, this helps us see the truth of the following extract from Dr Rick Warren's book, *The Purpose Driven Life*.

Rick writes, "Without God, life has no purpose, and without purpose, life has no meaning. Without meaning, life has no significance or hope."[42] A meaningless life is a life without hope or significance. This is a profound statement and one that everyone should spend time pondering. God gives purpose; Purpose gives meaning; Meaning gives hope and significance.

God in Christ ensures that we can live in His world of abundance and surplus, not scarcity and depletion. So, Ephesians 4:1 NIV: "As a prisoner for the Lord, then, I urge you to live a life worthy of the calling you have received" means just that. We are designed and created by God to live by giving away to others the understanding not only of salvation in Christ but of the incredibly fulfilling and joyful truths of living lives with Potential, Purpose, Meaning, Hope, Significance and the Intentionality of God for those who choose to live lives of His Higher Purpose.

John C. Maxwell asks three questions to help people discover their "why?" and their Best Lives:
Question 1: What Do You Cry About?
Question 2: What Do You Sing About?
Question 3: What Do You Dream About? [43]

What is your one word? What best describes you? That single word may inspire you, focus your attention, and help you to understand your why. Where will that one word take you? How does it relate to adding value to others? Why is it significant? Keep that one word in your mind as you go about your day in the coming weeks and see

---

[42] Warren, *The Purpose Driven Life*, p. 34.
[43] John C. Maxwell, *Intentional Living*, pp. 92–98.

where it leads you.[44]

Now you know how to live a life of purpose. You know that significance is within your reach. You know what it means to be intentional. So I want to ask you a series of questions. See how many you can honestly answer yes to:

➢ *Are you choosing to live a story of significance? Yes!*

➢ *Are you actively searching for your why so that you can make a difference? Yes!*

➢ *Are you choosing to live with intentionality, not just good intentions? Yes!*

➢ *Are you willing to start small but believe big to make a difference? Yes!*

➢ *Are you living with a sense of anticipation for making a difference? Yes!*

➢ *Are you seizing opportunities and taking action to make a difference? Yes!*[45]

If you answered YES! to all of these questions—or if you are willing to answer yes and take action now—then you have crossed over into the significant life. What Will Your Decision Be?[46]

If you join me in my dream of making a difference, together maybe we can start a movement—a movement toward a world of intentional living where people think of others before themselves, where adding value to others is a priority, where financial gain is second to future potential, and where people's self-worth is strengthened by acts of significance every day. If we each live a life that truly matters, we can change the world.[47]

A transformational leader intentionally engages people to think and act in such a way that it makes a positive difference in their lives and in the lives of others.[48]

So our Best Life is unique, our potential awaits to be unlocked, and our purpose awaits discovery. I can't wait to see you make a start!

God's Extraordinary Masterpiece People

God's Extraordinary Created Masterpiece People Live Intentionally and Growing Daily – these are living their Best Lives, and they:

---

[44] John C. Maxwell, *Intentional Living.* p. 101

[45] John C. Maxwell, *Intentional Living,* p. 265.

[46] John C. Maxwell, *Intentional Living,* p. 266.

[47] John C. Maxwell, *Intentional Living,* p. 182.

[48] John C. Maxwell, *Intentional Living,* p. 234.

> **AWAKE! To LIVE Their Best Life**
>> ➤ To Awareness of their Best Life
>> ➤ To Develop their Best Life
>> ➤ To Think Over Their Best Life
> **UNLOCK! Potential for Their Best Life**
>> ➤ To Breakout to their Best Life
>> ➤ To Grow their Best Life
>> ➤ To Engage themselves and others in their Best Life
> **ACT! Contributing For Others to Live Their Best Lives**
>> ➤ To Lead Others to their Best Lives
>> ➤ To Rally Others to their Best Lives
>> ➤ To Legacy Others to their Best Life Legacy

And they understand and Live in the Land of God's Transcendent Higher Purpose instinctively and permanently. They live Ephesians 2:10 NLT, "For we are God's masterpiece. He has created us anew in Christ Jesus, so we can do the good things he planned for us long ago." They are actively transforming and growing intentionally to live lives of significance and make a difference for Others, literally becoming, thinking and acting out in themselves for Others, the perfect human life that Christ did and modelled. Then I ask the question: "What does God's Higher Purpose look like?"

Professor Bob Quinn writes about this in a recent blog about "Contributive Vision".[49] The concept of wanting/needing to "Contribute" is vital to understand fully. I have lived with this, naturally, inwardly, for decades, but never fully considered the impact within *TRANSFORMED!* for God's Higher Purpose. "Contributing" involves us moving outside our normal self-centred lives and making not just a difference but a "connecting contribution" that stimulates fresh thinking, growth, and action and then further "connecting contribution" with others that could never have happened alone. "Contributive Vision" involves everyone at God's Higher Level and is fundamental to God's Higher Purpose. Professor Quinn has coined an intriguing phrase and states the "fundamental state of leadership (is) a state of internal motivation and disciplined contribution."[50]

I am living a "Contributive Vision" right now as I write! I am in the

---

[49] 'Contributive Vision', *Robert E. Quinn*
<https://robertequinn.com/uncategorized/contributive-vision/> [accessed 21 May 2020].
[50] 'Contributive Vision'.

fundamental state of leadership[51] and internally motivated, contributing (albeit humanly unseen) in a highly disciplined and focussed manner for God's Highest Purpose. And yes, supremely alone (at the moment), for I am carving out a masterpiece for God.

Transformational Leadership embraces Authentic Higher Purpose. Authentic Higher Purpose leads to Deep Engagement and feeds back to Transformational Leadership, which also grows and matures and moves to live permanently at the Higher Level. Connecting with, engaging with, and fully understanding Higher Purpose transforms those who have embraced it. The culture is transformed, thinking is transformed, action is redefined and transformed, and people self-lead and contribute by their empowerment. Before, they were low-level, "don't think, just do the work" employees. Now, they are fully engaged and continually renewed. When others discover their Higher Purpose, they also tend to become new transformational leaders. Authenticity increases, leadership increases, emerging potential in every situation, at every level, and in every person increases, and they build the bridge as they walk on it.

Higher Purpose work requires a person's transformation from conventional, hierarchical, organisational accepted beliefs, constraints and transactional management to a visionary leadership approach that believes in every person's transformation and their growth to fulfilment where unlimited individual Potential is fully engaged in the Higher Purpose for which God created them.

It requires the change from a traditional conventional, hierarchical, transactional organisation Mindset of People as Agents of that conventional organisational thinking to the dramatically different Mindset of People as God's uniquely created individuals whose potential is unlimited and whose purpose will yet be discovered.

Only a Higher Purpose-Driven Transformational Leader who has literally changed Mindsets can draw out from within a person their Unique Personal Significance.

Who We Are

As God's Extraordinary Masterpiece, God is calling from the very core of your created being good things placed there long ago. We are created by God and recreated by Christ as His Extraordinary Masterpiece to be connected with Him and with others, lifting and growing them for His Glory. We have placed within us God's extraordinary birth gifts – unlimited potential, capacities, capabilities,

---

[51] Quinn and Quinn.

talents, and vision that are summed up in unique potential and purpose found in our hearts, minds and spirits. He intends to unleash our unlimited potential in Greatness for Others, the Greatness described by Christ. He intends us to find "our voice" (Our God-created Unique Personal Significance) through Potential, Purpose, Intentionality, Inspiration, Vision and Destiny and help Others find theirs. Any response I make will inevitably be inadequate, but a God-created being must seek to respond to Him since not to would be to waste a God-created world of potential that would lie undiscovered, unused, and lost to Others.

> *"An unintentional life accepts everything and does nothing.*
> *An intentional life embraces only the things that will*
> *add to the mission of significance."*
> *John C. Maxwell, Intentional Living*

(Above quotation cited below.[52])

Please read the following for yourself:
"I matter to Him, and God has placed within me His Holy Spirit because of my trust in Christ for sins forgiven – I choose and commit to living as His Extraordinary Masterpiece today because I am Created to Make a Difference for Him – I choose to be a Transformational Leader to help others discover God's Salvation and Purposes for their lives and go and do something about it – am I living and understanding more fully both what a priceless privilege God has given me and how He designed me to firstly, to intentionally reconnect daily with Him with conscious consecration, decisive dedication, wholehearted commitment, connection by choice, all with discipline? Secondly, through personal transformation and growth to reach my fullest potential with servant leadership to make a difference, show others they matter, value others, and add value in others' lives today. Without these essential foundations and pinnacles, none of the following matters."

Living Intentionally

How we are to live Intentionally for God's Higher Purpose:
➢ **Transformation and Growth Living To Make A Difference** – My transformation and growth both towards and for God are unlimited. My Growth, I have discovered, matters because I will only reach my potential

---

[52] John C. Maxwell, *Intentional Living*, p. 34.

through Transformation and Growth through extraordinary awareness and expansion of my mind and thinking. The opportunity and potential for both are unlimited. My love and praise for God are potentially unlimited. I choose to live an extraordinary transformational life of growth for God and for myself and others today by unlocking and unleashing God-given unlimited potential in myself and others, to stretch to my fullest potential for God who has created me, with the understandings shown below – am I continually learning, growing, being transformed, reaching and stretching towards my fullest potential through the daily renewing, transformation and growth of my mind through greater awareness for God, so that I can make a difference for others, today?

➤ **Intentionality and Integrity Living To Make A Difference** – I choose to live an extraordinary life of intentionality and total integrity of character for myself and others as Jesus did, perfectly, today because this is the key to a life that matters – am I crossing over to an intentional life every day? Am I Thinking and Living each day with intentionality, becoming more intentional about my personal growth and living making a difference for others daily, today?

➤ **Significance and Meaning Living To Make A Difference** – I choose to live an extraordinary life of significance and meaning as Jesus did today – am I preparing and anticipating intending to be significant for others today? Am I crossing, daily, over to a Significant life that gives the meaning that we all crave?

➤ **Anticipation and Urgency Living To Make A Difference** – I choose to live an extraordinary life with a wonderful sense of anticipation and urgency as God intended, today – am I living with the anticipation of Transformation and Growth and a sense of urgency and expecting, planning, seeking, preparing and significantly positioning myself to make a difference for God and for others, today?

➤ **Abundance and Surplus Living To Make A Difference** – I choose to live an extraordinary life in significant abundance and surplus living as Christ did as a Masterpiece Abundance and Surplus Thinker (not default depletion and scarcity thinking), today – am I living with a Mindset of God's Abundance and Surplus for all of us as I intentionally live to make a difference for God and for others, today?

➤ **Focus and Commitment Living To Make A Difference** – I choose to live an extraordinary life of Focus and Commitment as God's Masterpiece of personal transformation, intentionality, significance and meaning, anticipation, abundance and focus, preparing daily for growth, action, service and sacrifice, all for being focussed on others, valuing them and adding value to others, today – am I focussed for God on these fundamental directions of the life He always created me to live, today?

➤ **Action and Opportunities Living To Make A Difference** – I choose to live an extraordinary life of intentional action today, fully engaged in the service of a cause larger and other than myself, and looking for and seizing opportunities to create a legacy of transformed lives for others as God intends me to do – am I growing and preparing (and always ready) with a positive attitude and focussed priorities, seeking opportunities and acting intentionally and significantly to unlock and unleash potential in others for their transformation and growth, today?

> *"Anticipation is a wonderfully proactive and intentional word for seeking out significance. People with anticipation plan to be significant. They expect to live a life that matters every day. They prepare to do significant acts. They position themselves physically, mentally, emotionally, and financially to make a difference in the lives of others. Their sense of anticipation for significance draws them forward."*
> *John C. Maxwell, Intentional Living*

(Above quotation cited below.[53])

This is simply how Christ lived as He grew His disciples. And all so we can live lives as God's Extraordinary Masterpieces, lives of intentionality, lives fulfilling our unlimited potential, lives full of meaning and discovered higher purpose, lives that matter, lives full of significance, to glorify our Creator and to lift Others to be fulfilled and do the same.

For me, Growth through Transformation, Intentionality, Significance, Anticipation, Abundance, Focus and Action are the fuel that ensures we can improve for God as He intended and get better every day, that tomorrow will be better because of them. Just Daily speaking, two of those words, thoughts-focus-decisions, Intentionality and Anticipation, causes an upwelling of hopefulness and purposefulness. The day before me transforms from fearful thinking of the responsibilities I need to undertake (and fearfully thinking about what will happen if I don't) to a state of fulfilled, directed and focussed self-leadership, which, if understood in the context of God's plans for you and me, informs my heart of what I am created for, daily.

---

[53] John C. Maxwell, *Intentional Living*, p. 217.

Then I use the *Daily Commitment Prayer:*

"Lord God, my Creator, I Choose to Love You, Trust and Delight in You, and Live and Commit My Best Life to You Today, Living for Your Transcendent Higher Purpose; You Chose, Designed and Created me to Live this Extraordinary Life, Fully Committed to You and Fully Connected with You, for Others, Today; To Live the Extraordinary Masterpiece Life, the Life of Conscious Consecration, Decisive Dedication, Wholehearted Commitment, Connecting with Choice to You; Trusting in You and Doing Good, Delighting in You, Focussed Intentionally on You; Living the Life of Transformation, Growth, Significance, Anticipation and Abundance, Connection and Contribution that you created me for, for Others, Today."

God created you and me to Live Extraordinary Lives so that whatever happens, you and I can say, *"I Intend to Grow,"* and, *"I Anticipate Growth, Making a Difference in the world to Value and Add Value to Others as God Intended and Planned, Today."* Speaking to myself, *"I Choose and Intend to Grow, and I Anticipate Growth Today For God and For Others,"* which Unlocks, Transforms and Renews my Vision for the day! This one simple "action of choice", more than any other, Lifts, Directs, and Focuses on "God's Higher Purpose" My Heart and Mind and Prepares Me to Make a Difference, Living a Life That Matters, Living a Life of Significance for Others. This is what God designed and created us for. A simple but constant daily commitment and focus (and for those of us like me, easily distracted, who need constant daily refocussing) repay dividends in the transformation and growth that we will experience. Over time, we will succeed with renewed minds with their new focus and commitment set in place.

40 Remarkable and Compelling Daily Commitment Choices

All 40 Choices below are about Our Significant Best Life. Building, Developing and Encouraging You and me to be more self-aware and, through that process, to be more God-aware as we Seek Him with all our Hearts, to be Part of Something Greater than Ourselves, even if we do not feel it. The simple "Choosing and Commitment to Action" of these Choices will lead to extraordinary changes in our minds and lives that are recognisable to us and others. But rather like the 50 Remarkable and Compelling Reasons for a Best Life, "How many Remarkable and Compelling Daily Commitment Choices do we need!?"

This is about embarking on a new journey, and not the predictable trudge through life, the "asking God to forgive and heal us every day" life, so beloved by traditional Christians, but an Indomitable spirit "Choosing and Commitment to Action" Escaping Breakout Journey that will Transform our Thinking, our

Lives, our relationship with God, and the Lives of Others and it starts with the simple choice and commitment to action:

The *Choice to walk hand-in-hand with God totally committed to Him*: He created you and me to be transformed, to live the life he created us for and intends us to live, and in that process, becoming a Significant Life of Profound Meaning, Purpose, and Passion, a Life of Focussed Intentionality, a Life that Matters, a Life that Makes a Difference, for Him and for Others.

Or the *Choice to walk away, alone,* back to self-focus, back to disappointment and the "lost-ness" that accompanies lives that are purposeless and have no meaning, lives that do not matter to yourself or anyone else, nor ever will.

> *God created us for His glory and gives us*
> *not only the freedom from, but crucially, the freedom to.*
> *Among all that we could mention of the freedoms to:*
> *to love Him with all our hearts with all our souls*
> *and with all our minds to live lives consecrated,*
> *dedicated and fully committed to Him*
>
> *To Live Our Best life, Intentionally Our Best Life*
> *to live lives that are intentional for others*
> *to live lives of contribution for others*
> *to live lives that matter for others*
> *to live lives that make a difference for others*
> *to value and add value to others.*
> *These are preeminent.*

Maybe this specific moment, as you read right now, is the "fork in the road" choice that only you can make. Maybe you are desperate to live a life of potential, meaning and purpose, to live a life that matters, the life that God created you for – because if You Choose, you can live the other side of Your YES!

- ➤ You Can Answer YES!
- ➤ You Can Choose to Live a Life that Truly Matters!
- ➤ You Can Discover Your Birthright that God has already placed in you.

Welcome home!

Welcome to the Real Life God Created You to Live. "Growing to Become the

Extraordinary Masterpiece God Created You to Be."

Personal Note: After I had written the above paragraphs, I felt the visceral response I seek to elicit in all of us, and I reached a mental tipping point that helped me recognise for the first time since starting the attempt at writing *TRANSFORMED!* that it could, after all, really happen!

So, together, we remind ourselves of our Commitment to God through faith in Christ and to Action Today. We are starting Every Day with that Commitment so that this "Daily Commitment" and the "Daily Choosing to Live" is the Extraordinary Life God Created Us For.

Now read on with a more profound understanding of the importance of and the freedom to "Choose". God created us for intentional activity, to be fully engaged in something greater than ourselves.

Our freedom to choose is unique to human beings. The freedom to choose is intentional activity and enables us to be fully committed, fully engaged and continually renewed, thereby living our Best lives if we Choose! And so the Masterpiece Commitment Prayers:

> *Lord God, my Creator, I Choose to Love You, Trust and Delight in You, and Live and Commit My Best Life of Contribution to You, Today, Living for Your Higher Purpose; You Chose, Designed and Created me to Live this Extraordinary Life, Fully Committed to You and Fully Connected with You, for Others, Today; to Live the Extraordinary Masterpiece Life, the Life of Conscious Consecration, Decisive Dedication, Wholehearted Commitment, Connecting with Choice to You; Trusting in You and Doing Good, Delighting in You, Focussed Intentionally on You; Living the Life of Transformation, Growth, Significance, Anticipation and Abundance that you created me for, for Others, Today.*

✓ *I Choose to Love You, Lord God, Today, with all My Heart, My Mind, My Soul, and My Strength.*

✓ *I Choose to Focus on You and Seek You Wholeheartedly with all My Heart, Lord God, Today.*

  ✓ *I Choose to Live the Life You Created Me for; Breaking Out, Escaping from and Leaving Behind my old life of mediocrity and status quo living; to Make a Difference in the Lives of Others by Adding Value to them and Living My Best Life, for You, Lord God, Today.*

- ✓ ***I Choose to Grow as Your Created Extraordinary Masterpiece in Loving You Today, Lord God.***
    - ✓ *I Choose to Live an Extraordinary Life of Transformation and Growth for You, Lord God and Others, Today.*
    - ✓ *I Choose to Live My Best Life of Contribution for You, Lord God and Others, Today.*
    - ✓ *I Choose to Anticipate Living an Extraordinary Life, My Best Life, of Transformation and Growth for You, Lord God, and I Anticipate Making a difference for Others, valuing and lifting them, Today.*
    - ✓ *I Choose to Walk on God's Extraordinary Masterpiece Highway that He created for Me, for Your Glory and for Impacting others for You, Lord, Today.*
- ✓ ***I Choose to Live a Life of Renewal, Transformation and Growth Thinking for You, Lord God, Today.***
    - ✓ *I Choose to Live with the Mindset of Transformation and Growth for You, Lord God, Today.*
    - ✓ *I Choose to Give my Life afresh to You, Lord God, Today.*
    - ✓ *I Choose to Unlock and Grow the Potential God has already placed in Me, the Seeds of Greatness for Him and for Others, Today.*
    - ✓ *I Choose to Build and Live in a Growth Environment for You, Lord God, Today.*
    - ✓ *I Choose to Deploy My God-given potential for You, Lord God, Today.*
    - ✓ *I Choose to Walk "Seeking and Finding God when I seek Him with all my heart", Today.*
- ✓ ***I Choose to Live with an Abundance and Surplus Mindset for You, Lord God, Today.***
    - ✓ *I Choose to Live in Your Abundance and Surplus of Transformation and Growth for You, Lord God, Today.*
    - ✓ *I Choose to Live a Life of Greater Awareness for You, Lord God, Today.*
    - ✓ *I Choose to Continually Breakout from My Old Life of self-centred sleepwalking for You, Lord God, Today.*
    - ✓ *I Choose to Be Fully Engaged and Continually Renewed to Intentionally Lift, Inspire and Grow others and make a Difference in their Lives for You, Lord God, Today.*
    - ✓ *I Choose to Be a Difference Maker for You, Lord God, for Others, Today.*
    - ✓ *I Choose to Live with Joyful Discipline, Enjoying Growing and Living the Life You, Lord God, Created me for, Today.*
    - ✓ *I Choose, Daring to be an Inspirational Transformational Servant Leader and Transformational Writer to Help Others Discover God's Authentic Higher Purpose for their lives and go and do something about it, Today.*

✓ *I Choose to Step Over and In to Live a Proactive "ALIVE" Life of continuing Transformation and Growth for You, Lord God, Today.*

✓ *I Choose to Lift Myself above the Ordinary to Live the Extraordinary Life God Created Me to Live.*

✓ *I Choose to Renew, Rebuild and Refocus my mind Intentionally on You, Lord God, Today.*

✓ **I Choose Expanding my Mind for God, Renewing it Daily, and Focussing on Inspiring and Impacting others for Him as He intended, not the default reactive self-centred life served up by countless generations of our dominating cultures and people-limiting churches, Today.**

 ✓ *I Choose to Live on the Assumptions of God's Creation, Abundance and Surplus for Everyone as Christ did for You, Lord God, Today.*

 ✓ *I Choose to be Focussed on You, Lord God, Living an Intentional, Significant, Anticipating, Abundant, Focussed, Actioning, and Joyful "Choosing To" Life, not a "fearful responding to" Life, My Best Life, Today.*

 ✓ *I Choose to Live a Joyful, Disciplined Life to be Aspired to and Enjoyed for You, Lord God, Helping Lift Others on Their Way, Today.*

 ✓ *I Choose to Focus on the Choices God created me for, not the conditions, direction and daily difficulties of life, the fearful responding to life, or the cultural impositions and constraints of others, Today.*

✓ **I Choose to Inspire Others to Find their Purpose, their Unique Personal Significance, their "Voice", Unlocking and Unleashing their Potential, just "Lifting the Lid off them" for You, Lord God, Today.**

 ✓ *I Choose to be an "Emanative Centre" that Inspires Others-Focussed lives to Lift and Help Others to Grow for You, Lord God, Today.*

 ✓ *I Choose to Do the Good Things You Planned for Me long ago, Lord God, Today.*

 ✓ *I Choose to Live a Life that Echoes in Eternity for You, Lord God, Today.*

 ✓ *I Choose to Live a Life of Significance that makes a Difference in the Lives of Others, Today.*

 ✓ *I Choose to Give Myself to Others, Lord God, as You directed, value them and add value, Living My Life in the Service of a cause greater than myself, Today.*

 ✓ *I Choose to Start and Restate and Underpin all my Life on the Foundations above for You, Lord God, Today.*

 ✓ *I Choose to rewrite the script for My Best Life, Every Day, Today.*

 ✓ ***I Choose to Live My Best Life on the Other Side of My "YES!" for You, Lord, Today!***

Three millennia ago, it was the transformational leader of his generation, Joshua, who, in the act of supreme commitment, proclaimed, "Choose for yourselves this day whom you will serve... But as for me and my household, we will serve the Lord." We still remember him.

So, as God's Created Extraordinary Masterpiece, I Choose, Lord God, to Anticipate, Aspire to, and Articulate that Vision, to walk God's Highway, the Christ Life, My Best Life Today, to Grow Intentionally, Connect with Others and Live as Jesus showed. I Choose to be a river, not a reservoir, an outpouring to bring life to others, not a holding back for myself. We are Created to Live and Should Anticipate Living:

> ➤ *Transformation and Growing Living*
> ➤ *Intentionality and Integrity Living*
> ➤ *Significance and Meaning Living*
> ➤ *Anticipation and Urgency Living*
> ➤ *Abundance and Surplus Living*
> ➤ *Focus and Commitment Living*
> ➤ *Action and Opportunity Living*
> *For the Purpose of Truly Lifting and Growing Others on the way as God always intended...*

This is the heart of human authenticity for God as it seeks to develop and add value to others.

Ephesians 2:10 NLT: "For we are God's masterpiece. He has created us anew in Christ Jesus, so we can do the good things he planned for us long ago."

Understanding Ephesians 2, v10, I am Called to Make a Difference in this world and Live a Significant Life of Profound Meaning, as God Planned for Me, Today! Romans 12:2 NIV: "Do not conform to the pattern of this world, but be transformed by the renewing of your mind. Then you will be able to test and approve what God's will is - his good, pleasing and perfect will."

I remember that my transformation and growth for God is a daily commitment and daily decision. I am reminded by 2 Chronicles 16:9 NLT of God's deliberate intentionality and focus for those who are totally committed to Him: "The eyes of the LORD search the whole earth in order to strengthen those whose hearts are fully committed to him." This is a foundational truth that underpins the whole of scripture. God's Abundance and Surplus flow from here. I remember those extraordinary verses that God spoke to His people: Jeremiah 29:13-14 NIV: "You will seek me and find me when you seek me with all your heart. I will be found by you," declares the Lord.

This is the remarkable underpinning thread of Divine Intentionality through all the scriptures, and it is simply this. God created you for a relationship with Him, and the one overwhelming aspect of that relationship is this truth: God says, "If you commit yourself to Me, I will commit Myself to you; I never planned for you to be alone; I created you for connecting and walking with Me; I created you to seek Me and find Me when you seek Me with all of your hearts; Let's journey, you and me together..." That is why He sent His Son, Jesus Christ so that through personal faith in Him, we can fully undertake that journey to completion, living the lives He always intended us to live.

I refuse to let the past be or control my destiny. I remind myself that God created me to be Intentional and Significant for Him and Live that Life of Significance, my Best Life, that Matters for Others, Daily (clearly understanding it is not about me) and that this will only come about by being Intentional. I remind myself that committing and crossing, daily, over from the default "fearful life" that is what happens to you, a life of inward-focussed reaction, and stepping deliberately onto the Highway of a God-Focussed Significant Life of Chosen Intentionality, Others-Focussed Significance, Eager Anticipation, Overwhelming Abundance, Directed Focus and Visionary Action all for Others, and choosing to GROW and BREAK FREE from *my old thinking* after 67 years was both essential and doable, but it was Never, Never, Never going to be easy. But I have discovered it is possible with *Conscious Consecration, Decisive Dedication, Wholehearted Commitment, Focussed Intentionality, Connecting with Choice, Delighting in You, and for You, Lord God,* to effectively transform from a self-centred fearful focus to an Others-Valuing and Lifting focus.

I remind myself that the Highway only exists when you intentionally take the first step, and the bridge only appears as you walk on it, and you will know you are on the right path because God in Christ walks with You and because it is Uphill all the Way!

And, if you are able to have faith in God through belief in Jesus Christ or even would like to have faith in God similarly, on the basis of God's Word, I can guarantee He will give His Spirit to you to ENABLE YOU as no one else can. But it takes that Daily Conscious Consecration, Decisive Dedication, Wholehearted Commitment, your Chosen Connection with God to Continue with your Intentionally Focussed, Intentionally Chosen Best Life, your Indomitable Spirit, and your Intentionally Growing God's Seeds of Greatness Within You to

SUCCEED!

Colossians 3:1 NIV:
"Since, then, you have been raised with Christ, set your hearts on things above, where Christ is, seated at the right hand of God."

Colossians 2:6-7 NIV:
"So then, just as you received Christ Jesus as Lord, continue to live your lives in him, rooted and built up in him, strengthened in the faith as you were taught, and overflowing with thankfulness."

Ephesians 4:1 NIV:
"As a prisoner for the Lord, then, I urge you to live a life worthy of the calling you have received."

Self-Leadership (notice, not self-centred or selfish leadership) must come by Personal Transformation and Personal Growth first, then Valuing, Lifting and Growing others to continue the extraordinary process God always intended. Simple, except transformation and growth must be intentional and a daily discipline. It does not happen by itself. It must become an intentional way of life that builds with potential interactively, daily. If growth can be adequately understood in the context of continuing transformation, a soaring heart seeing the bigger picture, enlarged potential and purpose, and inspiring vision and destiny, then discipline is the mortar that both builds and keeps the structure together.

This will become a Joyful Discipline. Far from being seen as a negative force requiring depleting effort, it becomes the foundation of the Abundance and Surplus thinking that ensues with Personal Transformation and Growth. Effective Joyful Discipline, if embraced and used correctly, can become, like Growth, an exhilarating aspect that builds continuous improvement and forward movement daily as we decide with confidence to anticipate and experience growth today. It will become a desired part of Your Life, Your Best Life for God, simply a "must-have" to enjoy the daily experience of deliberate growth. The feeling of daily achievement through Growth will become essential in your Life. I believe this is the "ALIVE" life God always planned for you to Live.

The flight preparation thinking for each of the three levels of *TRANSFORMED!* is instructive here. We start with intentional choice and planning; we continue with internal system training and upgrades; we become ready to launch from the runway of Higher Purpose to live the soaring, high-level life we are created for.

> *"Let me clarify what I mean when I talk about intentional living...Intentional living is the bridge that will lead you to a life that matters." p.29*
>
> *"Good intentions won't get you there." p.29*
>
> *"Do I live in the land of good intentions, or in the land of intentional living?" p.29*
>
> *"What's the key to a life that matters? Living each day with intentionality." p.4*
>
> *"When you live each day with intentionality, there's almost no limit to what you can do. You can transform yourself, your family, your community, and your nation. When enough people do that, they can change the world. When you intentionally use your everyday life to bring about positive change in the lives of others, you begin to live a life that matters." p.4*
>
> *John C. Maxwell, Intentional Living*

(Quotes above in citation below.[54])

Deliberately "LIVING" Today, in a growth environment (aided by Joyful Discipline), growing in some way every day by encouraging the discipline of growth will feed through to enhancing your unlimited potential. Ask yourself the growth questions Today and every day:

✓ Am I intentionally growing? Reply: Yes! Transformation and Growth is a choice! My Choice!

✓ What is my potential? Reply: It is Unlimited! And it is My Choice!

✓ Am I striving to reach my full potential? Reply: Yes! It involves stretching daily through growth! And it is My Choice!

✓ How can I value and add value to others today? Reply: This is where Significance starts! This is what God created you for – living a Life that Matters comes from the Intention to Add Value to Others. This also is My Choice!

✓ If I do not intend to grow, then I can be sure I never will!

---

[54] John C. Maxwell, *Intentional Living*, pp. 4 & 29.

✓ I choose and anticipate continuing transformation and growth! Even though it is a daily uphill path! Today!
✓ It is also a joy and a privilege to choose to become the extraordinary masterpiece God created me to be.
✓ I remember that a life of significance only comes from valuing and adding value to others, lifting them to discover all this for themselves so they can also become God's extraordinary masterpieces! For Others!
✓ If I am not striving to reach my full potential, I can also be sure I never will!
✓ I choose and anticipate stretching! Stretching to extend my potential for God! Today!
✓ If I am not aiming at "somewhere", I can be sure I am going "nowhere"!
✓ I choose and anticipate the direction of my goal and destiny! Today.
✓ I choose to Live My Best Life of Growing Transformation and Growth! Today.

Notice this is not a competition between individuals, competing via greater efforts to be more holy, more prayerful, closer to God, speaking in Christian language, and showing others! The whole point of "Growing to Become the Masterpiece God Created You to Be" is simply becoming all that You are Created to Be. Because of your unique creation and destiny, your unique personal significance, you are designed to be YOU.

❖ No one else can live Your Best Life for God, only you!
❖ No one else can or will love God as you does!
❖ No one else can live the life God created for you!
❖ No one else can fulfil the potential God has placed inside you from birth!
❖ No one else can fulfil God's purposes for your life!
❖ No one else can love and add value to others for God as you can!

Therefore, the daily choice for conscious consecration, decisive dedication and wholehearted commitment is not a race to the top! There cannot and must not be any "one-upmanship" in our hearts and intentions towards others. And most importantly (for me!), intelligence, age, race, colour, sex, anything, cannot help you or me! We are uniquely created human beings whose lives cannot and must not be compared with others since we all have God-given "Unique Personal Significance". We are created to Live Lives of Significance to value and add value to others, enabling them to be transformed themselves.

That is why I have written this book, not as a "this is how you become holier through long days of prayer and fasting" style book where the writers give very good impressions of virtue signalling how far they have got! I cannot and will not attempt that because we are all in this together.

A Simple Handbook

No, this is a simple handbook that resets the starting point where you turn up with God (hand in hand) and start from there.

➤ **A Handbook for Your Transformation and Growth**
(as God intended for your life) starting with Extraordinary Awareness
➤ **A Handbook for the Totally Committed**
(however inadequate or broken you may feel!) continuing with the Extraordinary Unlocking of Potential
➤ **A Handbook for Wholehearted Action**
(wherever you are starting from) continuing with the Extraordinary Commitment to Action
❖ **A Handbook for Greatness for God**
(the seeds of greatness for God are already within you)
❖ **With Potential, Purpose and Passion**
(your life that truly matters)
❖ **Called For God's Higher Purpose**

All of us are or can be as close to God as we want to be. Yes, you and I may mature in understanding, but our responses to the verses below are ours alone. No one can do or act them for us.

Jeremiah 29:11-14 NIV:
"For I know the plans I have for you," declares the Lord, "plans to prosper you and not to harm you, plans to give you hope and a future. Then you will call on me and come and pray to me, and I will listen to you. You will seek me and find me when you seek me with all your heart. I will be found by you," declares the Lord.

You can Choose to grow and become all you can be as God, through faith in Christ intends, for Himself and for Others, or you can Choose not to. What stuns me even as I write these words is the difference that choice, your choice and my choice will make. Either we take the human default lower path to Mediocrity, where potential is straitjacketed and effectively nullified and destroyed. Or we consciously walk God's upper path to Greatness, Transformation and Growth, where potential is unlocked and unleashed, and purpose fulfilled.

The paradigm of *TRANSFORMED!* is that God created you and me for

Greatness for Him, through our servant leadership, and for His Higher Purpose, to Become all He Created Us to Be, to Become like His Son, Jesus Christ, "to live a life of greatness, a life of real contribution, a life of significance – one that really makes a difference." To fulfil God's Higher Purposes in Our generation.

That is why unlocking potential, valuing and adding value to Others is the greatest act any human being can do for another. All the deliberate, intentional, focussed choices above are a life of significance and greatness for God. It is not simply a difference of emphasis, a difference of life "style", a different career, a different skill set. It is a choice that defines:

- ❖ the difference and direction of your fulfilled potential or not
- ❖ the difference between your transforming purpose or not
- ❖ the difference between your hope and meaning-inspired life or not
- ❖ the difference between your mind stretching vision or not
- ❖ the difference between your personal eternal destiny or not
- ❖ the difference of your life lived connecting with and partnering with God as He intended or not
- ❖ the difference between a life valuing and lifting others to be the same or not
- ❖ the difference between you daily choosing joyfully to live your best life for God or not
- ❖ the difference between the seeds of greatness for God, already created and placed within you from birth, germinating, and growing to the full maturity of a magnificent oak tree or not
- ❖ the difference between embracing transformation and growth, daily or not
- ❖ the difference between breakout from mediocrity daily, fulfilling God's purposes in your generation or not
- ❖ the difference between activating the 40 Remarkable and Compelling Daily Commitment Choices or not. How many more do we need?!

That choice "to Choose" will define your entire destiny. The Choice for Transformation and Growth is both life-changing and life-challenging. It is also continuous and uphill all the way. But God intends good things for those who come to Him in faith in Christ and fulfil His purposes for their lives. We can never be happy or fulfilled, living lives full of meaning and hope outside His created intentions and framework. Now, that may sound limiting, but your potential and purpose are unlimited. Only you can reach towards them, stretching every day to grow and develop yourself and others as God intended. And growth, your growth, like muscle, can only take place after stretching beyond the present, beyond where you are now. Your growth cannot take place

without stretching. So, the everyday questions are:
- ➢ What am I doing to stretch, develop and grow myself today?
- ➢ What am I doing to connect with others today?
- ➢ What am I doing to stretch, develop and grow others today?

One of the saddest and the most misunderstood failures of the last 2,000 years has been the failure to develop people as God in Creation intended. Jesus Christ came to live His extraordinarily "ALIVE" life to show how life should be intentionally lived as He actively connected with and transformed His friends and their culturally imprisoned thinking as they followed Him.

Far from continuing His example, instead, the formal Church chose the different path of human Graeco-Roman hierarchical philosophy as the basis for its thinking, and it and all of us have paid the price ever since. The focus of control became the sin-management ritual of the mass. Courageous efforts in the times of the Reformation in every shade of belief sought spiritual improvement and change, and they overcame overwhelming and vicious resistance to set people free from the dominatory traditions that had enslaved them to the cultural traditions of those times. We can never repay our debt of gratitude to those who gave literally all they had – their lives – to translate, print, distribute and preach God's Word in the everyday language of the cultures in which they lived. No one could have asked any more of these extraordinary people, many of whom were martyred and horribly abused simply because they "questioned" the established and self-maintaining position-controlling hierarchy. That work remains unfinished.

In England, one of our greatest heroes was William Tyndale, who had a prodigious gift for languages, for understanding and translating the Bible; he once famously said as a response to criticism, "If God spare my life, ere many years I will cause a boy who drives a plough to know more of the scriptures than you do. But God has ordained a better way to convey His truth into our hearts, and that is by a renovation of our minds and by the communication of a divine nature."

He knew what you and I might slowly be grasping! But why would he write these truths? Tyndale well understood the reasons. It was not so we could live lives of the lowest common denominator, as most do. It was because he understood those truths of Romans ch.2, vv 1-2, about not only the need but the absolute necessity of transformation, renewal, and growth of our minds to grasp the truth that you and I are divinely created to connect intimately with our Creator, and to live for others, valuing others, adding value to others! Ultimately, You and I matter, both connected to God and others.

In their days, the reformers gave all they had to recreate the rediscovered principle of life, faith and action based solely on the scriptures as the divinely inspired Word of God and understood by everyone in the vernacular of their times.

What is my bottom line? Unlocking and Unleashing Potential in Others to Grow and enable them to become the People God always Created them to Be. What would the Church of Jesus Christ look like if that was its bottom line? *TRANSFORMED!*

> 1. *"You can visualise tomorrow using it as a motivation to grow, but if you want to actually grow, your focus needs to be on today."*
> 2. *"Growth stops when you lose the tension between where you are and where you could be."*
> 3. *"Growth doesn't just happen—not for me, not for you, not for anybody. You have to go after it!" – John C. Maxwell*

(Quote 1 cited below.[55])
(Quote 2 cited below.[56])
(Quote 3 cited below.[57])

In every person's life, there is a constant context of past, present and future. Everyone who has ever lived will have been aware of this. In asking the question "Why?" we need to understand the greater, Higher Purpose context that God creates human beings in His own likeness within, and it is simply this:

We are Created by God as His Extraordinary Masterpiece for God and for Others!

When God said in Genesis 1:26 NIV, "Let us make mankind in our image, in our likeness", this was no "seems like a good idea" thinking. It was a deliberate act of God, who could not help but be true to Himself. His nature is not only to love, but He connects with others who seek to make their lives matter, growing and lifting others. This is the active love that His Son, Jesus Christ, personified.

All the above is *TRANSFORMED!* in a nutshell.

---

[55] John C Maxwell, *How Successful People Grow: 15 Ways to Get Ahead in Life,* (New York: Center Street, 2012), p. 42

[56] John C. Maxwell, *The 15 Invaluable Laws of Growth: Live Them and Reach Your Potential* (New York: Center Street, 2012), p. 156.

[57] John C. Maxwell, *The 15 Invaluable Laws of Growth,* p. 13.

- ❖ Jesus said, "believe in me because I am The Way, The Truth and The Life" – this is the start.
- ❖ Discover your "why?" – the purpose God created you for and living a life that matters with intentionality and significance. For me, it is Inspiring others to find their Purpose, Unlocking and Unleashing their Potential, just "lifting the lid off them".
- ❖ Lose yourself to become the significant person you are and become great for God through transformational servant leadership.
- ❖ Live with intentionality the masterpiece of a transforming and growing intentional, significant, meaningful, anticipating, abundance and surplus, focussed, actioned and perfectly fulfilled best life that God always planned for you to live, fulfilling God's purposes in your generation, repeating the legacy everywhere with everyone, so they know they matter, and do it with a sense of urgency.

50 Remarkable and Compelling Reminders of Your Best Life Success

(Because Being Wobbly is Normal!)

If you get up one morning feeling wobbly on all this, that is normal because God's Transformation for you is not so much a journey as a never-ending process of success upon success improvement. It can easily and almost casually happen, waking up to default living through worrying and problem-solving during the day to come. But almost inevitably, your courage level will need to be reset!

> *"Courage is not the absence of fear, but rather the judgement*
> *that something else is more important than fear."*
> **Ambrose Redmoon.**

(Above quotation cited below.[58])

We each need to find a personal mechanism for resetting our minds immediately to stop that Mindset in its tracks. Eventually, this will be normal, and we will live effortlessly in God's Higher Purpose. So, the issue is to move from problem-solving to purpose-finding. We are returning to Kurt Wright's concept of asking, "What's Right?" This appears deceptively simple:

What do I know is already right?
The agenda-setting question.

What is it that makes it right?
The energy-generating question.

What would be ideally right?
The vision-building question.

What's not yet quite right?
The gap-defining question.

What resources can I find to make it right?

---

[58] 'Ambrose Redmoon Quotes'
<https://www.goodreads.com/author/quotes/14958727.Ambrose_Redmoon>
[accessed 29 May 2020].

The action-engaging question.

It is very much a practical re-wiring of our minds, Mindsets and thought processes from our old ways of thinking to discovering God's plans for us. From "life is what happens to us" thinking to Transformation and Growth thinking. Personal Transformation and Growth for our Best Life are uphill all the way, but I can tell you, I affirm to you, you can do this if you choose and commit to Daily Living Your Best Life, Today:

✓ **Remind yourself you are Created, Chosen, and Called by God in Christ for Transformation and Growth, Daily, Today. It is your birthright.**
  ✓ Remind yourself that you are God's Masterpiece and of the story of your life and the truths that you have understood, Today.
  ✓ Remind yourself that Potential, Purpose, Passion and a Life that Truly Matters are Your Birthright from God Who Created You.
  ✓ Remind yourself that your personal Transformation and Growth for God are a Daily Decision, Today.
  ✓ Remind yourself that you can Renew, Rebuild and Refocus your mind, Today.
  ✓ Remind yourself that being fully engaged and continually renewed as you transform, grow, and seek to make a difference in the lives of others is your joyful discipline, Today.
  ✓ Remind yourself God has created you through His Abundance and Surplus to be Transformed and Grow, Today.

✓ **Remind yourself that entering the fundamental state of leadership[59] is your Choice to self-lead, Daily, Today.**
  ✓ Remind yourself that you can decide your thinking, psychological state and desired outcomes, Daily, Today.
  ✓ Remind yourself that transformation and growth are what your life is for, Daily, Today.
  ✓ Remind yourself that this is a daily battle that you can and will win, Daily, Today.
  ✓ Remind yourself why you were created, Daily, Today.
  ✓ Remind yourself who created you, Daily, Today.
  ✓ Remind yourself of your unlimited potential, Daily, Today.
  ✓ Remind yourself that you can stretch for your unlimited potential, Daily, Today.
  ✓ Remind yourself of your purpose, Daily, Today.

---

[59] Quinn and Quinn.

- ✓ **Remind yourself that becoming purpose-centred is your birthright.**
  - ✓ Remind yourself you have chosen a new Mindset of transformation and growth.
  - ✓ Remind yourself that transformation and growth fill you with purpose and hope.
  - ✓ Remind yourself of the good things that come with intentionality and integrity.
  - ✓ Remind yourself of the good things that come with significance and meaning.
  - ✓ Remind yourself of the good things that come with anticipation and urgency.
  - ✓ Remind yourself of the good things that come with abundance and surplus.
  - ✓ Remind yourself of the good things that come with focus and commitment.
  - ✓ Remind yourself of the good things that come with action and opportunities.
  - ✓ Remind yourself you are designed and born to be fully engaged in purpose.
  - ✓ Remind yourself you have chosen your new Mindset of transformation and growth because it is your birthright.
  - ✓ Remind yourself that this is your Choice; you can Choose this Path, Daily, Today.
- ✓ **Remind yourself you are Created, Chosen, and Called by God in Christ for Transformation and Growth, Daily, Today. Remind yourself to Choose to Commit to Him.**
  - ✓ Remind yourself to Choose to live a life of Significance.
  - ✓ Remind yourself to Choose to run the higher Road to Greatness for God.
  - ✓ Remind yourself to Choose to Commit to Him.
  - ✓ Remind yourself to Choose to live a life of Significance.
  - ✓ Remind yourself to Choose to Make a Difference.
  - ✓ Remind yourself to Discover God's Higher Purpose.
  - ✓ Remind yourself to move to Next Level Thinking.
  - ✓ Remind yourself to Unlock Your Unlimited Potential.
  - ✓ Remind yourself to Unlock Unlimited Potential in Others.
  - ✓ Remind yourself to Value and Add Value to Others.
  - ✓ Remind yourself of Transformation and Growth, and Choose to Make a Difference.
- ✓ **Remind yourself to Discover God's Higher Purpose.**
  - ✓ Remind yourself to Next Level Thinking.
  - ✓ Remind yourself to Unlock Your Unlimited Potential.
  - ✓ Remind yourself to Unlock Unlimited Potential in Others.
  - ✓ Remind yourself to Value and Add Value to Others.
  - ✓ Remind yourself to Live Transformation and Growth.

✓ **Remind yourself to Choose to run the higher Road to Greatness for God.**

    ✓ Remind yourself that you can Rewrite the script, Rediscover and Re-invoke Your New ideals and attitudes – Focus and Commitment, Dedication, Consecration, Focus with Intentionality, Transformation and Growth.

    ✓ Remind yourself that you are growing the seeds of greatness for God already within you from birth to Live the Best Life God always planned for you to Live.

    ✓ Remind yourself that Your Extraordinary, Best Masterpiece Life is ahead of you as you stretch and reach towards Your Next Level.

> *"When you find an authentic higher purpose, you acquire new feelings and thoughts. When you articulate and embrace a higher purpose, you enter a new life path"*
> *Professor Robert E. Quinn, The Economics of Higher Purpose*

(Above quotation cited below.[60])

---

[60] Robert E Quinn and Thakor, pt. 662.

Conclusions for Step 3

To Develop! Your Best Life

Key Thought – You Can Rewrite The Script

Sub-headings review:
> ➤ **Know Where You Are (and Where You Are Going)**
> ➤ **Create a Growth Environment**
> ➤ **Living Your Best Life**
> ➤ **God's Extraordinary Masterpiece People**
> ➤ **Living Intentionally**
> ➤ **40 Remarkable and Compelling Daily Commitment Choices**
> ➤ **A Simple Handbook**
> ➤ **50 Remarkable and Compelling Reminders of Your Best Life Success (Because Being Wobbly is Normal!)**

We can and must Intentionally Rewrite Our Best Life Script Today and Every Day as we Grow the Seeds of Greatness for God and Become the Extraordinary Masterpieces God Created Us To Be.

Intentionally Rewrite Your Best Life Script Today and Every Day. Intentionally Breakout to Intentional Transformation and Growth Every Day with the following 10 Actions for Success:

> ➤ Rewrite Your Best Life Script Today, Every Day, Every Morning (don't Stop!)
> ➤ Rewrite Your Transformational Growth Life Every Day
> ➤ Rewrite Your Wholehearted Commitment for God Every Morning (He will see it, and more importantly, respond to uphold and strengthen you – 1 Peter 3:12 NIV: "For the eyes of the Lord are on the righteous, and his ears are attentive to their prayer, but the face of the Lord is against those who do evil.")
> ➤ Rewrite or Reset Your Focus towards Growing to Become The Extraordinary Masterpiece God Created You To Be
> ➤ Rewrite or Remember Your Unique Personal Significance – Your Voice, Every Day
> ➤ Rewrite or Re-water the Seeds of Greatness for God in Your Mind, Every Day, Today
> ➤ Rewrite Your Position – I was, now I am... (your words here)

- ➤ Rewrite Internally, Rediscover and Re-invoke Your New ideals and attitudes – Focus and Commitment, Dedication, Consecration, Focus with Intentionality, Transformation and Growth. Why? – To be made complete with all the fullness of life and power that comes from God
- ➤ Rewrite or Reinstall Your Indomitable spirit to Fulfil God's Purposes in Your Generation
- ➤ Rewrite or Reconfigure Your Life the Other Side of Yes! Today
- ➤ Rewrite the plot, Rewrite Today, Rewrite the Ending, Every Day
- ➤ Because if you don't, circumstances and others will. Inspire, Challenge, and Help Bring People to the Point of Decision.

A practical graphical overview of my *TRANSFORMED!* Metacog is shown as a Metacog in Appendix B.

A Metacog, as by Dr Caroline Leaf in her book *Think, Learn, Succeed*, is merely the big picture of what goes on in a person's mind (my mind) as I think about *TRANSFORMED!*

It may be helpful for you to draw your own Metacog of how you are thinking at this moment, or even how you would like to be able to think. Yours will look completely different when you try it!

Step 4

To Think! About Your Best Life

God intends us to be TRANSFORMED!
from the "normal" downward cycle of depletion, scarcity and decline
to our God-intended Continuing Upward Cycle of His Abundance and Surplus,
Full Engagement and Continuous Renewal, Transformation and Growth!

~~~

"How do We Grow to Become the Extraordinary Masterpieces
God Created Us to Be?"
"What are God's Purposes for All of Us in His Planning?"
"Is not the secret behind all this – it is not about 'Us' but about 'Others?'"

~~~

Within every individual, there is potential that will never
be discovered outside God's purpose.
– Erwin McManus

~~~

An unintentional life accepts everything and does nothing.
An intentional life embraces only the things that will
add to the mission of significance.
– John C. Maxwell, Intentional Living

~~~

❖ **Key Purpose: This is the mortar that cements together all these Level One foundations. Create the Capacity, Commitment and Anticipation to Think Differently, Moving to Next Level Thinking by Asking the Right Questions.**

❖ **Key Learning (Always Facing the Unknown without Fear):** We learnt in the last step about the importance of intentional development, the benefits of intentional choices and the 40 (at least) choices that could underpin our actions. We learnt it is OK and normal to "Wobble". The essential comment in these choices that we make every day is "Thinking Differently". This may not be as easy at first sight to achieve. Our minds may have had decades to fester where they are!

We will learn about Next Level Thinking, where thinking is not just something that happens in a "normal, everyday, this is how I think" mode. Rather, it becomes an intentional "hands-on" thinking that may be structured but also always reaching toward the Next Level, whatever that might be.

❖ **Key Actions (Building The Bridge As You Walk On It):** The key actions required here are Focus and intentionality. Look out for Alan Mulally's Business Plan Review as former President and Chief Executive Officer of the Ford Motor Company. Stop and reflect on the simplicity, inclusiveness and effectiveness of it and how he turned top-down management on its head to draw out the best from everyone around him. That is what Real Thinking does.

Real Thinking

Dynamic thinking and dynamic multi-focus, not default reacting and default focus, should always be in place. "Seeing" what others cannot and will never "see" will encourage you forwards as you decide to break out from "normal life" to live the extraordinary masterpiece life God created you for, living intentionally to make a difference for others today every day.

Moving from your past to the Transforming present and into the Transformational emerging future with God's new life through faith in Christ within you forms the core of this book, *TRANSFORMED!*

Understanding the transformation process, the replacement of the old ways of thinking and acting of "normal life" is indeed extraordinary, and it is all about being transformed entirely by God's new ideals and attitudes within you and using your new core values for God and for Others. So: Be Transformed, Be Transforming, Be Growing, then always:

✓ Be Prepared always to act on the basis of your unlocked potential, discovered purpose, and new core values for God and for Others. Being prepared allows you to recognise and seize opportunities to make a difference, be significant, and undertake acts of significance for God and for Others.

✓ Be Alert always to act on the basis of your unlocked potential, discovered purpose, and new core values for God and for Others.

✓ Be Alive to Your Personal Agency, always choosing on the basis of your unlocked potential, discovered purpose, and new core values for God and for Others. "Between stimulus and response, there is a gap." That gap is your choice.

✓ Be Stretching towards Your Next Level because if you are not attempting and preparing for Your Next Level, be assured you will always stay where you are. The concept of stretching of the mind is vitally important to understand and act upon, such that if we are not stretching the limits of our learning and understanding, we cannot progress to new levels of preparedness, new alertness, new choices, next-level thinking and personal agency actions, and new stretching of our limits for God and for Others.

So all this is Dynamic Thinking, Dynamic Understanding and Multi-Focussed Living. It is all about holding dynamically within your mind truths that God has shown you in scripture, His plans for you, drawing forth your potential, discovering His plans, perceiving where you are now, where you need to be and the direction of travel, all at the same time, and then additionally intentionally valuing and adding value to others, all at once. You can do this!

It's the ability to hold multi-focus in your mind continually – where you are now in your everyday life and, more importantly, the emerging future and more significant focus on where you are going and then both where you need and are meant to be; understanding your current location, which has moved from yesterday, where you want to be and the direction of travel, then total clarity is absolutely vital, with the ability to be fluently bilingual in thinking and speaking about it all as you engage with others who already understand something of all this, along with those who do not yet understand.

Even if you have difficult situations in your life at this present time, you can choose all the above for your thinking because "when the opportunity comes to make a difference for Others, it is too late to prepare." Yes, there is no doubt that this will be difficult, but please remember this: God plans for You to Grow To Become The Extraordinary Masterpiece He Created You To Be.

Never forget, this is not about you but all about fulfilling God's purposes for your life as you intentionally value and add value to others.

Just Do It!

> ***If We Choose to Stretch towards our Next Level,***
> ***whatever that may be, then Next Level Thinking***
> ***and Action is Now, Today, not tomorrow.***

The fundamental thesis of *TRANSFORMED!* is:
- ❖ We are Created and Called by God to be Transformed.
- ❖ We are Created Extraordinary Masterpieces with the Capacity to Create.
- ❖ We are Created by His Higher Purpose and for His Higher Purpose.

But we have been separated from God by our sinful natures, and only belief in Christ as Saviour can start us on the road to eternal significance. And we have a pain problem within us that exists because we live lives without God, which are meaningless, and that creates the pain, but created we are. Thus, we long to matter, to live a life of God's Higher Purpose, to live lives that make a difference, and to live lives that are significant and consequential.

The truth is that since the time of Christ who showed us His better Way and His Way to Greatness, the world at large, our cultures, our education systems, and often our churches have all conspired against the simple truth that Christ came to set us free from not only sin but to unlock the greatness that God has created in each of us. He came to unlock and unleash our potential and to enable us to discover our purpose for Him, live our lives with passion, live our lives that matter, and, in Him, live our Mission and our Calling.

We are set free to be involved in something Greater and Larger than Ourselves.

None of the following will happen without Thinking Differently as God intends through the help of His Holy Spirit.

* ❖ Our Lives are a God-intended Mission and a Calling.
* ❖ Our God-Given Unlimited Potential may be hidden but is intended to be Unlocked.
* ❖ Our God-Given Higher Purpose may be unknown but is intended to be Discovered.
* ❖ Our God-Given Passion Maybe new, but it can be Maximised
* ❖ Our God-Given Lives are Lives that Truly Matter.
* ❖ Christ's Life and Actions are critical as examples for our Leadership of Ourselves to be Transformed by God and are a prerequisite.
* ❖ Leading and Impacting the Transformation of Others for God are the actions of Christ in Service to Others.
* ❖ Changing the Future by Transforming the Future is His Legacy to be aspired to.
* ❖ Focus, Commitment, Action, Service, Sacrifice. All of these come from Integrity and Character. And the outcome of all this is to Transform the world for the better through Transformed individuals as God intended. Are you ready to Fully Commit to this Mission and Calling?

Don't let your thinking be distracted by the sideshows of the unimportant, the irrelevant, or the simply subversive. The world in which we live defines everything in terms of the assumptions of limitations, depletion and scarcity. We do not start there with those assumptions. Jesus, in all His teachings, actions and prayers with His Father, spoke only of God, Who is "Abundant". We are redefining the biblical framework of the world God created in general and every human being with the assumptions of abundance, surplus and unlimited potential for the people God has created – you and me!

If You start to Walk over the Bridge of Transformation to Live the Life of God's Higher Purpose for You, I believe You will Discover the Freedom to Live a Life worthy of Your Calling and Greatness for God just as He Intended, knowing that it is not about You, but Others.

Dr Stephen Covey, in His overwhelmingly influential book, *The Eighth Habit: From Effectiveness to Greatness*, spoke of "Finding Your Voice And Inspiring Others to Find Theirs".[61] I now understand what he meant, but for those who are uncertain, he describes your "Voice" as your "unique personal significance".

One of the most profound questions we can ever be asked is:

"What is your God-created Unique Personal Significance?"

And one of the most profound realisations is that we live continually in the land of wrong assumptions.

The most famous phrase of the American Declaration of Independence is the following: "We hold these truths to be self-evident, that all men are created equal, that they are endowed by their Creator with certain unalienable Rights, that among these are Life, Liberty and the pursuit of Happiness."[62]

We rightly focus on the unalienable Rights of Life, Liberty, and the pursuit of Happiness. As a young man, I was profoundly affected by the concepts of these rights and freedoms. At the time of drafting, Thomas Jefferson and others appointed to create the document had the political realities of war with Great Britain to propel them to make the Declaration. Their biblical and religious realities brought forth the astonishing underpinning statement that "all men are endowed by their Creator with certain unalienable Rights".

TRANSFORMED! completes the Biblical status of the "Created", that is, you and me, with the sub-title: "Growing to Become the Extraordinary Masterpiece God Created You to Be" and taken from Ephesians 2, v10 NLT.

✓ "How do We Grow to Become the Extraordinary Masterpiece God Created Us to Be?"

✓ "What are God's Purposes for All of Us in His Planning?"

✓ "Is not the secret behind all this that it is not about 'Us' but about 'Others?'"

This is what God-focussed thinking does:

Jeremiah 29:11-14 NIV: "For I know the plans I have for you," declares the Lord, "plans to prosper you and not to harm you, plans to give you hope and a future. Then you will call on me and come and pray to me, and I will listen to you. You

[61] Covey, p. 26.
[62] 'Declaration of Independence: A Transcription', *National Archives*, 2015 <https://www.archives.gov/founding-docs/declaration-transcript> [accessed 30 July 2020].

will seek me and find me when you seek me with all your heart. I will be found by you," declares the Lord, "and will bring you back from captivity. I will gather you from all the nations and places where I have banished you," declares the Lord, "and will bring you back to the place from which I carried you into exile."

Vv13-14 are crucial in understanding the transformation of understanding taking place.

It is all about focus, commitment, and awareness and asking, "How can I make a difference for God where I am?" How can we transform the Church of Jesus Christ from where it is to where God always designed it to be?

The effects of high-level understanding through paradox thinking, paradox understanding, and paradox living cannot be overstated; seeing over the horizon to what might yet be if travelled towards with clarity and commitment is crucial.

From John C. Maxwell, *Thinking for a Change*:

✓ Understand the Value of Good Thinking: Do I believe that good thinking can change my life?

✓ Realise the Impact of Changed Thinking: Is my desire for success and to improve my life strong enough to prompt me to change my thinking?

✓ Master the Process of Intentional Thinking: Am I willing to pay the price to cultivate the habit of giving birth to, nurturing, and developing great thoughts every day?

✓ Acquire the Wisdom of Big-Picture Thinking: Am I thinking beyond myself and my world so that I process ideas with a holistic perspective?

✓ Unleash the Potential of Focussed Thinking: Am I dedicated to removing distractions and mental clutter so that I can concentrate with clarity on the real issue?

✓ Discover the Joy of Creative Thinking: Am I working to break out of my "box" of limitations to explore ideas and options that will enable me to experience creative breakthroughs?

✓ Recognise the Importance of Realistic Thinking: Am I building a solid mental foundation on facts so that I can think with certainty?

✓ Release the Power of Strategic Thinking: Am I implementing strategic plans that give me direction for today and increase my potential for tomorrow?

✓ Feel the Energy of Possibility Thinking: Am I unleashing the enthusiasm of possibility thinking to find solutions even for situations that seem impossible?

✓ Embrace the Lessons of Reflective Thinking: Am I regularly revisiting the past to gain a true perspective and think with understanding?

✓ Question the Acceptance of Popular Thinking: Am I consciously rejecting the limitations of common thinking to achieve uncommon results?

✓ Encourage the Participation of Shared Thinking: Am I consistently including the heads of others to think "over my head" and attain compounding results?

✓ Experience the Satisfaction of Unselfish Thinking: Am I continually considering others and their journey in collaborating with them in my thinking?

✓ Enjoy the Return of Bottom-Line Thinking: Am I staying focussed on results to gain the maximum return and reap the full potential of my thinking?[63]

Focussed Thinking

God's Extraordinary Created Masterpiece People Live Intentionally and Growing Daily, in the exact same method as our contents page they:

➤ **AWAKE! To LIVE Their Best Life of God's Higher Purpose**
   ➤ To Awareness of their Best Life
   ➤ To Develop their Best Life
   ➤ To Think over their Best Life
➤ **UNLOCK! Potential for Their Best Life of God's Higher Purpose**
   ➤ To Breakout to their Best Life
   ➤ To Grow their Best Life
   ➤ To Engage themselves and others in their Best Life
➤ **ACT! Contributing For Others to Live Their Best Lives of God's Higher Purpose**
   ➤ To Lead Others to their Best Lives
   ➤ To Rally Others to their Best Lives
   ➤ To Legacy Others to their Best Life Legacy

And they understand and Live in the Land of God's Higher Purpose instinctively and permanently. They live Ephesians 2:10 NLT: "For we are God's masterpiece. He has created us anew in Christ Jesus, so we can do the good things he planned for us long ago." They are actively transforming and growing intentionally to live lives of significance and make a difference for Others, literally becoming,

---

[63] John C. Maxwell, *Thinking for a Change: 11 Ways Highly Successful People Approach Life and Work* (New York: Warner Books, 2003), p. 254.

thinking and actioning out in themselves for Others, the perfect human life that Christ did and modelled.

These are my personal Thinking Priorities to Unleash the Potential of Focussed Thinking, Extraordinary Thinking that Fully Engages and Continually Renews:

➢ Creating both a God-focussed Growth Mindset and a God-focussed Growth Environment that Positively Influences and Unlocks Potential in People, every day

➢ Becoming Intentional in Transformational Leadership that Positively Influences, Develops and Equips Others, every day

➢ Becoming Intentional in Transformational Writing that Encourages and Positively Influences Develops and Equips Others, every day

➢ Being Intentional in Creating and Asking Great Questions to transform Myself and Positively Influence and Develop Others, every day

A process, all through:
✓ Making High-Quality Connections with Others
✓ Focussed thinking
✓ Asking great questions
✓ Eliciting a visceral response
✓ Showing them a vision of their better future
✓ Creating the desire, then the decision (the Choice) to change and breakout
✓ Energising and helping people (including myself) Transform themselves one at a time
✓ Energise People, Energise Organisations

The Challenge To Think Differently

I feel the imperative not to wake up to what I have to do but **to wake up to where I intentionally aim to be** by creating and seizing opportunities for growing and learning my way forwards in the face of uncertainty. My Focus and Commitment in My Best Life for God's Higher Purpose is to create the emergence, every day, of Awakening, Breakout, and Intentionally Preparing to Live a Life of Transformation, Growth, Contribution and Learning for Him, to Make a Difference For Others, Today.

> *"The greatest enemy of knowledge is not ignorance,*
> *it is the illusion of knowledge."*

(The above quotation cited and discussed. [64])

This is the extraordinary masterpiece life that God created me to Live. I commit to re-consecrate, re-dedicate, re-commit, re-focus and re-inspire myself for Him. I commit to continue being transformed, growing, learning, and fulfilling God's purposes for me by truly, intentionally, and with a mind directed by masterpiece significance thinking. I commit by intentionally contributing, making a difference for others, helping them do the same, and becoming the extraordinary masterpieces God always intended them to be. Ephesians 2:10 NLT: "For we are God's masterpiece. He has created us anew in Christ Jesus so we can do the good things he planned for us long ago."

> "Lord, Roll back the clouds of ignorance, lethargy, stupidity, and pointlessness of a life focussed on "doing" and enable me to take flight to a life that is continually "becoming" the Extraordinary Masterpiece Life You Created Me To Live." That is my vision, intentionally reaching and stretching to become that person of significance for others you created and designed me to be."

We must always be on our guard, but not on guard against attack, but on guard for opportunities. We can never relax because you never know when the opportunity may come, for which you need to be prepared. For when the opportunity comes, it is too late to prepare".[65]

The concept and implications of commitment, dedication and consecration to God help our vital understanding of Who created us, who we are, what we are meant to do and where we are meant to be. As recorded in scripture, God makes a definite distinction between those who are wholly committed to Him and the rest who are not.

2 Chronicles 16:9 NIV: "For the eyes of the Lord range throughout the earth to strengthen those whose hearts are fully committed to him."

---

[64] 'The Greatest Obstacle to Discovery Is Not Ignorance—It Is the Illusion of Knowledge – Quote Investigator'
<https://quoteinvestigator.com/2016/07/20/knowledge/> [accessed 2 June 2020].
[65] 'A Quote by John Wooden' <https://www.goodreads.com/quotes/8337239-when-opportunity-comes-it-s-too-late-to-prepare> [accessed 29 May 2020].

It is a distinction understood by those who are wholeheartedly and uncompromisingly committed to Him, and conversely, one sadly never understood by those who are not.

The burning question, therefore, is, "Who has created and called us and why?" And is the crux of our commitment simply reflecting back to God His commitment, compassion, dedication and consecration in such depth and at such a higher level that makes Him "break out in goose pimples", metaphorically speaking?

Leading inevitably to the questions within our hearts:

How can I not respond?

How should I respond?

Because if we understand the import and impact of all the above, our response must be clear and unequivocal. We must respond and live on the other side of, "Yes!" This is what God created you for!

We can be highly motivated, awake, aware, developing, thinking, unlocked, breaking out, and engaged; we can be actioning, leading, rallying, and living a legacy, but without total commitment and connection with God who designed and created us, we will never Live Our Best Life for God's Higher Purpose and fulfil His intentions and purposes for us. We will never stretch our potential, and we will never become what God planned for us; we will never become what we might have been, changing the Future. Living the other side of "Yes!" transforms everything!

Just hold that thought in your mind the next time you awaken with your mind all over the place. Steady it, Focus it on God, Embrace Him in your present, and say "Yes!" to Him daily, today and every day. The Breakout will occur again daily, today, and every day. Only by living the other side of "Yes!" can we ever live our Best Lives for God's Higher Purpose, making a difference, contributing, intentionally focussed and transformationally growing to become the extraordinary masterpieces God created us to be. Well, we were designed by God for this, and by His help, we can.

So, think differently by discovering God's Higher Purpose for you, living at God's Higher Level, and focussing on your strengths and not your perceived weaknesses. Daily, I tell myself/think out loud/focus on etc. In other words, we become what we think!

- ✓ I am a Transformational Leader!
- ✓ I am a Transformational Writer!
- ✓ I am an Inspirational Writer!
- ✓ I am Living a Life that Matters!
- ✓ I am Living a Life of Significance!

✓ I am Living a Life of Contribution!
✓ I am writing *TRANSFORMED!* to success!
✓ I am Living God's Extraordinary Masterpiece Life For Others!
✓ All for God and for Others!

Next Level Thinking

God's Masterpiece Thinkers are both thinking and living at a higher, different level, and a sample of that thinking is shown here, but yours may be different and in an entirely unique direction, so don't miss the chance to write your thinking patterns down, both where you are and where you need to be:

➤ Living Your Best life Thinking
➤ Unlocking Your Unlimited Potential Thinking
➤ Unique Purpose Thinking
➤ God's Transcendent Higher Purpose Thinking
➤ Growth Environment Creation Thinking
➤ Transformation and Growth Thinking
➤ Intentionality and Integrity Thinking
➤ Significance and Meaning Thinking
➤ Anticipation and Urgency Thinking
➤ Abundance and Surplus Thinking
➤ Focus and Commitment Thinking
➤ Potential, Purpose, Passion and Vision Thinking
➤ Intentional Choices Thinking-you become what you Choose.
➤ Indomitable Spirit Thinking – Jesus had it in bucketloads!
➤ "Seeds of Greatness" Thinking. God created You and me with the Seeds of Greatness already within us, deep in our hearts and minds, from birth.

You see, all the above and numerous others that you may have written down are at the heart of Transformed individuals growing to become the people God created them to be, and without these wholly different Thinking processes, we will stay where we are not meant to be, living unfulfilled mediocre lives of normality. We will either become or remain what we think!

> *Next Level Thinking is Absolutely Essential Because*
> *The Thinking that Got You Here*
> *Will not Get You There*

Jesus discovered, developed and deployed utterly different thinking from the culture where He was born. He alone could ponder His God-created role based on Servant Leadership, the Seeds of Greatness thinking and the Growing Others thinking that He had discovered around the age of 10, before His family's trip to the Temple in Jerusalem. It then took 20 years of growth to be ready before He both created and seized His Opportunities and displayed His unique thinking.

Continuing the quest to understand where we are and how to "break free from our current thinking" because it is hindering our future, here below are five admittedly longish quotes, but they are included to help us break out from the thinking that has kept us walled up for all our lives:

From *The Outward Mindset* by The Arbinger Institute:

We introduced the outward-Mindset way of thinking about one's role and obligations at work (and elsewhere). A hallmark of this way of working is a focus on the needs, objectives, and challenges of those toward whom one has responsibility. Those who work with an outward Mindset take responsibility for their impact on the results of their reports, their customers, their peers, and their managers. They hold themselves accountable for their full impact on the overall results of the organisation. As we have observed those who consistently work in this way, we have discovered a pattern—a way of working that such individuals demonstrate. They
1. see the needs, objectives, and challenges of others
2. adjust their efforts to be more helpful to others
3. measure and hold themselves accountable for the impact of their work on others
Engaging in these three steps is a practical approach to implementing and sustaining an outward-Mindset way of working. [66]

Now, some thinking from a top business perspective. Alan Mulally's Business Plan Review as former President and Chief Executive Officer of the Ford Motor Company was based on ten rules:

- People first
- Everyone is included
- Compelling vision
- Clear performance goals
- One plan

---

[66] *The Outward Mindset: Seeing beyond Ourselves: How to Change Lives & Transform Organizations*, 2016.

- Facts and data
- Propose a plan, "find-a-way" attitude
- Respect, listen, help, and appreciate each other
- Emotional resilience ... trust the process
- Have fun ... enjoy the journey and each other[67]

Mulally explains that "leadership takes courage, to have a point of view about the future and to pursue it in the face of resistance and doubt, in service of something great". These simple but compelling rules to effectively engage others (his top-level team) worked and turned around a failing multi-billion company. His effective simplicity was mind-blowing. At first, his fellow board members (working on the basis of fear of retribution as was the previous methodology) could not conceive the change happening but came around to embrace the inclusive "let do this together" approach that Alan personified. This is thinking differently, par excellence.

Now we turn, as earlier, to Kurt Wright of *Breaking the Rules*.[68] His simple route is to ask five simple but profound questions:
- ❖ What do I know is already right? The agenda-setting question.
- ❖ What is it that makes it right? The energy-generating question.
- ❖ What would be ideally right? The vision-building question.
- ❖ What's not yet quite right? The gap-defining question.
- ❖ What resources can I find to make it right? The action-engaging question.[69]

He goes on to explain:
The vast majority of us are negatively motivated. To be more precise, most of us are motivated to avoid pain. And the pain we most want to avoid is having to feel, once again, a negative emotion we've felt before and never, ever want to feel again. (Didn't you think all those "never evers" did a great job of demonstrating the intensity of this desire we have to avoid pain?) We are only kidding ourselves, however, if we think this approach is helping us. This is because, in our efforts to avoid negatives, we mistakenly keep ourselves on high alert to spot any and all negatives we might wish to avoid. And, in case you missed it, this is negative motivation, pure and simple. It is a compulsive focus on the negative, and all of the attention we put on the negative does more to create

[67] *The Outward Mindset*, pt. 803.
[68] Wright.
[69] Wright, pt. 629.

negatives in our lives than most of us would ever imagine.[70]

He talks of:

Energy Flow. It really is an energy issue, isn't it? Speaking of energy, do you know what a physicist would tell us about the flow of electrical energy? It causes a magnetic field to develop around that flow. Isn't it interesting how few people have thought about the way human emotional energy has a similar effect? Energy we focus on our weaknesses— whether to shield them from other people's view or to go in and dig them out by their roots—sets up a powerful "magnet-like" attraction for problems, obstacles, mistakes and failure.[71]

Yes, it's true! The energy we focus on negatives in our lives creates the magnetic effect of attracting the very undesired consequences we think we are trying to protect ourselves against. This is particularly true when our energy is focussed on trying to keep our weaknesses from being exposed. It is equally true, however, when our efforts are focused on trying to "fix" our weaknesses so they are no longer a source of concern. Wow! Did you get that? Could our notion of trying to find what's wrong and fix it be what's wrong and we've found it? You got it. Not only that, but it can't be fixed! Just think of how wonderful it will be to abandon this self-limiting illusion and discover an alternative that actually works![72]
How about all the energy we focus on our strengths? You guessed it again. This has the wonderful, effect of magnetically and effortlessly attracting to us the results we desire. This magnetic effect means those of us who master the discipline of identifying and building on our strengths will find ourselves achieving results we desire with far less effort than we would normally expect. Are you beginning to see the foundations being put in place to enable each of us to reach and sustain the wonderful state of effortless high performance?[73]

Do you also see, as mentioned above, how the whole notion of "find-what's-wrong-and-fix-it" may be precisely what's wrong, and that we have actually found it? Reminds me of that fun statement from Pogo: "We have found the enemy and it is us!" Keep in mind that effortless high performance is much more a by-product of energy management than of fact management."[74]

Now, back to Professor Bob Quinn, who, in his many books, elucidates the

---

[70] Wright, pt. 814.
[71] Wright, pt. 818.
[72] Wright, pt. 846.
[73] Wright, pt. 846.
[74] Wright, pt. 850.

concept of the Fundamental State of Leadership[75] , which is characterised by the individual's choice to become:

Purpose Centered - Your Highest Purpose and the Results you wish to create.

Internally Directed - Your Core Values with Authenticity and Authentic Engagement.

Other Focussed - Valuing and adding value to Others, Lifting them to Higher Purpose.

Externally Open - Open to external Learning Opportunities in every situation.

The choice to Lead and Live Your Best Life is just that, Your Choice. It is primarily first about the choice to self-lead, not out of selfishness, but the necessity to undertake that first and then lead others to the same.

Finally, from *Real Influence* by Mark Goulston and John Ullmen: "Persuade Without Pushing and Gain Without Giving In."

When you practice disconnected influence, you're stuck in what we call your here. You can see your position, your facts, and your intentions clearly. But to connect with the people you're trying to influence, you need to communicate from a perspective we call "their there". You need to see their position, their facts, and their intentions clearly. And you can't reach their there if you can't see it. From your point of view, these people are invisible.[76]

Put another way, good intentions often create a sort of intellectual and emotional laziness. We use our high-mindedness to justify failing to take the time to get where other people are coming from and why. Sure that what we want is best, we keep driving forward under the blinding confidence of our good intentions. We're convinced that we don't need to learn or hear more from others, that other options and alternatives don't exist, that our agenda is the single best plan possible, and that we're justified in using any means to achieve it. And we're nearly always wrong.[77]

The Solution: See past your Blind Spot.[78]

To reach people and win their long-term support, you need to stop pushing. You need to stop "selling." You need to stop focussing on what you want them to do. And you need to stop using sleight-of-hand schemes to trick them. Instead, you need to influence them in ways that spark a genuine connection. You need to see their vision and make it part of yours. You need to make them want to work with you to achieve amazing outcomes . . . and that means you need to start from their there. It's the secret for building long-term

---

[75] Quinn and Quinn, p. 202.

[76] Mark Goulston and John B. Ullmen, *Real Influence: Persuade without Pushing and Gain without Giving In* (New York: American Management Association, 2013), p. 11.

[77] Goulston and Ullmen, p. 12.

[78] Goulston and Ullmen, p. 14.

commitments—and for reaching big goals.[79]

Here are the core principles of the connected influence philosophy: It's about building a network of people who want to hear you out, help and support you, rather than leaving behind a list of people who feel disconnected, transacted, used, manoeuvred, or manipulated to serve your self-interest.

- *It's about making the journey from your here to their there so you can understand other people's points of view, learn from it, engage them based on it, and add to it.*
- *It's about identifying outcomes worthy of the people you want to connect with.*
- *It's about being open and transparent about what you're doing, rather than concealing tactics and techniques in the hope those hidden or secret sources of leverage will "work" on them.*
- *It's about easing the ache inside sceptical and even cynical people so they can trust safely.*[80]

The Connected-Influence Model
- *Go for great outcomes. This isn't just a once-a-year exercise in setting ambitious goals. It's about standing for something noble and worthwhile, and it's about going beyond where people want to be and showing them where they could be.*
- *Listen past your blind spot. To exert real influence, you need to have a willingness to learn, an open mind, and sometimes the insight to discover that you're wrong.*
- *Engage them in their there. Engaging strengthens the connection that comes from listening. It's about "getting" your audience—not using "gotcha" techniques to manipulate them into compliance.*
- *When you've done enough . . . do more. Doing more isn't just about the transactions you have with other people right now. It's about committing to making their great outcomes happen, both now and in the future, and leaving them awestruck by your generosity.*[81]

The three GETS of engagement:
The secret to reaching people in their there is to use what we call the "three gets of engage." By keeping these three "gets" in focus, you'll be able to shift quickly and effectively from your own perspective to another person. Here's a look at them.
- *Situational Awareness: You Get "It"*
- *Personal Awareness: You Get "Them"*

---

[79] Goulston and Ullmen, p. 14.
[80] Goulston and Ullmen, pp. 34–35.
[81] Goulston and Ullmen, pp. 37–38.

- *Solution Awareness: You Get Their Path to Progress[82]*

The best way to create real influence is to do more in ways that touch people's hearts and minds. Here are three ways to do this:
1. *Expand their thinking (the insight channel). Find ways to help them see new insights, reframe their situation, gather new information, and find new meaning in their lives.*
2. *Make them feel better (the emotional channel). Find ways to help them feel encouraged, capable, supported, energised, empowered, successful, happier, or valued.*
3. *Take effective action (the practical channel). Find ways to help them take action for themselves or for people they care about. Help them resolve issues, solve problems, build relationships, get projects done, or accomplish tasks.[83]*

If these three channels look familiar, it's because they link to the three "gets" of engagement we spoke about earlier. Back then, your goal was to understand where people were coming from. Now, your goal is to make things better for them in ways that will make you memorable. Here are some of our favourite examples of how it's done.

- *Adding Insight*
- *Adding Emotional Value*
- *Adding Practical Value [84]*

What we're going to say next might surprise you. We've told you how crucial it is to do more. We've told you to do more before, during, and after an interaction. We've told you to add value by offering insight, making people feel better, and providing practical help. But now we're going to tell you: Don't do too much. Right now, this advice probably sounds a little crazy. But what we're really trying to say is: To exert real influence, don't insist on doing more all on your own.

Instead, open your arms to other people who want to help. Just as you've invited them to join in your great outcome, allow them to make it even greater by adding value. When you do this, these people will contribute ideas you'd never think of on your own. By bringing them into the picture, you increase the chances that a great outcome will succeed, and, in turn, you increase your own positive influence. And here's another piece of advice: When you look for other people to add value, be careful not to limit yourself to "experts" or people with the same experience and background as you. Instead, look for people from different backgrounds who've done and experienced things you never have.[85]

Those are massive amounts to challenge our closed Mindsets. The challenge to

---

[82] Goulston and Ullmen, pp. 121–24.
[83] Goulston and Ullmen, p. 171.
[84] Goulston and Ullmen, pp. 172–78.
[85] Goulston and Ullmen, pp. 183–84.

think differently is just that, challenging. But without this core understanding of the fundamental need for Level 1 Awareness and challenging all our cherished thought processes and in-bred methodology, we will never break out of our old Mindsets to think differently, think better, think inclusively, or think transformationally, so that little progress will be made.

> *If I am not where I am supposed to be,*
> *I need to understand next level thinking.*
> *I need to be working towards the next level, a higher level.*
> *So, where is it and how do I get there?*
> *knowing I must start now!*

Foundations For Transformed Thinking

- In a world that denies and derides the existence of God,
  - ✓ *Value your ability and opportunity to Choose to Love Him with all your heart.*
- In a world that, like Nebuchadnezzar of old, demands you worship other Gods,
  - ✓ *Wholehearted Commitment to God Transforms Everything.*
- In a world that demands our attention to deflect us from discovering our purpose,
  - ✓ *Value Reflection to Discover His Higher Purpose.*
- In a world where so many are negatively impacted by the self-centred, self-absorbed, often narcissistic behaviour of both the "rich and famous" and our contemporaries,
  - ✓ *Draw out from yourself the gold within, your unlimited potential placed there by God, discover your Higher Purpose, take off to your emerging future and live the Best Life God Created You To Live.*
- In a world that would demean, devalue, deplete, and destroy us by default, as God's highest creation created human beings,
  - ✓ *Intentionally Grow To Become The Extraordinary Masterpiece He Created You To Be.*
- In a world that values money, fame, and trinket possessions above people,
  - ✓ *Whom You are is immeasurably more important than what you know or have.*
- In a world that hated and crucified Him,
  - ✓ *Intentionally Live the Transformational Growth Mindset of Christ, valuing and adding value to Others, every day.*

Conclusions for Step 4

To Think! About Your Best Life

Key Thought – You Become What You Think

Sub-headings review
- ➢ **Real Thinking**
- ➢ **Focussed Thinking**
- ➢ **The Challenge to Think Differently**
- ➢ **Next Level Thinking**
- ➢ **Foundations For Transformed Thinking**

Most of us imagine that thinking is what we all normally do. At the "normal" life level, that is absolutely true. Normal Life is a reactive life. What we are thinking about here is not that sort of thinking. Let's be brief for the point I am making for this conclusion demands it:

We become what we think.

But as we have seen in this step, To Think! About Your Best Life, we are to be thinking in ways that are totally transformational, totally focussed, totally directed and always seeking movement to the Next Level. This is very different from everyday thinking and very different from career thinking, profession-related thinking, business thinking, etc. It is deliberate, intentional thinking that creates outcomes. We are not trained to intentionally "think". All that is assumed is that thinking is normal, and therefore, we try to prepare at best or react at worst to life situations as they change around us. This truly is very different thinking. It is life-changing thinking, life-freeing thinking.

This is the transformational thinking that Paul writes about in Romans 12:2 NIV: "Do not conform to the pattern of this world, but be transformed by the renewing of your mind. Then you will be able to test and approve what God's will is – his good, pleasing and perfect will." This is the thinking that is vital and necessary to undertake as we grow to become the people God always created us to be. And always this thinking takes continuous effort to become our new normal.

Throughout this book, I refer to "Mindsets". Contrary to popular thinking, You Can Challenge Your Mindsets, and You Can Change Your Mindsets. Lazy people state, "I cannot change who I am." Transforming people state, "I must change and develop my mind to be fulfilled and effective, so I Can Move to Where I Need To Be."

➢ Write down the Positive Mindsets you think you have.

➢ Write down the Negative Mindsets you know you have.

➢ Make a note of how each list makes you feel.

➢ Write down the Mindsets you feel you need to have.

➢ Take Action to Transform yourself to create the Mindsets you need.

LEVEL 2

BE INSPIRED TO UNLOCK!

Level 2 – "On the Runway – Pre-flight Checks and Testing of Upgraded Avionics (aircraft software and hardware systems)" for God's Best Life for You – UNLOCK! Your "How?"

- ❖ **Breakout to Your Calling!** - With The Extraordinary Dynamic *Decision* to *Unlock!, Daily*
- ❖ **Your Key Thinking: Unlock!** Yourself To Your Potential and Daily Growth
- ❖ **Your Key Commitments to Dynamic Action 2** – *Facing and Growing Intentionally*, Daily, in the right direction.

  - ➢ **Step 5 – UNLOCK! Your Best Life of God's Higher Purpose:** Moves you seriously forwards, where you realise you have unlimited unused potential that awaits being drawn from within. Create the Willingness to Stretch and Reach and Unlock Unlimited Highest Potential in Yourself and Others and Discover God's Meaningful Higher Purpose for You through "Potential, Purpose, Passion and a Life that Truly Matters".
  - ➢ **Step 6 – To Breakout! To Your Best Life of God's Higher Purpose:** Create the Courage and Decision to Start The Breakout to Your Highest Calling, to Next Level Living, and Living a Life that Matters.
  - ➢ **Step 7 – To Grow! Your Best Life of God's Higher Purpose:** Create the Mindsets and Environments for Growth, Connection and Contribution. Draw out Greatness from within.
  - ➢ **Step 8 – To Engage! Yourself and Others In Their Best Lives of God's Higher Purpose:** Create Enrolled Hearts that are Fully Engaged and Continually Renewed.

Step 5

Unlock! Your Best Life

One word I use to describe what fires me continually,
what this book is all about, and what the
Gospel of Jesus Christ is all about,
for me.
The word is
<u>Unlocked.</u>

~~~

Hope is Believing that Tomorrow can be Better
because You're Growing Every Day.
We are Designed and Hard-Wired
for Inspiration, Growth and Making a Difference,
To Be Loved, To Belong, To Be Connected and To Matter With God.
We are Destined to be Unchained from Everything that has Enchained Us,
To Unlock Our Potential and To Discover Our Purpose
That God has already Placed Within from Birth,
And He has Provided Us with the Keys
To Soar With Him and with Eagles.

~~~

- ❖ **Key Purpose: Unlock moves you seriously forward, where you realise you have unique, unlimited, unused potential that awaits being drawn from within. Create the Willingness to Stretch and Reach and Unlock Unlimited Potential in Yourself and Others and Discover God's Meaningful Higher Purpose for You through "Potential, Purpose, Passion and a Life that Truly Matters".**
- ❖ **Key Learning (Always Facing the Unknown without Fear):** We learnt in the last step about the vital nature of Thinking Differently. You may notice you have survived to the next level. The first Level got you Awakening, Aware, Developing and Thinking. You can now understand the simplicity of this approach. I hope you also recognise the effectiveness of this as you move to the next level – the Unlocking Level and the Unlocking Step. This is where you will be able to "fill your tanks" with the fuel that will enable real forward motion, not just classroom learning. You will understand more about Potential, the discovery of Purpose, and how alignment with Purpose

provides the propellant of wholehearted commitment that will see you set free to fly because you were born for this.

❖ **Key Actions (Building The Bridge As You Walk On It**[86]**):** Your key actions will centre around your choice to unlock your potential and also the choice to transform your old Mindsets – trade them in for newer, transforming, much more effective ones! And as always, it requires intentionality to "Seize the Keys – Open The Gates" and "Start The Race". Hold on to your hat...

Your Choice To Unlock Your Unlimited Potential

We have two primary "unlockings" on the road to *TRANSFORMED!* The Unlocking of Our Potential and the Unlocking of Our Mindsets. Without Unlocking these aspects, we have no chance!

Discovering God's Higher Purpose for us and Living at God's Higher Level is all about human potential already within any individual. Tapping into that potential is about unlocking, releasing, developing and deploying that potential and enabling us to lift ourselves, lift our minds to rise above the ordinary, and then **"to choose the extraordinary".**

Those words, **"to choose the extraordinary,"** are significant. Because "potential" unlocked, unleashed and developed in individuals is **extraordinary.** Purpose discovered and aligned with creates Wholehearted Commitment and is utterly life-changing. Ninety-nine point nine per cent of people alive today have grown up under the "normal" assumptions of the conventional mental map and the fixed capacity Mindset. Very, very rarely does anyone attempt the breakout from those cultural prisons and succeed.

> *"Purpose is the deepest dimension within us—our central core or existence—where we have a profound sense of who we are, where we came from and where we're going. Purpose is the quality we choose to shape our lives around. Purpose is a source of energy and direction."*
> *Richard Leider*

(Above quotation cited below.[87])

---

[86] Robert E. Quinn, *Building the Bridge as You Walk on It.*
[87] Richard Leider, *The Power of Purpose: Find Meaning, Live Longer, Better,* Third Edition, Revised&Expanded (San Francisco: Berrett-Koehler Publishers, Inc, 2015), p. 1.

These people are doing "Leadership", whether they understand that term or not. Self-Leadership is a vital precursor to unlocking potential and breakout. The decision is just that; it is a "Choice". Let no one seek to disabuse you of the extraordinary choice that you have made if this describes what you have undertaken. It may have happened for you almost unnoticed, a gradual realisation and awakening to higher awareness, thinking and deliberate action.

The action itself is truly extraordinary simply because the individual choice to unlock and unleash one's potential is not only truly momentous, challenging, and, for some, in their cultures, downright dangerous; it is one of the world's greatest lies exploded. From birth, for every human being, every culture causes uniformity, convention and compliance within the often unseen expectations of that culture.

Overwhelmingly, then, in virtually every organisation where a hierarchical elite is in control, there is further total "misrecognition" of the true nature of the elite by the subjects of that hierarchy.

Carly Fiorina, speaking at the Global Leadership Summit 2014, Willow Creek Community Church, Illinois, said:

What things unlock potential? – Leadership; the highest calling of leadership is to unlock the potential of others. Everyone has more potential than they realise. Everyone has the capacity to lead. Leaders are made, not born. Leadership is changing the order of things. Leadership is unlocking the potential of others. Leadership is a profoundly human gift available to all. All of us have the potential to make a positive difference, to change the order, to unlock the potential of others.

True leadership requires faith. A love of God makes leadership easier. Faith gives us the gift of humility, and true leadership requires understanding it is not "about you" but about others and having a servant's heart. Faith gives us the gift of optimism – the leader must know things can be better. The most important gift is to have faith in others. You must know people can and will rise to the occasion and will use their potential to make a positive difference. Faith teaches us that all of us are gifted by God and that knowledge propels a leader forward.

Leadership is a choice. It can be exhausting, but there is a look that people get in their eyes when their potential has been unlocked, and that look is the same everywhere in the world, and that look is all the repayment a leader needs.

Choose to lead. Choose to change the order of things. Choose to fulfil your own potential and choose to unlock the potential of others. What we are is God's gift to us; what we make of ourselves is our gift to God.[88]

---

[88] '2014 Global Leadership Summit Session 2: Carly Fiorina #GLS14', *Live Intentionally* <http://www.liveintentionally.org/2014/08/14/2014-global-leadership-summit-session-2-carly-fiorina-gls14/> [accessed 21 May 2020].

Your Choice To Unlock Your Mindsets

What is a Mindset in reality?

Mindsets thinking and comment area:
Dr Carol Dweck writes in her book *Mindsets: Changing The Way You think To Fulfil Your Potential*:

> "For thirty years, my research has shown that the view you adopt for yourself profoundly affects the way you lead your life. It can determine whether you become the person you want to be and whether you accomplish the things you value. How does this happen? How can a simple belief have the power to transform your psychology and, as a result, your life?"[89]

> "You have a choice. Mindsets are just beliefs. They're powerful beliefs, but they're just something in your mind, and you can change your mind. As you read, think about where you'd like to go and which Mindset will take you there."[90]

Wow! Pretty straightforward? How come most of us live lives under the thumb of one or more (maybe many more!) of the list below? I suggest you read through them, and when you get to the end, stop and assess how you feel:

First, the Negative Mindset List = Fixed Mindset Thinking (primarily self-centred and self-limiting, where most of us stay):
- ≤ Fixed Mindset (conventional thinking)
- ≤ Reactive Mindset (normal life)
- ≤ Problem-Solving Mindset (also normal life)
- ≤ Hierarchical Mindset
- ≤ Self-absorbed Mindset
- ≤ Self-focussed Mindset
- ≤ Critical spirit Mindset
- ≤ Small-minded Mindset
- ≤ Egotistic Mindset
- ≤ Fearful Mindset
- ≤ Personal Entitlement Mindset
- ≤ Transactional Mindset (using others for what they can do for you)
- ≤ Fearful of Life Mindset
- ≤ Highly Critical Mindset
- ≤ Blaming Others Mindset

---

[89] Dweck, p. 6.
[90] Dweck, p. 16.

- ≤ Excessively Needy Mindset
- ≤ Hateful Mindset
- ≤ Constantly Complaining Mindset
- ≤ Comparison with Others' Mindset
- ≤ Negative Attitudes Mindset
- ≤ Know-it-all Mindset
- ≤ Pessimism Mindset
- ≤ Unforgiving Mindset
- ≤ Disloyal Mindset
- ≤ Deceitfulness Mindset
- ≤ Angry Mindset
- ≤ Immorality Mindset
- ≤ Cruelty Mindset
- ≤ Malicious Mindset
- ≤ Belittling Others Mindset
- ≤ Vengeful Mindset
- ≤ Selfish Mindset
- ≤ Envy Mindset
- ≤ Jealousy Mindset
- ≤ Greed Mindset
- ≤ Pettiness Mindset
- ≤ Hedonistic Mindset
- ≤ Narcissistic Mindset
- ≤ Dishonesty Mindset
- ≤ Untrustworthy Mindset
- ≤ Disrespectful Mindset
- ≤ Impatience Mindset
- ≤ Laziness Mindset
- ≤ Impoliteness Mindset
- ≤ Uncaring Mindset
- ≤ Thoughtless Mindset
- ≤ Self-imposed narrative of personal, educational failure Mindset
- ≤ Self-imposed narrative of personal inadequacy Mindset
- ≤ Self-imposed narrative of personal lack of potential Mindset
- ≤ Self-imposed narrative of personal failure Mindset
- ≤ Self-imposed narrative of personal unworthiness Mindset
- ≤ Self-imposed narrative of personal worthlessness Mindset

OK, you made it – so how do you feel? Do you feel elevated, or do you feel depleted and low? Here is the Positive Mindset list, and if you are not already "listed out", read this one next:

Second, The Positive Mindset List = Transformational Growth Thinking (primarily Others-focussed and potential unlocking with dynamic transformation becoming who we are supposed to Be):

- ✓ **Pro-active Life Mindset**
  - ✓ Growth Mindset
  - ✓ Others-Focussed Mindset
  - ✓ Transformational Mindset
  - ✓ Higher Purpose Mindset (purpose finding)
- ✓ **Transformation and Growing Living Mindset**
  - ✓ Intentionality and Integrity Living Mindset
  - ✓ Significance and Meaning Living Mindset
  - ✓ Anticipation and Urgency Living Mindset
  - ✓ Abundance and Surplus Living Mindset
  - ✓ Focus and Commitment Living Mindset
  - ✓ Action and Opportunity Living Mindset
  - ✓ Striving to reach my Fullest Potential Mindset
- ✓ **Consecrated to God Mindset**
  - ✓ Dedicated to God Mindset
  - ✓ Wholeheartedly Committed to God Mindset
  - ✓ Unlocking and Unleashing Potential in Others' Mindset
  - ✓ Extraordinary Masterpiece for God Mindset
  - ✓ Transformational Leader! For Others Mindset
- ✓ **Living a Life of Significance! For Others Mindset**
  - ✓ Living a Life that Matters! For Others Mindset
  - ✓ Living a Life of Contribution! For Others Mindset
  - ✓ Living Your Best Life for God and Others' Mindset
  - ✓ Living Your Best Life for God's Higher Purpose Mindset
  - ✓ Valuing and adding to Others' Mindset
  - ✓ Breakout to God's Calling Mindset
- ✓ **AWAKE! To LIVE Your Best Life of God's Higher Purpose Mindset**
  - ✓ To Awareness of your Best Life
  - ✓ To Develop their Best Life
  - ✓ To Think over your Best Life
- ✓ **UNLOCK! Potential for your Best Life of God's Higher Purpose**
  - ✓ To Breakout to your Best Life Mindset
  - ✓ To Grow your Best Life Mindset

✓ To Engage yourself and others in their Best Life Mindset

✓ **ACT! Contributing For Others to Live Their Best Lives of God's Higher Purpose Mindset**

    ✓ To Lead Others to their Best Lives Mindset

    ✓ To Rally Others to their Best Lives Mindset

    ✓ To Legacy Others to their Best Life Legacy Mindset

> *God created us for His glory and gives us*
> *not just the freedom from, but the freedom to.*

OK, you have made it through to this point. How do you feel now? Do you feel lifted and wanting to be transformed and grow? To live your life on a higher level? How can we transform from the negative first list above to the positive second list below it? The straightforward answer is this:

"We Become What Our Minds Think. We hold the Seeds of Greatness already within us by Our Decision to Wholeheartedly Commit the Totality of Ourselves to Our Creator. That fruit needs now to be grown."

It's not rocket science – all you need to do is choose where you wish to be.

Either: Back living the first list of depleting mediocrity and, ultimately, frustration and failure;

Or: Choosing the second positive list and Transformational Growth to Become the Extraordinary Masterpiece God Created You To Be.

Sadly, I suspect there may be not a few people who will choose to stay where they are simply because of the path dependence principle. In other words, your tendency is for your past to be defined by decisions you took in the past, to then determine your future, even though those conditions may no longer be relevant or wise to use – another negative Mindset! But the safety of the status quo smothers its disciples.

But for those who, like me, recognised a truth I had never really heard before and, through overwhelming emotion, could hardly breathe as I realised it for the first time, let me try to give you one now!

WHY?

"Transformed!" has been written
to help us all become truly alive as God intended,
simply because the world (and for many people, it's their churches)

have beaten out of them real living,
personal growth, fun, sharing, shared connections, creativity
wholehearted living, purpose, courage, compassion, empathy, shared vision;
It has beaten out of them the capacity
to lead lives of authenticity, passion, significance and consequence
and left them living lives of scarcity and depletion.
And what we are all simply designed and called
to do is discover God's purpose for our lives
unlocking daily our potential, then going with courage,
compassion and commitment, creating the bridge as we walk on it
leaning and learning into the unknown but emerging and developing future
knowing that we are living the lives God always planned for us to live,
God's Best Lives for Us, Lives of God's Surplus and Abundance.
Lives of Passion, Significance, and Consequence for Christ and for Others
To leave the world a Better Place than when we arrived.
To live for His Glory and not ours.
Are you that person God is calling...?

~~~

Ernest Rutherford, "The Father of Nuclear Physics", wrote: "If you don't do the best with what you have, You could never have done better with what you could have had!"[91]

George Elliot also wrote similarly: "It's never too late to be what you might have been."[92]

The commonality with these concepts within *TRANSFORMED!* is simply this: Where we are is not where we are meant to be. To journey to where we are meant to be, we must Unlock our Potential and then Breakout! And Breakout! specifically to our Second, The Positive List = Transformational Growth Thinking (primarily Others-focussed and potential unlocking dynamic transformation becoming who we are supposed to Be).

Because of our inherited and self-imposed negative narrative Mindsets, every one of us needs to break out of these internal conventional thinking Fixed Mindsets. Your Mindsets and thought-walls are needlessly trapping, sapping and depleting you and keeping you hostage to life's events and killing your future. Just to make this abundantly clear:

---

[91] 'Ernest Rutherford Quotes (Author of Radioactive Transformations)'
<https://www.goodreads.com/author/quotes/437411.Ernest_Rutherford> [accessed 21 May 2020].
[92] 'A Quote by George Eliot' <https://www.goodreads.com/quotes/619-it-is-never-too-late-to-be-what-you-might> [accessed 21 May 2020].

❖ The self-imposed narrative of educational failure is a lie that you have accepted.

❖ The self-imposed narrative of personal inadequacy is a lie.

❖ The self-imposed narrative of lack of potential is a lie.

❖ The self-imposed narrative of personal failure is a lie.

❖ The self-imposed narrative of personal unworthiness is a lie.

❖ The self-imposed narrative of personal worthlessness is a lie.

❖ Yes, others poured this venom all over us, and we believed it all.

❖ Why ever did we believe them?

❖ These false Mindsets must be removed and destroyed!

❖ They have straitjacketed, depleted and limited our minds and lives through ignorance, through cultural acceptability, personal imposition and also through religious beliefs and religious church systems of control.

However, your accepted history of fixed Mindsets can and must be challenged, confronted, removed, replaced, and the new Transformational Growth Mindsets above discovered, developed and deployed. Along with Other new, growing, life-enhancing Mindsets that overtake, eclipse, and finally destroy those old Mindsets that formerly held you unknowingly in their vice-like, slow death grip, you will be slowly transformed.

All Mindsets have results – whether results of uplifting beneficial/positive or depleting detrimental/negative consequences. They cannot be benign. They either uplift us or deplete us. And one of the worst Mindsets is that of the hierarchy, both in individuals and organisations. We will return to that theme elsewhere.

You Were Born For This – You Can Set Yourself Free

In a very real sense, *TRANSFORMED!* for me was born at the 2014 Global Leadership Summit autumn videocasts in Bristol, UK, when I heard Carly Fiorina speaking about unlocking potential in people and her mother's wisdom.[93] For me, it was one of those rare "hardly able to breathe" times when I first recognised a truth that resonated through my very being.

I have come to realise through that experience, through the leadership experiences at a local church, and particularly 20 years in a large organisation under the mushroom compost there is a very good reason why Carly's words created that reaction within my heart.

---

[93] '2014 Global Leadership Summit Session 2'.

> *"What we are is God's gift to us;*
> *what we make of ourselves is our gift to God."*
> *Carly Fiorina*

(Quote above cited below. [94])

God has created you and me. Through the life experiences He has allowed me to experience and come through, I believe the outcomes have enabled me to seek the unlocking of potential, the breakout from constraining Mindsets, and the discovery of God's Higher Purpose, not just for me but very especially for others. There is deep within my being a passion, born out of difficulties and honed through experience, to seek that unlocking, that discovery, that renewal, that aspiration, that inspiration, that redirection, that fulfilment of God's purposes and that attainment of God's destiny for me in the time I have left on this earth, for others. Nothing fires me up more than these possibilities.

The following are two straightforward statements. The first is a statement of belief, as a one-sentence distillation of *TRANSFORMED!* The second is a distillation statement of purposeful action. They represent, for me, the essentials of belief and purposeful action that drive me forwards.

"Every one of us is personally and specifically created by The Triune God, as witnessed in scripture. We are intended to come to faith in Him and then fulfil His Purposes planned for us individually in our Lifetime. We are intended to be filled with all the fullness of God in Jesus Christ and living the Best Life He always planned for us to live if we choose."

"You and I are created and called for God's Transcendent Higher Purpose, which is for our Salvation, Transformation and Personal Growth, to reach towards our potential for God, through Redemption in Christ, meaning: Re-creation in Christ, Renewal in Christ, Restoration in Christ, and Redirection in Christ; for His Purposes, for personal transformation and growth with joyful discipline reaching our fullest potential, for lifting others intentionally with us, to fulfil God's purposes in our generation, and to be filled to the measure of all the fullness of God in Jesus Christ."

We can choose this day to contribute by living a life of Total Commitment,

---

[94] '2014 Global Leadership Summit Session 2'.

Personal Growth, and an Intentional Life of Significance to Influence, Lift and Inspire Others to be the same in Jesus Christ. This is the Jesus Life.

The biblical results being:
- ➢ Discovering God's Higher Purpose for yourself;
- ➢ Being Transformed through Redemption, Renewal, Redirection, Fulfilment and Destiny;
- ➢ Unlocking your potential and others' for God's Higher Purpose;
- ➢ Stepping up and into God's Higher Level;
- ➢ Being Aware, Engaged and Wholeheartedly Living in God's Higher Level; Loving in God's Higher Level;
- ➢ Leading through Servant Leadership in God's Higher Level;
- ➢ Preparing yourself in God's Higher Level;
- ➢ Learning at God's Higher Level;
- ➢ Running towards all that God has for you in His Higher Level;
- ➢ Becoming an extraordinary, doing whatever it takes, human being for Him as He intended;
- ➢ Changing the Future;
- ➢ Creating and Sustaining the Legacy;
- ➢ Ready to be filled with all the fullness of God in Jesus Christ.

Jesus Christ said in John 10:10b AMPC: "I came that they may have and enjoy life, and have it in abundance (to the full, till it overflows)."

That life is rarely, if ever, attained through traditional belief systems. It is attained and sustained by discovering God's purpose for you and the potential already placed within you by your Creator for your life. The complete focus, vision and intentionality of Christ is the fullest redemption possible in this life and then the perfect redemption in the life to come for everyone. It is to create His kingdom of people who are conformed to His image and also seek that outcome for others.

The most important part of a leader's work is to both "unlock the potential of others" and "connect people to their purpose". That is why Jesus was so successful because He unlocked the potential that He saw in them and connected His disciples to the purposes He had for them individually. He ensured they discovered God's Higher Purpose for them and then lived at God's Higher Level for the rest of their earthly lives.

From John C. Maxwell, *The Power of Significance: How Purpose Changes Your Life*.

I often teach that we have two great tasks in life: to find ourselves and to lose ourselves. Ultimately, I believe we find ourselves by discovering our why. We lose ourselves while travelling the path of significance by putting others first. The result? The people we help also find themselves, and the legacy cycle can begin again. That cycle has the power to live on after us. When I die, I cannot take with me what I have, but I can live in others by what I gave. This is what I hope for you.[95]

Each of us right now has a lid on our potential. The only way to lift that lid is to develop and grow intentionally. As you do this, you will make a wonderful discovery—you can also lift the lids of others. I have always considered myself to be a lid lifter—someone who sees the greatest potential in others and then gives them what they need to rise up and fly.[96]

This, for me, is one of the most important statements made outside of scripture. We have mostly thought of Significance as an ego trip. But as you may remember, in Luke 22:25-26 NIV, Jesus said to them, "The kings of the Gentiles lord it over them; and those who exercise authority over them call themselves Benefactors. But you are not to be like that. Instead, the greatest among you should be like the youngest, and the one who rules like the one who serves."

In His eyes, greatness or significance is not wrong at all. If you decide that you seek to live like Christ, decide to live intentionally. Decide to live a life of significance and greatness through Servant Leadership.

Those two great tasks in life: to find ourselves and to lose ourselves, are the gold standard of God's plans for us as individuals, and for this reason, the Gospel of Christ is not only about salvation and eternal life but about the life that is real life as Jesus described it. This is also worth shouting about: a Life of God's Higher Purpose, AKA a Life of God's Higher Meaning.

God's Life of Significance was always planned for you and me. This is a life of soaring on eagles' wings, not pecking like turkeys by the side of the runway, unaware of the life they should have had if only someone had led them to discover it. Our lives yearn for meaning and significance, and God has provided fully for everyone a life of His Higher Purpose. We are born with this potential deep inside us.

Jesus specifically calls the elite "Benefactors". He totally understood the misrecognition that overtakes the subjects of hierarchy, whether in life, business and even the Church of Christ, because they misrecognise their overlords as

---

[95] John C Maxwell, *The Power of Significance: How Purpose Changes Your Life*, 2017, pt. 113.
[96] John C. Maxwell, *Intentional Living*, p. 142.

benefactors when, in fact, they are thieves, liars and destroyers of individuals and their potential.

Never forget, when Jesus talks about Life that is really Life, He is stating the blindingly obvious fact that where we live in our default culture is not where God planned for us to be. The sooner we discover His purposes already within us, decide to live a life of significance, then get out, get up and start adding value to others by lifting the lid off them, the better the world and ourselves will be.

> *"The essence of being human is being able to direct your own life. Humans act, animals and human "robots" react. Humans can make choices based on their values. Your power to choose the direction of your life allows you to reinvent yourself, to change your future, and to powerfully influence the rest of creation. It is the one gift that enables all the gifts to be used; it is the one gift that enables us to elevate our life to higher and higher levels."*
> *"Our birth gift: The freedom and power to choose."*
> **Dr. Stephen Covey**

(Above quotation cited below. [97])

God's primary objective with you and me is to conform us to the image of Christ as shown in Romans ch.8, v29, AMP: "For those whom He foreknew (of whom He was aware and loved beforehand), He also destined from the beginning (foreordaining them) to be moulded into the image of His Son (and share inwardly His likeness), that He might become the firstborn among many brethren." This is absolutely crucial to our correct understanding of God's purposes for us. Everything else is a sideshow.

Seize The Keys – Open The Gates

Come before God with anticipation, not on the basis of need, but on the basis of not only our position but precisely His chosen position for those of us made nearby faith in Christ. This is our standing with God and His avowed intentions for us – based on our God-given potential and purpose. What a difference. The transformation starts here, right now!

All the wisdom of God summed in 29 words:

---

[97] Covey, pp. 41–43.

Mark 12:30-31 NIV: "Love the Lord your God with all your heart and with all your soul and with all your mind and with all your strength."

The second is this: "Love your neighbour as yourself." There is no commandment greater than these.

As Paul wrote in Ephesians 4:1 NIV:

"As a prisoner for the Lord, then, I urge you to live a life worthy of the calling you have received."

Psalm 145:18 NIV:

"The Lord is near to all who call on him, to all who call on him in truth."

A calling received and a purpose to undertake whilst calling on the Lord.

A calling received.

A purpose undertaken.

A destiny reached.

Isaiah 40:31 NIV:

"But those who hope in the Lord will renew their strength. They will soar on wings like eagles; they will run and not grow weary, they will walk and not be faint."

In calling upon the Lord, we recognise daily:

❖ Who has created and called us?
❖ Why has He created and called us?
❖ What are His plans for us?
❖ Where is our destiny?

But Christians traditionally have focussed on their sin and God's forgiveness and tried to apply it to others who then go on to do the same. Coming to faith in Christ and forgiveness of sins is entirely biblically correct. No person of faith in Christ would disagree. But they have then made an incorrect assumption that as they continue to fall short of God's standards, they can never get close to God. This leads to further incorrect assumptions of never being good enough and always falling short of God's standards, being unable to do anything about it except through more extended prayer and quiet reflection.

Although it is personally useful, this reflective thinking will not get us out on the journey towards becoming the people God always created us to be. Paul wrote a very different slant on this in Ephesians 2: 10 NIV:

"For we are God's handiwork, created in Christ Jesus to do good works, which God prepared in advance for us to do."

The New Living Testament uses the word Masterpiece instead of handiwork.

Rather than the "sinful" road trudged by traditional Christian thought, we are presented in scripture with the very different ideas and concepts of creation, potential, purpose and destiny. This is why in Step 7, we look at a broader range of created aspects that are everyone's birthright but which, when back-lit by the actions of our Creator God, take on almost overwhelming importance for His plans and the transformation of individuals and the world.

Professor Bob Quinn, in a recent blog, notes: "To develop as a leader, one must overcome the social context and the pull of the culture. One must separate and contemplate. Doing so leads to increased consciousness. The highest possible purpose becomes clear. Committing to that purpose leads to failures and successes. From these new experiences, learning expands, and capacity emerges. We find that we know a new truth, and it makes us free from the culture. It allows us to act upon the culture with effectiveness. We operate at a new level of leadership." [98]

Purpose and Learning are inseparable. Purpose cannot be discovered and acted upon without learning. Learning cannot be effective without the search for and actioned discovery of Purpose. This concept is difficult and almost impossible for those people who, like me, have lived and breathed the greater part of their lives living within the constraints and expectations of their culture. It does not have to be like this.

It is even worse for those of us who have been in clearly declining churches where the focus is inwards, and the outcome of hierarchical management by clergy is where compliant congregations are taught every week like children who will never grow up. That being taught in rows by "teachers" who alone have the requisite knowledge has almost wholly obscured any sense of positive possibility by reinforcing the conventional mental map week after week.

It would be difficult to imagine a better methodology for burying any thought of personal breakout to discover God's Higher Purpose and His alternative Positive Mental Map for His people. Professor Quinn suggests increasing consciousness (awareness) and exposing people to this surprising alternative context and reality.[99] We really can rise above where we are, giving ourselves that permission, sloughing off the dead skin of past false assumptions that themselves were based on false assumptions.

Challenging culturally defined and assumed constraints is one of the essential starting points. So, by envisaging a different future, and by "seeing and sensing possibility" and believing that God has created us to be His Extraordinary

---

[98] Robert E. Quinn, 'How Culture Conspires to Prevent the Emergence of Leadership', <https://robertequinn.com/uncategorized/how-culture-conspires-to-prevent-the-emergence-of-leadership/> [accessed 21 May 2020].

[99] 'How Culture Conspires to Prevent the Emergence of Leadership'.

Masterpiece People who not only believe but that we are full of God-created Potential, we make progress – envisaging that we are created to be and do great things for God by living lives of Purpose and Fulfilling His Purposes in our generation.

WOW! COUNT ME IN! I'M READY, LORD!!!

This is the heart of Jesus Christ growing His disciples, who would escape their birth culture and turn the world upside down and change the future. This is not a self-absorbed ego working here but the birthright of every human being ever created on this planet. This is why, through faith in Christ, we are Redeemed and Renewed. Not to simply boost the numbers in heaven but to vitally impact everyone on earth. Never think any the less of God's plans for you by a false sense of unworthiness because of sin.

Start The Race

Moving from a reactive to a creative state, we can ask the question, "What results do I want to create?"

Professor Quinn practically writes: "Good people sometimes react unproductively to negative situations in a comfort-centred, self-justifying blame system, as we focus on problem-solving instead of purpose finding."[100]

A purpose is more than a goal. When people are purpose-centred,

1. *they envision and pursue extraordinary results that are not constrained by previous expectations or by the expectations that they receive from others*
2. *the results they pursue are energizing because they are self-chosen, challenging, and constructive*
3. *they provide a clear definition of the situation, focussing people's attention.*[101]

In their book, *Lift: The Fundamental State of Leadership*, Professors Robert E Quinn and Ryan E Quinn write of the concept of the Fundamental State of Leadership.[102] We have listed this before, but it bears reading again:

The Fundamental State of Leadership:

❖ *Purpose Centred with energy and focus (as against comfort centred- we seek comfort):*
   Clarify your Purpose continually.

---

[100] Quinn and Quinn, p. 44.
[101] Quinn and Quinn, pp. 59-60.
[102] Quinn and Quinn.

❖ *Internally Directed (as against externally driven - we react to situations automatically):*
Act consistently with your Values.

❖ *Others Focussed (as against self-focussed - we focus on our wants):*
Focus on engaging with others to thrive, grow, learn together and make a difference.

❖ *Externally Open (as against internally closed - we believe there is little we can do to improve):*
Believe you can breakout, learn, improve and lead others, be open to learning and receive and use feedback.

It's all about realising and creating new realities which did not exist before. Paul writing to the church of the Ephesians 3:19 AMPC shows, "That you may really come to know practically, through experience for yourselves the love of Christ, which far surpasses mere knowledge without experience; that you may be filled through all your being unto all the fullness of God may have the richest measure of the divine Presence, and become a body wholly filled and flooded with God Himself!"

God's Purpose is that we should be filled to the measure of all the fullness of God in Jesus Christ because of His Abundance and Surplus. This can only happen if we awake to new realities.

As we awake and breakout into these new realities, we enter the fundamental state of self-leadership. Leadership is a choice, not a position (so beloved of the Hierarchies). The calling and purpose of (Christian) leaders are to both unlock and unleash (God-given) Potential in their people <u>and</u> to Connect their people to their (God-given) Purpose. It is my sad realisation that the continuing sin-management charade they undertake every Sunday, in reality, depletes and prevents the realisation of God's potential in the lives of His people.

✓ Leading from the front – that's Christ, and He is entirely focussed on those not yet with Him.
✓ Leadership inspires others to choose to follow.
✓ Leadership is a positive cultural intervention.

Professor Quinn, in his book, *The Positive Organisation*, quotes Peter Vaill, who says:
Purpose is an unarticulated desire, and that,
First, higher purpose must be discovered. This means it already exists and must be found. It is an unarticulated desire. A leader must have the ability to listen to every stakeholder, reflect on what is said, and conceptualize the shared and unarticulated

purpose.

Second, the purpose must be acted upon. This means that the statement of purpose is real and that the leader uses purpose to govern personal and collective behaviour so that integrity fills the culture.

Third, the purpose must be continually clarified. In a world of constant change, purpose tends to get lost, and confusion reigns. In every action and in every conversation, the leader clarifies and creatively revivifies the purpose.

Fourth, executives avoid the work necessary to imbue an organization with purpose because it doesn't seem like real work. Executives want to complete tasks. Imbuing an organization with purpose is a requirement that never ends.[103]

Professor Quinn then elucidates four crucial aspects:

❖ *Leaders accept the responsibility for Purpose and live the 4 points above.*

❖ *Leaders see the link between Purpose and Listening, to deeply listen, hear and know the people, articulating their desires.*

❖ *Leaders embody the Purpose through "idealised influence" by transcending both self-interest and the conventional mental map and becoming "Transformational".*

❖ *Leaders meet the people where they are, starting where they are and inviting them to unlock themselves to a Higher Level of understanding, engagement, commitment and self-empowerment."*[104]

> *I should warn you that the journey to unlocking your potential won't follow a codified plan. In fact, the very first thing you need to do is become comfortable with a rather disconcerting idea: As you journey toward who you are meant to be,*
> *you will not always know where you're going*
> *Carly Fiorina*

(Above quotation cited below. [105])

We have come a long way in this Step 5, in Unlocking Your Best Life. Unlocking Potential, Transforming Mindsets, discovering new positive ones, and entering the Fundamental State of (self)Leadership are preparing you for the rest of your

---

[103] Robert E. Quinn, *The Positive Organization*, p. 39.
[104] Robert E. Quinn, *The Positive Organization*, pp. 38–43.
[105] Carly Fiorina, *Find Your Way: Unleash Your Power and Highest Potential* (Carol Stream, Illinois: Tyndale House Publishers, Inc, 2019), p. 17.

journey. You truly are "Building the Bridge as You Walk on It", as Bob Quinn writes.[106]

---

[106] Robert E. Quinn, *Building the Bridge as You Walk on It*.

Conclusions for Step 5

Unlock! Your Best Life

Key Thought – You Can and Must Unlock the Unique Unlimited Potential in Yourself (first), then Unlock it in Others.

Sub-headings review
- ➢ **Your Choice To Unlock Your Unlimited Potential**
- ➢ **Your Choice to Unlock Your Mindsets**
- ➢ **You Were Born For This – You Can Set Yourself Free**
- ➢ **Seize The Keys – Open The Gates**
- ➢ **Start The Race**

I discovered it was never too late to start unlocking the unlimited potential within. Okay, I had never even thought about it like this in over 60 years, so no wonder Carly Fiorina's words hit home, leaving me dizzy and gasping for breath.[107] No one ever told me anything like this. It is one thing to have personal skills that can be used in general life, business and, careers, etc. But it is transformational to realise not just another level of thinking but a new dimension of being and living, a new dimension of personal potential that lay within, dormant, unsuspected and unused until it was discovered. This is not any old potential but the potential to transform the world and change the future.

And it lies within every one of us. Who put it there? It was placed within you and me at birth by our Creator. This is staggering in its implications because the world in general and our culture laugh at and discount such a possibility. But you read it here, and I will not believe that you can remain untouched by such revelations. What an astounding way of thinking and living as you grasp the enormity of unlocking your unique and unlimited potential to make a difference in this world for Others if you choose.

So allow the last three sub-headings to direct you to take effective action:

- ➢ You Were Born For This – You Can Set Yourself Free
- ➢ Seize The Keys – Open The Gates
- ➢ Start The Race

---

[107] '2014 Global Leadership Summit Session 2'.

Step 6

To Breakout! To Your Best Life

~~~

God Created us His Eagles!
So, Soar like them for God!
Don't hold back! Don't be held back!
Breakout of whatever cage has imprisoned you!
Whether it's your culture, your country, your education, your religion,
all have an imprisoning effect of limiting your potential, your purpose,
your life and your destiny!
Make Breaking Out your default starting point!
Don't settle for a life of pecking the ground like turkeys by the runway,
never to understand its significance for you!
Live the Life God Created You for and Created for You!

"Slip the surly bonds of earth to Top the windswept heights with easy grace
Where never lark or even eagle flew.
And, while with silent, lifting mind tread
The high, untrespassed sanctity of space,
Put out your hand,
and touch the face of God."

After Pilot Officer, John Gillespie Magee
Royal Canadian Air Force
d. 11.12.1941

~~~

- ❖ Key Purpose: Create the Courage and Decision to Start The Breakout to Your Highest Calling, to Next Level Living, and Living a Life that Matters.
- ❖ Key Purpose: Unlock moves you seriously forward, where you realise you have unlimited unused potential that awaits being drawn from within. Create the Willingness to Stretch and Reach and Unlock Unlimited Potential in Yourself and Others and Discover God's Meaningful Higher Purpose for You through "Potential, Purpose, Passion and a Life that Truly Matters".

- ❖ **Key Learning (Always Facing the Unknown without Fear):** We learnt in the last step that Unlocking Your Unique Unlimited Potential is something you are born for. Never look backwards from now on because you are on the Breakout Step. This is not for the fainthearted. This is for the Fully Committed, someone who knows where they are, where they have come from, and has already invested substantial effort to get to this point. Breakout is where you intentionally (Yes, afraid so!) leave the pull-back of the gravity of the old status quo and achieve something approaching orbit – but not quite. You will learn about some of the issues that will always try to stop your take-off and bring you back to mediocrity and the "normality" of inward-focussed life.
- ❖ **Key Actions (Building The Bridge As You Walk On It[108]):** Your breakout must become second nature, even if you need to break out every day, as I have often discovered. We are human beings. The old Mindsets do not just lie down and die. The need for constant awareness and resolve to replace the old Mindsets may never completely go away. Breakout to Higher Purpose – that is hard work. Breakout to become so God-aligned He will show you His Joy.

Kickstart The Breakout To Your Best Life

Breakout is absolutely essential to becoming the person God always created you to be. Breakout needs to be dynamic! Hoping it will happen means it never will happen! It takes Intentional Living, Intentional Focus, and Intentional Action.

> *It is not my best life, but God's Best Life for me.*
> *He created me for this and planned for it to take place.*

Christine Caine from Hillsong Church in Australia, spoke passionately at the GLS, Chicago in 2013:

> *We do what we do out of passion. We have to understand that while we have a passionate hope for a lost and broken world, it will carry us beyond our gifts, beyond our talents, beyond our abilities, beyond our disappointments, beyond our discouragements. It is this passionate hope that Jesus can, will, and does make a difference in people's lives. Hope fuels our risk-taking. When you have no hope, you*

---

[108] Robert E. Quinn, *Building the Bridge as You Walk on It.*

play it safe. Everything just has to line up. You won't step out of the boat.

I believe in the days and hours in which we live, and the great adversity on the planet, and the challenges, and the great injustices, God is calling His Church to go places we have never been, by pathways we never even knew existed. You need hope to step out and take a risk. What many leaders do is we spend a lot of time praying for signs and wonders and miracles, and then we avoid the context in which a miracle can happen. God says, no, no, no. I need you to step out of the boat and take a risk. There is a lot of darkness out there. And rather than running away from the darkness, you and I need to step into that darkness and bring the light of Christ.

We don't need to fear the world; we don't need to fear the darkness. The hope on the inside of us, Jesus, this hope that we have as an anchor for our souls, both firm and secure, that hope compels us to go out into the darkness. We need to understand what is the purpose of light. It is not to be scared of the war, and the famine, and the poverty, and the injustice, and the big global issues, and the lonely person. God is saying, "I don't want you to run away from that. I don't want you to fear the world. I want you to take the light that I put on the inside of you. And I want you to penetrate that darkness and illuminate that darkness with the light and hope of Jesus Christ. That is the job of the Church." [109]

You see, friends, ultimately, *TRANSFORMED!* is all about the above. Believe that God has called you to His Higher Purpose, to make a difference in this world, to impact others. So, what is it that stops us?

Fear is at the root of all that holds us back. People not coming to faith, overwhelming internal focus, lack of clarity and purpose, the irrelevance of the church to most people, and blind adherence to the past and past methods and thinking are all produced by fear. These aspects are, of course, symptoms of the malaise. Fear is often incredibly subtle, subconscious, subliminal, and paralysing and must continually be reduced, removed and destroyed by Hope. Hope centred in our supernatural God who will act on our behalf in the days in which we live as we commit to Him unequivocally.

We need Hope and the Courage to look down the road of our journey to believe that God can and will act in the days we are called to serve. I believe that God created us for His Glory. Clearly, we are not where we should be or are meant to be. The global impact of thousands, maybe millions of people waking up to God's Higher Purpose for them, Unlocking their Unlimited Potential, and Acting to Really Make a Difference in the world will lead to the following

---

[109] 'Leading on the Edge of Hope - Christine Caine', *Global Leadership Network UK & Ireland, Partial Transcript*, https://globalleadershipnetwork.org.uk/lesson/leading-on-the-edge-of-hope-christine-caine/> [accessed 22 May 2020].

results:

We will see people coming to faith, marriages that were saved, children that were brought up in those loving, stable-marriage relationships, young people and their precious futures that were not lost to drugs, young men and women living wholesome, God-fearing, courageous lives, lives transformed, broken people healed, symphonies that were written, discoveries that were made, gardens that were tended, grandparents that were able to see grandchildren grow up, people lacking faith becoming worshippers of Jesus, members being mobilised for ministry and mission, because we stood up in the days in which we lived, took God at His word, and made the difference.

> *If I am not where I am supposed to be,*
> *I need to understand next level thinking.*
> *I need to be working towards the next level, a higher level.*
> *So, where is it and how do I get there,*
> *knowing I must start now!*

Friends, we have a breakout choice to make: The choice of continuing where we are, irrelevant, inward-focussed, fearful, and locked in to "doing church" on our terms, or we can break out of our current thinking, our current Mindsets, realise how short life is, and in the short time we have, stop wasting it on things that don't matter, and breakout to the Transformation and Growth that God always intended for us and start making a difference. And it all begins with Intentional Dynamic Breakout.

32 Daily Breakouts:

- ➤ **Breakout! from Where You Are**
    - ➤ Breakout! from False Assumptions
    - ➤ Breakout! To Awake!
    - ➤ Breakout! to Challenge Assumptions
    - ➤ Breakout! to Focussed Thinking
    - ➤ Breakout! to Full Awareness through Critical Thinking
    - ➤ Breakout! to Live Your Best Life
- ➤ **Breakout! to Where You are Meant to Be**
    - ➤ Breakout! to Full Commitment to God
    - ➤ Breakout! to God's Calling for You

- ➤ Breakout! to a Life of Contribution
- ➤ Breakout! to a Life that Matters
- ➤ **Breakout! to Transformation and Growth**
  - ➤ Breakout! to Intentionality and Integrity to Make a Difference
  - ➤ Breakout! to Significance and Meaning to Make a Difference
  - ➤ Breakout! to Anticipation and Urgency to Make a Difference
  - ➤ Breakout! to Abundance and Surplus to Make a Difference
  - ➤ Breakout! to Focus and Commitment to Make a Difference
  - ➤ Breakout! to Action and Opportunities to Make a Difference
  - ➤ Breakout! to God's Calling Mindset
- ➤ **Breakout! TO AWAKE! To LIVE Your Best Life of God's Higher Purpose Mindset**
  - ➤ Breakout! To Awareness of Your Best Life
  - ➤ Breakout! To Develop Your Best Life
  - ➤ Breakout! To Think over Your Best Life
- ➤ **Breakout! TO UNLOCK! Potential for Your Best Life of God's Higher Purpose**
  - ➤ Breakout! To Breakout to Your Best Life Mindset
  - ➤ Breakout! To Grow Your Best Life Mindset
  - ➤ Breakout! To Engage yourself and others in Your Best Life Mindset
- ➤ **Breakout! TO ACT! Contributing For Others to Live Their Best Lives of God's Higher Purpose Mindset**
  - ➤ Breakout! To Lead Others to their Best Lives Mindset
  - ➤ Breakout! To Rally Others to their Best Lives Mindset
  - ➤ Breakout! To Legacy Others to their Best Life Legacy Mindset

John C. Maxwell, writing in his book, *The Power Of Significance, How Purpose Changes Your Life*, notes:

> Now you know how to live a life of purpose. You know that significance is within your reach. You know what it means to be intentional. So I want to ask you a series of questions. See how many you can honestly answer yes to:

- *Are you choosing to live a story of significance? (my answer, Yes!)*
- *Are you actively searching for your why so that you can make a difference? (my answer, Yes!)*
- *Are you choosing to live with intentionality, not just good intentions? (my answer, Yes!)*
- *Are you willing to start small but believe big to make a difference? (my answer, Yes!)*

- *Are you living with a sense of anticipation for making a difference? (my answer, Yes!)*
- *Are you seizing opportunities and taking action to make a difference? (my answer, Yes!)*[110]

To me, anticipation is a wonderfully proactive and intentional word for seeking out significance. People with anticipation plan to be significant. They expect to fulfil their purpose and live a life that matters every day. They prepare to do significant acts. They position themselves physically, mentally, emotionally, and financially to make a difference in others' lives. Their sense of anticipation for significance draws them forward. What does a strong sense of anticipation do for us? It does five things:

1. *Anticipation Causes Us to Value Today*
2. *Anticipation Prompts Us to Prepare*
3. *Anticipation Helps Us Generate Good Ideas*
4. *Anticipation Prompts Us to Look for Ways to Help Others*
5. *Anticipation Helps Us Possess an Abundance Mindset.*[111]

In understanding the breakout to be *TRANSFORMED!* and to Live Your Best Life, the Life for God's Higher Purpose, I have deliberately injected John C. Maxwell's thoughts on a life of significance. Because that is what you are breaking out to. I can only add to his words above:

➤ Do it now!
➤ Possess the initiative
➤ Do it now!
➤ Stop procrastinating
➤ Do it now!
➤ Waiting until you "feel" ready will get you nowhere
➤ Do it now!
➤ Do whatever it takes!

As I write *TRANSFORMED!*, I ask myself these simple questions:

❖ Why am I doing this?
❖ Has God called me to do this?
❖ For whom am I doing this?
❖ What is the Purpose?

---

[110] John C Maxwell, *The Power of Significance*, pt. 1154.
[111] John C Maxwell, *The Power of Significance*, pts 605-806.

❖ What results do I seek to create?

My self-directed answers are:
- ✓ We are all created and called by God for His Higher Purpose.
- ✓ We cannot go on as we are.
- ✓ We are not where we are meant to be.
- ✓ God has placed within me certain gifts that need to be given to others.
- ✓ This is not about me, and I have no personal interest in this except the desire for personal growth and transformation.
- ✓ This is about unlocking and unleashing potential in others.
- ✓ I am aware of a growing conviction that we are not where God has planned us to be.
- ✓ I feel the growing conviction to do something about the situation, however inadequate I may be.
- ✓ I feel all my life has been leading up to this point in time.
- ✓ People are crying out for leadership that inspires them to transform themselves individually.
- ✓ As Christ did, we need to grow others and send them out to do the same.

But here is the reality, and it may be you will feel all of this and more as well, as you breakout to your Unlimited Potential and God's Higher Purpose for you:
- ✓ Yes, I feel wholly inadequate since I have no formal educational qualifications.
- ✓ Yes, I fear the laughter of others who will ask, "Who is this upstart to tell us what to do?"
- ✓ Yes, I am fearful of others' criticism, pointing fingers of laughter and scorn.
- ✓ Yes, I fear an adverse reaction, especially the "theologians" who may rip all this apart.
- ✓ Yes, I am fearful.
- ✓ But, I can delay no longer!

> **TRANSFORMED!**
> *Means To Intentionally Breakout every Day, Today.*
> *Breakout to Extraordinary Awareness*
> *Breakout to Unlock Extraordinary Potential*
> *Breakout to Extraordinary Action*
> *These are the reasons we put our feet*
> *On the floor as we get out of bed.*

I remind us because we all experience fear, of my favourite and especially encouraging quotation from Ambrose Redmoon:

"Courage is not the absence of fear, but rather the judgement that something else is more important than fear."[112]

Yes, you are ahead of me already! Someone has asked the question, "What would you do if you had 1% more courage?" That is a brilliant question on its own, let alone here. But that is my thinking: 1% would just tip the balance, 10% would rout the opposition! Therefore:

- ✓ I choose to overcome and rise above all those fears (lies to myself) to soar close to God on eagles' wings because l believe He created me for this.
- ✓ I am created for connection with my heavenly Father.
- ✓ I am created to be a servant leader to others.
- ✓ I refuse to come to the end of my life, having lived a life, even as a Christian, based on fear, procrastination and laziness with excuses, saying it was not my fault and not my responsibility to do something about it.

The result I seek to achieve is nothing less than the transformation of the Church of Jesus Christ from inward-focussed irrelevance (where it exists) via personal Renewal, Transformation and Growth to make a difference for Him, growing others where we are and live the lives He always planned for us to live. And to see this cascade through history. This is the real relevance of the Church of Christ – salvation and transformation and growth first for yourself and then for others as you make a difference where you are.

- ➤ So, I have said to myself, Just Do it now!
- ➤ Understanding an old reality anew (Christ's "adding value" to people through the transformation of His disciples) and doing something about it!
- ➤ I can help grow the Kingdom of God

---

[112] 'Ambrose Redmoon Quotes'.

> ➤ I can live a life of Transformation and Growth
> ➤ I can live a life that Matters and makes a Difference
> ➤ I can live a life of Significance and Meaning
> ➤ I can live a life that echoes in Eternity for God
> ➤ Just do it! Do it now!
> ➤ Do whatever it takes!
> ➤ Walk those pathways we have never known!
> ➤ Make a start and build the bridge as you walk on it!
> ➤ Go to places you never even knew existed as you transform and grow!
> ➤ Only you are called to walk those pathways and reach those unknown places!
> ➤ Do it now!

What Prevents The Breakout To Transformation And Growth?

Now, we may have all the enthusiasm and inspiration to breakout. Here is the reality check of helpful knowledge awareness and preparation you will need, which will mature your understanding as you breakout.

Paul wrote in Romans 12:2 AMPC: "Do not be conformed to this world (this age), (fashioned after and adapted to its external, superficial customs), but be transformed (changed) by the (entire) renewal of your mind (by its new ideals and its new attitude), so that you may prove (for yourselves) what is the good and acceptable and perfect will of God, even the thing which is good and acceptable and perfect (in His sight for you)."

We need to know what we are up against. I am introducing something here that is generally unknown, probably unacceptable to most people, but crucial in helping us understand where we are culturally. When Dr Stephen Covey wrote the opening quotation chosen in the introduction to this book (I paraphrase), "those who develop a vision of great things, who suspect there may be more to themselves than they realised, who take the initiative and tap into higher motivations, these people find and use their voice, and choose to influence and inspire others to do the same"[113], he was alluding to this breakout situation that all of us face.

It is a vitally personal act of self-leadership. We are undertaking "Leadership" whether we understand that term or not. Self-Leadership is a vital precursor to breakout. The decision is just that. It is a "Choice". Let no one seek to disabuse

---

[113] Covey, p. 25-26.

you of the extraordinary choice that you have made if this describes what you have decided. It may be that 1% extra courage is what it takes. It may have happened for you almost unnoticed, a gradual realisation and awakening to higher awareness, thinking and deliberate action.

The action itself is truly extraordinary simply because the individual choice to unlock and unleash one's potential is not only truly momentous, challenging, and, for some in their cultures, downright dangerous; it is one of the world's greatest lies exploded. From birth, for every human being, every culture causes uniformity, convention and compliance within the often unseen expectations of that culture.

Overwhelmingly, then, in virtually every organisation or culture where a hierarchical elite is in control, there is further total "misrecognition" of the true nature of the elite by the subjects of that hierarchy. Pierre Bourdieu[114] (French anthropologist, sociologist and philosopher) wrote extensively (relating to the Catholic Church primarily) about the pernicious effects of this misguided understanding and acceptance of the normality imposed upon the laity by their religious masters and supposed specialised superiors who create this system of colluding subordination to maintain their power and this dominating status quo of the dominated. This is difficult thinking, but it needs to be exposed for the truth it is.

"Somewhere within all of us there thus lurks a spirit of resistance, lying for the most part dormant and 'confused' under layers upon layers of misrecognition that dupe us into submission to the social order in all of its inequalities and injustices. Until, of course, a prophet (hopefully one who has read Bourdieu!) comes along to 'reactivate' it." – Dr Terry Rey, Bourdieu on Religion.[115]

The key word above here is "reactivate". "Lurking, dormant, confused"; this may well underline the Bordieuan concept of duped submission by misrecognition but then transform to enhance the created alternative to hopelessness. This is to recognise the existence of possibility in potential and purpose to be reactivated, which will enable the breakout of the people from submission to the social or religious order deemed normal by them and imposed by elites from above.

We cannot move forward in our personal growth without the full awareness and understanding of where we are. So, in asking the difficult questions below, we seek to become truly aware of the full horror of the conditioning of our Mindsets

---

[114] Terry Rey, *Bourdieu on Religion: Imposing Faith and Legitimacy.* (Routledge, 2014).
[115] Rey, p. 130.

by our cultural presumptions, cultural history and personal experiences. But always remember, we are both culture receivers/acceptors and culture creators in our own environment and spheres of influence. We cannot pass the buck by blaming outside influences. I ask the following questions:

What prevents Transformation? What prevents the renewal of thinking?

Alternative and better questions maybe because of the implications within them: What prevents the emergence of transformation, potential, purpose and positive thinking in individuals? What prevents the discovery and re-emergence of birth gifts created in us by God?

Professor Bob Quinn's book, *The Positive Organisation*, reminds us that The Conventional Mental Map assumes that an organisation is a pyramid, a hierarchy of positions.[116] That change derives from a formal plan conceived and implemented in a linear, top-down fashion and with the assumptions of expertise flowing down the hierarchy. Most organisations (and this includes churches) have a culture of hierarchy based on the notions of:

- hierarchy of positions
- hierarchy of importance
- hierarchy of authority
- hierarchy of sub-empires
- hierarchy of change from the top down
- hierarchy of expertise
- hierarchy of knowledge
- hierarchy of wisdom
- hierarchy of information
- hierarchy of information control
- hierarchy of information translation
- hierarchy of information flow
- hierarchy of decisions
- hierarchy of control
- hierarchy of direction
- hierarchy of manipulation

In other words, a pyramid of positions, importance, authority, knowledge, control, power and direction in every essential part of the organisation. What cannot happen in such a system is the emergence of individual potential and purpose. Because the hierarchical system will always destroy such thinking to

---

[116] Robert E. Quinn, *The Positive Organization*, pp. 28–29.

protect itself and those individuals who have attempted to break free. It is an unseen and secret sub-organisation with its own agenda, usually unnoticed by those at the bottom of the pyramid. And there will be many times when empires are built to satisfy personal ego rather than the organisation as a whole. It is a hierarchy of personal position and not personal function.

The assumption that some people are more important than others has been within humans since the dawn of time. Hierarchy is defined as "a system in which members of an organisation or society are ranked according to relative status or authority". Other similar words are oligarchy, monarchy, and anarchy, and all are related by organisational and governmental meaning. But the essential essence of the hierarchy is in its assumptions of power and the mechanisms that control, maintain and extend the influence and reach of that centralised power. It is not only the pinnacle of the pyramid that centralised, hierarchical power impacts. It is especially pernicious at lower levels as that pinnacle power moves only vertically downwards. All "subordinates" are simply that – subordinate and subordinate in position, status, power, leadership, moral power, titles, actions, thinking, awareness, relationships, and effectiveness. It is a hierarchy of controlling power that dangerously distorts all underneath, especially in relation to self-preservation and fear. It is all about position. Thus, we unknowingly collude in the continuation of the Conventional Mental Map.

Professor Quinn states, "The conventional map reflects the political nature of organizations. Inherent in the conventional mental map is a need for self-preservation and a fear of the vulnerability required in authentic dialogue. So many people hold this orientation that it is difficult to challenge it and to express an authentic voice." [117]

Now, that nuance will be lost on those who are within the hierarchical system. But those who can think outside of this cultural lead-lined coffin will be aware of the devastatingly different outcomes that this pernicious Graeco-Roman philosophy has produced in the centuries since it insinuated itself from secular thinking to infect, subdue and very effectively completely distort Christ's intentions for the early Christian church. The centuries since then bear tribute to both power battles and actual battles often viciously played out to jealously protect itself, its rites and its compliant congregations unaware of the wholly unbiblical nature of this beast. However, Jesus was only too well aware of this situation when He began to impact His culture in the duality of both the Jewish and Roman hierarchical systems of His day.

In a hierarchy, people are to be managed, used as the hierarchy decides, and fulfil the purpose of the hierarchy. Some are chosen to join the hierarchy and

---

[117] Robert E. Quinn, *The Positive Organization*, p. 48.

sometimes based on merit, but more often based on their usefulness to the hierarchy as "useful idiots" or their perceived acceptability, vis their "fit" within the culture. This is possibly benevolent, but more often, it is to support the hierarchy in their perceived superior knowledge-based actions, which may not fulfil the purpose of the organisation because of personal empire-building.

The horrific outcomes of the Conventional Mental Map are mainly found in the effects on those who form the base of the pyramid who, to a person, will:

- Feel fear and act out of fear and social rejection
- Feel deep frustration
- Feel deep resentment
- Feel a sense of powerlessness
- Feel a sense of hopelessness
- Feel a sense of being a small cog in a bigger wheel
- Feel a sense of insignificance
- Feel a lack of purpose
- Feel deep disengagement

And they then:

- Feel more fearful and rejected
- Feel more frustrated
- Feel more resentful
- Feel more powerless
- Feel more hopeless
- Feel more insignificant
- Feel more purposeless
- Feel a greater sense of disengagement
- Lose trust
- Lose open communication
- Lose authenticity
- Lose satisfaction
- Lose openness
- Lose willingness to participate fully
- Become alienated
- Pursue self-interest
- Disengage from the organisation
- Seek to limit personal hurt
- Posture for self-elevation
- Position themselves for self-preservation

- Compete with each other
- Battle for scarce resources
- Experience conflict daily
- Triangulate with others in venting frustrations
- Manipulate others negatively against the hierarchy
- Fail to see or seek opportunities
- Speak in politically correct ways
- Think within the "group think" boundaries
- Fail to grow as a person
- Stagnate individually
- Underperform by a substantial margin
- Make assumptions of constraint
- Are blinded by constraints to their own potential, excellence and possibility
- Hold back their discretionary energy and thinking
- Fail to learn
- Create hostility towards others at all levels
- Use theft justified as a means to get back at management
- Benefit from perks that are not for others but for them only
- Stay in their roles
- Minimise involvement with others
- Minimise personal cost
- Give up in the face of relentless rejection by the hierarchy of good suggestions
- Give up because of the fear of further failure and social rejection
- Keep silent, even as the organisation slides into oblivion, because they know they will be ignored, rejected and side-lined.

What a final ending of overwhelming tragedy and pathos. We keep quiet because we are afraid, frustrated and totally disengaged. No one wants to be rejected or laughed at for attempting to be positive and move forwards.

What a litany, nay a liturgy of fear, failure and deep unhappiness. Yet my experience is just that, and we live, often with the fear of rejection that causes many to silently give up in the local church. Experience shows that even helpful suggestions will have been rejected out of hand without discussion because it is a hierarchical system. I have discovered that it is a system of constraint where many people are disengaged, frustrated and fearful. And this is a church of Jesus Christ! Perhaps we should not be surprised because the Church, for two millennia, has been run on a completely unscriptural hierarchical basis.

In significant contrast and unknown to most people and organisations, the Positive Mental Map assumes very different "heretical views" compared to the Hierarchical-Traditional and Conventional Mental Map. This is because it is based on the assumption that an organisation is about people connected in personal relationships by respect, trust and authenticity.

Under the former, "The organisation" is a pyramid, a hierarchy of positions. Please stop and reflect on your experience of that fact. Under the latter, "The organisation" is a network of relationships where, along with getting things done, the equal and fundamentally more important focus is on valuing people, unlocking their potential within them and growing them to become the extraordinary people God always designed and planned for them to become. Maximised potential in people comes first and results second.

The primary driver and controller of the prevention of all above is the conventional mental map. What created or caused the growth of the conventional mental map? Primarily, Hierarchical assumptions, which became universal in western culture since the days of Greek and Roman culture, and are based on the concept of a descending pyramid of positions where power is both centralised and diffused or more correctly dispensed from the top and can only flow downwards. This has profound implications for those within the pyramid system. The terrible result is that the gifts existing latent in every human being are stifled from birth.

Contrast the above with the following uplifting statement from Professor Quinn: "The simplest definition of a positive organisation is a system in which the people flourish and exceed expectations. This means that the organisation has a culture in which the people are engaged, collaborating, growing, and performing at an extraordinary level. The Positive Mental Map recognises that people are full of potential and can do things not imagined from the conventional mental map."[118]

Possibility, potential, and purpose of people in collaboration underpin the Positive Mental Map. The fantastic result is the reversal of the conventional mental map imprisonment of people's latent birth gifts and the glorious freedom of the blossoming of Potential, the possibility of Growth, and the discovery of Purpose!

Having grown up and lived for seven decades under the conventional mental map, it is remarkably difficult to make the breakout and become free from that pernicious thinking. That is why if we can understand the reasons for the cultural and organisational difficulties we see, we can be all the more successful in circumventing and leaving the old hierarchical system behind. Because it is

---

[118] Robert E. Quinn, *The Positive Organization*, pp. 26–27.

universally assumed, it infects everyone's thinking and actions individually and organisationally and in every aspect of society. The breakout from its influence is both necessary and possible. The transcending of the cultural death cult of the conventional mental map, a forceful and admittedly brutal description of it, is essential.

We have within our grasp the possibility of the utter transformation of thinking from the conventional mental map with its hierarchical philosophy of inward-focussed self-preservation, and fear as underpinning assumptions, to what I define as the Transformational Mental Map, with its underpinning assumptions of people as God's Masterpiece Creations, and full of Potential, Purpose, Commitment and Growth for every human being alive today.

The Transformational Mental Map is based on the intentionality of Jesus Christ for people. Yes, folks, it's that simple. And just as the "infection" of conventional mental map thinking virulently and speedily spread out from the Graeco-Roman hierarchical assumptions of their day, so it is possible that this can be reversed and obliterated by the "proper infection" of the Transformational Mental Map that will develop and transform, as Christ intended, the potential of individuals and their collaboration in organisations in the church and everywhere else.

Under the conventional mental map, the past determines the present. Under the Transformational Mental Map, the future determines the present as we commit to a purpose. This leads to dramatic possibilities for people. And all they need is reactivation. A final question from Professor Quinn: "When does the future determine the present?" shakes most people with its unexpectedness. Two or three of his attentive students have offered their answers. He carefully and slowly offers his response: "When we have a purpose to which we are truly committed."

As You Awake to Breakout
Your Priorities are Reestablished Every Day
You Awake to Grow Every Day
Your Commitment Recommences Every Day
Your Potential is drawn from within You Every Day
Your Fulfilled Purpose is Recommenced Every Day
God Awakes You to Growth, Commitment, Potential and Purpose for Him Every Day
And God Honours Those Who Honour Him Every Day, Today

Breakout To Higher Purpose

Herein lies the beginning of a higher, increasing consciousness of God's Higher Purpose by:

> ➤ Increasing consciousness
> ➤ Increasing awareness
> ➤ Seeing possibility
> ➤ Challenging constraints
> ➤ Unleashing our own Potential
> ➤ Discovering our Purpose
> ➤ Believing in our own excellence and designed greatness, such that we are designed to impact and change the Future both for Others and God.
> ➤ This is why we are Created: the raison d'être, the bottom line.

In the context of the essential Breakout to Success, the beneficial outcomes of the Positive Mental Map are found in the deep integration of relationships that are built up over a period of time and which translate to positive outcomes, also over time, such that we can:

Conventional Mental Map	Positive Mental Map
Feel fear and act out of fear	Feel authentic connection with others
Feel deep frustration	Feel deep fulfilment
Feel deep resentment	Feel fully focussed on others
Feel a sense of powerlessness	Feel totally empowered
Feel a sense of hopelessness	Feel full of hope, vision and destiny
Feel a sense of being a small cog in a bigger wheel	Feel integrated with the whole
Feel a sense of insignificance	Feel significant for others
Feel a lack of purpose	Feel full of purpose
Feel deep disengagement	Feel fully, personally committed and engaged in something greater than themselves

It can all be turned around, but only if we Breakout! We are intended to be transformed, and if God is calling you and me to be transformed, the simple truth is that we are not and never were where we should be. The "transforming" is to be continuous forever, always recognising that we must not stay where we are because, although comfortable, it will metaphorically "kill us". We must break out from where we are to commence the journey to where we are meant to be!

John C. Maxwell, writing in his book, *The 15 Invaluable Laws of Growth*, states: "If you want to reach your potential and become the person you were created to be, you must do much more than just experience life and hope that you learn what you need along the way. You must go out of your way to seize growth opportunities as if your future depended on it. Why? Because it does. Growth doesn't just happen—not for me, not for you, not for anybody. You have to go after it!"[119]

Breakout To Become the Transformed Kingdom Christ Intended

Those of us who name the name of Christ serve the Eager and Lavish God who created us in the first place. We belong to Him, and we must be extraordinarily positive as God is about everything. For example, for me, instead of experiencing a steep mountain hillside trudged up in the rain by a dangerous raging torrent, others will "see" a fantastic 200m head of water just waiting to be transformed into a hydroelectric power scheme!

You see, we live our lives asleep repeating ad infinitum the status quo. We were born, awaking every day, to live lives of His Higher Purpose, and God has created in every human being an extraordinary life full of fulfilled potential. It is not unfulfilled but fulfillable potential that awaits the right moment of intentionality. That point of breakout from ordinary lives awaits most of us. *TRANSFORMED!* is for those of us who have not woken up and reached that God-intended point of breakout in our lives.

God's plans full of purpose and fulfillable potential for us are recorded for us in Jeremiah 29:11 NIV. "For I know the plans I have for you," declares the Lord, "plans to prosper you and not to harm you, plans to give you hope and a future". When we read the word "plans", we need to understand that God means His purposes for you and me being realised by kick-starting the fulfillable potential He has already created in us.

---

[119] John C. Maxwell, *The 15 Invaluable Laws of Growth*, pp. 12-13.

> *Just Commit*
> *Yourself Every morning*
> *to the God of all Creation and All Power*
> *Who Created You for Himself and for Others*
> ~~~
>
> *Never forget Who You Are*
> *Never Forget Who Created You*
> *Never Forget Your Gifts are Given to You*
> *To Live a Significant Life for Others*

But God is also saying, "When you get serious about me, then I can get serious about you! I am not joking." He will recognise your Intentionality, your daily choice to be serious about Today and your decisions to connect with Him and then your choice to be Significant for Him in lifting, impacting, and growing Others. When the scripture indicates the restoration from "captivity", of course, it does not relate in our day to physical captivity, but in reality, the default day-to-day "captivity" of lives lived as if God did not exist. These lives speak out loudly, "I don't care; I will not have anything to do with God. What has he ever done for me? This is my life, and I will live it like I want for me alone and nobody else until I die."

It is that "captivity" to which the scripture alludes. He sees the current state of the world, the state of our lives and other people's lives. He declares, "I have already purposed a better plan, and I will use My wholehearted God-seeking individual potential (they're looking for me and calling upon me, which gives me great pleasure, and I have my eyes and hands upon them right now), and they will fulfil My purposes, and by giving them My purposes and unleashing their potential, they will change the future and the destiny of millions for Me!"

God sees potential in all of His creation because He created it in us all. We are the result of His intentioned ongoing creation of human beings. Thank God He did not see just sinful people in us. When He looks at you and me, He sees extraordinary individuals with:

- ❖ Created origin
- ❖ Individual identity
- ❖ Personal significance
- ❖ Fulfillable potential
- ❖ Fulfilled purposes
- ❖ God-centred inspiration

- ❖ God-centred passion
- ❖ God-centred vision
- ❖ God-centred Focus
- ❖ Perfected destiny

And you and I are created by God in Christ to fulfil His purposes in our lifetimes by first discovering our purpose, discovering we have been gifted potential and then secondly, drawing out from ourselves and others those gifts already placed within us and then seeking to deliver them to the world, as Christ did His.

For far too long, the Church of Jesus Christ, in its more traditional form, has taken the almost imperceptible downward path of least resistance. This is the result of decades and centuries of the "decisions of comfort":

- ❖ We could, under God, as He intended, transform ourselves to be what God created us to be, or we can stay locked into irrelevance as we seek comfort before courage.
- ❖ We could seek God as He intended and collectively discover His purposes for us, or we can stay focussed internally on our building-centred decline.
- ❖ We could, with God as He intended, choose to be extraordinary for Him and change the future for Him, or we can stay where we are...

Or we could implement the "decisions of courage." You see, there is nothing predetermined about failing churches, church decline, church closure, or church irrelevance in the days in which we live.

All is the result of poor leadership, loss of purpose, loss of focus, loss of vision, wrong direction and function, all leading inexorably to failing, dying and closed churches. Christ never had anything like this in mind when He chose His disciples and created His Church:

- He could have bottled out of the purpose of His life.
- He could have said, "The cost is too great!"
- He could have made a pact with evil and walked away from the riches that were laid up for Him.
- He could have given up on His friends when they deserted Him at His death.

No, our Lord Jesus had settled all these questions and temptations at an early age. It is recorded in scripture. You may remember the incident of Him staying behind in the temple, astounding the religious leaders of the day, aged only twelve, stating, "I must be about My Father's business." He had already chosen to change the future because He had discovered the purpose of His life.

We are called to do likewise. Any other choice, any other vision, any other response is risible. What makes the difference between a self-centred ordinary life merely living to survive and an extraordinary life, when connected to and lived for God, is the discovery of His purpose, which indeed will enable you and me to change the future if we choose...

And so to the fundamental underpinning truth that this book seeks to elucidate, and it is this: God created you and me not just to accede to a system of belief, not just to attend church and do the same irrelevant, tedious rituals every week, not just to become self-righteous, and not just to be in community. But by discovering why He created us, discovering His purposes for us, to be fully engaged in His plans and purposes, to be wholly fulfilled in them, living at God's higher level, and through those experiences to be totally immersed in and merging our waking consciousness in relationship with Him forever. This breakout is the way of Jesus Christ.

Paul wrote in Ephesians 2:10 NLT, "For we are God's masterpiece. He has created us anew in Christ Jesus, so we can do the good things he planned for us long ago."

For far too long, the "Church" has been in the "ministry game", AKA making congregations comfortable. It has taught people to seek their own comfortable peace through belief in God. It is my profoundly held belief that this has done irreparable harm to the Church of Jesus Christ. We need to be rid of this self-centred, delusional folly because our God-created greatest need is not personal peace, however appealing that may seem, but the discovery and implementation of personal purpose in Christ. We will never live lives that glorify God at Christ's higher level unless we are led to discover our God-created purpose. And that is where you and I come in...

Jesus said, "You shall know the truth, and the truth shall set you free." – John ch.8, v.32. Wake up from your world, your thoughts, your limited vision, seek the Lord, discover His plans and purposes for you, and you will be shown truths and pathways you never even knew existed. This is the reality of God's truth and His promises to you and me in scripture. This is the life that He promised.

As I have reflected on the last seven years, I realised that, in a genuine sense, none of this book was planned. It is partly a cathartic response and a response to a time of overwhelming difficulty, which resulted in the "destruction" of my then "worldview".

TRANSFORMED! is not just my cathartic fight back, but it has become a discovered passion: to rediscover God's purposes for individuals and congregations that for centuries have been obfuscated by the Church and its dress-coded leadership and return to a new God-centred, God's-purpose-filled worldview as part of that necessary response. One that is scripture-based, one that would stand up to that test.

We all have our own internalised worldview through birth country, birth culture, parental influence, family, friends, religious affiliation, education, and the list could go on. It is what makes you, you!

But when one's worldview is destroyed, usually involuntarily, perhaps through personal tragedy, personal difficulties, or just plain nastiness from others, the slow road back from that destruction is long and, for many, painful. But for everyone, it can be transformational. This is quite normal, and though the transition and transformation may not be fully understood for years or decades, gratefulness will eventually shine through to thankfulness for those necessary painful experiences that God has allowed in our lives.

Along with extreme frustration during and subsequent to those difficult times, there was an unnoticed change taking place. Unknowingly, I realised I could not wait for change for the better to occur. It slowly dawned on my simple mind that destructive criticism and situational moaning would never impact anything or anyone unless they could be inspired to take greater action.

Through all my life experiences, I started to understand that all of them, whether good, bad (suffering) or indifferent, that God had somehow allowed them to mould me uniquely for understanding the essential necessity and requirement for transformation. To be moulded for God's purposes. Again, all painfully slow.

At that time, I subconsciously chose to attempt that necessary transformation of mind, asking awkward questions about where I was and the "Churchianity" system I had formally adhered to. That transformation of thinking and action that Paul spoke about being essential in Romans ch.12, vv1-2 was crucial in breaking out from my then status quo. Through that verse of scripture, I chose to attempt the transformation of my thinking to make a difference for God in my generation. Following on from that position, I simply made the conscious choice to seek to influence and inspire others to do the same for God.

But I did these things very uncertainly, with no idea of an end in mind, no plan, just a hunch that I was called to continue seeking God through simple prayers, reading, learning, and writing, although with considerable doubt about my lack of intellect and suitability for such a task. Still, slowly, new understandings filtered through, especially the biblical concept that we are God's highest creation, to be like Him in Jesus Christ. Therefore, we are created and called to be extraordinary individuals for God in the time He has given us on this earth. I find it strange that I have never heard a sermon on people living and being extraordinary for God because He has planned it that way.

Recently, I found a gem by reading John C. Maxwell's book, *Be all You Can Be*. He writes: "Purpose makes the difference between the ordinary and the extraordinary. A person with a purpose does things out of the ordinary, above average. Personality doesn't make a person extraordinary. Neither does intelligence nor education. What makes a person extraordinary is purpose—the consuming desire to accomplish something in life."[120]

Thankfully, for me, and I guess for many people, our personal inabilities do not disqualify us from personal transformation! God has provided for this in everyone's life. All this can be attempted by anyone, including you. It is not a spiritual competition with others! And in fact, knowledge cannot help you. Education, even to the highest level, is helpless here. Wealth cannot be used, and neither position advances you one iota. You see, no one else can or will live your life. Since you and I are utterly unique in the history of the world, only you and I can decide to seek God and love Him as only you and I can, as only you and I were created to.

I reiterate the earlier quote, again, as Dr Stephen Covey wrote in his book, *The Eighth Habit* (I paraphrase), "those who develop a vision of great things, who suspect there may be more to themselves than they realised, who take the initiative and tap into higher motivations, these people find and use their voice, and choose to influence and inspire others to do the same."[121]

That sums it all up.
And none of this is a Game.

I was recently reminded of Dr Martin Luther King's famous "I have a dream..." speech from 1963. And also of the UK singer Susan Boyle in her remarkable 2009 performance in the Britain's Got Talent competition:

I dreamed a dream in time gone by
When hope was high and life worth living
I dreamed that love would never die
I prayed that God would be forgiving

Then, I was young and unafraid
And dreams were made and used and wasted
There was no ransom to be paid
No song unsung no wine untasted.[122]

[120] John C. Maxwell, *Be All You Can Be: A Challenge to Stretch Your God-given Potential*, 3rd Ed (Colorado Springs, CO: David C. Cook, 2007), p. 72.
[121] Covey, pp. 25–26.
[122] 'I Dreamed a Dream', *Wikipedia*, 2020

<https://en.wikipedia.org/w/index.php?title=I_Dreamed_a_Dream&oldid=967382765> [accessed 31 July 2020].

But why are we so viscerally impacted by such powerful words in context? Here is the *TRANSFORMED!* dream list:

- ✓ God created us to dream
- ✓ He created us in His image
- ✓ He created us to realise and understand our relationship with Him
- ✓ He created us to respond to Him
- ✓ He created us to long for Him
- ✓ He created us to delight in Him
- ✓ He created us to be inspired by Him
- ✓ He created us to inspire others
- ✓ He created us to discover the wisdom of God
- ✓ He created us to aspire to great things for Him
- ✓ He created us to yearn for His vistas, unknown
- ✓ He created us to hope for His fulfilment beyond our wildest dreams
- ✓ He created us to soar to His realms, unknown
- ✓ He created us to go to His places we have never been, along pathways we never even knew existed
- ✓ He created us to be a dream team for Him
- ✓ He created us to see beyond ourselves and our limited situations, to see forever
- ✓ He created us deliberately with full-fillable potential
- ✓ He created us to be fulfilled entirely by Him
- ✓ He created us to be with Him forever
- ✓ He created us to be like His Son, who pleased His Father in every way.

We are not and never were the result of evolution with its undertones of hopeless humanistic philosophy. We are God's highest creation, endowed with aspects that are at once uniquely human and yet also uniquely divine. We are created in the image of God.

For far too long, those of us who put our faith in Christ have been on the back foot, almost fighting our own Dunkerque, our own strategic withdrawal. We are close to being annihilated or, at best, becoming completely irrelevant, a spent force in our country.

Not any longer. It does not have to be like this.

The time has come when those who name the name of Christ can rediscover who God created them to be, discover the Potential God has already placed within then, discover those Purposes God has for them to fulfil, if only they will wake up, breakout, step up to their high calling in Christ, trust Him completely and do what they are created to do, living the life He always created us to live.

> *I choose to use the past, with all its difficulties,*
> *unfairness and failure, not as an excuse to do nothing,*
> *but the reason to live and give*
> *my best life for God Today.*

God has always called you and me to step up and out and become the person He designed us to be by starting to live our life at that new level of consciousness of God's purposes for us, which Paul wrote about in Ephesians ch.2, v10. This is the answer to your "Why?" "Why am I created?" "Why do I live?"

For those of you whom God calls to lead, this will call forth from you a breakout of the most extraordinary transformational leadership, a breakout of extraordinary levels of transformed thinking, and a breakout of an extraordinary vision of where God would have you go in leading your people to impact others for Him. Are you ready to be that extraordinary person...?

Friends, this is my dream; that the time has come to shake off our cultural and "Churchianity" shackles, whatever they might be, and be personally transformed and renewed in our thinking, as Paul wrote in Romans ch.12, vv1-2. The time has come to re-consecrate, re-dedicate, re-commit ourselves to live wholeheartedly for God alone at a higher level as He intended, making a difference for Him through servant leadership and creating a legacy in the hearts and minds of others who will come after us, in the short time we have left on this earth. This is the new "normal". Everything else is a sideshow.

This book is a very different presentation of God's scriptural intentions and the work of His Son, Jesus Christ, to that given by the traditional Church, which, at worst, is about sin management and system continuity. At best, this leaves individuals and congregations immature, frozen in time and never able to grow up to embrace and discover their God-intended maturity. Congregations collude unknowingly with the clergy in their own inward-looking culture of immaturity, compliance, passivity, dependence, and continuity, leading to further helplessness and their eventual demise.

Today, at morning service, I was inspired by a sermon on John ch.20, v.19, where Jesus appears to the disciples behind closed doors when they sat in fear of the religious leaders' retribution after the crucifixion. Our speaker spoke of the fact that their fears turned to hope. But they were in a locked room. You see, the speaker challenged us to understand that Christ's followers could not stay where they were. They had to move and move out of that locked protective room:

➤ They had to leave the room.

➤ They had to wake up to their current reality.

➤ They had to make the choice to commit to the journey.

> **The Stretching of the Human Spirit to go**
> **Beyond the Extraordinary for God**

They had to deliberately start their individual journeys, bearing the message of the only essential news that God has for people. But it is not just sins forgiven by the crucified Christ. In John ch.15, v.16, Jesus says, "You have not chosen me. I have chosen you that you might go and bear fruit---fruit that will last---and so that whatever you ask in my name, the Father will give you."

They were chosen not only to put their faith in Christ but also to discover God's Purpose as Christ did for His life. That is the incredible significance of the incident recorded of Jesus staying behind in Jerusalem at around the age of twelve. He emphatically stated He <u>had</u> to be about His Father's business and God's Purpose for Him. He had discovered His Purpose and Vision. Once He had made that discovery, He was transformed. He would never be the same again. He was about to change the course of history.

TRANSFORMED! is written to help you be inspired to start on your own personal transformation and your personal journey for the purposes and future God always planned for you. Living the life God always planned for you to live is just that, but it takes an uncompromising decision to break out from your past, from current mediocrity and the status quo, commit to God and commence that journey. Do you not wonder what God has planned for you?

Conclusions for Step 6

Breakout! To Your Best Life

Key Thought – Be Extraordinary – Breakout! – Breakout To Live The Life God Created You To Live and Never Look Back.

Sub-headings review:
> ➢ Kickstart The Breakout To Your Best Life
> ➢ What Prevents The Breakout To Transformation And Growth?
> ➢ Breakout to Higher Purpose
> ➢ Breakout To Become the Transformed Kingdom Christ Intended

I cannot put it better than repeating the action from the Kickstart sub-heading:
> ➢ Just do it! Do it now!
> ➢ Do whatever it takes!
> ➢ Walk those pathways we have never known!
> ➢ Make a start and build the bridge as you walk on it!
> ➢ Go to places you never even knew existed as you transform and grow!
> ➢ Keep it simple; keep breaking out.

But remember, because you and I are utterly unique, this can never be a competition.

Step 7

To Grow! Your Best Life

~~~

Someone has said the only certainties in life are death and taxation.
This is scarcity and depletion thinking at its worst and is untrue.
There is another certainty.
Growth, personal growth, if undertaken intentionally, is also a certainty
and is the only guarantee that today and tomorrow will be better.
This is abundance and surplus thinking at its best.

~~~

❖ **Key Purpose: Create the Mindsets and Environments for Growth, Connection, and Contribution, all with Authenticity. Draw out Greatness from within.**

❖ **Key Learning (Always Facing the Unknown without Fear):** Breakout should now be a daily reality. You have decided to Live Your Best Life, and those who would seek to hold you back can be brushed off. This is hard, especially if your close family disagree with where you are going! It is rather like a second language – you speak normally with close family, but *TRANSFORMED!* with others who also speak your new language. Higher Purpose is a different world as you take on new concepts.

❖ **Key Actions (Building The Bridge As You Walk On It):** Breakout leads to Growth, although you will be very aware of your own transformation and growth to this point. John C. Maxwell shows up clearly here, offering pearls of wisdom about a life of Significance and Growth. You are born for these choices – you are hard-wired to grow – ensure nothing holds you back.

The Higher Level Actioned Life And Thinking

> *"Perhaps the most important vision of all is to develop a sense of self, a sense of your own destiny, a sense of your unique mission and role in life, a sense of purpose and meaning."*
> **Dr. Stephen Covey**

(Above quotation cited below.[123])

The concept of community is almost impossible to define since it has as many meanings as there are people! Many of us yearn for the closeness, connection, and safety that belonging to a community brings to us as individuals and which we accept as a member. But, what if the concept of "the church as a community", so beloved by many Christians, was a false concept simply because Christ had no intention of creating "community"? What if He had bigger plans than just warm fuzzy feelings experienced between people?

What if there is something called Cultural Deception? Culture (being solely in the minds of the people around whom it exists) is all about keeping what it thinks it has, protecting personal positions, defending itself against change, improvement and personal growth, only fulfilling personal needs, but which ultimately kills by slow depletion its adherents.

What if there is Cultural Depletion, whereby the Church's decline is so infinitesimal that no one notices and that carries on uninterrupted until challenged and transformed? Are the over 100 years of numerical decline in the Church of England an example of this phenomenon?

What if there is Cultural Death where those who cannot accept the reality of their situation and repeat the failing formulas of the past disappear from the pages of history, overtaken by events that they cannot accept are happening before their very eyes?

Jesus would have "none of this". He did not appear to be concerned about his disciples' needs because He had much bigger plans for His disciples and followers. His focus, intentionality and action were all about ensuring transformed individuals discovered God's purpose for their lives and were then filled with all the fullness of God in Jesus Christ. This is what Christ intended:

➤ Discovering God's Higher Purpose for yourself;

➤ Being Transformed through Redemption, Re-creation, Renewal, Restoration, Redirection, Vision, Fulfilment and Destiny;

---

[123] Covey, p. 71.

185

➤ Unlocking your potential and others' for God's Higher Purpose;

➤ Growing to become God's Extraordinary Masterpiece for Him and Others;

➤ Stepping up and into God's Higher Level;

➤ Being Aware, Engaged and Wholeheartedly Living in God's Higher Level; Loving in God's Higher Level;

➤ Leading through Servant Leadership in God's Higher Level;

➤ Preparing yourself in God's Higher Level;

➤ Learning into God's Higher Level;

➤ Running towards all that God has for you in His Higher Level;

➤ Becoming His Extraordinary Masterpiece and becoming a "doing whatever it takes human being" for Him, as He intended;

➤ Changing the Future;

➤ Creating and Sustaining the Connecting Legacy;

➤ Passing on the baton;

➤ Ready to be filled with all the fullness of God in Jesus Christ.

We are called in scripture as Christians to understand the following:

❖ For God's Higher Purpose – Sustain the Challenge – Action and Legacy must be from Day 1, not the end.

❖ Wake Up and walk Through the Wall of Your Cultural Prison that tradition, history and the world would enslave you inside.

❖ Ask Your Creator why you are created, why you exist, and what are the purposes He designed you to fulfil. He awaits to inspire you.

❖ We serve a Lavish, Abundant, Extravagant, Glorious, Omnipotent and Omniscient God who is Eager to connect with His people as they seek Him with all their hearts.

❖ The God-designed human aspects of Origin, Identity, Significance, Potential, Purpose, Inspiration, Passion, Vision, Focus and Destiny are extraordinarily shown in Jesus Christ; we are designed and destined to become like Him.

❖ Potential, Purpose, Vision, and Focus: the greatest unseen, unrecognised, undiscovered, and, for most Christians, unknown aspects of their lives. Unless personally found, followed, protected and fulfilled, most people take their unfulfilled purpose to the grave.

❖ Servant Leadership – Changing the Future as Christ did. Servant Leaders grow new Servant Leaders. They draw out of others the purpose that God has already placed within them.

❖ Inspire others to take action.

❖ For God's Higher Purpose – Sustain the Challenge – Action and Legacy must be from Day 1, not the end.

Then, if we almost casually throw in our new Mindsets from the previous chapter – they all bear repeating:

✓ **Pro-active Life Mindset**
    ✓ Growth Mindset
    ✓ Others-Focussed Mindset
    ✓ Transformational Mindset
    ✓ Higher Purpose Mindset (purpose finding)

✓ **Transformation and Growing Living Mindset**
    ✓ Intentionality and Integrity Living Mindset
    ✓ Significance and Meaning Living Mindset
    ✓ Anticipation and Urgency Living Mindset
    ✓ Abundance and Surplus Living Mindset
    ✓ Focus and Commitment Living Mindset
    ✓ Action and Opportunity Living Mindset
    ✓ Striving to reach my Fullest Potential Mindset

✓ **Consecrated to God Mindset**
    ✓ Dedicated to God Mindset
    ✓ Wholeheartedly Committed to God Mindset
    ✓ Unlocking and Unleashing Potential in Others Mindset
    ✓ Extraordinary Masterpiece for God Mindset
    ✓ Transformational Leader! For Others Mindset

✓ **Living a Life of Significance! For Others Mindset**
    ✓ Living a Life that Matters! For Others Mindset
    ✓ Living a Life of Contribution! For Others Mindset
    ✓ Living Your Best Life for God and Others Mindset
    ✓ Living Your Best Life for God's Higher Purpose Mindset
    ✓ Valuing and adding to Others' Mindset
    ✓ Breakout to God's Calling Mindset

✓ **AWAKE! To LIVE Your Best Life of God's Higher Purpose Mindset**
    ✓ To Awareness of your Best Life
    ✓ To Develop their Best Life
    ✓ To Think over your Best Life

✓ **UNLOCK! Potential for your Best Life of God's Higher Purpose**
    ✓ To Breakout to your Best Life Mindset
    ✓ To Grow your Best Life Mindset
    ✓ To Engage yourself and others in their Best Life Mindset

✓ **ACT! Contributing For Others to Live Their Best Lives of God's Higher Purpose Mindset**
   - ✓ To Lead Others to their Best Lives Mindset
   - ✓ To Rally Others to their Best Lives Mindset
   - ✓ To Legacy Others to their Best Life Legacy Mindset

Then what in God's Name (I use that in its most spiritual question form) do we supposedly imagine we are "doing" meeting every Sunday simply to decline slowly "in community" because the hierarchy, far from knowing the plot, never understood it in the first place. Would you want to return to the traditional church "community" thinking?

The twelve chapters and three levels of *TRANSFORMED!* almost without explanation reveal a dynamic world of transformation and growth for God unknown to traditional churches who will never understand what the Church of Christ intended to be all about – Transformed individuals who step up, lead, and help others be transformed!!

Dreary Sunday services with "building community" at the top of the list (that was never going to be a winner) and complex systems of belief (that incredibly subtly replaced a committed relationship with God) run by dress-coded clergy who divided themselves into the clergy and laity (you could not make a more divisive, God-dishonouring system of hierarchy if you tried) will never bring about what God always intended – You Living Your Best Life For Others!!! Yes, in community with Others, but a completely different form of community – one that seeks Others' Transformation and Empowerment for good through Servant Leadership.

> *Our Destiny Requires Choices in Our Lives:*
> *Choosing to Climb to Where We are Meant to Be*
> *Growing to Become the Extraordinary Masterpieces*
> *God Created Us to Be.*

The Servant Leadership exemplified by Christ is what He lived for and sought to instil in His friends. It is also the most misunderstood aspect because the world was overtaken by Graeco-Roman philosophy, which meant that leaders were and still are believed (especially subconsciously) to be the central part of the hierarchical grouping system where the people at the top are "superior" to others who are inferior and subordinate. This has mostly destroyed God's created human potential and purpose, especially in churches.

We are not important, but the gifts and purposes God has designed in us are. They must be released to the World. We must "draw out" from each other the potential within us and fulfil God's purposes in our lifetime. And God intends through our personally responsible leadership to do just that. Leadership, however, must be understood in the Jesus Way: It is not about you; It is not for you; It is not something you "do"; It is something you "become"; It is something you are born to be; It is already placed within you; It is designed to benefit others first. We are designed for Servant Leadership.

And when we understand the above, much of what Jesus spoke about falls into place.

Myles Munroe wrote in his book, *In Charge: Finding the Leader Within You*, "I believe the redemptive work of God as presented in the Scriptures is not just the salvaging and redeeming of a human soul but the reclaiming of a forest with a destiny. That is why He loves you so much because He knows what He put on the inside of you. Salvation means to salvage the forest. He did not save us to go to heaven; He saved us to do good works that were put inside us before the foundation. "For we are God's workmanship (masterpiece), created in Christ Jesus to do good works, which God prepared in advance for us to do" (Ephesians 2:10). So much is still inside of you." [124]

Not only living "FOR" God's Higher Purpose but living "IN" God's Higher Purpose, living "IN" God's Higher Level.

We must not fail to grasp this reality. It means having a total commitment system inside us. In Numbers 14:24 NIV, we read, "But because my servant Caleb has a different spirit and follows me wholeheartedly, I will bring him into the land he went to, and his descendants will inherit it." Caleb "followed the Lord Wholeheartedly." Our approach as Christians to God should not be based on our needs but on our desire to fulfil His purpose for our lives. He will respond eagerly!

The biggest question in my mind is, "How can we be transformed, renewed in our minds and fulfil God's purposes in our lives, honour the past, but not destroy the past, tradition and the earnest sacrifice of those who have gone before us?" It seems that Jesus bypassed all that existed before and went around it, not destroying it but rendering it redundant. He bypassed it for greater things and started creating the Kingdom of God as His Father intended.

---

[124] Myles Munroe, *In Charge: Finding the Leader within You*, 2008, pt. 1438.

> *"Be who God meant you to be and you will set the world on fire.*
> *Proclaim the truth and do not be silent though fear."*
> *Catherine of Siena, mid-14ᵗʰ C.*

(Above quotation cited below.[125])

Catherine of Siena gave us these timeless utterances, which we have forgotten and cast aside.

Grow – Through Significance

We will only know God, discover His purpose, maintain our passion, see our vision, live the life He always planned for us, and go with Him as far as we wish to go based on our committed desire to be serious with Him. If we desire none of the above, He will let us stay where we are.

It is no understatement to say this is the turning point for you as you read *TRANSFORMED!* This is a critical juncture. For if you desire what God desires for you and which awaits your decision, everything changes for you right now. If you decide not to go in God's direction, then this book is not for you. But, as scripture records, your commitment to God will open your life in ways that you could never imagine and lead you along pathways you never knew existed.

Keywords or phrases to understand here: Significance, Intentionality, Making a difference, Living a life that matters, Sense of Anticipation.

Live a culture of excellence in everything that you do, especially in a church. Not for its own sake or personal satisfaction, but because a culture of excellence, transformation and growth of individuals brings focus, energy and intentionality for God's Kingdom, which attracts others to service and, when this is celebrated regularly, grows the teams. It has an exhilarating, attracting, connecting, gelling, engaging, encouraging, and hope-filling effect of awareness.

The absence of a culture of excellence depletes, distracts, disconnects, disengages, diverges, disaffects, discourages and gives a hopeless future. Recognise where you are!? And we think this is all normal. Well, not where *TRANSFORMED!* is concerned.

John C. Maxwell writes in his book, *In The Power of Significance: How Purpose Changes Your Life:*

---

[125] 'Catherine of Siena Quotes (Author of Catherine of Siena)'
<https://www.goodreads.com/author/quotes/5794057.Catherine_of_Siena> [accessed 22 May 2020].

To be significant, all you have to do is make a difference with others wherever you are, with whatever you have, day by day.
No one stumbles upon significance. We have to be intentional about making our lives matter. That calls for action—and not excuses. Most people don't know this, but it's easier to go from failure to success than from excuses to success.[126]

If you want to live a life that matters, don't start when you get good; start now, so you become good.[127]

➢ *Start Writing Your Significance Story*
➢ *Embrace Intentional Living*
➢ *Be Willing to Start Small*
➢ *Live with a Sense of Anticipation*
➢ *Seize Significance Opportunities Every Day*
➢ *Share Your Significance Story* [128]

❖ *Every person was created to do his or her part to better mankind. That includes you!*
❖ *Every person has talents that will help him or her better mankind. That includes you!*
❖ *Every person is given an opportunity to better mankind. That includes you! Every person has a purpose for which he or she was created. That includes you!*
❖ *Every person must look within to discover his or her purpose. That includes you!*[129]

John then asks us:
❖ *Are you choosing to live a story of significance?*
❖ *Are you actively searching for your why so that you can make a difference?*
❖ *Are you choosing to live with intentionality, not just good intentions?*
❖ *Are you willing to start small but believe big to make a difference?*
❖ *Are you living with a sense of anticipation for making a difference?*
❖ *Are you seizing opportunities and taking action to make a difference?* [130]

---

126 John C Maxwell, *The Power of Significance*, pt. 67.
127 John C Maxwell, *The Power of Significance*, pt. 89.
128 John C Maxwell, *The Power of Significance*, pt. 20.
129 John C Maxwell, *The Power of Significance*, pt. 213.
130 John C Maxwell, *The Power of Significance*, pt. 1154.

Grow – Because God is Eager To Connect With Us

Jeremiah 29:13-14 NIV:
"You will seek me and find me when you seek me with all your heart. [14] I will be found by you," declares the Lord.

Ephesians 1:5 NLT:
"[5] God decided in advance to adopt us into his own family by bringing us to himself through Jesus Christ. This is what he wanted to do, and it gave him great pleasure."

We serve a Lavish, Abundant, Extravagant, Glorious, Omnipotent and Omniscient God who is Eager to Connect with His People as they Seek Him with all their Hearts. I feel compelled and drawn towards Him in this process to keep on seeking, and Psalm 37, v4, encourages us to "Take delight in the Lord" with almost a continuing sense of childlike wonder, discovery, and sensitivity while seeking.

As I read scripture, all I see is God intensely focussed on looking after and transforming those seeking Him. He responds actively, consistently and "trustfully" once the commitment to seek Him is entered into. It is a real relationship, yet I wonder at His allowing and encouraging me to seek Him with all my heart since fickleness is one human trait we can almost guarantee. Vv5 and 6 of the Psalm state that if we "commit our way to the Lord; trust in Him, and He will do this: He will make your righteous reward shine like the dawn, your vindication like the noonday sun."

Is that not strange? We come to Him in ignorance, in need, our created humanity naked, with nothing to bring Him and only the commitment and imperfect love of a sinful heart. So, why does He respond lavishly and extravagantly to what, at best, is inward-focussed, self-serving and fickle? These actions are shown for us in Psalm 37:3-7 NIV:

> **Trust in the Lord and do good;**
> **dwell in the land and enjoy safe pasture.**
> **Take delight in the Lord,**
> **and he will give you the desires of your heart.**
> **Commit your way to the Lord;**
> **Trust in him, and he will do this:**
> **He will make your righteous reward shine like the dawn,**
> **your vindication like the noonday sun.**

Be still before the Lord and wait patiently for him;
do not fret when people succeed in their ways,
when they carry out their wicked schemes.

Pray these prayers with me to encourage our Growth With and Towards God, Who Created Us in the First Place:

"**Eager God**, I trust in You, I feed on Your faithfulness, I delight in You, I commit my ways to You, I would be still and rest in You, I wait for You and patiently stay myself upon You, I stop fretting, I cease from anger, I forsake wrath, and I wait, hope and look for the Lord."

"**Lavish God**, You have chosen us before the foundation of the world;
You have destined us to be adopted as Your children by redeeming us in Christ;
You have opened our hearts and minds to Your wisdom and secrets;
You have planned for us a glorious inheritance and flooded our hearts with your unbelievable light;

You have enabled us to understand the extraordinary work of Christ in creation, redemption and His Lordship over everything and His Church;

You have filled everything everywhere with Him; to satisfy your intense love for us, You raised us above the mediocrity of ordinary life, showing and giving us the immeasurable riches of your free grace, which we cannot appropriate for ourselves in any way;

And You have done all this not just to bless us, but having recreated us and filled us with potential, and we are then destined to discover your purposes for us and live the lives You always planned for us to live." (Read this in Ephesians 1-2.)

"**Abundant God**, the world and the evil around us seek to distract, deplete and destroy our real position before You. Psalm 37:23 NLT, 'The LORD directs the steps of the godly. He delights in every detail of their lives.'"

"**Extravagant God**, I stand in awe of your creating me. I am unable to comprehend your ways with me. But I believe your word in scripture to be true, especially for a simpleton like me. So, I focus on You. You must become first in my affection despite whatever life throws at me. As Joshua stated so many centuries ago, 'But as for me and my house, we will serve the Lord.'"

"**Glorious God**, You call me to aspire to love you, to worship you and to reach towards your nature as shown in Christ."

"**Omnipotent God**, there is none like unto You, and none can stand in Your presence except through faith in Your Son Jesus Christ."

"**Omniscient God**, we live in your very presence, totally. As you are, so let your wisdom, understanding and vision inspire us to greatness for You."

Before such overwhelming good news, we stand open-mouthed and in wondering silence...

So, Eager, Abundant, Extravagant, Lavish, Glorious, Omnipotent, Omniscient God, I choose You, this day, to serve you. Please be first, Daily, in the life You have given me to enjoy, grow, control, guard, and direct my focus and the affections of heart and mind for You and towards You, the living God, this day. I choose to draw near afresh to You, Today, as You draw near to me according to Your word. Be first and last in my affections, my hopes, my desires, and in my fulfilment of your purposes.

> *Just ask God for His Heart, His Wisdom, His Mind, His Vision,*
> *and His plans to be Shared with Your heart,*
> *to impart His Wisdom,*
> *His Mind, His Vision and His Plans so you can*
> *join Him in Changing the Future.*
> *He has never refused anyone who asked for these.*

Join me in affirming your heart to God:
"I have chosen to believe in the God of miracles for whom all things are possible. I have chosen and sought to provide written servant leadership, understanding, vision, focus and direction and making a difference for the glory of God in the short time I have on this earth by writing *TRANSFORMED!*"

✓ I concur entirely with Abraham Lincoln's words, "Without the assistance of that divine being, I cannot succeed. With that assistance, I cannot fail. Trusting in Him, who can go with me, remain with you and be everywhere for good let us confidently hope that all will yet be well."[131]

---

[131] 'A Quote by Abraham Lincoln' <https://www.goodreads.com/quotes/715317-without-the-assistance-of-that-divine-being-i-cannot-succeed> [accessed 22 May 2020].

✓ I have realised the essential truth and the affirmative scripture that tells us, "We are God's masterpiece. He has created us anew in Christ Jesus, so we can do the good things he planned for us long ago." Ephesians 2:10 NLT.

✓ I have realised my life is lent to me by my Creator, God in Christ Himself.

✓ I am Chosen, Created and Called by God for His Purpose, to live for His Glory.

✓ I choose to live a life of expectancy with God.

✓ I choose to reach out towards God's aspirations for me, for He is eager to respond.

✓ **I aspire to a God-honouring life that constantly rises above and is totally opposite to the mediocrity of our lives touted as normal, especially in churches.**

  ✓ I aspire to live the life God always planned for me to live.

  ✓ Not for me a life of the dull and depleting, constant, impossible "sinfulness/Holiness" dance as promised and managed by so many churchmen. We realise we can never be completely "holy", but in Christ, we can live the life He planned for us, we can inspire others, and we can be used by God to change the Future for Others.

✓ **I aspire to consciously consecrate, decisively dedicate and courageously commit this life daily to God, who lent it to me in the first place.**

  ✓ I aspire to live a life of Christ-created origin, Christ-centred identity, lent significance, unleashed potential, discovered purpose, far-reaching and seeing vision, fervent directed focus, and fantastic destiny!

  ✓ I aspire to soar on eagles' wings because I was created to rise with my Creator above the everyday, the commonplace, to worlds unknown.

  ✓ I aspire to inspire others for God.

  ✓ All this is why I exist.

Why would we not understand God's word to us?

"For I know the plans I have for you," declares the Lord, "plans to prosper you and not to harm you, plans to give you hope and a future. Then you will call on me and come and pray to me, and I will listen to you. You will seek me and find me when you seek me with all your heart. I will be found by you," declares the Lord, "and will bring you back from captivity. I will gather you from all the nations and places where I have banished you," declares the Lord, "and will bring you back to the place from which I carried you into exile." Jeremiah 29:11-14 NIV.

Why would we not act as our Creator intended?

"Seek the LORD while you can find him. Call on him now while he is near. Let the wicked change their ways and banish the very thought of doing wrong. Let them turn to the LORD that he may have mercy on them. Yes, turn to our God, for he will forgive generously. "My thoughts are nothing like your thoughts," says the LORD. "And my ways are far beyond anything you could imagine. For just as the heavens are higher than the earth, so my ways are higher than your ways and my thoughts higher than your thoughts." Isaiah 55:6-9 NLT.

Why would we not reach out to Him daily to:

"Trust in the LORD and do good. Then, you will live safely in the land and prosper. Take delight in the LORD, and he will give you your heart's desires. Commit everything you do to the LORD. Trust him, and he will help you. He will make your innocence radiate like the dawn, and the justice of your cause will shine like the noonday sun. Be still in the presence of the LORD, and wait patiently for him to act. Don't worry about evil people who prosper or fret about their wicked schemes." Psalm 37:3-7 NLT.

I have been aware of a growing realisation that has turned to the conviction that much of what I have been fed for over 60 years, especially both from the world around me and also, surprisingly and sadly, churches, is an obfuscating smokescreen. There is much truth in it, but it lacks reality and vitality and supports the status quo. It is a cultural dead end. It cannot inspire but tends to deplete and deaden the lives of all who live within its shadow.

God in Christ is having none of it. And for Him, firstly, then His disciples and Apostles with Peter, then Paul, Transformational Growth and Breakout from the tradition-bound mediocrity of their day in God's power was the way forwards. Paul is the perfect example to us of a believer in Christ who had to break free from the culture of his day. And as we know, he also suffered and paid the ultimate price for his God-given freedom.

Jesus focussed on creating the Kingdom of God, and He said, "For behold, the Kingdom of God is within you." Luke 17:21 KJ. Fundamental to the above statement, I have come to a scripture-based realisation that:

"We are created to fulfil the purposes of God in our lifetimes, for the praise of His Glory." Ephesians 2:10 NLT reminds us, "For we are God's masterpiece. He has created us anew in Christ Jesus, so we can do the good things he planned for us long ago."

This is the purpose of life.

Don't just seek "your" personal peace.

Don't just seek "your" personal priorities.

Don't just seek for "your" personal needs to be met.

Seek the plans and purposes that God has created for YOU, then go and spend the rest of Your Life Fulfilling His Purposes. This is God's way. You will never need personal peace, priorities or needs ever again because God is Your Purpose.

It seems that most Christians, even though believers in Christ, are Cultural Prisoners in a Cultural Prison of their own acceptance. Traditional Christians are Culture Prisoners in a Cultural Prison, and we all are impacted. And like any prison, whether physical or mental, we were never designed to be there. Most cultures keep people in fearful and reactive states. It is part of the fallen nature of the world into which we are born. And Christ bursts on the stage of arguably the worst cultural double prison you could ever name. His world was dominated by the Jewish culture of His day and the Roman Empire's invasion culture that would one day destroy it.

Fundamental to the incredible life of Jesus is not only His ability to bypass, sidestep and uncompromisingly leave behind the prevailing culture of His time on earth but, more importantly, why and how He managed it. There are two words to describe His Mindset: **Vision and Focus.**

It is all about Vision and Focus

And not any old Vision and Focus. They need to be to a Christ-practised level:

✓ God-loving Vision and Focus
✓ God-centred Vision and Focus
✓ God-purposed Vision and Focus
✓ God-given Vision and Focus
✓ God-listening Vision and Focus
✓ God-motivated Vision and Focus
✓ God-honouring Vision and Focus
✓ People-Transforming Vision and Focus
✓ Future-Changing Vision and Focus
✓ Legacy-Ensuring Vision and Focus

> *In Romans ch.12, vv1-2 Paul exhorts us to:*
> *Daily Consecrated Connection with God and*
> *Transformation through the ongoing Entire Renewal of*
> *Our Minds through New Mindsets,*
> *New Purpose and New Vision*
> *Constantly Focusing on God's Plans and Purposes*
> *for us and For Others*
> *And that Process is to be a Continuing Discovery of all that He*
> *Created Us For.*

Jesus is creating God's new culture, the Kingdom of God, and what this culture is based upon is not personal internal focus and hierarchical control, but individuals connecting with their heavenly Father and living lives designed to fulfil God's purposes throughout their lives.

Grow – Authentically Connected Human Beings

We are hard-wired to connect with others. And during any connection with another, it is shown that human authenticity is foremost. It seems that "Authenticity" is a birth gift of potential placed in us when we were created, but it only shows through certain aspects of a good, other-focussed character. It is difficult to define, except we "know" it when we "see" it! It exists but too often has been smothered by bad choices, bad experiences, and bad thinking. Why is it difficult to define? Perhaps because of its scarcity? Or is it due to its indefinability? It can be seen and only recognised as it ensues from character. We cannot easily describe it, but we can recognise it instantaneously and without thinking! Is that not strange? Why is it so Important? Simply because, as Christ showed:

- ❖ It is fundamental to connect fully with others.
- ❖ It is fundamental in influencing others.
- ❖ It is fundamental in growing and lifting others.

Why is it so crucial in individuals?
Why is it so important in organisations?

It relates to who we are, how we connect and who we are meant to be. It is who we are at our very best when disinterestedly connecting with others when we own and display our own vulnerability, and seek others' highest good. That is our "authentic voice". It is a central part of us, our being, what we are all meant to be – Authentic in connecting with each other. Authentic people truly seek more *for* people than they require *from* them as they connect with others.

> *Someone has said the only certainties in life are*
> *death and taxation.*
> *This is scarcity and depletion thinking at its worst*
> *and is untrue.*
> *There are two other certainties.*
> *Potential, unlimited if unlocked, and*
> *Growth, personal growth, if undertaken intentionally,*
> *are the only guarantees that today*
> *and tomorrow will be better.*
> *This is abundance and surplus thinking at its best.*

Another fascinating aspect of Authenticity is the strange "parents" of authenticity, which allow it to shine through as a result of any individual displaying the following effects of good character:

- love
- joy
- peace
- forbearance
- kindness
- goodness
- faithfulness
- gentleness
- self-control
- sincerity
- vulnerability
- openness
- listening ability
- learning ability
- friendship
- integrity
- purpose

- consistency
- empathy
- wholeheartedness
- courage
- compassionate
- committed
- humility
- trustworthiness
- reliability
- patience
- abundance
- unselfishness

Interestingly, all of the above are others-focussed. There is nothing selfish or self-centred in any of the above. And the effects of "Authenticity" are an outflow of abundance and surplus from authentic people intentionally connecting with others to Grow and Lift them.

Another way to understand Authenticity is to state the opposite. The opposite of Authenticity is Posturing. Fascinatingly, it also is seen in its effects. It also cannot exist except when human beings connect. Posturing is in-Authenticity writ large! It is fake, and it also "ensues" as a result of that fakery. How does it make you feel? For me, immediately, I am reminded of my past failure, and it depletes me. I feel lower after being exposed to Posturing people than before the event. I feel drained emotionally.

Authentic people make Others feel good at their own expense; posturing people make themselves feel good at others' expense. That is why they drain you emotionally. We were never designed to be like that. One of the great benefits of Authenticity is that it is the gift that keeps on giving. You have filled yourself with the capacity, emotionally, to keep giving to others to connect with others positively. That, again, is another design aspect of human beings.

You see, Authentic people are like a river, as against a reservoir. Outflowing and not holding back is their hallmark. They continually give of the abundance they receive to Grow and Lift Others without any wish for reward. As they pour out what they have received, they are continually renewed and filled to give more.

I believe that these are the results of personal growth, which is why Authenticity is extraordinarily important. It cannot be faked. If anything, that is a brilliant definition of Authenticity and Character that cannot be faked, and it shines outwards towards others. You need others so that Authenticity can be seen and effective in both influencing positively and growing others. Ultimately, as seen at the beginning, "Who you are, is immeasurably more important than what you know or have experienced." And that is a function of character and acting authentically, most especially when no one else is looking. Authenticity cannot be undertaken, seen or recognised without human connection.

In his book *The Positive Organisation*, Professor Quinn comments:

"When people live in authentic communication, they tend to bond. They are more willing to pursue the collective good. As they do, the collective intelligence intensifies, and everyone begins learning, growing, and performing at a higher level. The organization then becomes a positive organization, and the people feel the activity is worthy of still more human investment."[132]

"The conventional map reflects the political nature of organizations. Inherent in the conventional mental map is a need for self-preservation and a fear of the vulnerability that is required in authentic dialogue. So many people hold this orientation that it is difficult to challenge it and to express an authentic voice."[133]

What a contrast to the experience of most of us in the organisations we have lived in, where posturing, self-interest and self-preservation are the main foundations of everyday life and the basis of interaction within them.

Grow – Because We Are Hard-Wired To Be Active, Engaged and Self-Directed

Daniel Pink, in his brilliant book, *Drive: The Surprising Truth About What Motivates Us*, makes the case that we are wired for Autonomy, Mastery and Purpose.[134]

We all desire Autonomy in the sense that the freedom to decide (for ourselves) is a fundamental human right and a hard-wired (God-created) desire.

We need Mastery, both the sense of doing something well and the pain of learning through repetition that leads to success and the knowledge that you are the very best you can be in the present moment.

Purpose is Why we are here, Why we are created, and Why we exist. Lack of Purpose is indeed the heartache most human beings experience. Most never find their purpose and live defeated and frustrated for all of their lives. But God has wonderfully designed us for purpose, for understanding our purpose and for fulfilling our purpose under Him.

---

[132] Robert E. Quinn, *The Positive Organization*, p. 58.
[133] Robert E. Quinn, *The Positive Organization*, p. 48.
[134] Daniel H Pink, *Drive: The Surprising Truth about What Motivates Us* (Edinburgh: Canongate, 2010).

Growth is essential in our relationship with God. Our growth is internal; it is in our thinking, and it is in our Mindsets. It is crucial as we connect with Others, valuing and adding value to Others. It is a Daily possibility if we Choose. It can be better understood in context as we make our choices and decisions, seek to improve and master what is best in us, and then fulfil the purposes God has for us.

Conclusions for Step 7

To Grow! Your Best Life

Key Thought – Authentic God-designed Growth is A Choice, Your Choice.

Sub-headings review:
- ➤ **The Higher Level Actioned Life And Thinking**
- ➤ **Grow – Through Significance**
- ➤ **Grow – Because God is Eager To Connect With Us**
- ➤ **Grow – Authentically Connected Human Beings**
- ➤ **Grow – Because We Are Hard-Wired To Be Active, Engaged and Self-Directed**

Transformational Growth is God-designed within you. All you need to do is unleash it. He created us for His purposes, His vision and His destiny; for consecration and dedication with courage, connection and commitment to Him; to lead lives that are consequential for Him. They are to be lives dedicated to God. They are to be lives of wholehearted connection with God. We are created to be inspired and transformed, not fearful. Christ restores us in Himself to God. But the foremost aspect of growth is that it must be daily, today. Stop and consider these aspects:

- ➤ **Firstly, Block out the noise.** Stop automatically listening to the noise of the world. Make time to listen to God. Meditate on His Word frequently.
- ➤ **Secondly, Realising who you are in Christ** and His Plans for you is infinitely more important than what you know or where you are from. He has set you free from the past through salvation and the past of pecking with turkeys to soar with eagles. He created you for this, to live life in all its fullness, as He said. To live the life He always planned for you to live. Do not ask, "What is God's will for my life?" but rather, "How can I give my life to fulfil God's Purposes?"
- ➤ **Thirdly, Wholeheartedness is of the highest importance.** Jesus's words, "Love the Lord your God with all your heart and with all your soul and with all your mind and with all your strength", is the call to a Wholeheartedness relationship with God and with others. It is not insignificant that He uses "heart" first. To love God wholeheartedly is a journey and a path of conscious

choice. Remember, Caleb in Numbers 14, 24 is described as "having a different spirit and follows me wholeheartedly".

➤ **Fourthly, Choose to become a Leader** for Christ and grow people as He did.

➤ **Fifthly, Connect with others for Christ,** valuing and adding value to them.

➤ **Sixthly, Ensure a lasting legacy continues to the next generation.**

Step 8

To Engage! Your Best Life

~~~

Anticipation is a wonderfully proactive and intentional word for seeking out significance.
People with anticipation plan to be significant.
They expect to live a life that matters every day.
They prepare to do significant acts.
They position themselves physically, mentally, emotionally, and financially to make a difference in the lives of others.
Their sense of anticipation for significance draws them forward.
John C. Maxwell – Intentional Living: Choosing A Life That Matters

~~~

Romans ch.12, vv1-2 AMP.
Paul exhorts us to:
Daily Consecrated Connection with God,
Transformation through the ongoing Entire Renewal of
Our Minds Through New Mindsets, New Purpose and New Vision,
Always Focusing on God's Plans and Purposes for us and For Others
And that Process is to be a Continuing Discovery of all that He Created Us For.

~~~

❖ **Key Purpose: Create Enrolled Hearts that are Fully Engaged and Continually Renewed.**

❖ **Key Learning (Always Facing the Unknown without Fear):** We have looked at the pivotal aspects of Significance and Growth, which are so closely linked with Purpose it is difficult to untwine any of it. In Step 8, we need to move to Full Engagement of hearts, minds, hands and brains in pursuit of our Higher Purpose. We will look at commitment and how it comes about, and after the example of Caleb from the Bible, see how we can be fully involved in becoming part of the solution, letting go of the past as we Fully Live Our Best Lives.

❖ **Key Actions (Building The Bridge As You Walk On It):** Purpose Discovery is fundamental. It may take time, but I can assure you your Purpose will be discovered. Let go of your past because it cannot help you where you are going. Intentionally commit to Living Your Best Masterpiece Life For God.

The Importance Of Purpose Discovery

What is God's Purpose? And what is the importance of Purpose Discovery? How does Purpose interact with Vision? Perhaps the question asked here is the wrong question, asked of the wrong people, based on the wrong assumption that purpose is foremostly about you and me.

> *Your purpose is "why" you put your feet on the floor in the morning.*
> *Your values define "how" you should behave*
> *to remain true to your purpose.*
> *Your vision will define "what" you want to accomplish.*
> *Mark Deterding, Leading Jesus' Way*

(Above quotation cited below. [135])

The whole problem of human beings is encapsulated in that simple error, the assumption that we are more important than our Creator, God Himself. Because, as Christ clearly demonstrated, it is not about us foremostly but about God and His plans and purposes for everyone.

Rather than seeking primarily, although vitally important, the answer to the question, "What is the importance of "purpose" and its discovery?" we should return to the creator of "purpose" in human beings and understand where it all started.

We read as Paul wrote in Ephesians 1:4 NIV, "For he chose us in him before the creation of the world to be holy and blameless in his sight." Along with Romans 8:29 NIV, "For those God foreknew he also predestined to be conformed to the image of his Son, that he might be the firstborn among many brothers and sisters."

These are the foundational scriptures that underpin and are the backdrops to everything. They show that purpose was always central to the heart of God, His planning, His thinking, His intentionality, His creation of human beings, His love for and intended relationship with us as individuals. He had a Vision of what He had planned. And for you and me, He has divine intentions.

So, the real importance of purpose is found in its divine nature, central to who

---

[135] Mark Deterding, *Leading Jesus' Way: Become the Servant Leader God Created You to Be*, 2016, p. 3.

God is and why we exist at the very heart of His being. And the most surprising and wonderful aspect of God's purposes and plans is that he reveals them so that we can enter an authentic relationship with Him if we choose aright, or alternatively choose not to if we so decide.

What did Jesus believe His Purpose was? Well, He had discovered God's Purpose for Him at age twelve, prior to the incident of Jesus (missed by His parents for three days) in the temple discussing with the leaders and asking them questions to which they had no answer. From the age of twelve until He bursts onto the world stage at eighteen years old. We can only surmise what happened to Him in that time, but it seems likely that He intentionally prepared for His ministry.

There are two related pathways that Jesus deliberately walked to fulfil God's purposes for himself. Firstly, He deliberately fulfils His Father's will for Him, and secondly, He intentionally creates Servant Leaders. And Servant Leaders produce Servant Seeders. These leaders were not any old leaders. They also acted intentionally by being Transformational Leaders.

John C. Maxwell brilliantly underlines the relevance and importance here in his book, *Be All You Can Be.* I am quoting it again to highlight these truths:

Purpose makes the difference between the ordinary and the extraordinary. A person with a purpose does things out of the ordinary, above average. Personality doesn't make a person extraordinary. Neither does intelligence nor education. What makes a person extraordinary is purpose—the consuming desire to accomplish something in life.[136]

Could it be that we need a mission bigger than ourselves, a purpose beyond our limited vision? [137]

Let me give you the three characteristics of people who have been willing to die for a greater cause than themselves.

- *A purpose worth the price. People who don't have to survive have a purpose that is worth the cost of their very lives.*

- *A vision that is bigger than life. They have the ability to see beyond their horizons. They are willing to make a sacrifice that they know will affect future generations.*

- *A power that is greater than theirs. People who don't have to survive aren't limited by their own weakness; they have a God-given power. Their purpose is God's*

---

[136] John C. Maxwell, *Be All You Can Be*, p. 72.
[137] John C. Maxwell, *Be All You Can Be*, p. 176.

purpose; their vision is God's vision; their power is God's power. His Spirit living in them makes the difference.[138]

> ***Purpose is a matter of life and death.***
> ***Your purpose reflects your ability to derive meaning***
> ***from your life's experiences as well as your ability to make***
> ***focused and intentional decisions.***
> ***Dr. Isaiah Hankel***

(Above quotation cited below.[139])

Without the discovery and knowledge of our "Purpose", Professor Bob Quinn writes that our lives are conventional and transactional. That is, we are primarily self-interested, and we view each social interaction as an exchange or "a transaction system" by which we can gain or negotiate with others via a "contract" the things we need or desire. He goes further to state that, "These assumptions are at the centre of every conventional culture and we are all continually trained to live by them. In conventional social theory, we live to acquire and survive."[140]

In other words, we are hopelessly trained by our cultures and the underlying, mostly subliminal assumptions to such a degree that we can never know anything different. We can never escape from the conventional to the transformational as Christ did.

The good news, of course, is that you "know and understand" already that the escape is not only essential and possible but also doable because you have read this far – you are on the right road!! Professor Quinn also writes of two paradoxes that people often feel:

"Overextended and Underutilized" is often normal.

And yet: "Fully Engaged and Continually Renewed" seems out of reach.

While the first paradox suggests a cycle of depletion that is not easily broken, the second suggests a cycle of renewal that is not easily believed.

When I show these two contrasting paradoxes to people, they immediately identify with, and emotionally react to, the first. They see its negative message as both real and inevitable. It is a downward cycle that always threatens organisational life.

---

[138] John C. Maxwell, *Be All You Can Be*, pp. 177–79.
[139] Isaiah Hankel, *Black Hole Focus How Intelligent People Can Create a Powerful Purpose for Their Lives* (New York, NY: John Wiley & Sons, 2014), p. 8.
[140] 'Culture Creation', *Robert E. Quinn*
<https://robertequinn.com/uncategorized/culture-creation/> [accessed 22 May 2020].

People react differently to the second paradox. They see it as an unreachable ideal. It is not something they experience or expect to experience. They believe, with good reason, that full engagement and continual renewal is not going to happen. Few people can envision it, and even fewer ever aspire to creating such a reality. The lack of vision and aspiration is crucial to this cycle.[141]

So, this question of engagement is crucial to our understanding of Level 2 Unlocking. That is why we turn to another person from three millennia ago who, like his friend Joshua mentioned earlier, was vital in the history of those days.

> **"If God is for us, who can be against us?"**
> **The very least we can do is respond with giving**
> **daily our lives in courageous intentional commitment.**
> **That is why He is active on behalf of those**
> **who are fully committed to Him!**

The Caleb Controversy – His Best Life

Caleb lived around 1500 BC. Joshua and Caleb went with ten other men to scout out the land promised to them by God. Although the expedition itself was a success, the ten others gave a very negative report of the difficulties they would face taking over the land and that it was impossible. But Joshua and Caleb had a different mind on this, and Caleb "quieted the people before Moses, and said, Let us go up at once and possess it; we are well able to conquer it." Number 13, 30, AMPC.

The overwhelming conclusion of the recorded scripture of Caleb is that he had chosen consecration and dedication, with commitment to God, before all other considerations that arose in his life. He had discovered the answer to the question, "Why?" He knew because he had discovered his "Why?"

And found here is this profound truth available to everyone that it was primarily a reflection of the character and intentionality of God Himself. He was so aligned with God and His purposes that he reflected God's character back to God. That gave God extreme pleasure and satisfaction to such a degree that one may even use the description "ecstatic". God felt so honoured that He had to write and tell us about it.

---

[141] Robert E. Quinn, *The Positive Organization*, pp. 1-2.

Caleb walked the different pathway of God's Higher Purpose, deliberately and wholeheartedly. He gave back to the Lord his Creator a life that was consciously consecrated, decisively dedicated, courageously committed, fully focussed, overflowing with extreme courage, with overwhelming wholeheartedness and a burning desire to lead people to the promised land, regardless of circumstances or timescales. Along the way, if all the preceding was not enough, he was inspiring others to take action! Does not that sound like someone we have read or heard about?

But a word of warning. A significant number of those who have chosen consecration, dedication and wholehearted commitment to God over everything else have paid the supreme price. Consecration may well prove costly for its adherents.

Of course, the characteristics before the warning are a description of the character of Christ. He reflected perfectly God's character and intentionality above every other consideration, above even His own life. Nothing stirs God more than an individual reflecting in their lives God's Character and Intentionality. Central to God's purposes for any individual are the key traits of Godly: consecration, dedication, commitment, focus, understanding, wholeheartedness, courage and connection with both Himself and especially Others. This is truly the character of Christ.

Caleb had it in bucketloads by living a God-focussed life in his day. The truth of God's Word in 2 Chronicles 16:9 NIV is plain to understand.

"For the eyes of the Lord range throughout the earth to strengthen those whose hearts are fully committed to him." Have you ever noticed personally the "actively strengthen" phrase? Do you feel that is your experience?

Dedication is the constancy of Wholeheartedness. Dedication can be described as the constant conscious choice of Wholeheartedness, especially in relation to a life dedicated to God. It does not waver in the winds of others' opinions or even events. Its destination does not vary with the winds of life. And when a life is consecrated and dedicated unreservedly and committed wholeheartedly to God, that is why God treasures that life beyond everything else. Because He actively searches out those people to act on their behalf. WOW!

So the key to all the above is not just a system of belief (as we have traditionally been taught), not just a relationship (which could be inadequately understood in human terms), but a deliberate and decisively dedicated, consciously consecrated, wholeheartedly committed "responding and reflecting relationship" with our Creator. Using a scientific example, you cannot reflect unless you are aligned to reflect. Pointing in any old direction does not reflect unless the alignment is correct. Caleb was such a person simply because his heart was aligned with God's heart and will, and being correctly aligned allowed him to reflect God's character and intentions.

It is a salutary reminder to us all to read of God's recorded anger and His sentence pronounced upon that generation in Caleb's time. This was that all over the age of twenty who had refused to follow God's directions and Caleb's lead would die in the desert and never reach the promised land. Numbers 14:24 AMPC: "But My servant Caleb, because he has a different spirit and has followed Me fully, I will bring into the land into which he went, and his descendants shall possess it."

Lord, give us hearts that are responsive and sensitive to You like Caleb's heart was.

Just as importantly, "Calebs" "see" what others cannot and probably never will, but they are not deterred because they think and live at a different level than others. They are living on God's Higher Level. Caleb is thinking differently. He is thinking on God's big-picture level. He is thinking on the consecration, dedication and commitment level. He sees himself within God's purposes for everyone, and for the whole world, for the whole of history. He follows the Lord on His level, saying: "I, however, followed the Lord, my God, Wholeheartedly." Joshua ch.14, v8,

Psalm 145:18 NIV: "The Lord is near to all who call on him, to all who call on him in truth."

> *You are hand-picked by God.*
> *You cannot become or discover all that*
> *you are created and meant to be until*
> *you wholeheartedly seek God*
> *to discover Him for all that He Is.*

As Caleb so eloquently showed in his life, his "seeing" resulted from his early dedication to God and his continually renewed mind that Paul underlined when he wrote the first two verses of Romans 12. You see, Caleb's heart and life had an internal compass that automatically aligned with God's bigger plans. And the passing of over 40 years before he was allowed to see the fruit of his heart's focus and alignment did not dim his wholehearted commitment and connection with God. "So every day, through conscious choice, make a decisive dedication of yourself to Him." Romans ch.12, 1 AMP.

Caleb had made the big decisions of life very early on, long before he was mentioned in scripture. He had recognised and discovered that God has a special relationship with those who Wholeheartedly have a special relationship with Him.

The verse above tells us an extraordinary truth that God reacts to the Wholehearted for Him and acts powerfully on their behalf. In Caleb's case, although it took a long time because of the disobedience of the majority, God would not be denied His show of strength on behalf of Caleb, even over 40 years later.

His Wholeheartedness was based on a Mindset of non-negotiable connection and contract with God that:

✓ had been decided early in his life
✓ was a daily consecration of his life to God
✓ was a daily dedication of his life to God
✓ was focussed daily on what was important to God
✓ was focussed daily on thinking differently to his contemporaries in order to reflect God's priorities
✓ was focussed daily on thinking on God's Higher Level
✓ was a continuous and constant conscious choice
✓ was unreserved and not withholding
✓ was not based on how long it took to see results
✓ was fixed on God's destination
✓ got him noticed by God
✓ was picked up by God's radar
✓ was based on a different mindset
✓ did not depend on others
✓ was entirely independent of circumstances
✓ was growing and renewed every day
✓ few others ever understood
✓ gave him his life's purpose for a God every day of his life
✓ was consciously renewed every day
✓ enabled him to live life on God's Higher Level
✓ was never weakened with the passing of time
✓ was more cemented and strengthened the older he became
✓ was infectious even in his 80s

Because of his early life decisions, Caleb's mind was different. He thought and acted differently because his entire being, his heart, soul, strength and mind, were founded on his profoundly different principles that naturally and inevitably grow from a God-focussed, decisively consecrated, dedicated and committed life. Caleb stood head and shoulders out and above his generation. He was intensely aware of God's Higher Purpose not only for himself but for his place in history and God's purposes for mankind.

Not for Caleb, the birth culture and wayward actions of his own people. Long before his first foray into the promised land, Caleb lived with a deep understanding of who he was before God, especially when no one else was around. And it was all because he was thinking differently. He had emancipated his mind from the culture in which he had been brought up to understand God's Higher Purpose. Very few people achieve this. But here is part of God's Good News in Christ: in scripture, we find He is the ultimate different thinker. Saying that helps us to understand that His actions came from His thinking. And His thinking was the outworking of His alignment with His Father.

Caleb, along with and alone with Joshua, stood and understood God's purpose and destiny for them. These were guys who breathed leadership with vision and focus and who had made a contract with God early in their lives. They did not need the approval of others to think and act as they did. They sought not the affirmation of others, especially of their own generation, because they could "see" what others could not and never would.

They sought only God's approval, and nothing, not even the disappointments and frustration of seeing the mob have their way (never forget this – the crowd are always wrong), would detract from or deflect their God-envisioned lives. Their identity was not only for God, in God, aligned to God, but had become synonymous with God. Their contract with God was rock solid, past, present and future. They were not religious "nuts" but "rocks", rock-solid in God. You see, Caleb understood what only people at his level understand. He understood his "Why?"

We may describe him as: "The most remarkable man of his generation." There is nothing to stop you and I from imitating Caleb because God has called and provided for us all to be "conformed to the image of Christ" if we so decide. You and I can decide that.

> **The simple truth is that**
> **we are as "close" to God as we want to be.**

None of this is a race or a competition with others; it is vitally about a heart, your heart, consecrated, dedicated, committed and here is the clincher, wholeheartedly connected to God through faith in Christ.

In its more traditional variants and elsewhere, the Church of Jesus Christ has moved from being a reality to becoming merely an activity. Where people are focussed on God in Christ, they will not be focussed on church and the Churchianity it breeds. One could describe the need for everyone who "is" the church to seek not for "activity", not even for "experience", but as Caleb did, to daily do the decisive dedication of "alignment" with God's heart, with God's priorities. Because as we have seen above, that is the one sure way of becoming noticed and set apart by God for His purposes.

Every single living person was designed for and has the capacity to live an extraordinary life of alignment with and reflection of God's character and intentionality in Christ. We were created for this. Christ has saved and re-created us for this purpose.

That is the reason why you are created: to be consequential for God in reflecting His Character.

The question for each of us is this: "Given what we now know, will you and I consciously dedicate our lives daily to God, Who gave us that life Himself in the first place and become the most remarkable people of our generation for Him in Christ?"

Are you that person that God created who will consciously become Intentional, Significant and remarkable for God? Because that is what He intended for you.

Most people, in general, and most Christians, in particular, see Jesus as a great leader with "followers". Nothing is further from the truth. His whole life and focus were upon growing the leaders of His Church. He called others to "become like Him", not to become only followers, but by His sacrificial servant leadership example to live and love others to "Become" the people God always planned them to become. He was creating tomorrow's God-aligned leaders like Himself. He was creating people who thought and, therefore, acted differently as He did. He was creating God-inspired originals who would act and do the same as He did. He intended a continuous cascade of God-focussed people who would consciously consecrate and decisively dedicate their lives daily to Him first and then intentionally connect with others to connect them to Him. He was creating and kick-starting the Kingdom of God.

So, a prayer of dedication:

"Lord, enable me, through the enabling of Your Holy Spirit, to reflect Who You are and Your Character as You transform me to the exact image of Your Son Jesus Christ. Because He is the perfect reflection of Yourself."

Finally, a thought for your future meeting with God when you leave this world. Given the absolute importance of all the above, what will be your answer to the inevitable question, "Did you consecrate and dedicate your life daily to God as Caleb did? And if not... could you please tell me... why not?"

"Why did you decide not to be the most remarkable person of your generation for God? Because that was a choice, and your choice if only you had taken that opportunity."

"What level of distraction or importance was so great as to stop that event taking place?"

"What level of aimless distraction did you allow and encourage in your life that effectively closed the door on a consecrated life dedicated to God that, as Scripture testifies, was God's intention for you?"

Only you and God know the answers to all the above.

One last question. Now that you know all the above, the Caleb story and God's assessment of his life:

"Will you today, right now, as you read these words, decide to become the person God always planned for you to be and become the most remarkable person of your generation for God?"

> Only you can make that choice.
> Live the Life God always planned for you to Live. Or not.

And spend the rest of the life God planned for you, wandering in the metaphorical desert of that chosen life, aimlessly, until you pass.

It's Your choice, and that "response-ability" is yours alone.

Will You Choose a Life of Total Commitment and Connection to Your Creator?

He planned for that. Let's be unequivocally clear about this:

Only you can make that decision to walk away, or not.

Masterpiece Commitment Living – Our Best Lives

Don't stay where you are; Constantly step up and step out and "Grow to Become the Masterpiece You were Created to Be". God's Extraordinary Created Masterpiece People Live Intentionally and Growing Daily, they:

> AWAKE! To LIVE Their Best Life of God's Higher Purpose
> To Awareness of their Best Life
> To Develop their Best Life
> To Think over their Best Life
> UNLOCK! Potential for Their Best Life of God's Higher Purpose
> To Breakout to their Best Life
> To Grow their Best Life
> To Engage themselves and others in their Best Life

> ➤ ACT! Contributing For Others to Live Their Best Lives of God's Higher Purpose
> ➤ To Lead Others to their Best Lives
> ➤ To Rally Others to their Best Lives
> ➤ To Legacy Others to their Best Life Legacy

And they understand and Live in the Land of God's Transcendent Higher Purpose instinctively and permanently. They have deliberately moved on from the normal problem-solving focus that limits everyone. They live Ephesians 2:10 NLT: "For we are God's masterpiece. He has created us anew in Christ Jesus, so we can do the good things he planned for us long ago."

They are actively transforming and growing intentionally to live their Best Lives of significance and make a difference for Others, literally becoming, thinking and actioning out in themselves for Others, the perfect human life that Christ did and modelled. They are transforming the future by committing to God's Transcendent Higher Purpose in the present. Daily, They awake and recommit to that Higher Purpose, thus genuinely making a difference as they change the future through their commitment to God's Purpose. In short, God's Masterpiece People being fully engaged, awake, Daily, to Fulfil His Transcendent Higher Purpose and Reach the Higher Destiny He Created them for.

You may write your own purposes that you realise you are called to undertake by God. I list the ones that fire me up, and there is no boasting or disgrace in believing the position you are called to – I use these often to remind myself of what I aspire to:

✓ I am a Transformational Leader!
✓ I am a Transformational Writer!
✓ I am an Inspirational Writer!
✓ I am Living a Life that Matters!
✓ I am Living a Life of Significance!
✓ I am Living a Life of Contribution!
✓ I am writing *TRANSFORMED!* to success!
✓ I am Living God's Extraordinary Masterpiece Life For Others!
✓ All for God and for Others!

Because of the above, I feel the imperative not to awake to what I have to do but to awake to where I intentionally aim to be by creating and seizing opportunities for growing, and learning my way forward in the face of uncertainty. My Focus and Commitment in My Best Life for God's Higher Purpose this morning and every morning is to create the emergence, again, of Awaking, Breakout, and Intentionally Preparing to Live a Life of Transformation, Growth, Contribution and Learning for Him, to Make a Difference For Others, Today.

Be Part of The Solution

"We are created and called for God's Higher Purpose, which is for our Transformation through Redemption, Re-creation, Renewal, Restoration and Redirection for His Purpose, Vision, Fulfilment and Destiny, lifting others intentionally with us, to fulfil God's purposes in our generation. To be filled to the measure of all the fullness of God in Jesus Christ." Anon.

Our goals and values for God in Christ must mirror the extraordinary people we are becoming, as Fully Engaged People we are to be.

- ➤ Be Inspired to Act.
- ➤ Unlock Potential in Others.
- ➤ Living a life of Intentionality and growth for God and others;
- ➤ Discovering God's Higher Purpose for yourself;
- ➤ Being Transformed through Redemption, Renewal, Restoration, Redirection, Fulfilment and Destiny;
- ➤ Unlocking and unleashing your potential and others' for God's Higher Purpose;
- ➤ Stepping up and into God's Higher Level;
- ➤ Being Aware, Engaged and Wholeheartedly Living at God's Higher Level;
- ➤ Loving in God's Higher Level;
- ➤ Leading through Servant Leadership in God's Higher Level;
- ➤ Preparing yourself in God's Higher Level;
- ➤ Learning in God's Higher Level;
- ➤ Running towards all that God has for you in His Higher Level;
- ➤ Becoming an extraordinary (doing whatever it takes) human being for Him as He intended;
- ➤ Changing the Future;
- ➤ Creating and Sustaining the Connecting Legacy;
- ➤ Passing on the Baton;
- ➤ Ready to be filled with all the fullness of God in Jesus Christ.

> *"Let me clarify what I mean when I talk about intentional living. I'm describing a life that brings you daily satisfaction and continual rewards for merely working to make a difference—small or large—in the lives of others. Intentional living is the bridge that will lead you to a life that matters." p.28*
>
> *"When you live each day with intentionality, there's almost no limit to what you can do. You can transform yourself, your family, your community, and your nation.*
> *When enough people do that, they can change the world.*
> *When you intentionally use your everyday life to bring about positive change in the lives of others,*
> *you begin to live a life that matters." p.4*
> *John C. Maxwell, Intentional Living*

(Above quotes cited below.[142])

Living for God in Christ through wholehearted, God-focussed and God-centred conscious consecration, decisive dedication, courageous commitment, and a continuously connected seeking of Him as my considered response to His calling in scripture is the very least I can undertake. These are my responses to God that I have decided to live out daily. I choose to move towards the Lord daily in these simple but profoundly committed actions.

My three primary goals in light of the above statement are:

❖ Loving God and living for Him and His Higher Purpose with His Grander Vision at His Higher Level to fulfil His Purposes in my generation, and live an extraordinarily transformed, redeemed, re-created, renewed, restored and redirected life for His purpose, vision, fulfilment and destiny that echoes in Eternity for God, living a legacy for Him.

❖ Unlocking and unleashing God's prepared potential and significance in others by connecting with them through servant leadership, creating new realities that did not exist before, inspiring and encouraging others to grow, be transformed and redirected, doing whatever it takes in Christ, to become themselves the extraordinary significant, fulfilled, productive, purpose fulfilling and focussed people he always planned for and expects us to be.

---

[142] John C. Maxwell, *Intentional Living.*

❖ Calling and challenging the Church under Jesus Christ to be transformed, renewed, restored, and redirected by being "purpose-driven, internally directed, others focussed and externally open,"[143] leading to fulfilment and destiny by moving from comfort (with complacency) to courage because you cannot have both.

This is the question I seek to ask of myself: "Today, by His Spirit, will I courageously and wholeheartedly, by consecration and dedication, commit myself to love and seek God with all my heart to fulfil His Purposes in Jesus Christ, for His Church, for others, and for myself, and live the extraordinary life that He created for me and recreated me to live, walking the pathways He created for me to walk in and do those good works He created for me to do?"

What will I choose? What will I achieve? How will I respond to the realisation that "You, the Lord, are in me"? Almost any response is inadequate, but for me, of greater scriptural importance is that every response of personal commitment will be instantly understood, recognised and acted upon by God. In 2 Chronicles 16:9 NIV: "For the eyes of the Lord range throughout the earth to strengthen those whose hearts are fully committed to him."

How will I do it? By conscious and intentional awakening, by awareness, by alignment, by engagement, by looking, by longing, by learning, and by wholeheartedly calling on and seeking the Lord daily, imitating by action with the heart of Christ, with His Greatness, His Wholeheartedness, His Courage, His Compassion, His Commitment, His Vision and His Focus.

My desire is to be part of the solution. It is not about me, but about Unlocking and Unleashing Potential in Others for God, Fulfilling His Purposes in my generation and leaving a connected legacy for the next.

Loving and knowing God in a relationship with Him is critical. We must move past only theoretical theological knowledge and even statements of belief and faith to seek an ever-deepening relationship in connection with Him for His own sake to "know" Him and fulfil His purposes. We need to practice God-directed "mirroring". It works in this way. If you and I entrust all that we are to God determinedly, only then can God start to entrust His Heart and plans to you and me.

We want to need this so badly that God recognises this fact. Can you see the difference we are trying to understand here? You and I seek the Lord with all our hearts. He will respond. Become desperate to get close to God. Become as desperate as a drowning person needs to take that next breath. He will draw

---

[143] Ryan Quinn and Robert Quinn, *Lift*, *2nd Edition*, 2015, p. 2
<https://www.safaribooksonline.com/library/view//9781626564039/?ar> [accessed 21 May 2020].

close to you. Simple, wholehearted action towards the Lord initiates His equal response. You and I draw as close to God as we "want to", and in that process lies the foundation of becoming the extraordinary human being He created us to become for Him.

Jeremiah 29:13-14 NIV:
"You will seek me and find me when you seek me with all your heart. I will be found by you, declares the Lord."

Lord God, by Your Spirit, grant me a heart that seeks You with all its God-endowed faculties of Trust, Delight, Commitment and Wholeheartedness today.
Grant me Your transformation
Grant me Your heart renewal
Grant me your vision
Grant me Your heart
Grant me Your mind
Grant me Your focus
Grant me Your intentionality
Grant me Yourself
For the sake of Your Son Jesus Christ, who gave everything He could and His giving echoes for all eternity.
Because You created me, Lord God, for Yourself, I realise I am created to fulfil Your purposes in this world.

> *Go and Invest and Re-invest all yourself, who you are, your mind, your soul, your heart, your hands, your time, your vision, your desires, in God Your Creator and He will invest in you!*

For those who name the Name of Christ, fully grasping who He is, what He is doing, how He does it, and what results He is creating are all of vital importance to us as individuals and as local churches. This is because He is all about people and His relationship with you and me and our personal response to Him. Therefore, it is critical to our awareness, understanding, engagement, and life that we clearly discover the purpose and practice, values, and vision of Christ in Scripture.

God created us for His purposes, His vision and His destiny; for consecration and dedication with courage, connection and commitment to Him; to lead lives that are courageous and consequential for Him; to lead lives that fulfil His purposes for us.

They are to be lives dedicated to God.
They are to be lives of wholehearted connection with God.

We are created to be inspired and transformed, not fearful and inward-focussed, as Christ restores us in Himself to God, and we are to discover our identity in Him. Living for God in Christ through conscious consecration, daily dedication, and courageous commitment as my considered response to His calling in scripture is the very least I can undertake. These are my responses to God that I have decided to live out daily. I choose to move towards and reinforce them every day in this act.

Myles Munroe wrote in his book, *Maximising Your Potential*, "Releasing what you have received benefits you and others. Holding on to a treasure forfeits the blessing inherent in the treasure, and no one profits from it. Like the seed, you must release what God has stored in you for the world. You do this by releasing seeds into the soil of the lives of others. Rise above circumstances and maximise your potential for others." [144]

What are my defining values, those values which I have built my life around?

❖ For God: Consecration, Dedication and Commitment daily to Him and treating others as I would be treated; all these are non-negotiable.

❖ For myself: Integrity, Trustworthiness, Honesty, Wholeheartedness, Authenticity, and Vulnerability.

I ask myself this question, "What are the outcomes that I seek?" All I want to do is switch the outcomes that I experience every day from being diminished and depleted by my Christian experience to being inspired by the same as God intended, and inspiring and encouraging growth in other people for God. It is that simple.

I would love to be in a church where I can be authentic, purposeful, valued, engaged, growing and growing with others, for others, for God.

> ### Unlocking and Unleashing God-Created Potential in People

Then I ask the question, "What can I focus on?" My answer is, "To write a compelling book that will enable people who are stuck where they are, people

---

[144] Myles Munroe, *Maximizing Your Potential: The Keys to Dying Empty*, 2008, p. 129.

who are living lives less than what God intended even if they cannot see their difficulties, to become the fulfilled and productive people God always planned for them to become." As a result, I have the focus:

➢ To unlock and unleash potential in others.
➢ To start the journey, grow, mature and become the fulfilled people God always planned for us to be.
➢ To understand the process, pathway and purpose of discipleship through purpose, values and vision.
➢ To find a way through the difficulties and forge a route for others to follow.
➢ To inspire others to action under God.

All this is my purpose and goal for God. I hope to: FOCUS – Follow One Course Until Successful.

Lead others for God. It is all about living for God, leadership for God and legacy for God. It is all about a responding relationship with God through understanding His timeless truths in scripture.

I feel I was created for this purpose. It is as if my name is on this. It is as if I have been waiting for and working towards this all my life. Living for God's Higher Purpose with His grander vision is what I was created for. I feel my whole life has been moving towards and readying for this purpose.

"Lord, lead me by your indwelling Holy Spirit to discern, understand, prepare and grow towards your grander vision not just for me but for your church.

To escape the ordinary mind-numbing mediocrity of our lives to become extraordinary for You, simply by discerning your purpose, potential, values and vision for me.

To escape the mud-hole of the status quo, to rise above and beyond where we think we are, to envision Your grander purposes, to understand and then act out Your plans and future for us.

To stop pecking like turkeys by the runway you created for us and placed us next to, then take off, fly, and rise on eagles' wings to the destiny you have for us if only we would open our God-given minds and realise we are created to fly closer to You.

To simply stop burying daily the talent you gave to every one of us to use for Your glory.

God grant us Awareness of Your plans, Alignment with Your plans and Action for Your plans."

Here are some goals for both individuals and organisations under God-centred,

God-focussed transformational Leadership continually reinforcing generational legacy and helping to:

➢ **Unlock and Unleash Potential in others and oneself**
  ➢ Discover God's purposes individually and corporately
  ➢ Inspire to conscious awakening
  ➢ Inspire conscious consecration
  ➢ Inspire to decisive dedication
  ➢ Inspire to courageous commitment
  ➢ Inspire to action
➢ **Reinforce values consistently**
  ➢ Create and revisit vision consistently
  ➢ Establish a laser focus
  ➢ Engage hearts, minds, bodies and souls
  ➢ Inspire others for Christ
➢ **Be a Multiplier for Christ**
  ➢ Discovering our identity in Christ
  ➢ Challenging and disrupting the conventional culture as Christ did
  ➢ Utterly transform and overturn assumptions as Christ did
  ➢ Aspire to reach the unreachable and transform the hierarchy who "diminish" others "below them" by helping them "see" what they cannot "see".
➢ **Help others discover their actual status in Christ**
  ➢ Making a difference for God in the time I have left on this earth
  ➢ Consecrate consciously and decisively dedicate my life daily to Christ
  ➢ Transform my thinking for Christ to His thinking for others
➢ **See the Church transformed from its fatal inward, self-absorbed focus to what Christ intended it to be**
  ➢ Be focussed and intentional like Christ
  ➢ Plan long-term with a vision for growth and improvement
  ➢ Get people started on their journey of transformation for Christ
  ➢ Grow others, then cascading that process for Christ
➢ **Motivate to Intentionality**
  ➢ Inspire to wholehearted commitment
  ➢ Draw out courage, compassion and connection
  ➢ Draw out potential and purpose in people
  ➢ Demand authenticity
  ➢ Ensure accountability
  ➢ Map results

- ➤ **Frame the future**
  - ➤ Define the present
  - ➤ Complete the past
  - ➤ Run towards Destiny
  - ➤ Resonate with others
  - ➤ Realise real and deep understanding
  - ➤ Resolve the minds of others
  - ➤ Attract talent
  - ➤ Liberate thinking
- ➤ **Transform, Grow and Renew minds**
  - ➤ Challenge assumptions
  - ➤ Challenge culture wherever it is
  - ➤ Allow inclusive debate
  - ➤ Stimulate investment in people
  - ➤ Create transformation in people
  - ➤ Encourage potential in people
- ➤ **Fully engage people's discretionary thinking**
  - ➤ Fully engage people's discretionary action
  - ➤ Fully deploy people's discretionary gifts
  - ➤ Continually reinforce generational legacy

All for God
Wow!

- But how to stimulate and engage others and introduce new assumptions and thinking?
- How to overthrow the assumptions and thinking that keep us enslaved and colluding in our dis-empowerment?
- How to break out from "normal" thinking, which is killing us?
- How to recognise that where we are is a tragic charade and illusion of being "normal" when the reality is that God never intended our lives to be "normal"? They are to be individually "extraordinary" if only we can break out of "normal" culture to discover God's planned purposes for our lives.
- How to break the shackles that hold most people in the poverty of untapped potential and undiscovered purposes?

"Most ailing organizations have developed a functional blindness to their own defects. They are not suffering because they cannot solve their problems but because they cannot see their problems." – John Gardner.[145]

I add that they are also incapable of seeing the possibility of solutions, or even possibility itself because the focus is on problem-solving rather than discovering purpose in people and growing them as God intended. They cannot dream or envision that God in Christ always planned a dramatically different way for us to live and fulfil His purposes for us in our generations.

> *In Romans ch.12, vv1-2 Paul exhorts us to:*
> *Daily Consecrated Connection with God,*
> *Transformation through the ongoing Entire Renewal of*
> *Our Minds through New Mindsets,*
> *New Purpose and New Vision*
> *Constantly Focusing on God's Plans and Purposes*
> *for us and For Others,*
> *And that Process is to be a Continuing Discovery*
> *of all that He Created Us For.*

Organisations and individuals constantly deny and ignore the possibility of something better having been purposed for them. We need to challenge, change and live out an alternative mental map.

As I wrote the following paragraphs on my mobile phone in Evernote, I recognised that for the first time in 6 years since 2011, in seeking to write *TRANSFORMED!* I was getting nearer to the heart of the book and its focus, and that my intellect was slowly, almost imperceptibly, understanding what I really sought to convey. The growing conviction had given way to a deeper understanding of thought, intention and action for a believer in Christ like me. It was as if the long climb in the mist up the precipice of gaining wisdom and understanding was at last showing results with the bigger picture and easing slightly as I climbed onto the upper slopes of *TRANSFORMED!* It seems that Christ calls us to go to places we have never been by pathways we never even knew existed.

I also feel I am engaged in a great endeavour. That it is utterly beyond me is self-evident, but I am drawn, nay, compelled to be in its engagement and driven by the concern that I might die before its completion (which, paradoxically, I am

---

[145] Gordon L. Lippitt and Warren H. Schmidt, 'Crises in a Developing Organization', *Harvard Business Review*, 1 November 1967 <https://hbr.org/1967/11/crises-in-a-developing-organization> [accessed 7 August 2020].

sure will not happen). The "constraints and limitations of my history and life, especially cultural constraints", always seem to loom large and continually, and there appear more questions than answers, but God has called me to this task.

So, may God afford me the courage to continue and with similar brevity of language to inspire and draw people to God's Higher Purpose. No one I know has been down this road before. I build it as I walk this road.

But this should be true for every Christian, to discover God's purpose for each of us. In that process of a personal journey, consecration, dedication, commitment, and discovery, we are learning and maturing that we become truly those people He intends to live for Him alone.

If the Church of Christ in this country is to awaken and transform to be both collectively and individually what God always planned for it to be, then there needs such an understanding of His purposes, such clarity of vision and such integrity of action as it has never seen since its inception. Even to the simplest onlooker, doing more of the same in the mad and vain hope that some different outcome can ensue is the recipe for further decline, disaster and ultimately, congregational and personal spiritual "death".

Did Christ intend His Church to be so lacklustre and inward-focussed? Of course not. So who "screwed up"? The answers to this and other stark questions are elsewhere in this book. But here, it is all about us as individuals growing in Christ and realising that God has a calling for us. God placed within us undiscovered potential and purpose with our names on it. These need discovery under a dramatically redirected local church leadership away from the "Churchianity" that imprisons us each week towards an individual learning Transformational and Growing church living at a different level entirely under God.

Let Go of The Past – Fully Engage With Your Purpose

It has been almost impossible for someone like myself brought up in churches for over six decades to start thinking differently, to get to God's heart in Jesus Christ. The status quo and respect for church systems are overwhelming. But called we are, and sooner or later, one must take the first step on the road that one is called to and leave to God, whatever the results may be. One must break free from the illusory constraints that hold us in collusion with the currently overwhelmingly accepted system of "Churchianity" that does indeed hold us all in suspended animation. We never become either the church or individuals that God planned us to be.

I have also discovered that perhaps after much water has gone under the bridge, there is a genuine sense of needing to let go of the past, deeply reflect on the present, and purposefully contemplate the future that God calls us to reach out for. All the negative childhood memories and others' thoughtless, unkind comments and actions towards us, we remember and have carried with us from our earliest times. The more recent hurts, the feelings of rejection, of being made to feel I did not matter, all needed to be let go.

Professor Susan David's book *Emotional Agility* was just what this helpless child needed: To finally let go of the baggage that we all carry with us but are too afraid to let go.[146] But you see, there was God's Higher Purpose compelling me onwards. I realised that carrying all that "normal" emotional dead weight held me back from God's purposes.

Perhaps I read the book at just the right time. Aged 66, and having finished as a churchwarden (the most defining experience of my life) over three years earlier, I have felt able to grow up, that I must grow up, let go and move on to become the person God always intended me to become. It was as if I was free at last to choose and place them, the baggage I had carried, almost gently, into the river I had crossed and stayed by for those three years and watch as the current took them from me until they were out of sight. I will not need them where I am going as God has His Way with me.

The metaphor of crossing a river is apt for me. In my work on river surveys, I have many times undertaken that task. It can only be successfully completed with a staff! One can look across to contemplate the current, the depth, the roughness of the bed, the edge of the bank. But until that first step is taken, you cannot know that reality of hesitantly stumbling, often tripping and slipping, then finding the location too deep, or the velocity of the water too great, but also discovering a shallower but still rough crossing nearby.

And so it seems as though it took over three years of sitting on the far bank. Only then could I let go of the past and not only the very personal baggage that I clung to. For me, there was also the overwhelming cultural baggage, both secular and religious. These are the most lethal, constraining influences on people's lives. Not that they are all wrong. Our parents did their best in early post-war Britain. I did my best with our three children, the oldest now over forty. What cultural and religious baggage did I load them with?

Yet I cannot and will not deny my Lord and Saviour Jesus Christ. I will always hold to Scripture as the unique, solely and divinely inspired Word of God, all of it. And it was amongst Paul's letters to the early Church that *TRANSFORMED!* had its beginnings. God's promised land for me will not be won by blindly following and repeating the constraints and chains of the past or

---

[146] Susan A David, *Emotional Agility Get Unstuck, Embrace Change, and Thrive in Work and Life*, 2017, pt. 1475.

recent present. I am called to daily conscious consecration, decisive dedication and courageous commitment to God. Nothing less than total commitment and focus, as epitomised by Christ, can suffice. Begone self-interest and ease of life. God's sacrifice demands a greater response than we can possibly conceive, but to which we give our lives in praise of His Glory.

We are called to walk on roads that do not exist (that we must create as we walk on them) if we are to get to His places we never even knew existed...

I submit that the primary heart of a Christian for Christ is to be:
- ✓ Fully engaged and continually renewed by Christ
- ✓ Fully aware and continually connected to Christ
- ✓ Fully committed and continually consecrated for Christ
- ✓ Fully dedicated and continually growing in Christ

We are by God:
- ✓ Created
- ✓ Connected
- ✓ Conformed

in Christ to the praise of the glory of His glory.

That is the grand vision and plans of God for mankind in three words. These are indeed eternal truths and are shown throughout the scriptures.

I am a Transformational Writer for God in Christ.

I was created for this task.

Whether anyone else understands or believes these statements is irrelevant because they have not experienced my life.

> *I am Hand-picked by God, my Creator.*
> *Am I prioritising my day, every day, to Live My Destiny?*

I believe I am called by God in Christ to this task. I feel that all my life has been but one long learning experience leading to these moments. Especially the difficult times. And God allows those times to do His unique work.

- The 20 years at the bottom of the work "pile" – brought forth the hunger to matter, to make a difference, to leave a legacy.
- The four years as a Church Warden – these effectively sharpened the edge of my saw and commenced the clarification towards writing *TRANSFORMED!*

- These produced the dual pains of palpable disengagement and lost unfulfilled potential in people in most churches.
- My sadness for closed churches when passing by. For the loss of their people and the vision that opened them, now no more.

All created their own unique pain in me when I thought of them. You see, our culture traps each of us. Professor Quinn in *The Positive Organisation* states, "Instead of moving toward an ever more positive culture where people sacrifice for the common good, most organizations maintain conventional cultures full of self-interested people. The people continually splinter, and the organisation moves toward a slow death."

The Apostle Peter awoke from his old life when, as a fisherman, he met Christ, who, bypassing the culture of those times, immediately started Peter's awakening process. Scripture records the battles. All the time, their culture fought to stop this work. God calls all of us, and He does not change His mind. We can decide not to respond. But for those who do respond, give up any current ideas of your Christian life being "a wandering in the wilderness" so beloved by earlier romanticising generations of Christians. God has greater plans for you than you can ever conceive.

So, what are we to be, to do, to seek? The only answer to these questions can come from you. Only you know your heart. Only you can answer for yourself and your decision.

Just do it. Just say "yes" to God who created you. Don't make it complicated.

Just consciously, consecrate and decisively dedicate your life to Him daily. Become the "Caleb" of your generation.

Those who honour me, I will honour. – 1 Samuel, ch.2, v.30
Seek the Lord while He may be found. – Isaiah ch.55, v.6.
If you seek Him with all your heart, He will be found by you. – Jeremiah ch.29, v.11-13

> *I am chosen, created and called by God for His purpose, to live for His Glory with my Destiny for Transformation in Christ. I am designed by God for His purpose:*
> *for wholehearted living*
> *for connection with Himself*
> *for connection with others*
> *To grow others through servant leadership like Christ*

Now, interesting thought.

I started out seeking transformational change in churches, and here I am pushing my goals:

✓ Living for God's Higher Purpose with His grander vision for me.
✓ To live a life that echoes in Eternity for God.[147]
✓ Inspiring others to grow and be transformed in Christ to become the fulfilled people he always planned them to be. To discover and unlock potential in others for God and to connect them to God's Higher Purpose for them.

To find a way through the difficulties and forge a route for others to follow. To start the journey, grow, mature and become the fulfilled people God always planned for us to be. This is total engagement. It is all about living for God, leadership for God and legacy for God.

Daily Choice – Daily Commitment To Your Best Life

We face every day Our Daily Choice and Our Daily Commitment. It is a deliberate choice, a considered choice, a consecrated choice, a choice of decisive dedication. It is the daily choice to seek God every day. It does not just happen, and it is not a warm fuzzy feeling that mysteriously washes over you from time to time, as some would characterise it. It is hard, intentional, deliberate work. Remember from our introduction the statements about Wholehearted Commitment and how it all fits together with Purpose:

---

[147] 'Ready to Fly: Finding Your Greater Yes by Dr. Dan Erickson', *People Matter Ministries*
<http://www.peoplematterministries.com/store/ready-to-fly-finding-your-greater-yes> [accessed 7 August 2020].

❖ Wholehearted Commitment is achieved and experienced when we are committed to our Purpose.

❖ We are Wholeheartedly Committed when we are Fully Aligned with our Purpose.

❖ Wholehearted Commitment ensues from Alignment with Our Purpose.

❖ "When we Commit to a Purpose" is firstly about Alignment with that Purpose, then effortlessly riding the wave of Commitment that ensues.

God created us for His purposes, His vision and His destiny; for consecration and dedication with courage, connection and commitment to Him; to lead lives that are courageous and consequential for Him; to lead lives that fulfil His purposes for us. They are to be lives dedicated to God. They will be perfectly God-fulfilled lives. They are to be lives of wholehearted connection with God. We are created to be inspired and transformed, not fearful, as Christ restores us in Himself to God, and we are to discover our identity in Him.

Bishop T.D. Jakes, in his book, *Identity* writes:

> *Once you realize that you were created on purpose and created in the image of the Creator, you begin to recognize that there are secrets stored up inside you. These are the very secrets that must be discovered and unleashed to a purposeless planet and a purposeless people.*
>
> *There are secrets inside you that God has planted—secret talents, secret gifts, and secret wisdom—that have been divinely orchestrated. These gifts, talents, abilities, wisdom, solutions, and creativities are uniquely yours. God the Creator is multidimensional enough to create you uniquely. Trust His design. The moment you start to embrace how you have been formed and fashioned is the moment you step into the very purpose for which you were created.[148]*

Given this level of investment God has made in creating you and me, the very least we can do is to respond. You see, Friends, we have a choice to make, a choice of profound engagement with God, a choice either to step out in a God-honouring direction or we can choose to stay where we are and remain irrelevant, purposeless, confined and constrained by our mediocre status quo Churchianity and its inward-focussed culture.

We can choose to break out of our culture as Christ did, our culturally

---

[148] T. D Jakes, *Identity: Discover Who You Are and Live a Life of Purpose.* (Place of publication not identified: Destiny Image), pt. 107.

compromised thinking, the baggage we carry of our pasts, the supposed failures, the criticisms of others, and let God transform our minds and hearts to become the people God always planned for us to be.

Or we can stay pew-bound. We have to choose either comfort or courage because we cannot have both.

One final comment. Those who desire to be fulfilled for God must be fully available and fully committed to God. They must be Fully Engaged, finding that they are Continually Renewed.

> 2 Chronicles ch.16, v9 NIV:
> "For the eyes of the Lord range throughout the earth to strengthen those whose hearts are fully committed to him."

> 2 Chronicles ch.16, v9 MSG:
> "God is always on the alert, constantly on the lookout for people who are totally committed to him."

King David was described in Acts ch.13, v22 NIV: "After removing Saul, he made David their king. God testified concerning him: 'I have found David son of Jesse, a man after my own heart; he will do everything I want him to do.'" Here was a man whom God told the world unequivocally in scripture, was utterly committed to God and would seek to do whatever God asked of him.

If you want to be close and connected to God, on His side, working for Him, you can be. You are as close and connected to God as you want to be. And if you are fully committed, or totally committed, like Christ, like King David, like the Apostle Paul, then 2 Chronicles 16:9 AMPC promises three God-actioned events: "For the eyes of the Lord run to and fro throughout the whole earth to show Himself strong in behalf of those whose hearts are blameless toward Him."

1. He, the Lord, will be the first to recognise and notice that total commitment instantly.
2. He will commit Himself to You.
3. God will show Himself strong on your behalf.
4. He will strengthen that commitment and the connection you have made towards Him.

Wow! That is a stunning set of declarations. And you and I often feel weak, worthless, insignificant and useless. Never again need you doubt God's heart and actions for you. If you make a total commitment to God, he makes a declaration of His intentions towards you! Guaranteed! Rock-solid and declared in scripture!

All this now helps to be the background as to why you and I are hard-wired to discover your God-installed sense of your Origin, Identity, Significance, Potential, Purpose, Vision and Destiny. You are created by your Maker for understanding, commitment, courage, focus and action. Christ discovered all this as a young man of twelve years of age.

Now we can start to understand why, for centuries, the Church has been so weak, distracted, infighting, gossiping, distracted and irrelevant. Yes, we have been taught to "believe" and say creeds, to attend, to undertake ritual, to follow and repeat liturgy, to sit in rows facing the dress-coded professionals at the front we pay to act for us. But we rarely have, if ever, been led to discover and act upon God's simple truths for ourselves. Because we are taught to attend a structured show, not personally discover all that God in Christ has for us. That would be dangerous!

"Today, by His Spirit, I will courageously and confidently commit myself to seek God with all my heart to fulfil His Purposes in Jesus Christ, for His church and for myself and live the life that He created and recreated me to live, walking the pathways He created for me to walk in and do those good works He created for me to do."

This is the Cross that Christ personally asks you daily to take up. It means dying to self. It means crucifying your natural thinking. It means breaking out of that thinking.

You and I are called to:
- ✓ Understanding
- ✓ Commitment
- ✓ Courage
- ✓ Focus
- ✓ Action

And
- ✓ Know your Creator
- ✓ Know you are created
- ✓ Know why you are created
- ✓ Know you have been recreated in Christ Jesus
- ✓ Know your "WHY?"

Because None of this is a Game.

Conclusions for Step 8

To Engage! Your Best Life

Key Thought – Let go of the past. It will not help you. Grasp and fully engage your Best Life with your emerging future because that is where you are going.

Sub-headings review:
- ➢ The Importance Of Purpose Discovery
- ➢ The Caleb Controversy – His Best Life
- ➢ Masterpiece Commitment Living – Our Best Lives
- ➢ Be Part of The Solution
- ➢ Let Go of The Past – Fully Engage With Your Purpose
- ➢ Daily Choice – Daily Commitment To Your Best Life

The end of Step 8 is two-thirds through *TRANSFORMED!* So, you are well over halfway and ready for the final push. There is no downhill glideslope!

These Step 8 concluding thoughts are not looking back. They are designed to help you look forward. All to this point has really been the preparation for a continuing breakout and now to Action. You have worked through the first two levels and eight steps to this point. You stand on the cusp of great actions if you choose.

In effect, all leading to this point was the pure training for Transformation and Growth you needed. All of it is essential, dynamic, and absolutely worthwhile as you walk this unique path to where you are meant to be.

I wonder how you are feeling? Even as I write, I feel elation, purpose, direction, even escape from the past, and yet also a feeling of anticipation for the future. Be encouraged. The path you are on can only be walked by you. No one else can fill your shoes. It is the path created by God uniquely for you to travel. Can you now comprehend how this cannot be based on the old hierarchical traditions of comparison and position grasping, climbing "the greasy pole"?

You are becoming a Masterpiece for God as He intended and designed you, and all it took to start was your "Yes!"

Level 3 is Take-Off. You are ready, you are prepared, and you are self-trained. But you will also be circumspect and know enough not to expect an easy flight. You will also see how you got here. Daily consecration, daily dedication, and daily commitment have served you well.

Take courage, and choose the actions God created you for.

LEVEL 3

BE INSPIRED TO ACT!

Level 3 – "Take-off To High-Altitude Supersonic Flight" and God's Best Life for You – ACT! Your "What?"

- ❖ **Breakout to Your Calling!** – With The Extraordinary Dynamic *Transformation* to *Act!, Daily*
- ❖ **Your Key Thinking:** Act! Fulfilling God's Purposes in Your Generation by Leading, Transforming, Developing, Equipping, Deploying, and Changing the Future for God and Others
- ❖ **Your Key Commitments to Dynamic Action 3** – *Actioning and Leading Intentionally, Daily*, by doing the right actions for take-off

  - ➢ **Step 9 – ACT! For Others for Their Best Lives of God's Higher Purpose:** Create Cultural Transformation and a prerequisite to action: Create Leaders with the Skills and a Sense of Urgency to Build, Develop and Equip People to Act.
  - ➢ **Step 10 – To Lead! – Others To Their Best Lives of God's Higher Purpose:** Create a Compelling Vision to Inspire with Clarity and Connection to Lead Yourself and Others to God's Higher Purpose, Starting The Journey, Building a new Culture of Empowerment, and the Outcomes that God plans.
  - ➢ **Step 11 – To Rally! – Others To Their Best Lives of God's Higher Purpose:** Create Leadership to Continue for God in the Service of Something Greater than Yourself.
  - ➢ **Step 12 – To Legacy! – Others To Their Best Life Legacy of God's Higher Purpose:** Create a Leadership Legacy that is Eclipsing the Past, Transforming the Present by Investing in Others, and Changing the Future so that You and I, and Others, can be TRANSFORMED! just as God Planned for Us to Be.

(Always Remembering it's Not About You, but for God and Others.)

236

Step 9

Act! For Others For Their Best Lives

~~~

Do not be silent.
There is no limit to the power that may be released through you.
Don't ask yourself what the world needs.
Ask yourself what makes you come alive, and then go do that.
Because what the world needs is those people who have come alive.
Howard Thurman, Author
Theologian, Civil Rights Leader [149]

~~~

God's Good News in Jesus Christ is found in Ephesians 2:10 NLT.
"For we are God's masterpiece.
He has created us anew in Christ Jesus,
so we can do the good things he planned for us long ago."
In other words:
"I came to Transform You So You Can Do The Good Things
I Planned For You Long Ago."
"Will you please move from all those
unnecessary and outdated assumptions
of sinful, needy supplicants to
Understanding Through Your Faith in Me?
I AM TRANSFORMING YOU!
I Created You My Extraordinary Masterpieces
SO - ACT - LIKE - THEM!"

~~~

- ❖ **Key Purpose: Create Cultural Transformation and a prerequisite to action: Create Leaders with the Skills and a Sense of Urgency to Build, Develop and Equip People to Act.**
- ❖ **Key Learning (Always Facing the Unknown without Fear):** Congratulations again, you have reached Level 3 of your journey. This is a real milestone. In Step 8, we have learnt the importance of Purpose

---

[149] 'Howard Thurman Quotes (Author of Jesus and the Disinherited)' <https://www.goodreads.com/author/quotes/56230.Howard_Thurman> [accessed 20 May 2020].

Discovery, about being part of the solution – whatever that might mean to you; we have discovered the importance of commitment and how alignment with our purpose creates confidence and commitment.

❖ **Key Actions (Building The Bridge As You Walk On It):** We now move to Level 3, Step 9 and the Take-Off to Action thinking. Part of pre-flight checks before take-off is checking the weather ahead, going over the flight plan, and having enough fuel for the flight. The Creation of Transformational Cultures cannot be ignored or delayed. It is up to you as a leader to fully understand that, "You get what you allow." We will see the dangers confronting us, which must be dealt with before we can move ahead. Success in these endeavours is dependent on action – Our Action. Leading to stop Silos from forming as you lead is essential at this juncture. You might wish to taxi down the runway fast enough to take off, but Step 9 is critical in your understanding at this point. Please study and don't commence take-off without carefully planning ahead!

From Transactional to Transformational Cultures

We now turn to what may arguably be the most critical and challenging Level of *TRANSFORMED!* The moment when all that preceded the Awakening, the Unlocking, was but a preparation for this point in time of Action. All the previous difficult work of challenging personal Mindsets, changing personal Mindsets, and changing from personal transactional thinking to personal transformational thinking has started and is well underway. What we look at shortly will be painful to many since we deal with the relevant difficulties that overtake many organisations.

Before we dive into Cultural Transformation, we need to understand that neither failure nor success just happens. They are often the result of doing nothing, allowing failure to happen or stopping success by inaction or lack of forward planning. Dr Henry Cloud, in his book, *Boundaries For Leaders – Why Some People Get Results, and Others Don't,* explains with overwhelming clarity:

✓ Leadership matters and Leadership competencies must be in place for a vision to become a reality.

✓ Leaders lead people who need to be led to give all of their discretionary input to get things done to thrive by using all of their capacities.

✓ Leaders "Always get what they create and what they allow." [150]

We need to understand the bigger picture, the broader landscape where the above personal transformations must become culture-wide transformations. And if the purpose of Step 9 is to become a reality, then "Create Leaders with the Skills and a Sense of Urgency to Build, Develop and Equip People to Act" must be built on prepared ground with solid foundations.

It would be misleading to allow the progress undertaken so far to give the impression that we are almost "there". We have all walked up mountains where the steeper lower slopes gave way to sunlit uplands, and then we discovered that the rise ahead was not the penultimate slope before the summit. Solid progress had been made, but we misled ourselves into the "almost there" thinking.

The real push is now if we are to conquer this particular mountain. To prepare for the summit push, it is entirely relevant to ask essential questions again, which may be recognisable from earlier in the book but now take on a very different level of importance in the ACT! arena of leadership.

What did Christ intend for His Church?
➤ **Growing to Become the Masterpiece You Were Created to Be.**
(Ephesians 1-2)

What cultural change is required now?
➤ **Transactional to Transformational.**

How do we achieve this level of cultural change and transformation?
➤ **Transform Mindsets from fixed to growth.**

How do we sustain it?
➤ **Create legacy.**

We saw in Step 6, Breakout, how hierarchy tends to disintegrate organisations by disengaging individuals. Our normal lives and day-to-day interactions often consist of the accepted mediocrity of hierarchies, "silos" (more below), and fixed Mindsets, which are the result of the cultural limitation of the status quo ably underpinned by scarcity and transactional thinking. Hierarchies, silos and fixed mindsets stymie Transformational Leadership.

---

[150] Henry Cloud, *Boundaries for Leaders: Results, Relationships, and Being Ridiculously in Charge,* First Edition (New York, NY: HarperBusiness, an imprint of HarperCollins Publishers, 2013), pp. xiii–xvi.

All grow from and are based primarily on a self-centred focus. These challenges that confront the Transformational Leader are at their most difficult and dangerous unless adequately understood and fully appreciated for their ability to derail and destroy Transformational work unless neutralised. In other words, You get what you allow.

You see, we need to move our thinking and learning from the personal-cultural to organisational-cultural level. What worked for you is unlikely to work for others, especially not in an organisational context. What was a personal Mindset is now especially unpleasant, rearing its ugly head as a "silo" in an organisation. If it was difficult for you personally, it is impossible for organisations unless cultural surgery is undertaken.

As always, Professor Bob Quinn gives us a head start in an extract from his blog: "From Silos to Collaboration: The Process of Cultural Surgery."

> *The work of the cultural surgeon is to create experiences that change beliefs. For every surgical act, there is a feedback loop that changes the surgeon and the surgery. The success of the operation is dependent on the capacity of the surgeon to maintain focus on the highest purpose while learning and changing in real-time.*
>
> *My highest life purpose is to inspire positive change. My purpose for the day was also to inspire positive change. To do it, I needed to let go of my ego and become more virtuous. I had to model the living of contrasting, positive virtues tempering each other. In this case, I had to model disciplined persistence of purpose while I modelled human sensitivity and transformational influence. I needed to simultaneously challenge and support; I needed to practice tough love.*
>
> *Conventional thinking desires to do this through authority, expertise, and telling.*[151]

So, Cultural Surgery, and now Silos? What are you talking about? Well, at its most fundamental base, organisational dysfunction, disintegration, and breakdown is something most of us will have been aware of and experienced. So how does this happen? Is it normal just because we see it everywhere? Is it inevitable? Are we just pawns in the terrible grip of the disengagement many of us feel towards the organisations we are connected to?

Let's get to grips with this latter term. Some may not have come across this before, and others will wince painfully within at its very mention due to past experiences.

"Silo" is a description that has come from business management but is now

---

[151] 'From Silos to Collaboration: The Process of Cultural Surgery', *Robert E. Quinn* <https://robertequinn.com/uncategorized/from-silos-to-collaboration-the-process-of-cultural-surgery/> [accessed 22 May 2020].

understood to be endemic in every organisation. A silo can be as small as one person, isolated on their own within the organisation, or a more substantial but still small group, maybe within an office or a specific function or department within a larger organisation.

In other words, a Silo is simply an insular, inward-focussed group of people, often in management, mostly in hierarchical organisations, who have created (sometimes deliberately, sometimes unknowingly) a negative behavioural culture that is manifested primarily by the exclusion of and towards others. Now that exclusion and exclusivity may include the exclusion of information, beliefs, finance, Mindsets, even parking spaces, and generally an inward circling effect that can be as simple and thoughtless as keeping seats around a table for friends to the exclusion of everyone else, however needy!

For individuals, it can be overwhelming and unpleasant. For organisations, it can be fatal if left unchecked.

> *Our cultures subdue the human spirits God*
> *creates through the suffocating work of the status quo.*
> *Our Christian Church systems prevent*
> *the unlocking of our potential;*
> *they prevent the discovery of purpose;*
> *they halt the transformation and growth of individuals*
> *who would otherwise grow to become*
> *the Extraordinary People God*
> *created them to be.*
> *Period.*

The Dangers – SILOS – How We Must Master Them Before They Master Us

Dr Gillian Tet is a trained anthropologist. She's no stranger to questioning the assumptions and practices of a culture. In her brilliant book, *The Silo Effect*, she writes:

We all do need to think about the cultural patterns and classification systems that we use. If we do, we can master our silos. If we do not, they will master us.[152]

We live in a world that is hyper-connected, yet often we barely know what is

---

[152] Gillian Tett, *The Silo Effect: Why Putting Everything in Its Place Isn't Such a Bright Idea.* (Little Brown Book Group, 2015), pt. 831.

happening around us. That begs the question: what can we do? We cannot entirely abolish silos any more than we could abolish electricity and maintain our modern lifestyles. Mastering silos is not a task that is ever truly completed. It is always a work in progress.[153]

We cannot live without silos in the modern world. But we can avoid succumbing to the problems they pose. Looking at how we organize the world with an insider-outsider perspective—as anthropologists do—is one way to combat the risks. Being an insider-outsider enables us to see our classification systems in context.[154]

In today's complex twenty-first-century world, we are all faced with a subtle challenge: we can either be mastered by our mental and structural silos, or we can try to master them instead. The choice lies with us. And the first step to mastering our silos is the most basic one of all: to think how we all unthinkingly classify the world around us each day. And then try to imagine an alternative.[155]

The Dangers – SILOS – How they have killed the Church in post-Christian West

All this is difficult to discuss openly, and I am well aware that we have tried to uplift and inspire so far. To allow you to go beyond this point without the dangers highlighted would be foolish and set you, the reader, up for failure. Because of my knowledge of church systems, I am using "the church" as the organisation under discussion.

Information Silos significantly and negatively impact organisations across the world along with departmental Silos. The term "Silo Mentality" refers to a group of people suffering from the hidden effects of working within this strange construct known as a "Silo". These apparently intelligent, committed, and even professional groups of people may exhibit "group thinking" inability to share information and knowledge across functions and departments, along with a similar inability to relate to the rest of the business. They may forcefully act in defence of their small group, but they also limit their thinking to the culture of the Silo.

Of course, the analogy relates to an actual vertical steel vessel used for grain storage. They may exist in considerable numbers in a grain storage facility, but they are simply self-contained containers that remain that way.

But Silos especially proliferate in the rigid structures of the traditional

---

[153] Tett, pt. 3910.
[154] Tett, pt. 3996.
[155] Tett, pt. 4034.

hierarchical Church. The official "Churches" may be described as "Super-Silos". They are simply very large Silos that are brilliant at remaining so but much less effective in impacting the world for Jesus Christ. In reality, their need to exist and retain their hierarchical systems has effectively overruled the founder's original plans, instructions and intentions.

Silos are the most lethal of all the difficulties faced, the least seen, and the most unnoticed and unaccepted enemy of Christ. And they exist surreptitiously everywhere, almost always negatively impacting the lives of every Christian alive today.

Welcome to the cancer of the Silo. The most secret and successful weapon that, if not treated early in its growth, will always insidiously impact, debilitate, potentially limit and destroy (spiritually and emotionally speaking) every individual, every local church, and every super-church denomination. Silos have the power, especially within traditional clergy-led churches, to:

- Ensure a self-contained culture within the local church Silo
- Inhibit personal growth in individuals
- Inhibit the growth of congregations
- Inhibit the unleashing of potential in individuals
- Prevent personal growth and maturity
- Limit relationships
- Polarise relationships
- Polarise groups
- Stifle innovation
- Stifle healthy debate
- Prevent questioning
- Cement the hierarchy in place
- Cement hierarchical positioning
- Give undue prominence to hierarchy and clergy
- Allow unhealthy action undertaken by favourites of the leaders
- Allow the sustaining of unhealthy cliques
- Create a glass ceiling
- Encourage virtue signalling
- Encourage small group silos
- Encourage a Silo of the church itself
- Cement current Silos
- Encourage the group to inward focus thinking
- Uphold the status quo of the inward focus

- Encourage group-think
- Institutionalise group-think
- Favour those at the pinnacle of the clergy hierarchy
- Favour their immediate circle
- Favour their supporters
- Favour certain individuals
- Encourages transactional leadership
- Prevents transformational leadership
- Create inward focus within the Silo
- Prevent innovative thinking
- Prevent global thinking
- Prevent focus on the things that matter
- Prevent understanding of the bigger picture and vision
- Foster silo limited thinking
- Create church organisation rigidity
- Allow fragmentation into sub-silos
- Shut down dissent
- Prevent questioning
- Prevent fresh thinking
- Create tunnel vision
- Create an increasingly inward-focussed culture
- Allow poor leadership to thrive
- Allow focus on what the clergy want
- Allow conflicting views to fester
- Encourage competition for a position
- Encourage sub-silos and sub-cultures to thrive
- Encourage the slow loss of the primary focus of the church
- Encourage the inward focus in contrast to the outward focus on those not yet with them
- Encourage the inward focus on the needs of the congregation
- Create cultural rigidity
- Create compliant and dependent congregations
- Create a culture of dependence on the hierarchy
- Prevent the discovery of God's purposes for the church
- Prevent the discovery of God's purposes for individuals
- Prevent the emergence of tomorrow's leaders

- Prevent the discovery of new opportunities
- Focus on system continuity
- Forget the importance of legacy creation

None of the above just happened out of the blue. Where any organisation loses its primary focus, its central vision, and its reason to exist, allied to weak and ineffective leadership, especially transactional leadership, like weeds in the garden, Silos slowly seed, grow, mature, and eventually choke the growth of other plants around them. In other words, as someone has sensibly deduced, "Churches (and their Silos) are the way they are because they have never been led to be anything else." These aspects are particularly pernicious, especially where churches describe themselves in terms such as "Church family", "Church community", etc.

> *Every week, these traditional churches run through the same sin-management routines. Parishioners turn up to seek God's forgiveness of last week's sins. They sing hymns, listen to a sermon, beseech God to bless, preserve and heal Tom, Dick and Harriet and generally use the language of scarcity and depletion in their relationship with God.*

They are never led to grow up and grow to a higher level of practice and experience. Indeed, because of the relationship between the clergy and the laity, both terms not recognised in the New Testament, they can never live the lives God always planned for them to live, and they stay in a state of suspended animation of unintended immaturity.

If anything is the basis for this cultural failure, it is in the omission of action and not necessarily any deliberate acts of cultural vandalism that allow Silos to succeed in their deadly work in organisations. It is the blind and unquestioning acceptance of current culture in any organisation that creates its eventual collapse.

Congregations collude unknowingly with the clergy in their own inward-looking culture of compliance, passivity, dependence, and continuity, leading to further helplessness and their eventual demise. If you asked any of these groups to state their purpose, it would likely be in terms of "showing God's love to others". Something nice, warm, fuzzy, woolly, and totally lacking Christ-honouring commitment. It would not be in terms of "reaching out" or "leading irreligious people to faith in Christ".

If churches and their leaders fail to continually and frequently check out where they are compared to the original intentions, design, and practice of the founder, they will always tend to conform to the culture they have allowed. In other words, "You get what you allow in Leadership."

Don't make all of this complicated. Human society always defaults to carrying on what it has always done. Doing nothing to change or improve is the default. Don't rock the boat, keep things on an even keel, and other nautical analogies are the order of the day.

Equally true, if you do not know where you are headed, you cannot set a course. And famously, you will be all at sea and going around in circles unless the organisation has a crystal-clear vision and direction supported by defined values. We may find a commonality of experience in these simple, almost homespun truths, but "you get what you allow". No one else can be blamed!

The inescapable conclusion is that unless you weed your garden, it will be overrun by weeds that continuously grow unless kept in check. They can only be kept in check by carefully weeding from time to time. This is a never-ending battle.

None of this is rocket science. But most of us simply accept in churches that because a culture exists, it exists in stone. Most people will literally fight to keep it that way. They will metaphorically "kill" to get their own way, which is usually the continuance of the status quo.

Now that we understand better the fatal effects of Silos and organisational hierarchy, it is obvious why Christ bursts on the scenes of His time and why He does what He does. He deliberately moves beyond and bypasses the culture of His day to start His Church. He is biting in His condemnation of the dress- and status-coded religious hierarchy of His birth culture. He takes no prisoners as He successfully connects with those not yet with Him in His Church. One may ask the entirely understandable question why our major traditional churches are still run by dress- and status-coded religious hierarchies, the sort against which Christ railed?

There is a better way.

Professor Quinn Blogs:

> *People often speak to me about the problem of silos. Their organization lacks collaboration. To imbue an organization with purpose is to create a climate of shared intention. Each person understands the collective purpose and sees how their individual tasks contribute to that purpose. The people create a positive organization, and silos disappear. Unfortunately, this seldom happens. Culture prevents it.*
> *In order to survive, animals are constantly scanning for threat. By detecting danger early, they can react in a way that allows them to survive. The same is true for us. If we are standing in a corner reading a book and suddenly we hear screeching brakes, we look up*

and assess the possible danger. In capturing human attention, negative cues are more powerful than positive cues.

If we are in a meeting and the boss loses his or her temper with a colleague, we glance at each other with knowing looks. While the boss did not intend it, his or her expression of negativity just set an expectation that is likely to become a boundary. Our fear is going to keep us from going anywhere near the line just crossed by our colleague.

The existing culture is the collective comfort zone. In most organisations, we tend to stay on the path of least resistance: we do that which is safe. While we claim to value the creation of new outcomes or contributions, our behaviour often demonstrates self-interested risk avoidance.

Living in this organized hypocrisy gives rise to a severe problem. The external context keeps changing, and the organization does not adapt. The organization becomes dis-integrated or unaligned with the external world. Silos arise. This increasing dis-integration requires that we practice further self-deception and tends to lead to a loss of energy. Centred on our comfort, we languish and stagnate. We do not reach our individual or collective potential.[156]

Only the emergence of authentic Transformational Leadership will make the difference.

Transformational Leadership

Given all the above salutary warnings of hierarchies, silos and fixed Mindsets, is it impossible to transform organisations so that they do not lose vision, focus or momentum and success?

The good news is that it certainly is possible. It is doable, but it will not be easy. We must transform and transition from transactional to Transformational! The old normal must envision a better way. We must use our minds to imagine the better way of Jesus that has been hidden for centuries. Since I love lists to help give a bigger overall perspective, here is one for the Transformational Leader. A Transformational Leader must:

➤ **Transform themselves first, then:**
  ➤ Move outside experience, convention and normal expectations

---

[156] 'The Source of Silo Behavior', *Robert E. Quinn* <https://robertequinn.com/uncategorized/the-source-of-silo-behavior/> [accessed 26 May 2020].

- ➤ Initiate and Inspire transformations to positive change and growth
- ➤ Expand awareness
- ➤ Engage and expand hearts and minds
- ➤ Encourage Shared purpose
- ➤ **Envision a better way**
  - ➤ Create experiences that change beliefs
  - ➤ Change from the usual hierarchy and conflict to authentic collaboration
  - ➤ Become high on task and high on people
  - ➤ Model disciplined persistence of purpose
- ➤ **Co-create a new culture and behavioural contract**
  - ➤ Co-create a new vision and strategy for transforming themselves
  - ➤ Co-create a new vision and strategy for transforming the world
  - ➤ Co-create a new vision and strategy for transforming Others
  - ➤ Get out of their way!

All at the same time!

Let's remind ourselves what "normal culture" looks like through the Transactional Mindset. The transactional Mindset is based on the "normal" assumptions of:

- Hierarchy
- Positions
- Status
- Potential for conflict
- The layering of people, especially of ability, social standing and usefulness to the system
- Pecking orders exist
- Fixed Mindsets are just that
- People cannot grow or change
- People stay where they are
- People have value insofar as they are useful to the system
- Some are elevated if they are useful to the system
- Others are discarded or left behind as of no use to the system
- Positive attempts to change and challenge the system are met with fierce opposition
- These people are marked as troublemakers to be avoided, excluded and eliminated

And all the above is assumed subconsciously! All this is normal! But is it? We know these things, but they rarely surface in our consciousness. In a "normal" transactional culture, people are subservient to the system; the system is foremost, and they collectively die because they can never grow.

In any system, if you are not growing, then you are slowly dying, mentally and spiritually.

Most people and their potential are, therefore:

1. Trapped under layer upon layer of cultural expectations and limitations that preclude breakout
2. Locked behind doors that hold them and stop any potential for Transformation and Growth
3. Submerged under their own misrecognition of the intentions of the system
4. Held back by their personal self-assumed untrue stories of their histories

We can only grow when we choose to transform ourselves and move from transactional leadership to transformational leadership.

In transformational cultures, people are foremost. These people recognise that they are designed for Transformation and Growth, and they seek to improve their capacity continually. More than that, they choose to lift Others along with them.

Growth is simply: **"Growing to Become the Masterpiece You Were Created to Be."**

> *But the concept of challenging and changing culture is unknown, it is foreign. It is no exaggeration to state that the conventional mind cannot conceive either the need, the possibility or even the actuality of carrying out such a concept. So, it is impossible, using the conventional mental map to achieve solid, lasting change, let alone transformation. It does not compute or make conventional sense. That is why it is strongly resisted because path dependence, the misrecognition of the hierarchy, and the status quo, and the silos prevent change however necessary and desirable it may be.*

Seeing The Whole

The Overall Picture:

Personally uniquely created by God for:

✓ Personal faith in Jesus Christ

- ✓ Personal responsibility in seeking God
- ✓ Personal greatness for God through becoming a servant
- ✓ Personal Calling that comes from God
- ✓ Personal Purpose that is for God
- ✓ Personal Leadership that influences others for God
- ✓ To personally inspire others to do the same

Discover God's Purpose for you and me to inspire others to do likewise.

The Big "But"

We have moved an enormous distance from the intentionality of Christ because the "Church", far from desiring and seeing transformed lives as the intentions of Christ, actively subverts and continues with its attendees and adherents to its own perverted form of apostolic Christianity, which can be named as "Churchianity". Congregations collude unknowingly in their own disempowerment with the clergy in their own inward-looking culture of community with compliance, passivity, dependence, conformity and continuity, leading to further helplessness and their eventual demise. The result is a frightening dependency that leads to failure as the inevitable result.

The Big Picture:

The most significant problem for the traditional church is staticity. Continuity of the church systems is the focus and, with it, the fatal pew mentality. The people cannot get anywhere near where God would have them be despite their best efforts and the urging of the clergy class from the front of the church. They are led down a one-way tunnel towards an inward-focussed community. And when they get there, they can only stay there, their inward focus getting worse week by week.

It is like a golf game where no layperson (a term unknown in the New Testament) can hole the putts. They can get it close, but the ball never rolls in. In fact, because of the nature of ordained clergy who manage this unbiblical system, they are not even allowed to be on the green! That is the analogy. How can we avoid the clergy class always leaving their congregations dependent and compliant in this God-dishonouring system? Its effect is spiritual abuse across the Church, which does not have to be.

Now, I am sure that very little of this is deliberate, except for a few people who love the power and the position. Most clergy are hardworking and indefatigable, becoming worn out and exhausted by the continuous care they express for their church. But if they were cognizant of the extreme nature of the adverse effects they unknowingly unleash on congregations, they would immediately seek God's better way for them to follow.

Individuals and congregations need to become fully committed to God in their daily lives. The Church of Jesus Christ was never about them and their needs. The sooner they realise that, the better. The everyday cross-hoisting of lives not just "surrendered" but "fully committed" to God and the actions He asks of them is the vital precursor to a God-centred life laid down for His Glory. The recent concept of "surrender" appears to have come from revival and evangelistic "meetings" where it was a device for a decision for Christ. God's word uses "full commitment" as a more intentional and, ultimately, game-changing concept. In scripture, people who had taken that "fully committed" decision for God early in their lives changed the Future.

The Big Difficulties:
- **Complete mismanagement** by the unbiblical, hierarchical, dress-coded clergy class who effectively glass ceiling their "position". Their system focus is primarily on community. This is transactional management and relies on the clergy/laity divide. A division between Christians that has no precedence in scripture because it was unacceptable to Jesus.
- **Completely wrong focus** by keeping the "Churchianity" creaking on with systems of belief, creeds, effectively sin management with absolution still present, and church "attendance" leading to community, togetherness, dependence and compliance, rather than the biblical relationship with God that Christ focussed on. Congregations and individuals become like children who can never grow up and reach maturity.
- **Completely wrong choice** of leading or allowing their congregations to choose comfort over courage.

> *"We can choose courage or we can choose comfort, but we can't have both."*
> *Dr. Brene Brown, Rising Strong*

(Above quotation cited below. [157])

The Big Solution:
- ➤ **Institute Inspirational Transformational Leadership** compared to traditional transactional management.

---

[157] Brené Brown, *Rising Strong*, 2015, p. 4.

> ➢ **Lead the people** (make the big ask) as Christ did to the choice for full commitment to God.
> ➢ **Lead the people** to break out from poor leadership, mediocrity and inward focus.
> ➢ **Lead the people** to start and continue moving on the journey God always planned for them, embedding scripture in their underpinning thinking to encourage God's outworking in their lives.
> ➢ **Lead the people** to discover their potential.
> ➢ **Lead the people** to discover God's purposes for them.
> ➢ **Lead the people** to their destiny.
> ➢ **Lead the people** to step out and step up to new levels of commitment.
> ➢ **Lead the people** to their release for leadership where they are.
> ➢ **Lead the people** to connect effectively with others who are not yet with us and lead for legacy.

Lead the people as Christ did. Lead at every opportunity. I think you get the message. Our Churchianity systems perversely create inward focus, dependence, compliance and continuity. Christ would have none of it.

The Leadership And Mindset Of Christ

God created us for His purposes, His vision and His destiny; for consecration and dedication with courage, connection and commitment to Him; to lead lives that are consequential for Him. They are to be lives dedicated to God. They are to be lives of wholehearted connection with God. We are created to be inspired and transformed, not fearful. Christ restores us in Himself to God.

Before time began, God started the process of:

- ❖ Creation, which man spoils and then, at last, He completes His plan of
- ❖ Redemption for mankind through the death of His Son Jesus Christ that precedes His great Plan for
- ❖ Transformation of Individuals who were chosen before time began, which
- ❖ Christ recommenced to complete,
- ❖ To be Conformed to the Image of Christ
- ❖ For God's Glory for Eternity

Transformation in individuals of:

- ✓ Purpose
- ✓ Character
- ✓ Thinking
- ✓ Acting

The Leadership of Christ is all about Transformation. To this end, He is continually:

252

✓ Living the Life He is created humanly for
✓ Understanding the Big Picture
✓ Thinking and acting at a higher level
✓ Keeping momentum by seeing and seizing opportunities
✓ Focussed
✓ Preventing the culture from dragging Him back

At no stage does He stop doing all the above, but the question of "how" He continues is significant. Christ starts transforming people from "the inside out". So, He connects with individuals and immediately shakes their thinking to grab their attention. He transcends His own culture to associate Himself with them and redirect their focus towards God, His Father. He is utterly focussed on and dedicated to the transformation of people and enabling their growth.

Jesus's Life of Leadership, Purpose, Values and Vision, How he lived, and the life He invites us all to live, and as Creator and Head of the Church, His Body, He is literally essential to every person alive today, and never more so than in His Church.

Because if we cannot effectively emulate what He did, then we have no legitimacy for our work in the local church. Asking relevant questions (to spotlight the irrelevant) may well be awkward, difficult and probably life-changing for many of us. As we confront what it is we do in whatever our local culture is, why we do it, and discover the irrelevance of much of it, only then can we start the long road back to the Christ-centred living of His understanding, His focus, His intentionality, His action and His results.

He is not only creating discipleship in us, but He is also calling us to become His vital friends, and He is focussed on developing tomorrow's leaders who will cascade that focus to the next generation. He is focussed on people and their growth in Him.

> *Transformational Leadership will be needed to kick start individuals and congregations on the journey.*
> *Specifically the journey to discover and*
> *unlock their potential and purpose for God.*
> *To discover what God has called them to do, and how to do it.*

Christ's awareness, engagement, thinking, wholeheartedness, clarity of mind, His capacity and speed at which He makes His astounding behavioural choices are legendary in scripture. But most importantly, his assumptions are the complete opposite of His people, His culture, and the political situation in which He grew up. Everywhere around Him are those who wish to control, manipulate, and effectively diminish and often destroy others, whether they are religious or civil authority.

Jesus is the exact opposite. He is going to multiply Himself through His Church. His assumptions are based on God, His Father's thinking, and it is simply this. He has come to "seek and save that which was lost". Don't make the false assumption that you know those words only in the context of salvation from sin. Jesus is focussed on people and their relational response to Him, and not just their salvation. Because it is also the context of the restoration of their God-created lives both now and for Eternity. It was no coincidence that Jesus uttered those words after His meeting with Zacchaeus. At the moment of their meeting, this man was one of the most despised and socially peripheral people amongst his contemporaries, but God had plans and big plans for him as a person.

Welcome to the Higher Purpose life that you were created for by God in Christ. He discovers His Higher Purpose, He lives for that Higher Purpose, He loves for that Higher Purpose, He leads for that Higher Purpose, He Prays for that Higher Purpose, and He dies for that Higher Purpose.

And the only question here is, "What was it that He had discovered?" It was that He, Jesus, was The Christ, and His Purpose was to recreate and connect people back to God, and to conform people to His Image. Absolutely central to that Purpose is this profoundly simple core aspect, the truth that "People Matter".

> *God created us for His purposes,*
> *His vision and His destiny;*
> *for consecration and dedication with courage,*
> *connection and commitment to Him;*
> *to lead lives that are courageous and consequential for Him.*
> *They are to be lives of wholehearted connection with God.*
> *We are created to be inspired and transformed, not fearful.*
> *Christ restores us in Himself to God.*

Jesus commences His public life (called His Ministry – but in fact, it is far greater than that) and immediately:

> ➤ **N.B. He had already discovered His Purpose at age 12. Luke 2:46.**
>   > ➤ He discovers who He is and His Father's Business. Luke 2:46.
>   > ➤ He fully understands who He is and, more importantly, why He exists.

- ➢ He becomes fully aware and wholly engaged in His life's work, purpose and destiny.
- ➢ That business is the transformation of people, one person at a time.
- ➢ **He is now entirely focussed on His Father's business.**
  - ➢ He discovers His Father's Purpose and His Father's Plans for Him. Luke 2:49.
  - ➢ He discovered what was already present and awaiting Him. He did not invent it. Luke 2:49.
  - ➢ He lives for Higher Purpose, His Father's will, "not mine, but your will be done". Mark 14:36.
  - ➢ He is laser-focussed on His Purpose for God, His Father.
  - ➢ He is laser-focussed on people, their growth and their legacy for God.
  - ➢ He continually clarifies that Purpose. Matthew 17:22.
- ➢ **He is the ultimate transformational leader, not the normal transactional manager.**
  - ➢ He lives with and exhibits perfect integrity.
  - ➢ He lives with and exhibits perfect vulnerability. Matthew 18:3-5.
  - ➢ He chooses to be vulnerable to carry out His Father's Purpose.
  - ➢ He focuses on God's plans and purposes in the ordinary and also the extreme times
- ➢ **He is Wholeheartedly Committed with Courage, Compassion and Connection.**
  - ➢ He is consciously consecrated and decisively dedicated to God, His Father.
  - ➢ He is authentically engaged – He chooses to if need be, embrace pain and sacrifice pleasure.
  - ➢ He is "fully engaged" and "continually renewed".
  - ➢ He seizes the initiative.
- ➢ **He seeks to unlock potential and create personal growth in everyone He meets and connects with.**
  - ➢ He recognises strengths in people, not weaknesses, and builds on them.
  - ➢ He seeks to connect everyone to God through Himself. John 14:6.
  - ➢ He has made a conscious decision already to rise out of and move beyond His birth Culture.
  - ➢ He then dangerously ignores His birth and simply bypasses culture and convention.
- ➢ **He calls individuals to Himself.**
  - ➢ He imparts the staggering truth in calling fishermen, tax collectors and other people of low social standing that "who you are is immeasurably

more important than what you know", or your social status or your wealth. In complete comparison, our "Churchianity" culture is based around clergy and their hierarchy, position, status, knowledge, and power that flows only down from the top.

➢ **He then continually reinforces all the above as He speaks and teaches and heals.**

> ➢ He uses the language of abundance and surplus as He speaks, teaches and prays (we use the language of scarcity and depletion, especially in prayer).
>
> ➢ We pride ourselves on being a "knowing and believing" organisation in the Church. This is inadequate simply because God has always called us to be a "learning and growing" organisation as we are transformed by Him.
>
> ➢ Christ points to the simple fact that bricks and mortar will collapse and be replaced.
>
> ➢ In the "normal" UK experience, we "think" that the Church is the destination. Wrong. See the next point.

➢ **Transformed people living transforming lives in Him are Christ's intention. These then produce others who, likewise, are committed to the transformational pathway.**

> ➢ He creates and expects His transformed people to be like Him, understand and think like Him, and act like Him with understanding, focus and intentionality.
>
> ➢ He lives in a full-time value-finding mode.
>
> ➢ He refuses to judge anyone. He has a zero-based strengths perspective.

➢ **He does not condemn but encourages constructive direction.**

> ➢ He challenges and changes culture.
>
> ➢ He helps people transform themselves from their conventional cultural Mindset.
>
> ➢ He helps people transform themselves into a Christ-centred Mindset.
>
> ➢ He embodied the scriptural and Godly notion of Personal Responsibility before God.

➢ **He calls people to His higher purpose. John 14:1.**

> ➢ He kick-starts "Cultural Transformation".
>
> ➢ He is wholeheartedly focussed on other people.
>
> ➢ He is in the people-building business.
>
> ➢ He seeks to connect people to their God-planned purpose.
>
> ➢ He sees unlimited potential in other people.
>
> ➢ He seeks to unlock that potential in people.

➤ **He engages Others' hearts, minds and souls as has no other.**
  ➤ He lives the profoundly simple truth that "Everyone Matters".
  ➤ He challenges Church systems.
  ➤ He does not compel people to be subservient to a Church system.
  ➤ He does not subjugate people to a Church system or any other system of authority.
  ➤ He asks questions and gives them as gifts.
➤ **He helps His people fulfil the purposes of God in their lifetime.**
  ➤ He does not condemn people. John 4:17-18.
  ➤ He encourages people when they stumble. John 21:15-18.
  ➤ He cares for the well-being of all.
  ➤ He acts and speaks to others in such extraordinary ways that people have never seen before.
  ➤ He connects people with God's purposes, which draw out purpose and destiny.
  ➤ He "grows" His own mind in His people by example.
➤ **He leads people to discover Himself, who He really is.**
  ➤ He leads people to discover their purpose.
  ➤ He leads people to discover His Father.
  ➤ He leads people to reconnect to God, which is the greatest result ever.
  ➤ He creates a Living Legacy of Leadership.

> *His thinking, focus and intentionality are seismically different to our accepted culture and thinking, which is primarily to "Do Church on our Terms", because that is what we do and we focus on getting people to attend church (the building), and we will never understand the reality of God's intentionality, as shown in Christ, that we "are" the church and "transformation" is God's primary focus and game plan.*

So, far from focussing on the people who come through our church doors, helpful as that may be, we need to be transformed in our thinking to "see" the process of transformation as one of connection first, assimilation second, and then accountability third. This will ensure that their movement/journey of personal transformation is a continuum. We need to understand that the model of "Churchianity" we blindly follow every week is no longer the model that carries on what Christ started (if it ever did).

257

The focus on the weekly Sunday morning Protestant service has become a dangerous distraction because it focuses the local church on a resource-costly repetition that forces dependent congregations to sit passively in rows being "taught" by dress-coded paid professionals. This is traditional Christian "worship". Nothing fundamentally wrong with that, you may ask, is there? Read your Bible through opened eyes, strip away the cloying effect of your current culture and "see" through Christ's eyes His intentionality as He connects with individuals.

The result of this system and systemic slavery is horrific, both in results and implications. Dependent congregations are kept in this mode by default, not intention. The focus is on this weekly event, and not the focus of Christ, which is individual transformation for life through a relationship of permanent connection with Him and then seeking to connect with others for Him so that they, too, would join Him.

What on Earth is He doing?
- ✓ The Son of God comes to the earth to be about His Father's Business.
- ✓ He discovers His Position and Purpose at the age of Twelve.
- ✓ He then spent nearly 20 years preparing Himself before bursting onto the World stage.
- ✓ He has a specific plan for the world
- ✓ He has a specific plan for His new Leaders
- ✓ He has a specific plan for His Church

And:
- ✓ Everything He does and also does not do is intentional.
- ✓ Everything He does and does not do is not incidental.
- ✓ Everything He does and does not do is predestined, predetermined and calculated.
- ✓ Nothing he does is without intention. We were told at Sunday School that Jesus went about doing good, right? Absolutely wrong. He did not wander aimlessly. Everything He said and did was uniquely aligned with His Purpose.
- ✓ He is ruthlessly focussed and intentional on two aspects: His Mission and Transforming His People.
- ✓ He came to enable and give people Life in all its Fullness.
- ✓ He specifically connects, by intention and design, with His people.
- ✓ Every one of His Disciples gets an individual call that is for no one else.
- ✓ He deliberately connects with individuals in their own individual way.
- ✓ He grows everyone with Purpose.

- ✓ Everyone is grown relationally to Christ.
- ✓ Everyone He calls is involved in His Church.
- ✓ No one is to be above another.
- ✓ He deliberately inspires others to action for His Glory and His Church.
- ✓ He deliberately connects with individuals so that they belong.
- ✓ There are no outcasts with Jesus.

This is no ordinary Man. He has moved out of His birth culture, and He creates a new one in the individuals whose lives He touches. Fundamentally, Christ establishes a culture of:

- ✓ Connection, firstly to Himself and His Father, secondly with others
- ✓ Belonging
- ✓ Growth
- ✓ Love with:
- ✓ Respect
- ✓ Compassion
- ✓ Shared purpose
- ✓ Shared Vision
- ✓ Shared knowledge
- ✓ Mutual respect
- ✓ Inspiration
- ✓ Renewal with:
- ✓ Seeing their potential
- ✓ Unlocking their potential for God
- ✓ Helping them discover their gifts and talents for God
- ✓ A Mindset of growth

In other words he is not "ministering",
not in any shape or form. He is transforming people,
through a new transforming culture, identity and "language" in
ways no one has seen before or since.
Therefore, we need to be transformed by Christ,
rising above the culture we inhabit, and in doing so,
we escape to live the lives He has already planned for us to live, as
He intended and spoke about.

So, here are the big-picture aspects of Jesus's personal life:

❖ Jesus, as the incarnation of God, was a uniquely created human being.

❖ He discovered His Purpose around the age of twelve years.

❖ He lived His life in His Father, His wholeheartedness was evident to all, and His life was one of surplus and abundance, even in the midst of His death and resurrection.

❖ He was completely focussed and perfectly balanced regarding both God's eternal plans and His daily connections with others. No one was turned away, and all, especially people doing wrong, were treated with love, respect and compassion in His temporal and eternal purposes.

❖ He, alone, has the willingness and power to restore, transform and perfect (in eternity) all those who come to Him.

❖ He asks us to embrace His priorities, seek to act always in ways consonant with His priorities, and actively grow and mature continuously in Him, both as individuals and as unique members of His Church.

❖ He embodied the world-transforming purpose that His task was to help other people fulfil their God-created purpose.

❖ He was resolute, focussed, and continuously moving forwards into uncertainty, danger and opposition to fulfil His Purpose.

He is the "I AM", and He also states:

❖ I am The Christ, John 4:24

❖ I am The Light of the World, John 6:48

❖ I am The Bread of Life, John

❖ I am from above, John 8:23

❖ I am The Good Shepherd, John 10:14

❖ I am The Resurrection and The Life, John 11:25

❖ I am in The Father, John 14:11

❖ I am The Way, the Truth and The Life, John 14:6

❖ I am The True Vine, John 15:1

If we ask the "What's right?" and, "What is it that makes it right?" questions, we start to understand more easily, correctly and more emphatically what sets apart Jesus, what He was doing, how He did it and most importantly, what the outcomes were.

Note: "created in the image of God", we always need to ask the question, "If Jesus is what God is like, how are we to respond to transform ourselves in the light of that revelation?"

Wholeheartedness, as a way of living and wholehearted commitment as the outcome is crucial.

"Seeing the whole" – Jesus' life and leadership is all about connection to His

Father, to Himself, and crucially between His Disciples, those who have given their lives to Him. When Jesus taught of the Kingdom of God, He was thinking of a place where purposeful activity is taking place; thus, he creates: Caring/loving Connection, communication, collaboration, and coordination.

> **God's call to each of His People is to His Higher Purpose. It is not to a life little differentiated from the world, but crucially and overwhelmingly different by each of us discovering their God-planned purpose and in thinking and acting in a Christ-emulating manner.**
> **That is what Paul is talking about in Ephesians 10:10.**

I recently heard Josh Groban – "You Raise Me Up". Loved by many and used extensively, to me, suggests a singular lack of awareness of God's provision and scarcity in our lives such that:

- Our "normal" Christian life is based on depletion, scarcity and lack of abundance as we stumble along, our need-filled prayers and worldview reflecting those normal human life values.
- As we discover our unique purpose, we should be living lives based on God's unlimited blessings, surplus and abundance. When we live a life of wholehearted commitment, we are in full alignment with the purpose we have discovered because that creates permanent, internally sustaining commitment that brings this constant up-welling of renewed energy.
- Jesus's worldview was, despite His sacrifice, when with His disciples, seeking to grow them to understanding, maturity, and leadership. This was one of God's plans for them (with His overruling, the defeat of evil, the coming of His Spirit, the birth of His Church, the body of Christ), and lives lived in "surplus and abundance". There it is.

In his thoughtful book, *Transformational Leadership,* Kyle Patterson writes:
Connecting people with God's purposes draws out purpose and destiny. That's a leader's job, and that's what Nehemiah did. He connected hundreds of people to the vision for Jerusalem and drew out of them purpose, and they fulfilled destiny in their generation. Likewise, God's not looking for the most qualified, educated, or influential. He is looking for those with a yes in their heart to the things of God. As leaders, we must spiritually discern where people are at and, like Nehemiah, call them forth into the destiny and

calling of God.[158]

Oswald and Jacobson wrote with clarity in their book, *The Emotional Intelligence of Jesus*:
People with a scarcity mentality focus on limits, are able to see only their immediate needs, are fearful of loss, have diminished impulse control, focus on the short term, and see themselves in competition for scarce resources.
People with an abundance mentality, on the other hand, focus on possibilities and are willing to take risks. Scarcity thinkers tend to be resentful of the success of others. They are into hoarding, into defending what they have. Abundance thinkers are generous and willing to share what they have. They have confidence that there will be enough for everyone."[159]

It is becoming increasingly clear that the current world (culture) that traditional Christians inhabit, that of "church attendance" (we can call it "Churchianity") and so on, is the result of 1,800 years of misunderstanding because of the overlayering of the Graeco-Roman culture of hierarchy (including ordination as a sacrament) on the Christian culture of that time. This effectively overwhelmed, sidelined and then largely destroyed what Christ and the Apostles had intended in scripture. After all the momentous upheavals of the Reformation, we have ended up with a national Church that is, in every practical estimation, dedicated only to "continuity in community".

Frank Viola, in his book, *Reimagining Church*, rather subversively but very effectively writes, quoting Christian Smith:
The clergy profession is fundamentally self-defeating. Its stated purpose is to nurture spiritual maturity in the church— a valuable goal. In actuality, however, it accomplishes the opposite by nurturing a permanent dependence of the laity on the clergy.
Clergy become to their congregations like parents whose children never grow up, therapists whose clients never become healed, and teachers whose students never graduate. The existence of a full-time, professional minister makes it too easy for church members not to take responsibility for the ongoing life of the church. And why should they? That's the job of the pastor (so the thinking goes). But the result is that the laity remains in a state of passive dependence.[160]

---

[158] Kyle Patterson, *Transformational Leadership* (Independently published), p. 48.
[159] Roy M. Oswald, *The Emotional Intelligence of Jesus: Relational Smarts for Religious Leaders* (Lanham: Rowman & Littlefield, 2015), pt. 537.
[160] Frank Viola, *Reimagining Church: Pursuing the Dream of Organic Christianity.* (David C. Cook, 2012), pt. 2037.

"The sad comment for most individual churches where struggle is occurring, where the Vicar/Pastor/Minister, etc. is worn out and disillusioned, where the congregation retains its fatal inward focus is that if only the leader could have understood that his purpose is to lead his people to discover their God-created purpose(s). God has provided in His people an extraordinary potential and capacity for vision, action, caring and creativity along with their hands, heads, and hearts if only they had known how to ask." – Anon.

> *"The quickest way to reinvigorate a plateaued or declining church is to reclaim God's purpose for it and help the members understand the great tasks the church has been given by Christ."*

(Above quotation cited. [161])

Dr Rick Warren helpfully shows in his book, *The Purpose Driven Church*: *"Leading your congregation through a discovery of the New Testament purposes for the church is an exciting adventure. Don't rush through the process. And don't spoil the joy of discovery by simply telling everyone what the purposes are in a sermon. Wise leaders understand that people will give mental and verbal assent to what they are told, but they will hold with conviction what they discover for themselves. You're building a foundation for long-term health and growth."* [162]

It is the illusion of spirituality and leadership that the clergy effect to create in their hierarchical system. Power can only flow vertically downwards from these people. This creates a deeply distorted impact on churches and diminishes everyone. The diminisher and one who kills ideas and who focuses on system continuance at the expense of growing people is effectively saying, "I don't need or even want your input."

True Multiplier leaders like Christ grow everyone because they are seen as equally important, have hidden potential that calls out and needs to be unlocked, and each has a unique part to play in their response to God's calling.

Primary Question: what are the evident assumptions that Christ makes about His people?

❖ They are essential to God

---

[161] Rick Warren, *The Purpose Driven Church: Growth without Compromising Your Message & Mission* (Grand Rapids, Mich.: Zondervan Pub., 1995), p. 87.
[162] Warren, *The Purpose Driven Church*, p. 96.

- ❖ They are worth dying for
- ❖ They already exist, and He finds them

So, what is important in all of this stuff?

- ❖ My purpose: To engage in and seek Revitalisation through the Transformation of the Church of Jesus Christ in the World.
- ❖ Embrace and discover God's revealed priorities and purposes in His Son Jesus Christ.
- ❖ Ephesians 1:11. So we must understand God's purposes first, then discover His purposes for us as unique individuals.
- ❖ Ephesians 2:10. We are recreated in Christ Jesus.

Some vital ingredients:

- ❖ The Great Commandments and the Great Commission are central.
- ❖ People who have discovered their higher purpose in Christ.
- ❖ Servant Leadership - anyone who holds him or herself accountable for finding potential in people and processes and seeks to connect people to their purpose.
- ❖ Transformational culture changers.
- ❖ Wholeheartedness and Wholehearted Living with Courage, Compassion and Connection.
- ❖ Full engagement that continually reverses disengagement in our organisations, churches and communities.
- ❖ Authenticity Living and Authentic Connection
- ❖ Understanding before being understood
- ❖ Deep Listening and valuing others
- ❖ Clarity of vision
- ❖ Action in Teams
- ❖ Externally open
- ❖ Internally driven by their core beliefs
- ❖ Other focussed
- ❖ Purpose-driven

Our normal way of life shows the Conventional Mental Map of (church) culture, presenting notions of:

- ≤ Hierarchy – a pyramid-shaped organisation.
- ≤ Position – layered authority led by a person at the top who has power.
- ≤ Power – the ability and function to use it for control.
- ≤ Control – those beneath the leader must be controlled and directed by those who "know".
- ≤ Knowledge is power.

≤ Information flows down to those who need to know.
≤ Leadership is a position of authority directing others.
≤ Leaders are focussed on problem-solving using people.
≤ People get privileges based on their perceived status.
≤ A few people are close to the Leader and the hierarchy, and others feel excluded.
≤ Change is conceived at the top and driven down the system to those who need to know.
≤ Management and clergy specialist control.
≤ Fear, especially of getting things wrong, but also of being Christians in a hostile world.
≤ Scarce resources focus.
≤ Conflict avoidance by allowing issues to fester.
≤ Focus on problem-solving.
≤ Organisational predictability.
≤ Confusion and chaos.
≤ The delusion of doing church on our terms.
≤ Exhaustion, both personal and corporate.

And Our People:
≤ Disengage and withdraw.
≤ Suffer exclusion.
≤ Personally stagnate.
≤ Pursue self-interest.
≤ Live with an inward focus.
≤ Engage in self-absorbed conflict.
≤ Minimise personal cost.
≤ Are fearful.
≤ Prefer the status quo.
≤ Stay in their roles.
≤ Speak in politically correct ways.
≤ Compete for scarce resources.
≤ Experience conflict.
≤ Complain about leadership because of the above situation.
≤ Triangulate by discussing with others the problems they see but cannot solve.
≤ Triangulate because leaders are deaf and blind to solutions.

The conventional mind, seeing to some degree each or all of these aspects, simply and automatically chooses to apply more of the same thinking that created all the above.

Thus, hierarchical positioning, control, micro-management, creation of greater predictability, procedural compliance, and cost control lead to a stifling bureaucracy, rigidity, and scapegoating of individuals who are perceived to be part of the problems, not the solution, which is normal. These normal actions are blindly followed in the (vain) hope by (Christian) leaders that just once in a lifetime, something may change, and the organisation may be turned around from negativity and hopelessness to "success".

> *Jesus goes much further.*
> *His primary task through Courage, Compassion,*
> *and connection is to carry out His Father's plans for Him*
> *and the world and connect himself with people, and then help*
> *connect those people with God.*
> *Along that road is the connection of His people*
> *to their purpose.*

Does this define the life of Jesus? I believe it does insofar that we can ever discover what drives the Triune God. And "Vulnerability" is the key that allows us to unlock the door to understanding the truth about Jesus and His life, example, purpose and ultimate success.

A dictionary definition of *vulnerability is from the Latin word "vulnerare", which means "capable of being physically or emotionally wounded" or "open to attack or damage".*

So, it is evident that we have utterly mistaken vulnerability for weakness, and it is true that weakness can ensue from a lack of vulnerability.

I believe the primary reason for the ongoing catastrophe occurring in the Church of Jesus Christ in the post-Christian West is "Disengagement". Disengagement follows disconnection as night follows day. Disconnection starts the moment leadership stops its true function of connecting people to their purpose to grow and morphs into the management of people where they are treated as objects to solve management problems, or worse still, subjects of "Sin Management".

Leaders need to begin moving to a transformed organisation by dealing a death blow to the conventional organisation, nurturing authentic conversations and connections. Encourage people to find their "voice". The opposite of posturing is authentic connection and conversations. These come about when people in a group are invited to reflect, assess and publicly own their shortcomings and declare what personal changes they are willing to make to bring about the collective future they desire. When conversation and group discussion are so real, people are held accountable both by themselves and their group to their deepest moral responsibility or personal vision.

Because of fear and posturing, people can never commit to a higher cause until they ask themselves to commit. Again, our quiet friend in the background, vulnerability, is the key to starting the changes that a group of people need. Authenticity gives rise to cultural change.

Emotional Intelligence

Emotional intelligence is part of understanding Jesus's Leadership, but vulnerability is the foundation. Jesus comes, he connects, he creates.

He has an abundance mentality, not a scarcity mentality.

He creates a unique community where everyone is treated as a full human being. No one is disregarded, sidelined, underutilised or left behind. And he creates connection through authenticity. Authentic connection is the bedrock of the church of Jesus Christ.

He also speaks a language that is fundamentally different from the culture he was in and the culture where we are.

Key leadership suggestion for Jesus' style – he perfectly demonstrated how to lead/grow his own guys using methods effective for their needs and God's plans for them.

And interestingly, look at Jesus and Zacchaeus – what a fascinating example of Jesus alert to and interacting with marginalised and peripheral people, calling them by name and making sure they are included and matter. He makes sure they are central.

Pastors – You seek to Love like Jesus, You seek to Live like Jesus, You seek to liberate sinners like Jesus, and now is the time to Lead like Jesus. "But I am," you protest. Who are you, Richard Flew, to counsel or tell me something I am not doing? Righteous indignation and hurt will be a normal reaction. I understand your reaction, your outrage, your indignation, your exasperation. You exclaim, "I cannot do any more; I am flat out and fast on the way to burnout and perhaps physical and mental collapse."

Pastors, Vicars and current church leaders – You are fully committed to your calling, you are beyond conscientious in undertaking that calling, you are caring beyond belief.

But you are slowly, irrevocably, and irreversibly killing the church you lead.

I believe with all my heart that if you can embrace the concept that there is a way forward that requires you to transform your thinking and focus, you can see change, improvements and transformation. There is good news for you. Start the painful process of Transforming the way you think and work. Change from traditional management methods to Jesus Leadership.

Can I suggest you consider leading like Jesus by Unlocking Potential in People? The purpose of leadership is foremost to create new leaders who understand that!

> *The high cost of both lack of leadership and bad leadership is found in people and specifically in their feelings.*
> *Get leadership right and anything is possible.*
> *Get it wrong, and the decline and possible destruction of your organisation, your church, or your business is assured.*

As Dr Henry Cloud shows:

In the end, as a leader, you are always going to get a combination of two things: What you create and what you allow. Good leadership boundaries give direction, establishing norms and behaviours that drive success. They build unity and energy, focusing that energy and attention on what is important. They build optimism and empower people to do what they have to do. They set conditions and standards for great teams and culture. On the flip side, good leadership boundaries diminish bad behaviour and forge an immune system that automatically Identifies, isolates, and stamps out toxins, infections, or other viral patterns that make the organisation sick or lead it away from its values, mission, purpose and results.[163]

Wow! What clarity.

So, the effects of poor or non-existent leadership are found in the people who have suffered it. As listed above, feelings lead to disaffection, dissatisfaction, being disrespected, rejection, feeling diminished, unwanted, unloved, isolated, uncared-for, unrecognised, anger, frustration, pain, anguish, unworthiness, confusion, despair (yes, there are that many and more).

---

[163] Cloud, pp. 14–18.

These are normal feelings when good leadership is lacking. They are often accompanied by the complicating emotions of personal guilt (this is my fault), depression (I can't help feeling this way), hatred (focussing my anger and frustration on others), and seeking relief from the situation either by being a thorn in an organisation (getting your own back) or planning an exit strategy (removal from the painful experience). The last aspect, the exit strategy, is almost inevitable. God never designed His Church to be like this.

These feelings come inevitably as a result of leadership that allows these feelings to occur. Remember, leaders get both what they create _and_ what they allow. But how come this is all so unseen?

Instead, so often, churches have to be content with the less-than-adequate control of a leader who vainly imagines that directive management and "nice" people manipulation is the way to go. It is the road to deep unhappiness for those who would and did seek to give their all for God in the church they were called to serve. These faithful people were destroyed by directive leadership that, unknown to the leader, diminished those being managed and left them sidelined as favourites took their place, and bad management created dysfunctional leadership throughout the church. They were left feeling let down, unworthy and discarded. Worse still was the feeling that they were wrong to have these feelings, and blamed themselves!

It surely cannot go unnoticed that Jesus, as He built His team, did not suffer any of these issues. If ever there was a case of the blindingly obvious, this is it.

Leaders who do not and will not have the humility to deeply respect and genuinely listen to learn from those they lead together fool no one but themselves. Instead, their legacy is often dysfunction, dissatisfaction, and unhappiness, while they blithely battle on stubbornly regardless of the chaos and confusion they give birth to. One can only conclude this delusion that they are right, masquerading under humility, is arrogance hidden under Christian love.

People are uniquely able to reflect and turn the pain of painful experiences into positive outcomes.

For those involved with churches, this is my take on the basics of church transformation – this is where it can begin, and without a deep understanding of the implications of these simple definitions, nothing can change. It is all about effective leaders and their effective leadership.

Patrick Lencioni says, "Why should someone want to become a leader? Because they want to sacrifice themselves for the well-being of others, even when they don't know whether they will get any return on that investment."[164]

---

[164] '2014 GLS Highlight', _Dotsub_ <https://dotsub.com/view/359fba1a-0d3f-4e05-9021-e085d5e56137> [accessed 7 August 2020].

It is heartbreakingly sad to compare the prescriptive reasons that Vicars exist. These are very important, but Jesus's leadership is all about focus and people.

From Bishop Alan Wilson's Blog:

> *What are parish clergy actually there to do? The answer lies in Canon C24 of the Church of England. Such is the variety of circumstances in which clergy work that these norms are indicative, taken in context, not exhaustive and literally applied. Bear in mind that nobody scores 100% in any or all areas, but these are their core functions.*

- *Prayer*
  Maintaining a pattern of prayer in the parish, traditionally understood as drawn from the Daily Office - the prayers of the whole Church provided for in Prayer Book and Common Worship.

- *Celebration of Holy Communion*
  They should provide for the regular celebration of Holy Communion, especially on Sundays and Holy Days.

- *Preach*
  Clergy should provide for regular preaching in the Churches for which they are responsible.

- *Teach*
  Clergy should teach, both adults and children, being willing to visit schools when invited

- *Present candidates for Confirmation*
  having prepared them for discipleship within the life of the Church.

- *Visit*
  both the sick and housebound, and make themselves available for spiritual counsel and advice.

- *Consult with a Parochial Church Council*
  about matters of general concern and importance to the parish. This should meet at least four times a year.

- *Arrange substitutes*
  when unable to perform their basic duties themselves.[165]

The focus is on maintaining the system, which is largely an internal focus, and God-honouring Leadership is nowhere to be seen. No wonder churches stop

---

[165] Bishop Alan Wilson, 'Bishop Alan's Blog: How to Change Your Vicar (Part Two)', *Bishop Alan's Blog*, 2012 <http://bishopalan.blogspot.com/2012/09/how-to-change-your-vicar-part-two.html> [accessed 26 May 2020].

growing and fade when the focus is so inward, maintaining the system. We need both Faithfulness and Fruitfulness.

We need to become effective and relevant communicators, but evangelism is a problematic word for many Christians. We hold in our hearts and minds and hands God's eternal truths. And the reason we were brought into a relationship with God is to pass on to others of a new generation the good news of His love and eternal plans for them. But as someone has said: "The Church is irrelevant, broken, not fit for purpose, and in greater need of salvation than those it seeks to save."

Instead, collectively, corporately as churches in maintenance mode, we created a culture of dangerous complacency, fuelled by the status quo, towards a slow death. We need to reverse this situation via a new culture of commitment in a Church revitalised by God in missional Transformation mode.

> *We have created a theology to be believed*
> *and a system to be sustained,*
> *when we should be proclaiming*
> *from the roof tops the revelation of God in*
> *Jesus Christ to be personally discovered.*

Stop the norm of trying to solve problems. Instead, move to seeking purpose and the four key aspects of the transformative leader. True leaders are, as Professor Bob Quinn states in his book, *Building the Bridge as You Walk On:*
- ✓ Externally open
- ✓ Internally driven by their core beliefs
- ✓ Other focussed
- ✓ Purpose-driven[166]

If ever we needed effective leadership in the Church of Jesus Christ, it is now. Only effective Transformational Leadership will start the long road back to success for God. Consider the following quotes and see whether they resonate with you. Why? Because you could be just the right person God is Calling to Make a Difference where you are!

"Yesterday is not ours to recover, but tomorrow is ours to win or lose."

---

[166] Robert E. Quinn, *Building the Bridge as You Walk on It*, pp. 21-25.

– Lyndon B. Johnson[167]

"A true leader has the confidence to stand alone, the courage to make tough decisions, and the compassion to listen to the needs of others. He does not set out to be a leader, but becomes one by the equality of his actions and the integrity of his intent."
– Douglas MacArthur[168]

"The call and need of a new era is for greatness."
– Dr Stephen Covey, The 8th Habit.[169]

Jesus said in Matthew Ch.20, v.26, "Whoever wants to become great among you must be your servant."

"There is a revelation of God to be discovered, His pathways to be walked, and God's equipping to be completed for those who are called by Him."
– Psalm 143, verses 8-10.

So, what is God calling you to do?
If the situation where you are is impossible, don't focus on the people roadblocks or the overwhelming difficulties (which you cannot change). Instead, transfer your focus to God, who has precisely placed you there, and wait patiently for Him to break a way through supernaturally. Keep asking, "Lord, What are you calling me to do?" and keep asking until you receive the answer!

No easy gospel.
So be ready for God's opportunities.

Two Simple Questions:

What is the current state of the Church of Jesus Christ?
First reply – because it is a straightforward question to ask. But there are many who dare to think that the modern Church, despite its best intentions, especially the traditional element, is based on arrogance, mediocrity and self-interest

---

[167] 'A Quote by Lyndon B. Johnson' <https://www.goodreads.com/quotes/3276-yesterday-is-not-ours-to-recover-but-tomorrow-is-ours> [accessed 26 May 2020].
[168] 'A Quote by Douglas MacArthur' <https://www.goodreads.com/quotes/359193-a-true-leader-has-the-confidence-to-stand-alone-the> [accessed 26 May 2020].
[169] Covey, p. 4.

towards survival. One particularly brutal description is that it is blind, deaf, ignorant, arrogant and deeply institutionalised. What's new, the cynic might reasonably ask. Has it not, historically, always acted in these ways?

Now to the second question. Stripping away all our knowledge, all of Church history and all our current experience, "What did Christ plan as its purpose, and therefore, what should it be and look like? What should the Church of Christ look like as He planned it?"

He stated in Luke 10:27 NIV:

❖ He answered, "'Love the Lord your God with all your heart and with all your soul and with all your strength and with all your mind'; and, 'Love your neighbour as yourself.'" This must be the starting point. Here is found the grand vista of His Vision. That is His starting point. But to understand God's viewpoint, we need to understand Christ's intentions when He was alive and then how His disciples grew when he had left them. Plus

❖ Love each other as I have loved you.

How is this achieved? Through the simplicities of Servant Leadership that grow people to become the people God always planned for them to be. Grow tomorrow's Leaders, not yesterday's followers.

273

Conclusions for Step 9

Act! For Others For Their Best Lives

Key Thought – Action involves Leadership, and Leadership is a Choice

Sub-headings review:
- ➤ From Transactional to Transformational Cultures
- ➤ The Dangers – SILOS – How We Must Master Them Before They Master Us
- ➤ Transformational Leadership
- ➤ The Leadership And Mindset Of Christ
- ➤ Emotional Intelligence
- ➤ Two Simple Questions

You had already decided to Lead yourself when you started Step 1. Whether you like that fact, intended that fact, desired it or ever considered it, you are a Leader. You have Awoken, Unlocked, and now you are Acting. Those actions are the actions of a leader. But not any old leader. It has been said that Leaders create followers. That was under the proscribed cultural assumptions of the past.

Your Leadership demands Next Level Thinking and then beyond Next Level Thinking. You are creating tomorrow's Leaders, not collecting followers. Your job is not to minister to their needs but to Unlock their Potential.

Got it?

Step 10

To Lead! Others To Their Best Lives

~~~

Christ inspired and transformed those with whom He connected.
They sensed His Purpose for them, and by responding,
they transformed the world through Him.
Often at the cost of their lives.
In contrast, our churches are generally led by those
who manage hierarchically and transactionally
through "kindly manipulation" of their followers;
eventually, most of these churches die.
We desperately need Christ-centred leaders who inspire others to action.
We desperately need those who were thus inspired
to discover God's purposes and
calling for their lives.

These are tomorrow's leaders who will inspire
the next generation for God
Just as He intended.
For the believer in Jesus Christ
who wishes to define God's Purpose for their lives in a word
for me, there is only one: Transformation.
That is it. Don't add to it.
Don't compromise it.
Don't forget it.
Period.
Christ inspired and transformed those whom He connected with...

~~~

❖ **Key Purpose: Create a Compelling Vision to Inspire with Clarity and Connection to Lead Yourself and Others to God's Higher Purpose, Starting The Journey, Building a new Culture of Empowerment, and the Outcomes that God plans.**

❖ **Key Learning (Always Facing the Unknown without Fear):** Step 10 is a huge chapter both in length and importance. We have learnt of the need for Cultural Transformation, and Transformational Leadership is essential in Leadership, and Step 10 will give you the details of the road map required.

❖ **Key Actions (Building The Bridge As You Walk On It):** You will need to expand your knowledge, understanding and vision – taking in the bigger picture of where you are, where those with you are, and where you all need to be. Note the short piece at the end on the status quo – it will never give you rest in this battle, but you can bypass it and lead Others to become the People God Always Created Them To Be.

Please note – Step 10 is a long and vital Step, so it has been divided into three parts: 10.1, 10.2, and 10.3

10.1 A Compelling Vision

Your compelling vision:
* ❖ Must to be perfect in inspiring, challenging and directing those who read to unlock their potential and discover their purpose for action.
* ❖ Must Inspires and Challenge to unlock Potential to discover purpose and lead to action.
* ❖ Must Inspire, Challenge and Bring People to the Point of Decision to Choose to Change.
* ❖ Must Inspire Others to Find Their Voice.
* ❖ Remember, God's Higher Purpose is all about Contribution and our desire to make a difference.

> *"God is a visionary God. And you, God's servant, have been given the profound ability and responsibility to dream." p.8*
> *"Think long because God thinks generationally." p.29*
> *"Perhaps the most compelling reason we should think long-range is that our ultimate shared vision as God's people is beyond time itself." p.29*
> *"If you think long, you are more likely to dream big and attempt great. " p.36*
> *From "God Dreams", Will Mancini*

(Above quotes cited. [170])

If God designed and created us to be extraordinary, flourishing, soaring, living

---

[170] Will Mancini and Warren Bird, *God Dreams: 12 Vision Templates for Finding and Focusing Your Church's Future* (Nashville, Tennessee: B & H Publishing Group, 2016).

beings connected to Him with our potential, purpose and vision, how come most of us settle for the status quo of the inward-focussed (church) culture we live in? The simple answer is that we have never been led to be or understand anything else. And without vision, none of this happens. This is the missing ingredient. Vision starts with the Potential already inside of you seeing possibility. Possibility morphs into purpose. Purpose births Vision. And Vision is for those who have come to faith in Christ, seeing the future from a God-positioned standpoint.

"Vision is important for leaders because leadership is about going somewhere. If you and your people don't know where you are going, your leadership doesn't matter..." — Author and management consultant Ken Blanchard.[171]

As before, Professor Bob Quinn often asks, "When does the future determine the present?" The answer is, "when we have a purpose to which we are truly committed."[172]

This occurs when we "see" a vision to which we are truly committed. He continues, "Leaders do not focus on empowering us. They seek instead to build a culture where a critical mass of people will be enticed to take the risk to empower themselves. Leaders do this by asking us questions instead of giving answers. They refuse to play the expert role we expect them to play. They refuse to take responsibility for decisions we need to make. Instead of creating comfort, they bring challenges and require that we make our own decisions."

The two absolute essentials in this whole Transformational Leadership concept are leaders who:

Firstly, choose to lead with purpose, create vision.

And secondly, but equally importantly, create transformed cultures of self-empowerment that grow new leaders. You cannot have one without the other. They are all mutually indivisible ingredients.

Choosing to Lead By Empowerment

Myles Munroe, writing in his book, *In Charge, Finding the Leader Within You*: *But always remember, Leadership is not for you; it is for others. If you wish to lead, you must serve. If we all discovered the gift God gave us and served it to the world, we could solve all the needs of humanity.*[173]

---

[171] John Blanchard and Jesse Stoner, 'The Vision Thing', *Leader to Leader, No.31 Winter 2004*, p. 2.
[172] 'When Does Future Determine the Present?'
[173] Munroe, *In Charge*, pt. 1502.

Leadership is for the benefit of others.[174]

Leaders are simply people who have discovered themselves and decided to become who they really are. Leaders are simply people who dare to be who the Creator made them to be and are committed to expressing themselves fully to the world through their gifts.[175]

Be Inspired
Be Transformed
Become a Leader for Christ

Who are we designed to be, what is our purpose, and how do we start the journey in pursuit of that discovery? We Discover, We Decide, We Deploy.

Transformational Leaders create a culture of Empowerment (Intentionality) by growing and empowering intentional people who:

➤ **Start the Journey consciously, making it a personal decision.**
  ➤ Understand preparation is essential.
  ➤ Seek God's Vision for your life – it is the only one that matters.
  ➤ Remember, I/we need inspiration like a drowning man.
  ➤ Being inspired is the lifeblood of God's Higher Purpose.
  ➤ "God is a visionary God. And you, God's servant, have been given the profound ability and responsibility to dream." – Will Mancini.
➤ **Start Building The bridge as You Walk on it.**
  ➤ Don't wait for others; decide to go it alone anyway because leadership is alone (initially).
  ➤ Decide to discover your authentic self.
  ➤ Decide to become a self-empowered person because only you can empower yourself, and no one else can do it for you.
  ➤ Understand the only other being that knows your purpose is God because He placed it inside you.
  ➤ Understand that purpose is in God's Vision for you.
  ➤ Seek to prove His Vision as yours and be transformed by it.
➤ **Create a culture of empowerment – only leaders can do this: Build safety, Share vulnerability, Establish purpose (from Culture Code).**

---

[174] Munroe, *In Charge*, pt. 1668.
[175] Munroe, *In Charge*, pt. 2176.

- ➤ Create a culture of inspiration, literally, blow the flame to a powerful white heat.
- ➤ Empower yourself: Research by Gretchen Spreitzer suggests that people experience self-empowerment when they feel meaning and purpose in their work; Feel a sense of competence – that they can do their job well; Have a sense of autonomy – that they have self-determination in how they do their work; Feel a sense of impact – that their work is indeed making a difference.
- ➤ Escaping the negative gravitational pull of your own and your culture's assumptions and others' comments about you from the past.

➤ **Discovering the extraordinary leader within.**
- ➤ Discover, Develop and Deploy your God-given gifts and talent.
- ➤ Choosing to lead.
- ➤ Choosing Self-Awareness.
- ➤ Choosing to transform.
- ➤ Choose to move from problem-solving to purpose-finding
- ➤ Choosing to flourish in your God-created life.
- ➤ Choosing Isaiah 40:31 NIV: "But those who hope in the Lord will renew their strength. They will soar on wings like eagles; they will run and not grow weary, they will walk and not be faint."

➤ **Become intentional in all these aspects – none of this just happens without intentionality.**
- ➤ Model the behaviours that reflect and enhance Transformational Leadership (see below).
- ➤ Understanding Trigger Events.
- ➤ Unlock, release, realise, recognise and discover your potential.
- ➤ Create a culture where Potential is continuously unlocked and unleashed.

➤ **Discover the purpose for which God placed you on this earth.**
- ➤ Create connectedness and destroy fear.
- ➤ Transcend from hierarchical authority and its directive perspective to a co-creative perspective and capacity, growing others.
- ➤ Believe in self-efficacy.
- ➤ Become your best self.
- ➤ Engaging with your own learning.
- ➤ Turn your disengagement on its head.

➤ **Engage in new learning to transformatively learn.**
- ➤ Choose to avoid slow death (AKA Colluding in your own diminishment).
- ➤ Deep learning through Self-Reflection.
- ➤ Deep change.

- ➤ Gaining a more complex understanding.
- ➤ **Developmental Readiness – Entering the Fundamental State of Leadership.**[176]
  - ➤ Be ten times as clear, in a never-ending loop, about purpose, vision, and priorities as you think you should be.
  - ➤ Leadership transforms from the hierarchical model to the co-creative facilitator model, learning and developing jointly with others at the highest level of engagement.
- ➤ **Transform from hierarchical telling/teaching mode to facilitator mode.**
  - ➤ Transformational influence is now possible.
  - ➤ It is not about knowledge but about transcending and rising above who we have been told we are, ourselves and our cultures, to rise above these things to learn, develop and become the people God always planned for us to become. See Isaiah ch.40, v.31.
  - ➤ To fully become the people God meant us to be, if only we could stop acting like turkeys pecking the ground literally beside the runway we never even knew existed and take flight like the eagles God purposed us to be.

We are living our own part of the incarnational life of Christ when we discover God's purpose for our lives, and we transform ourselves to transform others as Jesus did. This is true transformational leadership. The whole purpose of Jesus Christ and the whole of scripture is not only that we should be saved but that we should be transformed by our Creator and transformed for Others. This is transformation for multiplication, which is primarily what the kingdom of God is all about!

> *"The Primary Purpose of a Leader is*
> *to Connect People to Their Purpose "*
> *Joe Robles, USAA*

(Above quotation cited. [177])

Building A Culture of Empowerment

Unlock and Unleash Potential Perpetually

---

[176] Quinn and Quinn.
[177] Robert E. Quinn and Anjan V. Thakor, 'Creating a Purpose-Driven Organization', *Harvard Business Review*, 1 July 2018 <https://hbr.org/2018/07/creating-a-purpose-driven-organization> [accessed 2 June 2020].

In *The Best Teacher in You*, Professor Bob Quinn, transformational leadership is reflected in the four kinds of behaviour described below.

Idealized influence. Transformational leaders operate with moral power. They model high standards of ethical and moral conduct. They do things that gain respect, build trust, and increase the willingness to believe. This may result in higher-quality relationships.
Inspirational motivation. Transformational leaders provide collective meaning by articulating an appealing, inspiring vision, offering challenging standards and communicating optimism. This may result in a shared vision and the emergence of a collective purpose.
Intellectual stimulation. Transformational leaders challenge assumptions, take risks, and solicit input from followers. They value learning and encourage independent thinking and creative outcomes. This may facilitate the desire for and the emergence of knowledge generation. An intellectually stimulating leader is one who helps followers think in new ways. The leader helps people reexamine their own assumptions, look for new perspectives, and consider different ways to think about a problem.
Individualized consideration. Transformational leaders act as respectful mentors or coaches. They listen and attend to individual needs. They provide empathy and support, emphasize the need for respect, and celebrate each person's contributions. This may lead to the emergence of intrinsic motivation.[178]

He envisages building an empowering culture by growing and building self-empowered people who practice:

- Idealised influence
- Inspirational motivation
- Intellectual stimulation

Individualised consideration who also live the Fundamental State of Leadership[179] being:

- Purpose centred
- Internally directed
- Others focussed
- Externally open

All the above are impossible under hierarchical leadership as currently practised

[178] Robert E Quinn, *The Best Teacher in You: How to Accelerate Learning and Change Lives*, 2014, pt. 2020.
[179] Quinn and Quinn.

by the traditional Church. Transformational leaders change assumptions and Mindsets. This is all about Servant Leadership, which is less about doing and rather more about a state of being. Jesus exemplified servant leadership.

He epitomised The Fundamental State of Leadership[180], "which is all about seeing, realising and releasing potential and acting with purpose based on inner integrity to create new realities for others while continually being open to learning."

God's highest purpose for everyone is to connect with Him through faith and total transformation by renewing our minds.

So first, faith; second, a transformation of the mind.

- Jesus took 18 years to get to where He started His ministry.
- Paul took 3 years (in Arabia) before he started to teach.
- So the transformation of the mind is from one Mindset to another, and it does not happen overnight; from a mind focussed on finite transient things of the natural Mindset to a Mindset that not only seeks God but, more importantly, is deeply connected with Him as He intended.

Jesus Himself when He discovered His purpose at the age of 12 and became:

- Purpose centred
- Internally Directed
- Others Focussed
- Externally Open

Reflection questions:

- ❖ What is God's Highest Purpose in this situation?
- ❖ What result does God want me to create?
- ❖ What outcome would be most meaningful and best for God's purposes?
- ❖ What would be the most ambitious and exciting goal I could pursue (for God)?

Finally, Professor Quinn states:

When we, like Richard Thurman, create new purposes that shed the inappropriate expectations that come with being comfort-centred, we lift ourselves with new ideas, new direction, and new energy. We assume leadership, and we lift others.[181]

Leaders do not focus on empowering us. They seek instead to build a culture where a critical mass of people will be enticed to take the risk to empower themselves. Leaders do

---

[180] Quinn and Quinn.
[181] Quinn and Quinn, p. 65.

this by asking us questions instead of giving answers. They refuse to play the expert role we expect them to play. They refuse to take responsibility for decisions we need to make. Instead of creating comfort, they bring challenges and require that we make our own decisions.

> **"Leadership has nothing to do with ruling people.**
> **It has more to do with your gift—identifying it, maximizing it, and**
> **serving that gift to the world."**
>
> **Myles Munroe**

(Above quotation cited. [182])

If you, a leader, are not leading your people to discover the leader within them, to discover, develop and deploy their God-given gifts and talent, then you are simply a controller and manipulator of your people. You may imagine that you are doing great things for God. The simple truth is that you have set your people on the slow path to decline and ultimately organisational (church) death since hierarchical controllers manipulate their people and deplete them one day at a time, destroying them slowly so they can never become the people God created them to be.

So, here are some helpful thinking actions:

➢ **As you lead, do it focussed and faithfully.**
  ➢ Lead with a Sense of Urgency.
  ➢ Caring and Clarity: with conviction and credibility.
  ➢ Connecting: with passion, confidence and gratitude for themselves (perhaps, particularly with millennials).
➢ **Inspiring: with the right words and a clear action plan.**
➢ **Remember, Personal Transformation and Growth are unknown concepts amongst most Christians.** They are solely focussed on the status quo because they have never been led to understand or see anything different.
  ➢ How to Kickstart thinking differently?
  ➢ We need to provide the Why, not just the What. This gives the context for decision-making and focus.
➢ **Build a Sense of Urgency.**
  ➢ We cannot go on as we are.
  ➢ Enlarge Your Vision.

---

[182] Munroe, *In Charge*, pt. 477.

- ➤ Enlarge their Vision.
- ➤ Keep your destination in sight!
- ➤ Show them there is Hope.
- ➤ **Show them how to Discover their "Why?"**
  - ➤ Aligning yourself with the purpose God created you for Daily, is key.
  - ➤ Vision creates a picture of the future that people can understand.
  - ➤ Purpose and Hope provide the Energy to Move Forwards towards that Vision, Daily.
  - ➤ Clarity provides both individuals and groups with Direction.
- ➤ **Begin with the End in Mind.**
  - ➤ Show them they are God-designed for His Fulfilled Transcendent Higher Purpose.

But never forget that none of this happens without your Conscious Decision to Awake, Unlock and Act, to Consecrate, Dedicate, and Commit to God Daily, Living the Life God created you for, Living Your Best Life, Living for Jesus Christ, who is transforming you, and Living in the service of a cause greater than yourself.

Ask yourself, by Leading, How can I create anticipation in Leading?

Ask yourself, by Leading, How can I draw myself forward to express the deepest understandings within me for Others?

Remember, by Leading, you are helping them Awake to Awareness, then Breakout, Unlock, Grow, Connect, Lead, and Legacy.

For Legacy: We need to become bilingual in thinking and action, understanding the past, unlocking the present, and allowing the future to determine the present as we commit to a purpose that will fulfil our potential.

Remember all this as you Lead:
- ➤ **Take them on a pathway, and lead them on a journey with you.**
  - ➤ Help them think and act differently, breaking free from their cultural constraints, status quo thinking and expectations.
  - ➤ Create a Sense of Urgency.
- ➤ **Ask challenging questions.**
  - ➤ Ask thought-provoking questions.
  - ➤ Use lots of stories, illustrations and examples.
  - ➤ Draw out from them a different way of thinking.
  - ➤ Understand their fears, frustrations and desires.
- ➤ **Meet and understand them where they are.**
  - ➤ Help them know you care.
  - ➤ Challenge them.

➢ **Help them understand the scriptural truth that God created them individually for His Glory.**

    ➢ Help them understand the scriptural truth that God has a Higher Purpose for their lives and that the potential already within them awaits being unlocked and their purpose for Him being discovered.

    ➢ Help them understand there is hope.

    ➢ Help them understand there is a way forward.

    ➢ Help them see a vision of their unlimited potential, of worlds unknown.

➢ **Help connect them to God's Higher Purpose.**

    ➢ Help them to grow as God intended.

    ➢ Help them understand, create and live with renewed and redirected focus.

    ➢ Help them appreciate a longer timescale.

➢ **Help create a "critical path" to follow.**

    ➢ Help them with a workable game plan.

    ➢ Help them with ongoing practical things to action.

    ➢ Help them to live dynamically, constantly acting as they were designed.

    ➢ Set them free to fly and soar as they are meant to! John Gillespie Magee – High Flight: "Oh, I have slipped the surly bonds of earth..."

➢ **We need to become bilingual in thinking and action, understanding the past, unlocking the present,** and allowing the future to determine the present as we commit to a purpose that will fulfil our potential.

    ➢ This cannot succeed by telling someone they need to change. They will push back and turn away.

    ➢ We need to provide the Why, not just the What. This gives the context for decision-making and focus.

Do What Christ Did – Inspire!

Manipulation is what occurs in churches where ordained clergy "manage". It is the opposite of the actions of Christ with His disciples, and it destroys God's intended plans for people. If you are in a position of leadership already, or if you understand that everyone is a servant leader for Christ (simply because leadership at its simplest level is about influence and everyone has the capability to influence others for good and for God), lead your people to discover God's purposes for them individually and corporately.

Because that was Christ's intention with His disciples.
Christ certainly did not manipulate; He Inspired.

So, we need to start with our "Why?"

Why do I feel passion for God's Higher Purpose?

Why do I feel the passion for unlocking potential in others for God?

Why do I feel the passion for inspiring others and encouraging God's profound vision for people to be fulfilled in His Church?

Why do I feel the passion for fulfilling the purpose of God in my generation?

Because I was created with this end in mind.

On a personal level, I reflect on my life and all the aspects of it. All the significant changes, the more extended periods that I can see and all the good times, times of stability, of God's blessings, along with all the hurts, embarrassments, difficulties, the throwaway cutting comments of teachers and others from my earliest days, the wrongs done to me, all these (I have reached my seventh decade) God has planned and used to mould and make me what I am. I am still with the potential to be used effectively for God. That is why I have these passions:

✓ Passion for God's Higher Purpose

✓ Passion to unlock potential in others for God

✓ Passion to inspire others and encourage God's profound vision for people to be fulfilled in His Church

✓ Passion to fulfil the purposes of God in my generation

These are my compelling visions.

> *"There are only two ways to influence human behaviour: you can manipulate it or you can inspire it.*
> *Manipulations Lead to Transactions, Not Loyalty."*
> *From Simon Sinek, "Start with Why"*

(Above quotation cited.[183])

I reflect and understand that those painful moments of my life, the cutting criticisms, the failure of exams, the waste of human potential inside organisations, the wrong use of power to humiliate and control, especially in churches, all of these things God has allowed so that I might use all that I am for His Glory, in the days I have left on earth. God will never waste any experience in our lives. I feel that my whole life has been but a preparation for

---

[183] Simon Sinek, *Start with Why: How Great Leaders Inspire Everyone to Take Action* (New York; London: Portfolio/Penguin, 2011), p. 16.

TRANSFORMED! Yes, the world may have beaten and crushed out of us our potential and purpose, but in Jesus Christ, as God overcame all the evil and sin of the world, so He will use all of our experience to change the world through us for His Glory; to change the future and destiny of others, you may have contact with; to bring hope, to draw out purpose, to help others understand they matter, to bring significance to others, and that they matter to God.

It makes no difference whether your personally perceived character is introverted or extroverted or anything else in between. This is not the focus of this book. We are created by God individually. Therefore, comparison with others or, worse, still wishing to imitate others in whatever way we perceive to be in our best interest is madness. Only you can ever be you. Never let others, either now or from the past, ever direct or dictate who you might think you are or limit who you imagine you became. God has bigger and grander plans for you than you can ever imagine.

7 Human Perfections of Jesus that He Calls us to emulate (Ultimate Transcendent Higher Purpose):
* ❖ Beyond Extraordinary for God and for Others
* ❖ Servant Leader
* ❖ Others Focussed
* ❖ People Imagineer or Visionary
* ❖ People Transformer
* ❖ People Grower
* ❖ People Multiplier

TRANSFORMED! is about growing towards and living that life. The complete focus, vision and intentionality of Christ is the fullest redemption possible in this life and then the perfect redemption in the life to come for everyone. It is to create His kingdom of people who, like Him, seek that outcome and become like Him.
In Step 2, To Awareness! Of Your Best Life, I showed that for every person on this earth, God has designed in you the aspects that make you human, that make you, you. They were created, present and perfectly expressed in Jesus Christ. They are in every person unique, individually created aspects of:
* ❖ Creation
* ❖ Identity
* ❖ Potential
* ❖ Purpose
* ❖ Inspiration
* ❖ Passion

❖ Vision
❖ Intentionality
❖ Focus
❖ Anticipation
❖ Significance
❖ Destiny

They are vital to every human being, and these are the reasons:

✓ Because every one of us has our beginning and creation in God.
✓ Because every one of us has our true identity in God.
✓ Because every one of us has potential placed in us by God.
✓ Because every one of us has a God-planned purpose.
✓ Because every one of us was born to be inspired.
✓ Because every one of us was born to be passionate.
✓ Because every one of us can receive God's vision for ourselves and His Church.
✓ Because every one of us has been created with a conscience.
✓ Because every one of us is significant and matters to God.
✓ Because every one of us is designed to live an intentional life.
✓ Because as we focus intently on our Maker, He will respond.
✓ Because every one of us has a God-given Destiny that awaits us.

And all these God-created aspects were present in Jesus Christ. That is why His humanity and His likeness that we recognise inspired the first generation of His servant leaders. God's ultimate visionary is His Son, Jesus Christ. In history, all things are created by Him, flow towards Him and from Him in scripture. Colossians ch.1, vv16-20.

What is a "visionary", and why does God seem to use them throughout scripture to carry out His plans?

Hebrews 11:13-16 NIV:

"All these people were still living by faith when they died. They did not receive the things promised; they only saw them and welcomed them from a distance, admitting that they were foreigners and strangers on earth. People who say such things show that they are looking for a country of their own. If they had been thinking of the country they had left, they would have had opportunity to return. Instead, they were longing for a better country – a heavenly one. Therefore, God is not ashamed to be called their God, for he has prepared a city for them."

God's Extraordinary Masterpiece people live with a God-centred view:

✓ They "see" what others are not aware of, they "see" what others cannot see, and they "see" what others will never see.
✓ They have a raging dissatisfaction and impatience with the status quo.

✓ They "see" a picture of the future that creates Passion in them.

✓ They "know" they are created for God's Higher Purpose.

✓ They "know" they are created for a relationship with Him in His kingdom.

✓ They "know" they are created to connect with God and His people to fulfil His purposes.

✓ They desire something better.

✓ They are triple-A people who are aware, aligned and actioning.

✓ They are triple-C people who are created by, connected to and being conformed to the image of Jesus Christ.

> *"Leadership is rallying people to a better future.*
> *Vision is seeing it before you see it.*
> *All people matter."*
> *Ronnie Floyd*

(Above quotation cited.[184])

God's Big Picture (AKA The Plan)

❖ Before time began, God started the process of

❖ Creation, which man spoils and then, at last, He completes His plan of

❖ Redemption for mankind through the death of His Son Jesus Christ that precedes His great Plan for

❖ Transformation of Individuals who were chosen before time began, which

❖ Christ recommenced to complete,

❖ To be Conformed to the Image of Christ

❖ For God's Glory for Eternity

His Transformation of:

➢ Purpose

➢ Character

➢ Thinking

➢ Acting

---

[184] Ronnie Floyd, '30 Leadership Lessons from 30 Years at the Same Church', *CT Pastors*
<https://www.christianitytoday.com/pastors/2016/november-web-exclusives/30-leadership-lessons-from-30-years-at-same-church.html> [accessed 26 May 2020].

So, the leadership of Christ is all about Transformation and to this end, He is continually:

✓ Living the life He is created humanly for
✓ Understanding the Big Picture
✓ Thinking and acting at a higher level
✓ Keeping momentum by seeing and seizing opportunities
✓ Focussed
✓ Preventing the culture from dragging Him back

At no stage does He stop doing all the above, but the question of "how" He continues is significant. Christ starts transforming people from "the inside out". So, He connects with individuals and immediately shakes their thinking to grab their attention. He transcends His own culture to associate Himself with them and redirect their focus towards God, His Father. He is utterly focussed on and dedicated to the transformation of people and enabling their growth.

He appears at the crossroads of time in one of the worst imaginable religious and political situations on earth. He proceeds to ignore both, focussing on His mission with laser precision, and starts to transform His people from the inside out.

He is brutally honest in warning about the religious tradition of His time, almost benign about the political system, but utterly intent on creating and building the kingdom of God in individuals without delay. And all of this without a church building or any formal system structure, no liturgy, no dress-coded, vision-limiting hierarchy, no pulpits, no clergy, no creed, nothing but a crystal-clear focus on growing His people and creating the necessary legacy of tomorrow's leaders to follow His example.

He is all about people, and specifically His people in the Kingdom of God, those who would come to faith in Him. He is all about their growth, their God-given purpose, and their effectiveness in fulfilling His Purpose for their lives, both now and in eternity with Him. He is focussed on the birthing of the Kingdom of God.

So, where did it all go wrong? It was a loss of focus. The Church lost focus, then forgot its mission and was taken over by forces who viewed the focus of Christ as secondary to their personal advancement and ended in the organisational structures they put in place. And insidiously, "They" and "Their" titles and positions became the focus. For anyone who has read even a little of Church history since the Apostles' times, it does not make encouraging reading.

The major events recorded show nothing but conflict, schism and often war. The most significant upheaval and the split was, of course, the Reformation. But there never was a time when the "Church" was ever really doing what God planned for it, except in small, isolated locations. It seems as if the owner's manual was continually being rewritten by those who thought they knew it all when, in fact, they had never understood Christ's intentions in the first place. Their culture, traditions and history ensured they could never break out from where they were to discover and appreciate anything different. If they were properly cognisant of and aligned with God's purposes, they would never have acted as they did. It is recorded that even John Calvin, although not personally responsible for the individual's death, supported the execution at the stake of a supposed heretic Servetus in Geneva in 1553.

We rightly shudder at such unbelievable abuses, but remember these were carried out by people who thought they were right. And that is the key that unlocks our awareness, and it is simply this. The humility that accepts, loves, and grows others despite who they are and what they might or might not believe first started with Jesus Christ.

I believe the current organisational ignorance, arrogance, blindness, deafness and deep institutionalisation, which is also present in every church I know and which accepts frustrated and disengaged individuals as normal, is one of the greatest evils ever perpetrated on that organisation. For most people, the far-seeing vision has been cut back to myopic vision and then to the fatal inward focus.

Indeed, it can be said, "We are blinded by the knowledge we think we have."

Because it will stop you from even starting the road of fresh thinking and new understanding. It is indeed a frightening thought that what you or I may think we know and believe with all our understanding may be hurting the God who created us in the first place.

So, what is the exact vision and focus of Christ, and should we do the same, or is it just about building a community that loves each other?

> **TRANSFORMED!**
> is at its heart the transferring of my dream of the possibility and goal for every individual, of being Fully Alive and Fully Engaged whilst being Continually Renewed and Transformed, Reaching and Accomplishing their God-Given Potential and Purpose.
>
> In writing I seek to transfer my dream to your reality as you seek this transformation to God's higher purpose that is your birthright.

10.2 Inspire Others To Take Action

By God, we are:

❖ Created

❖ Called

❖ Conformed

   ✓ For consecrated connection with Christ

   ✓ To love Him and align ourselves with His Purpose

   ✓ For connection with others

   ✓ To create and sustain cultures that unleash potential, purpose, growth and originality in others as God intended.

For a considerable number of years, I have felt a growing conviction that all was seriously not well in the Protestant traditions that I was brought up in and in which I played a small but vital role in recent years. The final catalyst was the four years I served as a churchwarden, where, for various reasons, I concluded that we could not go on as we were in perpetuating the "Churchianity" that we had come to accept as normal against the backdrop of the written biblical accounts both of the incomparable life of Christ and the letters of Paul.

In short, I have found a profoundly concerning incompatibility between what we do where church is seen and modelled as an event to attend rather than a life and calling to be discovered and lived.

Dr Brene Brown talks about the need for clarity of purpose in a world of constant change in every area of life. She also states, "Vulnerability is the core, the heart, the centre, of meaningful human experiences."[185]

We are in the People Development Business. We are created to grow and develop. I believe this is what God in Christ planned for His Church to be focussed on. It was, in fact, Christ's overwhelming focus. My personal calling is for this.

Paul writes, "This grace was given me: to preach to the Gentiles the boundless riches of Christ." Ephesians ch.3, v8. We have come to faith in Christ. But what precisely are Christ's boundless riches? How can we know, receive and act upon this understanding? Well, our eternal status is now apparent to us as believers in Christ. But Christ called us to live a real life that is in Him. I believe that it is His purpose for us individually that we must understand more fully based on that understood status.

God's Purpose and Destiny for us start now, at this very moment. Because we are created for His Purposes. So every day, through conscious choice, make a decisive dedication of yourself to Him. Romans ch.12, v1 AMP.

God is the author of His Purpose, Planning Provision, Alignment, Fulfilment, Vision and Destiny for us. In Christ, this is fulfilled; our task is to wake up, seek Him

---

[185] Brown, *Daring Greatly*, p. 10.

with all our hearts, discover, understand and then align to be "full-filled" in Christ; it is this simple. God calls us individually to discover what already exists, but what has been hidden for centuries and is mostly hidden by the Church. He creates us, then through Christ fulfils us, then calls us to grasp the enormity of it all. This is the thrust of Paul's triumphant letters to the churches at Ephesus, Philippi, and Colossi, even though written from prison. It is our true status in Christ, what we are created for, what we arrive on this planet for, and what God purposed in Christ before time began for everyone who trusts in Him. And the answer to the greatest question ever, "Why?", is found in Paul's letter to the church in Rome, ch.11, vv.33-36 NIV: "Oh, the depth of the riches of the wisdom and knowledge of God! How unsearchable his judgements, and his paths beyond tracing out! "Who has known the mind of the Lord? Or who has been his counsellor?" "Who has ever given to God, that God should repay them?" For from him and through him and for him are all things. To him, be the glory forever! Amen."

This is why the following paragraph of the original text (artificially separated from it by a chapter heading is beyond crucial for our understanding): Romans 12, vv1-2 NIV: "Therefore (in view of my preceding comments), I urge you, brothers and sisters, in view of God's mercy, to offer your bodies as a living sacrifice, holy and pleasing to God—this is your true and proper worship. Do not conform to the pattern of this world, but be transformed by the renewing of your mind. Then you will be able to test and approve what God's will is—his good, pleasing and perfect will."

This truth must also be vitally understood – the transformation is not only an injunction to be undertaken and a goal to be reached but, more dramatically, a birthright to be discovered and claimed. You were and are created for this moment, a moment of understanding that does not stop. Once you have awoken to these glorious truths of scripture, you cannot go back to the ignorance of the past. What happens when simple faith and trust (which we must never despise) grow to the deeper understanding of this: the "I now give or commit myself without reservation"? God will take and lead you out onto the mountain top of "you shall". Not "you must", but "you are enabled to". Which essentially is what we are Created for: a dynamic two-way connection of uninhibited receiving and giving of unlimited love to God in Christ.

Coming to faith in Christ, with the forgiveness of our sins, is merely the starting point of our transformation. But for most of us (and more than likely, our spiritual culture has done this), we stopped. We stopped at the point of salvation because those who should have known better unwisely did not and probably could not lead us beyond our birthright of not just maturity but a sincere connection with the God who created us for it. Friends, as shown above, this is both our birthright and destiny already provided for us by God in Christ. Never deny it to anyone.

Taking Flight

The situation is analogous to an aircraft, fully fuelled, loaded, checked, flight plans filed, air traffic control has cleared us for take-off... and then we wait... and we wait... Eventually, we switched the engines off. Why? Because we have never been led (or better stated, trained and encouraged) to understand or even discover our purpose and take off. We are stuck at the point of salvation simply because, traditionally, our churches aimed for that. It was merely a numbers game. And the biblical growth and maturing that was often preached about never occurred, simply because our Churchianity systems were not designed for it. They are still not today. What a catastrophic and outrageous waste of God's human potential.

Friends, the awesome truth of scripture is that we are designed to fly (metaphorically, of course) with God in Christ, close to Christ and for Christ. Instead, like flightless birds, we move to the side of the runway and live lives of turkeys pecking the ground. Because we were never led and trained to be otherwise. The clergy have ruled that roost, and the blame for this mess is at their feet. This artificial layer of hierarchical management has succeeded in almost every church in producing infantile Christians. They can never grow up and will never reach the true potential God always planned for them. The clergy singlehandedly, through unbiblical hierarchical management (not Christ-emulating leadership), create dependent, compliant and passive congregations under the guise of creating or building community. This is profoundly dishonouring to God's purposes for us. It is deeply insulting to our scriptural status in Christ, which is clearly stated in scripture!

Indeed, Isaiah, ch.40, v31 NIV, writes this: "But those who hope in the Lord will renew their strength. They will soar on wings like eagles; they will run and not grow weary, they will walk and not be faint." God designed us to soar with Him. This will be true in Eternity, but it is also clearly true for our lives as we prepare for that time.

So, this is all about relational alignment with God in Christ. We can understand this as converging towards God's ways. "Just live a life worthy of the divine calling you have received," Paul states in Ephesians ch.4, v1.

God speaks through Jeremiah. "Then you will seek Me, inquire for, and require Me (as a vital necessity) and find Me when you search for Me with all your heart. I will be found by you," says the Lord. Jer. ch.28, vv13-14 NIV.

Seek to move from the common mistruth that life is a "journeying" in the Wilderness (along with its fellow fake ideal, that of creating community) to living the life of conscious transformation and purposeful fulfilment that God always planned for you to live. St. Paul's words in Romans ch.12, v2 are the basis for our transformation, and it starts with our minds so that we are transformed by thinking and imagining differently from the inside out. But he also calls for a "decisive dedication" to sacrifice ourselves for God's Glory, not our own. If you ever hear yourself saying inwardly, "I now decide to... whatever, for God," that is it.

You see, Paul understood the dangers of living under the yoke of traditions and comforting activity. He had enthusiastically lived that. He knew first-hand where that led. Here, he rightly calls us to recognise this and to consciously "do decisive dedication daily!" This allows the daily growth of the human spirit that God created within us. I love this quote from Erwin McManus, who says this:

> *"Somewhere between our first breath and our last breath the extraordinary nature that God placed in us is beaten out of us... broken out of us... lost to us... and the Church needs to be the nurturer of the human Spirit."*

(Above quotation cited.[186])

And when Paul adds in his letter to the Ephesian church: "As a prisoner for the Lord, then, I urge you to live a life worthy of the calling you have received." this sense of dynamic living for God is made clear.

Growth is normal. But clearly, however much we may preach about it, if the church where you serve is not consciously and deliberately aligned and geared up for it, the status quo will always suffocate and prevent any attempts at real personal growth and transformation.

"Do decisive dedication daily!"
"Make the commitment because commitment is the Key!"

When you commit to, God will move for you.

---

[186] Erwin Mcmanus, *The Church Should Be the Nurturer of the Human Spirit*, 2011 <https://d15greoaou1b27.cloudfront.net/YR/Erwin%20McManus/FS201112/FS2011 12-McManus_2011_00-35-45_ChurchLeadership_HopeoftheWorld_ChasingDaylight-640x360.mp4> [accessed 29 May 2020].

> **2 Chronicles 16:9 NIV**
> **"For the eyes of the Lord range throughout the earth to strengthen those whose hearts are fully committed to him."**
>
> **Psalm 37:23 NIV**
> **"The Lord makes firm the steps of the one who delights in him."**

So God promises strengthened <u>and</u> directed hearts, and direction for those who are committed to Him.

But it can only be undertaken by you alone.

John C. Maxwell writes in his book, *Be All You Can Be*:

> *Until I am committed, there is a hesitancy, a chance to drawback. But the moment I definitely commit myself, then God moves also, and a whole stream of events erupt. All manner of unforeseen incidents, meetings, persons, and material assistance which I could never have dreamed would come my way begin to flow toward me—the moment I make a commitment. The greatest days of your life are the days when you sense your commitment to its highest degree. Your greatest days are not your days of leisure. Your greatest days are not even times when you have your closest friends around you. When something has seized you and caused you to have a high level of commitment to it, those are your greatest days. They may be your days of struggle, they may be your days of suffering, and they may be the days of your greatest battles in life, but they will be your greatest days.*[187]

It is about choosing not to take easier the path to mediocrity but choosing the less-trodden path to greatness, not for you, but greatness for God's Glory, the Servant Leader path. God calls both you and me to attempt greatness for Him, to make a difference for Him in the days He has given us on this earth. To live a life that echoes in Eternity for Him.

The start of the breakout from the default "aimless distraction" life we live, for both individuals and churches, is often through the wake-up call of crisis. This leads to awareness, awakening to reality, then confronting the brutal facts, accepting painful reality, Is/Should be discernment, discovering the Vision Intersection Profile, creating and maintaining a culture of excellence/greatness – making a difference for His Glory.

---

[187] John C. Maxwell, *Be All You Can Be*, pp. 179–80.

Unashamedly, we need to make the Church of Jesus Christ great again for Him. Come out of the shadows, come out of the foxholes, come out of the inwardly focussed clubs that practice "Churchianity", and let's start the long haul back from irrelevance to greatness for God.

It can be done; it must be done for His Glory.

Because your Destiny starts now. It starts with your commitment to God, making the decision to move from comfort to courage because you cannot have both. And only you can make that commitment to God. No one else can do it.

So, Clergy, as a body, stop your "good thoughts" of ministry and community, and LEAD the people under your care from community, which creates dependence, compliance and passivity (which never appear in scripture, except in connection with disobedience to God). Lead them to the mountain tops of maturity of understanding of their true status in Christ, prepare them for take-off and then "get out of their way" to gloriously "take off and fly" and live the lives God always created them to live.

Dramatically, stop this metaphoric wandering in the desert life while practising community – that was for the disobedient losers of Joshua's time. Lead and properly lead people, with purpose, vision and destiny in mind, to become the "Calebs" of their day because "Wholeheartedness" for God is essential on the road to maturity in Christ. We were born for this: a life of connection, commitment and contribution with God. That defined who Caleb was before God.

It is my profound belief that if the Church of Christ is ever to start the long, painful, but ultimately worthwhile road back to biblical relevance, the "clergy" as a "separate class" must be disbanded, redirected in focus and transformed. Scripture never allows a separate class of pseudo-priests, and yes, even if you think you are not, that is the sad truth. Get away from your dress-coded management of dependent congregations leading towards the mistruth of community, and start to do what most of you are not trained for.

- ✓ Lead.
- ✓ Lead like Christ.
- ✓ Lead your people to become the people God always planned for them to become.

And if you feel outraged, you should do. Because only taking and accepting the culture handed to you has led to the difficulties we are in today. "The Lord says: "These people come near to me with their mouth and honour me with their lips, but their hearts are far from me. Their worship of me is based on merely human rules they have been taught." Isaiah ch.29, v13.

"Jesus replied, "Isaiah was right when he prophesied about you hypocrites; as it is written: 'These people honour me with their lips, but their hearts are far from me. They worship me in vain; their teachings are merely human rules.' You have let go of the commands of God and are holding on to human traditions." Mark ch.7, vv6-8.

In its more traditional variants and elsewhere, the Church of Jesus Christ has moved from being a reality to becoming only an "activity". Where people are focussed on God in Christ, they will not be focussed on church and the Churchianity it breeds. One could describe the need for everyone who "is" the church to seek not for "activity", not even for "experience", but as Caleb did, to daily do the decisive dedication of alignment with God's heart, with God's priorities. Because as we have seen above, that is the one sure way of becoming noticed and set apart by God for His purposes

One of the most significant difficulties facing the Church in pursuit of its Churchianity agenda is "groupthink". It displays itself in the unquestioning following of the dress-coded leaders, the willingness to act on their behalf to suppress dissent or alternative views, often in extreme or unpalatable ways, and the essential in-group activities that quietly create the out-group unwittingly.

It denigrates and dilutes the work of Christ as He focussed intensely on the creation of the early leaders of His Church. He focussed intently on growing His people. Above all else was His incredible courage in speaking out actively on the abuses of the Church of His day, the proud dress-coded clergy priesthood.

Bottom-Line Stuff

Don Stephens, the co-founder of "Mercy Ships", the hospital ships bringing healing and hope to thousands of people every year, reports:

> *Although the greater story of Mercy Ships is about the thousands of supporters and volunteers who helped make this dream a reality for the past 40 years, four key events motivated me to launch out: a storm, a ship, a son, and a saint.*
>
> ***Storm:*** *In 1964, my wife Deyon and I went to the Bahamas with a youth group of about 120. A 100-year storm, Hurricane Cleo, struck the Bahamas. Various small groups gathered to pray, and someone prayed for a ship to show God's love in the midst of disaster.*
>
> ***Ship:*** *The ship that became the seed for the vision was the hospital ship of the Eisenhower administration, the SS Hope. I was fascinated by Dr William Walsh's idea of taking the hospital to the poor.*
>
> ***Son:*** *In 1976 our son John Paul was born. 'JP', as we affectionately call him, was a special needs child who is now a special needs adult who cannot care for himself, nor speak. This son, whom we dearly love, became an inner catalyst for my wife Deyon and I to look for ways to serve others in difficult circumstances.*

Saint: In 1977, I spent 10 days in Calcutta, India. A friend arranged for two of us to meet Mother Teresa. She arranged for a tour of the Sisters of Mercy home for the disabled. The impact on me was profound. I left with a sense that Mother Teresa was saying to me to be the eyes, ears, hands, and heart for others like John Paul, who had no voice.

So a saint, my son, a 100-year storm, and a hospital ship of the past became strong threads woven into my inner being. I had found something worth investing my life to bring it into a reality. Now, no one does anything alone. The real story of Mercy Ships is the thousands of volunteers and supporters who are now a part of this journey. These are the ones at the 'coal face' of bringing hope and healing as we follow the 2,000-year-old model of Jesus.

> **Stephens said he had prepared questions beforehand he'd wanted to ask Mother Theresa, but she insisted instead on asking him three questions:**
> **Why were you born?**
> **Where is the pain in your life?**
> **What are doing about your dreams?**

(Quote above cited.[188])

Stephens recounted that visit with what he described as a diminutive, but direct nun.

The first question is a fundamental one, Stephens said, in determining a purpose in life.

The second question can be a difficult one to answer, particularly for people who'd rather dismiss or ignore the pain in their lives, he said.

The third question constitutes a call to action, he said.

In answering the questions, Mother Theresa posed, Stephens decided his purpose in life was to launch a hospital ship that would provide medical services to the poor.

One of the pains in his life, he said, is the challenges faced by a severely autistic son who can't talk. Stephens said Mother Theresa told him that if he pursued his dream of a hospital ship, his son's voice would be heard by thousands.

Shortly after visiting with Mother Theresa, he began looking for a ship that

---

[188] M3 Contributor, '2019 M3 Plenary Session – Don Stephens | M3 | Mobilizing Medical Missions', 2019 <https://m3missions.com/2019-m3-plenary-session-don-stephens/> [accessed 28 May 2020].

could be converted into a floating hospital.[189]

The Big Plan

God has placed within every human being, in their heart, mind, soul and body, His characteristics of Origin, Identity, Significance, Potential, Purpose, Vision, Focus and Destiny. He planned for every single human being to live with Wholeheartedness, Courage, Compassion and Commitment.

We have a choice. To stay where we are or step up to become the person God always planned for us to become. Yes, we are imperfect, sinful people who fail, but having put our faith in Christ, never let those aspects hinder you from becoming God's person as He intended. Never let anyone or any church system hold you back.

> Your identity is Christ-defined – rediscover it.
> Your significance is unique to Jesus Christ – realise it.
> Your potential in Jesus Christ is unlimited – unleash it.
> Your purpose is just perfect for you and what God planned – carry it out.
> As you consecrate, dedicate and fully commit yourself to Him daily, He will impart His Vision to you – don't let it out of your mind.
> Your destiny is assured and beyond human understanding, now and forever; grasp it, and go for it.

Or:
> Feeling you don't know who you are? Truth: Your identity is Christ-defined – rediscover it.
> Feeling you are insignificant? Truth: Your significance is unique to Jesus Christ – realise it.
> Feeling you have no potential? Truth: Your potential in Jesus Christ is unlimited – unleash it.
> Feeling your life is purposeless? Truth: Your purpose is just perfect for you and what God planned – carry it out.
> Feeling lost in this world? Truth: As you daily consecrate, dedicate and fully commit yourself to Him, He will impart His Vision to you – don't let it out of your mind.

---

[189] 'Sight Magazine - THE INTERVIEW: DON STEPHENS, CO-FOUNDER OF MERCY SHIPS' <https://www.sightmagazine.com.au/features/12647-the-interview-don-stephens-co-founder-of-mercy-ships> [accessed 28 May 2020].

➤ Feeling there is nothing to live for? Truth: Your destiny is assured and beyond human understanding, now and forever; grasp it, go for it.

Our Leadership focus should be to: Lead people to discover and connect with their Purpose in Christ.

Our Leadership focus for The Church:

The Body of Christ becomes alive with the individual's potential, purpose and possibilities and connects with the world outside.

Its focus is to connect with and grow people just as Christ did when He walked this earth. His entire focus is both His Father's plan of salvation and growing His people to become the people individually that God always planned for them to become.

> *"Our duty, as men and women, is to proceed*
> *as if limits to our ability did not exist.*
> *We are collaborators in creation."*
> *Pierre Teilhard De Chardin*

(Above quotation cited. [190])

Questions:

Where am I trying to go? – I must understand my purpose completely and what I am trying to achieve.

What is my goal? – I must clearly state my purpose. I must clearly know where I am going.

How am I going to get there? – I must understand what the vehicle is. (Do what you can with what you have where you are.)

How does all this stuff fit together for God?

TRANSFORMED! is a similar theme, that we are created and endowed with God-given gifts and unique attributes. Your life experience is just as God planned it. No one else can live your life for you. No one can replace you, and God's purpose for you. You are unique and irreplaceable but also uniquely filled with potential and purpose. The salvation that Christ completed, once accepted personally, opens the door to the unleashing and, indeed, the unlocking of the potential and purpose that God has for you. What will you do with your life?

---

[190] 'A Quote by Pierre Teilhard de Chardin'
<https://www.goodreads.com/quotes/38263-our-duty-as-men-and-women-is-to-proceed-as> [accessed 26 May 2020].

Will you waste it on the overwhelming, aimless distraction that holds most people in its grip?

Or will you wake up and realise that God gifted you a different life to be lived and that it is yours for the living if only you will give your life back to the one who created you in the first place and use

- ✓ every ounce of your strength,
- ✓ every aspect of your intellect,
- ✓ every aspect of your creativity,
- ✓ every aspect of who you are,
- ✓ to influence and help others to live the life God always planned for them to live, if only someone had told them soon enough.

Here's the deal – God has created and gifted you to be an utterly unique person. What you do with your life is your gift to God. Live it up, live it out, give it back to the One who created you.

Quotes:

"Live the life you have been entrusted with."[191]

"If you live in the past, you die to your future."[192]

"God never calls us into our past; He is always calling us into His future."[193]

"Don't allow fear to steal your future, die empty."[194]

"Whatever God has planned, we need to get prepared for it. When we finally get there, we need to be ready. We need to be ready for those unexpected moments when we're called to elevate, those moments so much bigger than we are that we can hardly breathe. We must be battle-ready."[195]

"The great tragedy would be to live your life waiting for that moment to come instead of living your life preparing for when the moment comes. In God's economy, nothing is wasted. Everything you do today that seems insignificant will find its significance. You should never see any task as too small for you. If small is what you are entrusted with, that's your stewardship."[196]

"To live the life God created you to live, to ensure that everything within you is unleashed for the good of humanity, even if your ultimate longing is to find

[191] McManus, *The Last Arrow*, p. 28.
[192] McManus, *The Last Arrow*, p. 34.
[193] McManus, *The Last Arrow*, p. 43.
[194] McManus, *The Last Arrow*, p. 22.
[195] McManus, *The Last Arrow*, p. 194.
[196] McManus, *The Last Arrow*, p. 194.

yourself, you need to find your people." [197]

"We live our lives holding on to the status quo, and we are terrified of breaking away from the pack to become uniquely the person who God created us to be." [198]

All the above Quotes from Erwin McManus's book, *The Last Arrow*.

> **Be courageous enough to pursue Destiny. Stand up in this world occupied by more than seven billion people, and say, "I have a unique purpose and a destiny that is distinct from any other person who has ever lived."**
> **Know that you have a role, an idea, a plan, or a vision to make a contribution to humanity.**
> **from Destiny, by T.D. Jakes**

(Above quotation cited. [199])

To those who have hurt, hindered and kept us back from discovering our purpose, this must be our reply – "I have a unique purpose and a destiny that is distinct from any other person who has ever lived." God has called me to respond in this way and write *TRANSFORMED!* because I believe the Church of Jesus Christ needs total transformation as Christ intended. It needs to rediscover God's Identity, God's created potential, God's Purpose, God's Vision, and God's Destiny for it both as individuals and corporately.

- ✓ Lord God, here I am: Count me in!
- ✓ Yes, I will be seen as simple,
- ✓ Yes, I will be disdainfully rejected by traditional theologians,
- ✓ Yes, I will be shunned by others who cannot see my vision,
- ✓ Yes, I will be ridiculed by the various church leaders who blindly repeat every week the same depleting rituals in the vain and mad hope that a different result will ensue.

But you see, what started all this was the simple pain of seeing failed, closed

---

[197] McManus, *The Last Arrow*, p. 165.
[198] 'GLS18 Session Notes–Erwin McManus–The Last Arrow', *Global Leadership Network*, 2018 <https://globalleadership.org/articles/leading-yourself/gls18-session-notes-erwin-mcmanus-the-last-arrow/> [accessed 26 May 2020].
[199] T. D. Jakes, *Destiny: Step into Your Purpose*, First edition (New York: Faith Words, 2015), p. 234.

churches all over Wales and the South West of England. All has not been well with the Church of Christ in the UK for over 100 years. My heart would literally feel that pain when I saw thousands of closed churches and chapels across Wales and the South West in every town and village. The question that surfaced was this: "Who screwed up? Was it God or the people?" And then, "Who am I to imagine that I could help this situation?" But then again, no one else seems able to make a difference as the traditional churches, on their slow downward decline, have simply given up, lost the plot, sidelined themselves down the cul-de-sac of "community", and "loving each other" as ends in themselves.

The Church of Jesus Christ was always designed to break out of the cultures it grew up in to become what God intended it to be. And it is plain to be seen that the Churchianity we blindly pump out is not what God intended despite the protestations of the clergy. We cannot go on as we are in the foolishness of pretence that all is well.

So, I decided to make a difference under God to the best of my ability, such as it is, and *TRANSFORMED!* was born.

TRANSFORMED! was written to seek God's way forward out of this desert. And it will take the personal discovery of God's true individual origin, His true individual identity for you, His true individual significance, His true individual potential, His true individual purpose for you, His true individual vision for you, and His true individual Destiny for you, to undertake this task.

It was fundamentally for all these closed churches, the loss of focus, the growth of the fatal inward-looking nature, and the insidious cancer of deep institutionalisation along with the unbiblical hierarchical ordained clergy that stopped these well-meaning congregations from realising that God intended them to grow personally and numerically. Someone has written with intense clarity, "Churches don't grow because they don't want to grow." They did not, and the catastrophe that overtook these churches was as sure as it was complete.

There is a way back to the original church health that God will honour. And it is this: that through effective, focussed, visionary leadership that leads their people to connect with God's purposes for them, and the encouragement of courageous commitment, both personally and corporately, that the transformation spoken of in Romans ch.1, v2 will take place. Only through the rediscovery of your origin, identity, significance, potential, purpose, vision and destiny by individuals saying, "Lord Jesus, count me in," by conscious consecration and decisive dedication, will the Church of Jesus Christ become great again as He first intended.

So, every individual's transformation and renewal in the Church of Jesus Christ, under His effective leadership, is God's Big Plan. Lord, count me in!

10.3 Transformational Leadership

> *"A transformational leader intentionally engages people to think and act in such a way that it makes a positive difference in their lives and in the lives of others."*
> *John C. Maxwell, Intentional Living*

(Above quotation cited. [200])

Mac Pier wrote in Consequential Leadership: "Mellado (Jim) saw the American church trending in the same direction as the church in Western Europe, where cathedrals are empty and Christian influence is minuscule. He concluded that America was potentially one generation away from a European non-Christian reality.'" [201]

Sadly, I have lived and "attended" church in that reality, thinking it was normal all my life. I thought that the "ordained" hierarchical leadership of a church was normal. I sought to excuse the unsavoury sycophantic results of that unbiblical format by imagining that it also was normal. Christ never intended such a God-dishonouring system to be the leadership of His Church.

In the spirit of Bill Hybels's book, *Holy Discontent*, I realised I had "had enough" of dead churches going through the motions. I could not stand it anymore! I had to do something about it. Not that I was in the least bit qualified in any way, shape or form. Looking at the CV of RJF, you might say that God was "having a laugh". No one could be less qualified in the traditional academic or ordained ministry senses to attempt to see the need, discover the deep issues that have long held us back, and start the long and inevitably painful transformation of the Church of Jesus Christ from its tradition-bound and inward-focussed retreat mode, to the properly functioning growing group of personally focussed people fully engaged in a relationship with the living Christ!

I feel the need to somehow "nail" the issues behind this book (at least my simple understanding of them), the issues of:

- Inadequate biblical understanding and practice: we are created by God for His Higher Purpose, for relationship with Him, and to fulfil His Higher Purpose for us individually. Instead, we try to exist with:
- Inadequate and simply bad hierarchical leadership.

---

[200] John C. Maxwell, *Intentional Living*, p. 234.
[201] Mac Pier, *Consequential Leadership: 15 Leaders Fighting for Our Cities, Our Poor, Our Youth, and Our Culture* (Downers Grove, IL: IVP Books, 2012), pt. 1700.

- We imagine the "Churchianity" that we "do" and the church buildings we "attend" are somehow what Christ intended! It beggars belief that we dutifully support this travesty of God's intentions every week in the mad hope that something, somewhere, may happen if we repeat it often enough!
- Wrong assumptions: that God will revive us if He wills.
- Wrong focus on community.
- Wrong direction – touting a system of tradition and beliefs rather than a relationship with the living Christ.
- Passive congregations comprised of compliant and disengaged Christians.
- Dead churches whose visible trajectory is a slow decline.
- The complete inability for anyone to stand up and state, "We cannot go on as we are," fearful of being seen as troublemakers for the current church hierarchy with the inevitable ostracism by the "leader followers" and their sycophancy for rocking the boat.
- Congregations locked in to "doing" church (Churchianity) on their terms.

In understanding the UK figures for church attendance, we do not have comparable statistics to attempt a serious comparison with the US situation. But if one takes, say, 1913 as the start date, look at the attendance then, look at the overall population then and compare it with now, we get a picture of a continuing, unbroken decline. The figures are horrific, but what is worse is that no one has been able to do anything about it! Being effective in assessing and understanding where we are is an essential part of understanding where God would have us be and go.

The turning against God by a nation and the consequence of that decision to turn away is the imperceptibly slow "disintegration" of a society that abandons God and His revealed Word. That abandonment of Scripture's laws and truths is never without painful results and, indeed, a disaster for a nation that literally turns its back to its Creator.

That we could reach such depths of societal disintegration could not have been apprehended or imagined 50 or even 100 years ago. Divorce, for example, once seen as horrific, is now often encouraged by a society of individuals who have never been shown or understood that God's ways were laid out in scripture as the best way to live. Now, we reap what we have sown, and the Harvest is almost too terrible to contemplate. However, this was not part of Christ's focus, but it is tempting to think/argue, etc., into that area, except this takes away from the central theme of "We are Created for Higher Purpose". Negative arguments never lead people to their purpose and destiny for God. Negative arguments cannot be sustained because they do not inspire. They do, however, stir human emotions in short-lived ways that are unsustainable and depleting.

God created us for His purpose, His vision and His destiny; for courage, connection and commitment; to lead lives consequential for Him. They are to be lives of wholehearted connection with God. We are created to be inspired and transformed, not fearful.

For those reasons, negative argument acts only on the fearful parts of human thinking. Creating fear is not part of Christ's focus. Those who use such arguments can be effective at a certain level, but we end up being known for what we are against, not for the glorious purposes of God, Who created us individually. We end up in the middle ages thinking of heresy, heretics, and burnings, which Christ condemned unequivocally, but which the negative culture and thinking of those times, such as actively seeking out of heretics, justified as God's will for them! With hindsight, it seems impossible that such things could happen, but even John Calvin agreed with the burning alive of a man called Severus, who disagreed with the current theological thinking of their day.

What Christ did over a period of time was to transform both individuals and cultures as a result of their trust and relationship with Him. For the first generations of people brought up in a Godless society, we see the opportunities that God would have us take to transform ourselves and our culture, once again, as in history and return to the Lord our God and seek His face earnestly. Always remember this: that changed society is the result, not the reason.

"You see, we spent time with visionaries. We hung out with people of great faith. Yes, they are fallible and sometimes sinful persons, but God has used them in extraordinary ways. Some of the visionaries served on the staff. Some were senior pastors. Some were laypeople. But all were visionaries. They believed in a God of miracles. They attempted things that would be impossible without a supernatural God. They went into the promised land of God's possibilities, and they will never be the same." *Breakout Churches*, Dr. Thom Rainer.[202]

---

[202] Thom S. Rainer, *Breakout Churches: Discover How to Make the Leap* (Grand Rapids, Mich: Zondervan, 2005), pt. 1946.

> *I am reminded of Brene Brown's book 'Daring Greatly',*
> *"That it is not about winning or losing. It's about courage.*
> *It is also about finding your voice,*
> *insisting with courage that you be heard."*

(Above quotation cited.[203])

In our calling as Transformational Leaders, we are to live by expressing God's heart. In other words, live or do what is on God's mind, what He is thinking, and that means checking that out. He will create His Plans as we create the bridge by walking on it. Instead of leaning backwards in comfort as we sit in our pews, we need to lean forwards in expressing His thoughts so that we can be alive.

Leighton Ford writes in his book, *Transforming Leadership*:

If Jesus' venture in leadership was to invest and reproduce himself (and his Father) in those he chose at that time, then his leadership is more than a historical curiosity. It is an ongoing reality. It is his continuing reproduction of himself in human beings in every generation until the consummation of all history.[204]

It is my deep conviction that the understanding of Jesus' leadership is not only important but essential to our time. He was able to create, articulate and communicate a compelling vision; to change what people talk about and dream of; to make his followers transcend self-interest; to enable us to see ourselves and our world in a new way; to provide prophetic insight into the very heart of things, and to bring about the highest order of change. Because of the great paradigm shifts which our world is undergoing at the end of a millennium, we need both a supreme model and the source which Jesus provides for transforming leaders - leaders who can enable us to see beyond our narrow and often selfish horizons, who can empower us to be more than we have been. Transforming leaders are those who are able to divest themselves of their power and invest it in their followers in such a way that others are empowered, while the leaders themselves end with the greatest power of all, the power of seeing themselves reproduced in others.[205]

According to Bernard Bass

---

[203] Brown, *Daring Greatly*, p. 248.
[204] Leighton Ford, *Transforming Leadership: Jesus' Way of Creating Vision, Shaping Values & Empowering Change* (Downers Grove, Ill.: InterVarsity Press, 1991), pt. 88.
[205] Ford, pt. 72.

- *Transactional leaders work within the situation; transformational leaders change the situation.*

- *Transactional leaders accept what can be talked about; transformational leaders change what can be talked about.*

- *Transactional leaders accept the rules and values; transformational leaders change them.*

- *Transactional leaders talk about pay-offs; transformational leaders talk about goals.*

- *Transactional leaders bargain; transformational leaders symbolize.*[206]

- *Transactional Leaders consult about what followers want: transformational leaders talk about higher objectives.*[207]

How does all the above make you feel? Helping to grow others by:
- ✓ Seeing their potential.
- ✓ Unlocking and Unleashing their potential for God.
- ✓ Helping them discover their gifts and talents for God.
- ✓ Helping them lead lives of significance for Christ.
- ✓ Helping them make a difference for God in the days He gives them on this earth.
- ✓ Creating a living Mindset of growth and development from the inside out.
- ✓ Helping others succeed to live a life of greatness for God.
- ✓ Helping those who feel disengaged, disregarded and peripheral (especially in churches) that they matter in God's sight.

---

[206] Ford, pt. 134.
[207] Ford, pt. 3154.

> *Lord Jesus Christ, I long to be involved in Your plans,*
> *in something bigger than myself:*
> ✓ *where I matter*
> ✓ *where I can make a difference*
> ✓ *where I am heard*
> ✓ *where I can grow*
> ✓ *where I am inspired*
> ✓ *where I can contribute*
> ✓ *where I am part of that intense environment that requires*
>   *people's best contribution*
> ✓ *where I am challenged*
> ✓ *where I can be included in rigorous debate*
> ✓ *where I am invested in*
> ✓ *where I can be led to greater things*
> ✓ *where I am totally engaged in this*
> ✓ *where I can give all my discretionary time, emotions and love*
> ✓ *where all my faculties can be used by God for His Glory*

Lord God, the world You created needs my contribution – I believe that You created me on purpose for Your Purpose. I long to be part of Your plans, to be fully engaged in something bigger than myself, where I matter, and I am encouraged to contribute.

My Compelling Vision

Living for God in Christ through conscious consecration and daily dedication as my considered response to His calling in scripture is the very least I can undertake. So, my compelling vision:

The Purpose:

My two primary goals in light of the above statement are:

- ❖ Living for God and His Grander Vision of Higher Purpose for me and to live a life that echoes in Eternity for God.
- ❖ Inspiring others to grow and be transformed in Christ to become the fulfilled people he always planned them to be. To discover and unlock

potential in others for God and to connect them to God's Higher Purpose for them.

The Picture:
- ➤ To find a way through the difficulties and forge a route for others to follow.
- ➤ To start the journey, grow, mature and become the fulfilled people God always planned for us to be.
- ➤ To understand the process, pathway and purpose of discipleship.
- ➤ To unlock potential in others.
- ➤ To inspire them to action under God. All this is my purpose and goal for God.

The Values:
I submit that the primary heart of a Christian is to be:
- ✓ Fully aware and continually connected to Christ.
- ✓ Fully aligned and understanding in Christ.
- ✓ Fully engaged and continually renewed by Christ.
- ✓ Fully committed and continually consecrated for Christ.
- ✓ Fully dedicated and continually growing in Christ.

It is all about living for God, leadership for God and legacy for God. These are my compelling visions.

> *Today, by His Spirit, I will seek God with all my heart to fulfil His Purposes in Jesus Christ, for His church and for myself and live the life that He created me to live, walking the pathways He created for me to walk in and do those good works He created for me to do.*
>
> *Anon.*

In Romans ch.12, vv1-2, Paul exhorts us to continually consecrate and dedicate lives and transformed minds in our relationship with God in Christ. We are created for this, and Paul tells us this in Ephesians ch.1, vv 4-6 that God chose us in Christ before the world began, planning that we <u>should</u> be consecrated to the praise of His Glory. Our work is to discover and unlock that potential in every human being so that firstly, by faith, they might come to God in Christ and then, secondly, become in their lives the people God created them to be. To the praise of His Glory. Ephesians ch.1, vv12 and 14.

Paul is saying behave and think like Christ towards others with focus, intentionality and courage, unlocking their potential for God. That is an almost impossible task, except for one thing – He has given us His Spirit, not only to believe but to be transformed in both thinking and behaviour.

In the Church of Christ, the first priority has, in the past, sometimes been achieved. The second priority has rarely been either recognised, understood or realised.

There will never be a single human being on this planet that is not of such significance to God but that God chooses to die to save that person. It then follows that our response to that love is of unbelievable importance.

We cannot be effective for God if we seek to live our lives with the illusory assumptions of our culture. Unless we assume the premises of the mind of Christ, we will live lives that are simply an illusion.

Stop living your accepted, normal, cultural-assumptions-based life of scarcity and depletion. Start living your life transformed by the assumptions of Christ as He lived His Life.

So one of the most influential and important questions we can ever ask ourselves is this: "What are the assumptions of the mind of Christ clearly stated in Scripture?"

Instead of seeking to manage an organisation in normal mode, AKA "survive with scarce resources", we should aspire to inspire to have flourishing, growing people. Don't focus on problem-solving, but on growing your people. When you change your organisation's underlying assumptions, a very different culture will appear, and the results that will follow that change will be transformed and growing people.

Can you grasp the significance of this? Continuously repeating the same things (normal mode) in the vain hope that some different result will ensue is the definition of madness. The constant weekly repetition of Sunday services is depleting the Church at every turn. Every Sunday morning, God's people turn up at their church building and depart unchanged as their God-created potential and talents are left locked inside them by the ruling clergy, unrecognised, undiscovered, unused, unfulfilled and wasted. They are continually depleted rather than being developed for God's purposes. And the Church systems that control this charade continue every week to deplete further and disengage the people of God.

Instead, change the organisation's assumptions from solving daily problems and the repetition of the denominational cultures towards the growth and development of the individuals in it (and outside it), and a completely different outcome will naturally ensue. And it will be the result of the change of assumptions of the organisation away from problem-solving {the old normal) to a dynamic and inspiring culture of people development.

That, simply, is what Jesus did, and He is still transforming the world 2,000 years later. I rest my case.

Lead Where You Are

Let's get a few things straight:

➢ Being a leader is a choice, not a position.
➢ Never underestimate yourself if God has gifted you with this Mindset.
➢ You are a leader if you have chosen to undertake this path for others.
➢ Never allow others, who may officially be leaders in the organisation or church where you are, to put you down because you are not Clergy or part of the hierarchy.
➢ Never allow others to discourage you. Only you can do that!
➢ Give yourself permission to lead where you are.
➢ Realise no one can stop you from becoming the person God always planned for you to become.
➢ God has called you to live Christ-inspired leadership for Him.
➢ Remember that this is not about you but for others whom you are created and called to grow for God in Christ.

Integral to all of the above is the concept, the truth, that God has entrusted us with life. It is not ours, yet we must live it. The concept of it being stewarded fits perfectly with Christ's parable of the talents.

> *Let your vision be determined by*
> *what your Creator has put inside you.*
> *— Jossy Chacko*

(Above quotation cited.[208])

People are created by God for His Purposes, and my job as a leader is to draw out and help them discover their true God-given gifts and talents. You see, Christ calls us to transcend our current limitations, to start our journey to grow, mature and transform, to become all that He intended.

✓ Transform, Inspire, Equip

---

[208] 'QI201710523', *Global Leadership Network*, 2017
<https://globalleadership.org/quote/leading-yourself/qi201710523/> [accessed 26 May 2020].

✓ Develop a compelling vision that will outlast you.

✓ As shown in Christ, we "are" the church and "transformation" is God's primary focus and game plan.

✓ As Christ instructed Peter, "feed my sheep", which meant "grow My people" to become all I designed them to be.

✓ Christ is the greatest multiplier of people.

You are called by God in Christ so that in loving God, make these conscious choices daily:

✓ Be Consecrating, Dedicating, and Transforming yourselves because you are created to grow in Christ.

✓ Take ownership of yourself for God.

✓ Live your life worthy of His Calling.

✓ Challenge assumptions as Christ did everywhere. Your own, those of others, your culture, your church system, all of them. Most are wrong. But you will notice He never challenged Scripture, for it speaks of Him. Start thinking like Christ towards people.

✓ Decide to become a multiplier of people for Christ as He did.

He showed the world that one person in Christ could affect not just contemporaries but Nations and the World itself. There is no limit to what God can do with a single human being who daily consecrates, daily dedicates, and daily transforms their hearts, minds, and lives to Him. I find that both incredible and frightening in equal measure. Just live your life worthy of His Calling.

So why are our churches so full of needy consumers of religion? Because they have never been led to be anything else. What a criminal waste of God-created human potential masquerading as accepted spiritual practice that has kept individuals and congregations dependent, compliant, inward-focussed and immature like children who cannot and never will grow up. We vainly imagine that our inward-focussed club is what Christ intended. The "Church of Jesus Christ" was never planned to be about "you" or "your" needs, likes and dislikes, or "your" style of worship. The saddest truth is that the Clergy, in complying with their denominations' directions, has led us nowhere.

They have led us to dead ends and left us in suspended animation simply because they have never understood that if they aspire to be like Christ, then ministry is a fallacy. It was not his intention to "minister" to anybody. Yes, of course, He had compassion for those who could not help themselves, but as you will remember, He could and did rope-whip the commercial thieves out of His Father's house. This was not merely because of that activity directly, but more likely, they had perverted the dress-coded priests of that time, colluding with them through back payments to defraud the people.

Christ's intention was to lead every one of those who called on Him to become the leaders of His Church, His visible body, and to always look outwards for those who were not yet with Him. Mollycoddling church members was definitely not on His agenda. And those who mistakenly misunderstood His intentions would be told in no uncertain terms that He viewed them as a Satanic attack on Him.

Every human being that Christ connects with is designed to grow. It is in our genes. If we are not aware of that personal growth taking place inwardly and self-evidently, then we are highly likely in a state of suspended animation. And most churches, because of their deep and depleting inward focus, are in that state.

We have been conned and effectively lied to for over 1,800 years by the dress-coded hierarchy known as "the clergy". To be fair, they were never designed to grow their congregations but to control and effectively manipulate them into pursuing the status quo while maintaining their own power and position. The result is dependency, compliance and immaturity. In many churches, traditional and otherwise, the Protestant Sunday morning service serves only to create its own continuity while stopping the release of God's created Purpose, Values and Vision within the individuals present. They turn up as needy consumers of religion, and they depart unchanged, unchallenged, unreleased, their God-created potential locked firmly in place. This is the reality that the clergy-controlled hierarchy working in transactional mode has achieved for centuries.

Hierarchical management of churches creates a deeply distorted version of the Church of Christ. Power can only move vertically and flows only downwards in hierarchical systems. And don't let anyone use cynical, spiritual-sounding language to put you down in that area because you can unequivocally say that Christ would not countenance such practice. Far from a hierarchical, transactional mode, He epitomised transformational leadership simply since He let nothing get in the way of growing His people. Such are you and me if we name the name of Christ.

It's time to change. We cannot and must not go on as we are. We must be transformed to become the people God always planned for us to be.

God created us for His purposes, His vision and His destiny; for consecration and dedication with courage, connection and commitment to Him; to lead lives that are consequential for Him; to lead lives that fulfil His purposes for us. They are to be lives dedicated to God. They are to be lives of wholehearted connection with God. We are created to be inspired and transformed, not fearful, as Christ restores us in Himself to God, and we are to discover our identity in Him:

✓ Rediscovering the uniqueness of the human spirit in God's sight.
✓ Rediscovering the incredible importance of every human being.

- ✓ Rediscovering your part in God's plans for you because you are an original in God's sight.
- ✓ Rediscovering the truth that our identity is found in Him.

It is all about being inspired to action, keeping focussed on Christ, keeping His focus and connecting with people. It is not necessarily about stopping everything you do. It's genuinely understanding Christ's priorities correctly and then deciding how to align your priorities and your habits/culture and what you do with that fresh knowledge.

The gap between where we are and the intentions of God in Christ for each of us is enormous. Our assumption that the Churchianity that we "do" is where we should be is a life-wasting fallacy. God has called each and every one of us to His life of Higher Purpose, and if we cannot awaken to that new reality, then we can never grow to become the person God always planned for us to become. It is that simple. Our problem is that what we think we know gets in the way and stops us from growing into God's new reality for us. Every one of us has potential beyond our understanding and beyond our wildest dreams. God calls each of us to discover that life, start soaring like eagles close to Him and stop pecking with turkeys by the side of the runway.

Maturing in your relationship with God in Christ is not just a "nice to do" or "good to do" thing. It is about fulfilling God's purposes for you, in you, and through you forever. It is about taking hold firmly, consecratedly, dedicatedly, and fully understanding God's grace and intentional plans for you. It is more effectively realising *your* status in Christ. Then, acting on that understanding. So, "Just live a life worthy of the calling you have received."

Simply wake up and realise that God created you to:

- ✓ Grow to become the person God always planned for you to be.
- ✓ Wake up to all God has for you right now and start the transition to transformation.
- ✓ Understand, start living and start acting the status He gives you in Christ.
- ✓ Realise you are not where you should be.
- ✓ Transform and become Transformational.
- ✓ Break out of your cultural silo, stop your Churchianity culture acting, stop conforming to the status quo, and become the person He always meant you to be.
- ✓ Live a life worthy of His calling.
- ✓ To re-align our lives with God in connection, commitment and contribution to Him as He designed.

✓ "To lead a life that echoes in Eternity for God." – Dr Dan Erickson. [209]
All this is to help people become the people God always planned for them to become. By starting the Awakening, we move with courage through personal ownership to commitment and contribution.

"For we are God's handiwork, created in Christ Jesus to do good works, which God prepared in advance for us to do." Ephesians ch.2, v10.

The once-great Church of Jesus Christ in the post-Christian West has declined primarily because of a loss of courage, focus, leadership, vision, discipline, and connection, where comfort has replaced courage. The remedy is to be found in the rediscovery under God of the same.

That same courage, focus, leadership, vision, discipline, and connective ability took our Saviour from obscurity in Nazareth to the heights of Calvary, and all in servant obedience to the Higher Purpose that His Father had planned for Him.

We also are called to discover personally God's Higher Purpose for our lives. Those same qualities will be drawn forth from those who commence this walk into the unknown, trusting in the Eternal Being who created them in Christ uniquely for this task.

This loss of courage, focus, leadership and vision etc., is primarily the result of human Silos (the word is used in social anthropology to describe the default human, rational compartmentalisation in organisations). The roots of this are grown in the default human nature of sin, selfishness, greed, and fear. These inevitably give birth to the need to rule over others by power, influence and manipulation for self-gratification. Jesus said, in response to His disciples starting to act in this way, "not so with you. Instead, whoever wants to be great among you must become your servant." Mark ch.10, v43, NIV.

All the above come from the twin natural human assumptions of scarcity and depletion. God's economy is based on surplus and abundance. What a sharp distinction and contrast.

Christ was having none of it. He was ruthless in stopping Silos in their tracks. He knew that if you cannot master Silos, they will master you.

And holding people back are the Churchianity's unseen cultural rules, especially those of the established traditional churches where the dress-coded hierarchy is king. This is not only the hidden rules of that hierarchy (especially the glass ceiling of the clergy), but equally important are the assumptions that

---

[209] 'People Matter Ministries', *People Matter Ministries*
<http://www.peoplematterministries.com> [accessed 26 May 2020].

flow from traditional practices for the people in a church that sin management along with transactional leadership is more important than their spiritual growth and the unleashing of their potential for God.

Fortunately for everyone, the Bible shows unmistakably that Jesus Christ, who is firstly Creator, then Saviour, is unmistakably the greatest culture transformer ever. We are called, in scripture, to be like Christ, to challenge current culture and then help people transform past and beyond their culture and beliefs, whatever they may be, to reach God's culture that He planned for us. It is not an understatement to say that God created us for His Culture, which Christ exemplified.

So, invest in your future and seek under God to become the person He planned and, actually, the person you always wanted to be.

Lead For Your Calling

Paul writes in Ephesians 4:1 NIV, "Live a life worthy of the calling you have received." We rightly ask:
- ✓ **Who is calling us?**
  - ✓ We are called because we are uniquely created for God's purposes.
  - ✓ We had better be aware of this.
  - ✓ We had better be sure of Who is calling.
  - ✓ We had better be sure of what He is saying.
  - ✓ We cannot afford to ignore God.
  - ✓ We cannot afford to get it wrong.
  - ✓ We must discover His plans and purposes individually.
- ✓ **Why is He calling us?**
  - ✓ Because He knows the plans He has for us.
  - ✓ Because He decided this for us before the world began.
  - ✓ All the rest of Romans 8 28-30 and Ephesians 1, etc.
- ✓ **What is this calling?**
  - ✓ We are royally called because this is no ordinary human calling.
  - ✓ We are uniquely called to faith in Christ.
  - ✓ We are uniquely called to be focussed on Christ.
  - ✓ We are uniquely called to a relationship with Christ.
  - ✓ We are uniquely called to live lives centred on Christ.
  - ✓ We are uniquely called to be conformed to the image of Christ.
  - ✓ We are uniquely called to suffer for Christ if need be.

✓ We are called to be disciplined like Christ.

✓ **How can we implement this calling?**

   ✓ We are to discover His Higher Purposes for us.

   ✓ We are to follow those Higher Purposes, once discovered.

   ✓ We are to live the life that is really Life given by Christ in pursuit of those Higher Purposes.

   ✓ We are to give our lives for those Higher Purposes if need be.

✓ **What are we to do?**

   ✓ Make daily a decisive dedication, a conscious consecration of all that you are and have been given.

   ✓ Just live a life worthy of the calling you have received.

   ✓ Become a Multiplier for God.

   ✓ Continue to ensure that your calling continues.

   ✓ Be prepared to follow God's calling for the rest of your life.

   ✓ Never allow yourself to deny, renege or bale out on this calling.

   ✓ Carry out continuous self-leadership.

   ✓ Continuously reaffirm your calling.

   ✓ Rise up on eagle's wings and soar close to God as He intended.

✓ **To Whom is this life to be dedicated?**

   ✓ Understand first your status in Christ (not the "journey" in the desert or "in community" nonsense you have been led to believe).

   ✓ Become a consequential leader like Christ, who is transformational, not hierarchically transactional.

   ✓ Make a decisive dedication of yourself to God every day.

   ✓ Create a culture of shared values, vision and passion, where authenticity creates Christ-like transparency.

   ✓ Create Teams where everyone on the team defers to one another, where they celebrate one another's gifts and create opportunities for one another to succeed.

   ✓ Activate God's vision where you are to connect with others for Christ wherever they are.

   ✓ Fight to ensure that this mission is the boss and never gets sidelined.

   ✓ Inspire others to take action!

   ✓ Stop filling potholes; start building peaks.

   ✓ "Just live a life worthy of the calling you have received."

And all because God calls us Transformed people to transform the world one life at a time, as God intended and Christ exemplified, by helping people start the journey God has created them for and to which He called them. In other words, as Christ showed us clearly, we are to be like Him, a Multiplier for God.

We believe we are people whom God has called for His purpose, His Higher Purpose. Those whom He calls (and no one is excluded), He not only equips but, more importantly, He gives them the life that is really Life and gives them His Vision and Purpose, which is a never-failing upwelling of motivation, understanding and commitment to that purpose. This is what Christ not only talked about, but from day one of His earthly ministry, He lived and kept a razor-sharp focus on.

We will not rest until we have achieved His Purpose for our lives. We were born for this. A life of consecration, dedication, courage, connection, commitment and contribution with Christ in God. It was never merely about a system of belief and religious practice of the culture we grew up in, as important as those are in salvation. In New Testament terms, faith in Jesus Christ is always presented in terms of a "believe then act" process that never stops as we mature in our relationship with Jesus Christ.

The inescapable assumption of the people outside the "church" is that we don't care, and they don't matter. Otherwise, we would be amongst them, showing that not to be the case.

Continue To Escape Your Status Quo

Our Churchianity systems are not designed for movement and action. Church has become simply an activity we "attend". All they achieve is to create an inward-focussed, dangerous, frustrated, calamitous and outrageous waste of God's human potential. Instead, much of our Churchianity is simply an exercise in futility, stupidity and groupthink covered with a gloss of religiosity.

The start of the breakout from the default "aimless distraction" life we live for both individuals and churches is often through the wakeup call of crisis. This leads to awareness, the awaking to reality, then confronting the brutal facts, accepting painful reality, the Is/should be discernment[210], discovering our purpose (discovering the Vision Intersection Profile [211]), then creating and maintaining a culture of excellence/greatness – making a difference for His Glory. It is about choosing not to take easier the path to mediocrity but choosing the less-trodden path to greatness, not for you, but greatness for God's Glory, the Servant Leader path. God calls both you and me to attempt greatness for Him, to make a difference for Him in the days He has given us on this earth, and to live a life that echoes in Eternity for Him.

---

[210] Rainer, pt. 1138.
[211] Rainer, pt. 1135.

Despite the clergy's best intentions, it is now clear that they are incapable of moving their people in any meaningful way. Vast amounts of talent for God are squandered continuously because of the inward focus on the "Churchianity" we do in general, and the Sunday morning charade that consumes the efforts of those favoured by the clergy leaves the rest of us as dependent and compliant congregations.

Effectively, everything we do in traditional churches simply is a handed-down culture that we imagine is "Church". Simply culture. It would be laughable if it were not such a sad charade that we unthinkingly run through every week. We never ask whether this is what God wants or planned for us to do. We repeat this charade 52 Sundays a year and never stop to think differently. Most of the church resources are focussed on the need to "feed this beast", who seems insatiable!

We have a morning service where we begin by "seeking God's forgiveness for our sins". This could be described as "sin management" or "shame management" at best and the last vestiges of the Reformation from Catholic priestly indulgences. Of course, we need to seek God's forgiveness for our wrongdoings. But this "sin management" continuation is an insult to the positional integrity that Christ defined for those who trust in Him. Its continuity week by week severely and continuously depletes us by its focus on a clergy-centred sin-management system using the language of scarcity and depletion instead of God's message to us that is one of His calling to everyone and the communication of His abundance and surplus.

Wake up! Grow up! Transform yourself away from this traditional religious hierarchical management to become the person God created you to be. Stop the futility of "church attendance as an activity" and replace your thinking by realising that you are "the church", someone whose actual status and responsibility in Christ before God is immeasurably greater than you have been falsely led to believe.

This will be a tough and challenging road for anyone to walk. Because it calls forth from any individual starting this road unusual depths of courage, impossible heights of vision and the unique calling of commitment to the higher purpose for which God created you. If ever there was a case for the "practice of courage", this is it.

> *Only you can love God like you do.*
> *No one else can take your place.*
> *You were created for this reason and purpose,*
> *and God designed you to fulfil this task of love with Him in this life*
> *and to worship and adore Him for Eternity.*
> *It is why you were born.*

Victor Frankl spoke of the uniqueness of every human being:

"The same holds for human existence. One should not search for an abstract meaning of life. Everyone has his own specific vocation or mission in life to carry out a concrete assignment that demands fulfilment Therein, he or she cannot be replaced, nor can their life be repeated. Thus, everyone's task is as unique as is their specific opportunity to implement it."[212]

Note: R.F. modified to include genders.

For the Christian, this means simply, as Christ manifestly showed, a life of courage, connection, commitment and contribution to God.

So, are the primary underlying reasons for the failure of the Church in the post-Christian West merely a loss of courage, leadership, vision, focus, and connection?

In other words, have we forgotten and lost God's calling to each of us personally, lost our focus on those not yet with us, lost our connection with Him and seeking to connect with others; have we lost the courage to act while turning inwards to our own comfort in the buildings we created accepting our own traditions as the basis for action?

This situation is fundamentally a failure of leadership for and focus on Christ by clergy in the church system that they and their hierarchical management dominate, rather than the Transformational Leadership exemplified in Jesus Christ. Tradition has trumped Transformation. It alone, almost singlehandedly, has killed the church, which placed so much emphasis on its value. No outside agency is responsible for the decline.

The inescapable conclusion is that we cannot go on as we are because more of the same will be more fatal than the irrelevance we have sunk to in our once Christian nation.

Fortunately, God has always had bigger plans than we can ever imagine, and the necessary transition from inward-focussed decline to both personal and church-wide transformation will take place under courageous and visionary leadership that alone follows the unique example of Christ.

---

[212] Viktor E Frankl and others, *Man's Search for Meaning*, 2014, pt. 1400..

Conclusions for Step 10

To Lead! Others To Their Best Lives

Key Thought – It is all about Vision, Inspiration and Transforming Leadership, growing tomorrow's Leaders.

Sub-headings review:

10.1 A Compelling Vision
  - ➢ Choosing to Lead By Empowerment
  - ➢ Building A Culture of Empowerment
  - ➢ Do What Christ Did – Inspire!
  - ➢ God's Big Picture (Aka The Plan)

10.2 Inspire Others to Action
  - ➢ Taking Flight
  - ➢ Bottom Line Stuff
  - ➢ The Big Plan

10.3 Transformational Leadership
  - ➢ My Compelling Vision
  - ➢ Lead Where You Are
  - ➢ Lead For Your Calling
  - ➢ Continue To Escape Your Status Quo

A huge chapter that would be difficult to split or change other than sub-divide. This is the heart of *TRANSFORMED!* It is why you and I decided to stand up and stand out for God in the decisions that have brought us here. Be encouraged because you are transformed in your thinking, potential, and desire to make a difference for God.

We now turn to the fruits and further responsibilities of Leadership for God because, as you may have suspected all along, all this never stops!

Step 11

To Rally! Others To Their Best Lives

~~~

My greatest fear is getting stuck in yesterday.
My greatest opportunity is today.
My greatest focus is today and tomorrow.
Intentionally preparing to make a difference,
living and giving my best life so that others will
be lifted and transformed today and tomorrow.

~~~

You Cannot Add Significance and Value to Yourself alone.
We Can and Must be Significant and Add Value to Others
Because That is What We Are Created For.

~~~

- ❖ **Key Purpose: Create Leadership to Continue for God in the Service of Something Greater than Yourself.**
- ❖ **Key Learning (Always Facing the Unknown without Fear):** You have learned of leading others to Live Their Best Life. This Step 11 may seem unnecessary at first. But the significance is not in the having "done it" of the last step, but the genuine requirement to continue to remind and to rally others, your church, your team, whoever, we all need refreshing reminders of where we are, why we are here, and the encouragement to keep going, maybe in the face of heavy opposition and oppression.
- ❖ **Key Actions (Building The Bridge As You Walk On It):** After Step 10, this is one of the shorter Steps to undertake on your journey. But its importance is out of all relationship to its length. We all become tired, lose energy, feel depleted, and lose alignment with purpose. All these things will conspire against you to lose heart, and others will lose heart in the process. The key Actions are the listed sub-headings below:
- ❖ **Rally Others – Action Steps To Change The Future**
- ❖ **Rally Others – Sustain The Challenge**
- ❖ **Rally Others – Revisit The Dream**

Rally Others – Action Steps To Change The Future

Because this is what it is all about: Growing transformed people who Change their Future, Change their Destiny, make a difference in this world and help others do the same.

Our churches should be less Care Homes for the Elderly – More Boot Camps for Tomorrow's Leaders and Tomorrow's Christ-Centred People whose vision, understanding, and intentionality for Christ and His people are off the scale and out of this world. We need to move from our self-centred mediocrity and the status quo to wake up and live the lives of the magnificence and munificence of God our Saviour as He intended.

It is essential to start from the assumption that where we are in our churches is not normal and that we are most definitely not where we should be. If that is correct, then the vision- and direction-setting questions must be, "Who is God calling us to be, Where is God calling us to go, What is the road we must take, and How is God calling us to get there? What has to change in a church to ensure the move from comfort-centred irrelevance towards becoming the courageous prevailing Church of Christ that Jesus worked to create before His death?"

It is all about counting the Cost.

Am I willing to pay the price that Christ did for me and give my life to fulfil His purposes in me, at the cost of my life...?

- ➢ Do not conform to the pattern of this world but be transformed by the renewing of your mind, then you will be able to test and approve God's purpose for you. Romans ch.12, v2.
- ➢ Wake up! Get up! Step up! Call upon the Lord daily!
- ➢ Break-out of the culture (every day) that is holding you down and back!
- ➢ Break-in to unleash the potential God has created in you!
- ➢ Don't look back!
- ➢ You can stop the cycle of depletion and scarcity – your culture is continually "killing" you!
- ➢ You and I are designed, deployed and destined for God's Greatness, for Him already placed within us!
- ➢ You and I are created extraordinary people by God, living the life for his Glory that God always planned for us to live!
- ➢ You can wake up and realise your status in Christ!
- ➢ You can choose to become that person God always planned for you to be!
- ➢ It is all a choice...!

Jeremiah 33:3 NIV:

"Call to me and I will answer you and tell you great and unsearchable things you do not know."

Romans 12:2 NLT:
"Don't copy the behaviour and customs of this world, but let God transform you into a new person by changing the way you think. Then you will learn to know God's will for you, which is good and pleasing and perfect."

Jeremiah 29:11-13 NIV:
"For I know the plans I have for you," declares the Lord, "plans to prosper you and not to harm you, plans to give you hope and a future. Then you will call on me and come and pray to me, and I will listen to you. You will seek me and find me when you seek me with all your heart."

> *It is all about consecration, dedication and commitment*
> *to the living God as discovered in scripture.*
> *It is all about Living the Life that Jesus Lived fully Aware,*
> *Fully Engaged, Fully Leading.*
> *It is all about vision, focus and our connection*
> *with God our Father.*

This biblical concept of God asking us to "call" on Him is very significant. The reason for this is that when we "call" on God, our focus is on Him, and He has our attention. For those who are fully committed, we have the following dramatic promise in 2 Chronicles 16:9 NIV. You see, God desires our totality. No half measures, no conflict or compromise of views and thinking. Adam lost his focus on his creator, and the rest is history. But because God has created us and the future is not yet with us, we are called like Jesus to step up and change the future for others round about us.

All of us, if we name the name of Jesus Christ, are not only called by God, we are called to aspire to be like Christ and change the future for God as we connect with others.

What is the difference between those who make a difference for God in the time God has given them on this earth and those who don't, those who will never make that difference?

It is simply these three aspects.

Firstly, those who aspire to change and do change the future for God have a relationship with God, their heavenly Father and Creator.

Secondly, they are completely and utterly focussed on God in ways that we can only imagine.

Thirdly, that relationship is deeply connected, and these people call upon God because He has asked them to.

Can you name any of the following list of God's heroes and heroines noted in scripture who failed the above definitions? I have listed them in a prayer elsewhere, but their personal characteristics bear repeating here because they illuminate the point being made.

Lord, give me:

- ✓ the heart of David
- ✓ the love of Jonathan
- ✓ the obedience of Moses
- ✓ the integrity of Joseph
- ✓ the decisiveness of Joshua
- ✓ the commitment of Caleb
- ✓ the heart seeking for God of Ezra
- ✓ the courage of Esther
- ✓ the perseverance of Ruth
- ✓ the wisdom of Solomon
- ✓ the authenticity of Jeremiah
- ✓ the consecration of Samuel
- ✓ the vision of Daniel
- ✓ the steadfastness of Meshach, Shadrach and Abednego
- ✓ the intentionality of Elijah
- ✓ the dedication of Isaiah
- ✓ the leadership of Nehemiah
- ✓ the boldness of Peter
- ✓ the faith and intensity of Paul
- ✓ the servant leadership of Christ

For the praise of your Glory.

What stood them apart was their connection with God, calling upon Him and His name, and their single-minded focus on Him and His ways, acknowledging their needs and position before Him. Yes, they were sometimes less than perfect human beings with deeply personal flaws, and their lives bore witness to their almost inevitable human failings, but they perfectly show the truth of these inspiring aspects, and God used them for His purposes.

Here is the simple truth, paraphrased from Jeremiah ch.29, v12-13: "Then you will call on me and come and pray to me, and I will listen to you. You will seek me and find me when you seek me with all your heart."

Each had God's purposes in their hearts and minds, and when they called upon the Lord, seeking Him with all their hearts, God unlocked and unleashed the potential He had already created and placed within them and used them for His Glory.

These were no stained-glass saints. They were people who had said, "Yes!" to God, called upon Him, focussed their minds on Him, and deeply connected with Him, and they were never the same again. They had chosen to live at God's Higher Level for God's Higher Purpose, and He graciously used them to change not only the future but the destiny of an untold number of people who chose to believe in Christ and His Word:

➢ Changing the Face of History.
➢ Changing the Course of History.
➢ Changing Others Lives in the Future.
➢ Changing the Trajectory of Others Lives.
➢ Changing and Transforming their Destiny.
➢ Changing and Transforming the Future.
➢ Changing Destiny for Millions of People.

All I am reading is that Christian traditional hierarchical management/leadership is about doing the work of running a church, solving the daily and weekly problems that arise, providing services of worship on a Sunday, and hopefully encouraging people to come to faith.

I believe this approach has dramatically disadvantaged the Church at least and kills it at best. Why? It has not helped that the primary means of leadership is hierarchical management, where "subordinates" carry out work for the leaders. And the focus is on problem-solving and not on people-growing as Christ intended.

"Hierarchies tend to be knowing organizations not learning organizations." – Bob Quinn.

This is the very start of the slow-decline slope, when "knowing" (with undertones of pride and inward focus) rather than learning (together in humility with shared vision) becomes the focus. From such innocuous seeds, hierarchy, posturing, knowing, spiritual one-upmanship, and superiority with the cancer of silos growing all lead to Church and organisational death. What characterised the Church that Jesus started was:

✓ Personal People Focus
✓ Personal People Growth
✓ Personal People Learning
✓ Personal People Serving

✓ No hierarchy

Stop the slogging away at the declining traditional Transactional Church and become the Transformational Church as Christ intended.

Borrowed from *Creating a Purpose-Driven Organization* by Robert E. Quinn and Anjan V. Thakor:

1. Envision an inspired workforce.
2. Discover the purpose.
3. Recognize the need for authenticity.
4. Turn the authentic message into a constant message
5. Stimulate individual learning.
6. Turn midlevel managers into purpose-driven leaders
7. Connect the people to the purpose.
8. Unleash the positive energizers.

We can clearly see Jesus at work here as He created His Transformed disciples. Jesus had discovered His Purpose, and He had a plan. The above is pretty close to the biblical accounts of what happened in the gospels.

> *My greatest fear is getting stuck in yesterday.*
> *My greatest opportunity is today.*
> *My greatest focus is today and tomorrow.*
>
> *Intentionally preparing to make a difference,*
> *living and giving my best life so that others will*
> *be lifted and transformed today and tomorrow.*

Rally Others – Sustain The Challenge

What God Calls us to Do

This is not "an optional, leave legacy" to the end of the book because we imagine legacy is about the future. Wrong. Christ's legacy started on day 1. He did not leave it until the end of His time with His disciples. If it is not there on day 1, don't start. Build this underpinning action from the start. Legacy thinking (notice, not "planning") must be present and underpinning. Growing people must become the highest priority.

Here is my take on a God-honouring Survival Action Plan (because we cannot stay where we are) with a simple underpinning prayer at every stage and every day: "Lord God, show me the opportunities that you want me to take this day":

➤ Firstly, Create.
➤ Secondly, Understand.
➤ Thirdly, Act.
➤ Fourthly, Keep it simple.
➤ Fifthly, Make it a way of life.
➤ Sixthly, Sustain the challenge.

❖ <u>Create</u> courageous leadership, especially in laypeople.
❖ <u>Understand</u> by asking the questions, "What is our purpose? Where might God need us to be in 5 years? Where are we? Are we fit for purpose? What is our vision?" Face up to the "brutal reality" of our situations. All this will require clarity of purpose.
❖ <u>Act</u> by discovering for ourselves where God might want us to be. This will require a singleness of purpose both personally and congregationally under clear leadership. We need "boots on the ground" co-operating to reverse and redirect the current Church behaviours and culture and be externally focussed in pursuit of the unchurched.
❖ <u>Keep</u> it simple. Keep everything externally focussed on the unchurched by doing nothing but a "Saddleback" – Members, Maturity, Ministry, Mission, as people come to faith in Christ.
❖ <u>Make it a way of Life</u> personally and congregationally. Build people who know they are growing. Encourage and build new habits. Measure progress and celebrate even small successes. Ensure that people don't stop and settle.
❖ <u>Sustain the challenge</u> by growing the next generation of leaders – hand on the baton to them. Galvanise at the local level a new breed of lay leadership and congregations with clear authority not to accept anything less than outward-focussed, missional action to bring irreligious people to a transformed life in Christ.

Do all these things as far as you are able at the same time. A tall order, but necessary. Because we do not have the time to waste doing things that are not effective. We must also remember:

✓ A clear purpose builds morale.
✓ A clear purpose reduces frustration.

✓   A clear purpose allows concentration.
✓   A clear purpose attracts cooperation.
✓   A clear purpose assists evaluation.[213]

(With thanks to Dr Rick Warren, Saddleback Church)

So, God requires us to have clarity, to be focussed, and to be pro-active.
"Lord God of all, continue to lead me on the road of your opportunities. I long for your Church to grow as people come to faith in your Son, Jesus Christ. I long to be part of a vibrant, missional community whose focus is on those who are not yet with us. Please continue to direct my heart, soul and mind, as you see fit to work, to bring irreligious people to a transformed life in You."

Rally Others – Revisit The Dream

Lord God, more than anything, I dream that everyone can and will be transformed and grow to become the people full of purpose and potential you always planned us to be, transforming and growing others in turn. Sadly, your Church has lost this dream if it ever understood it in the first place. It's time to challenge and change all that. It's time to wake up, break out, and intentionally carry out your plans as Christ lived. Grant Your plans, understanding and vision to my heart as I live this dream for Your glory.

I dream of a Church where no one will put me down or ignore my heart for God for dreaming all the Longings below. I choose to live for your Praise and Glory alone. I decisively dedicate myself to you in consecration with commitment again today. I choose to live with anticipation that I can make a difference for others in this world. I choose to live a significant life for You. I choose to live intentionally for You. I choose Your abundance and surplus as I live and dream for You.

These simple, heartfelt prayers are for Your Glory so that we can live the lives you always planned for us to live.

God created us for His purposes, His vision and His destiny; for consecration and dedication with courage, connection and commitment to Him; to lead lives that are significant and consequential for Him; to lead lives that fulfil His purposes for us.

✓   They are to be lives dedicated to God
✓   They are to be lives lived intentionally for God

---

[213] Warren, *The Purpose Driven Church*, pp. 86–93.

✓ They are to be lives that make a difference and matter.

✓ They are to be lives of significance for God

✓ They are to be lives of wholehearted connection with God.

✓ We are created to be inspired and transformed, not fearful, as Christ restores us in Himself to God, and we are to discover our identity in Him.

I dream of a Church...

➢ **Where everyone matters with the passion that God has for us.**

    ➢ Where Christ, His Mission and His Purposes are central and understood by everyone.

    ➢ Where the mission and focus are on "those who are not yet with us".

    ➢ Transformational leaders intentionally engage people to think and act in such a way that it makes a positive difference in their lives and in the lives of others. John C. Maxwell.

➢ **The Transformation of being and thinking towards Inspirational and Transformational Servant Leadership is normal.**

    ➢ Where people are transformed and grow by the renewing of their minds, thinking and actions.

    ➢ Where the vision, focus and purpose of the Church are red hot, and everyone is on board.

    ➢ Where Christ's vision leads people from comfort and complacency to courage, commitment, contribution and action.

    ➢ Where God's purpose for individuals is not only recognised but encouraged to be discovered.

➢ **The Potential God has placed inside of everyone is drawn out by Transformational Leaders.**

    ➢ Where the anticipation that God will act is palpable and believed.

    ➢ The vision is not just a mission statement but a God-defined picture of the future that creates passion and understanding in people.

➢ **Personal Potential, Purpose, Vision and Courage are used by God to enable them to soar with eagles' wings as they were intended.**

    ➢ Where everyone turns up to contribute, not to receive.

    ➢ Where passivity is translated to passion.

    ➢ Where passion translates to contribution.

    ➢ Where contribution leads to purpose and action.

➢ **Consecration, Dedication, Commitment and transformation are everyone's daily experience.**

    ➢ Where God-honouring visions are turned in to reality.

    ➢ Where we decide to live lives that are significant.

> ➢ Where significance leads to being consequential.
> ➢ Where a compelling vision of the future is being translated into reality.
> ➢ Where I can live a life worthy of the calling I have received.

➢ **We can align our hearts and minds with God's heart and mind.**

> ➢ Where we are connected to Christ with wholeheartedness and commitment, enjoying lives of His surplus and abundance, not the world's scarcity and depletion, and purposefully engaged in something bigger than ourselves, to dare greatly for Him.
> ➢ Where I can do what God has called me to do and to do it with people I love.
> ➢ Where being inspired is normal.
> ➢ Where inspiring others is normal.

➢ **Being motivated and inspired to do great things for God is normal.**

> ➢ Where people understand how short life is and want to make a difference for God in the short time they have.
> ➢ Where people are living lives that are passionate, significant and consequential.
> ➢ Where seeking God together deeply to understand where He would have us be in the future is normal.
> ➢ Where everyone matters and is valued.
> ➢ Where courage, compassion and commitment are central, valued, lived and practised.
> ➢ Where Potential is continually unlocked in individuals.
> ➢ Where the assimilation from the first-time attendee to maturity in Christ is an essential and planned development for everyone.

➢ **I am inspired to become the person God always meant me to be.**

> ➢ Where I can discover, grow and release my gifts, talents and unrealised potential, purpose and possibilities.
> ➢ Where we can all discover, grow, develop and deploy our God-designed potential.

➢ **Christ's culture of people development is normal.**

> ➢ Where my desire to lead is recognised, celebrated and fulfilled.
> ➢ Where Purpose and Destiny in Christ are properly understood.
> ➢ Where our purpose is defined with overwhelming simplicity so no one can be unsure of what we are doing.
> ➢ Where we know with assurance in our hearts what results we want to create.

➢ **Shared vision and shared values are continually reinforced.**

> ➤ Where we are all encouraged to be authentic through vulnerability like Christ.
> ➤ Where breaking out of our status quo is always assumed to be normal.
> ➤ Where leaders are Multipliers and not Diminishers.
> ➤ Where leadership is created and encouraged by those Multipliers.
> ➤ Where leaders have made the jump over the chasm from being transactional to transformational.
> ➤ Where tomorrow's leaders are discovered and grown to their fullest potential.

➤ **We can grow as human beings.**
> ➤ Where space is intentionally created for that to happen.
> ➤ Where space is created for others to contribute.
> ➤ Where that space allows conflict to be transformed into creativity.
> ➤ Where creativity leads to commitment.

➤ **We all turn up to contribute.**
> ➤ Where we are all committed connectors with others where we are all expected to do extraordinary work.
> ➤ Where we can grow to be inspiring influencers and grow others to do the same over the long term.
> ➤ Where we can experience and lead a profoundly meaningful life, growing others and creating tomorrow's leaders who are not defined primarily by tradition, comfort and continuity.
> ➤ Where individual longing is perfectly satisfied by being inspired, and people live the lives God always planned for them to live.

➤ **Living life in all its fullness because of all the above is both understood and a reality.**
> ➤ Where I can love God as only I can because I am created uniquely for this.

Conclusions for Step 11

To Rally! Others To Their Best Lives

Key Thought – Sustain The Challenge Because It Does Not Just Happen

Sub-headings review:
- ➤ **Rally Others - Action Steps To Change The Future**
- ➤ **Rally Others – Sustain The Challenge**
- ➤ **Rally Others – The Dream**

"Because this is what it is all about: Growing transformed people who Change their future, Change their Destiny, make a difference in this world and help others to do the same."

Embed Rallying Others in the Culture from Day 1. This is Day 1 Legacy creation and building it into the transformed and transformational cultures you create for God. Imagine transformed and growing leaders that you have helped Awaken, Unlock and Act.

You get what you allow in life in general (and in failing and ineffective organisational cultures). The corollary of that statement is that you get and become what you think, what you dream about, what you discern and "see" in the future. Success is won or lost at this juncture. Fail to Rally Others, and you will create the conditions for failure.

In effect, Step 11 is the changing up a gear or supercharging simile for *TRANSFORMED!* Now is the time to set in stone the new and successful cultures you are creating for the future.

Step 12

To Legacy! Others For Their Best Lives

WHY?

"Transformed!" has been written to help us all become truly alive as God intended,
simply because the world (and for many people, it's their churches)
has beaten out of them real living, personal growth, fun, sharing,
shared connections, creativity, wholehearted living,
purpose, courage, compassion, empathy, shared vision;
It has beaten out of them the capacity to lead lives of authenticity,
passion, significance and consequence
and left them living lives of scarcity and depletion.
And what we are simply designed to do is discover God's purposes for our lives
then go with courage, compassion and commitment,
creating the bridge as we walk on it,
leaning and learning into the unknown but emerging and developing future
knowing that we are living the lives God always planned for us to live.
Lives of God's surplus and abundance,
Lives of passion, significance, and consequence
for Christ and for Others.
To leave the world a better place than when we arrived.
To live for His Glory and not ours.

Are you that person God is calling...?

~ ~ ~

❖ **Key Purpose: Create a Leadership Legacy that is Eclipsing the Past, Transforming the Present by investing in Others, and Changing the Future so that You and I and Others can be *TRANSFORMED!* just as God Planned for Us to Be.**

❖ **Key Learning (Always Facing the Unknown without Fear):** The real importance of the Rallying of the last Step 11 **To Rally! Others To Their Best Lives** will now become apparent here. Because this is where the harvest of all your efforts comes to fruition. It is, of course, the legacy. It may be your legacy, but what good is it that when you die, what you built just stops or dissipates like fog on a spring morning? Legacy (or heritage) for God is what you leave in others after you have gone. Ask yourself these questions: What will happen to the dream after I am gone? What will I leave in Others? Will they carry the baton of the dream or the purpose that I was given? Will it just die?

❖ **Key Actions (Building The Bridge As You Walk On It):** Thinking of the death of purpose, dreams, ideas and visions above brings us to the key actions here: "Save nothing for the next life, to do what must be done, to say what must be said, to write the words that must be written, and to live the life that must be lived. Don't settle for so little. Die empty – leave nothing for the next life. Choose to live without regret."[214]

Legacy! – The Breakout Continues

God's Vision for His Church is TRIPLE A Churches with Triple C People Who have broken out from where they are to create and travel the road to where He wants them to be. Breakout for God's Higher Purpose.

Knowing what God has called them to be for Him, they are Triple-A Churches:

➤ Awakened to become:
➤ Aware and engaged
➤ Aligned and understanding
➤ Actioning and transforming

They are also importantly:

➤ Breaking out from mediocrity to become:
➤ Aware and engaged
➤ Outward focussed
➤ Impacting the community

God's plans and vision are simply to redeem and restore every person on this planet through His Church, which has woken up from mediocrity and broken out to connect with the people God has already prepared to meet.

Most churches and their congregations are:

• Un-Aware of God's plans and non-engaged.
• Un-Aligned with God's plans and misunderstanding.
• Non-Actioning and status-quo-conforming for comfort.

They are also:

---

[214] McManus, *The Last Arrow,* p. 24,59.

- Internally focussed on their needs.
- Not impacting the community.

OK, God, "grant us Your vision of the Church you always planned for it to be." We are under God planned to become Triple C People:

✓ Created in Christ to the praise of the glory of His glory.
✓ Connected in Christ to the praise of the glory of His glory.
✓ Conformed in Christ to the praise of the glory of His glory.

That is God's grand vision and plans for mankind in these three words – Created, Connected, and Conformed. These are indeed eternal truths and are entirely and continuously shown throughout the scriptures. It is necessary to awaken and break out of who you think you are, yourself, your limited understanding and your experience, culture, and even your church. I submit that the primary heart of a Christian is to be:

✓ Fully aware and continually connected to Christ.
✓ Fully aligned and understanding in Christ.
✓ Fully engaged and continually renewed by Christ.
✓ Fully committed and continually consecrated for Christ.
✓ Fully dedicated and continually growing in Christ.

Breakout by God's Spirit, hand in hand with God under scripture, to become the person God always planned for you to be, to fulfil His purposes in your generation! To Be:

✓ Aware and engaged
✓ Aligned and understanding
✓ Actioning and transforming

To Be:

✓ Outward focussed
✓ Impacting the community

Unlock the unique potential in others and inspire them to action because:

✓ God is the God of Purpose.
✓ Keep your eyes on the God of Purpose.
✓ Seek faithfully to be prepared for His Purpose.
✓ Be prepared for God's moments and timings.
✓ God will invite you to a higher level of experience and trust.
✓ Breakout into the new identity God always planned for you to have.

"*God created us for His purposes, His vision and His destiny; for consecration and dedication with courage, connection and commitment to Him; to lead lives that are consequential for Him; to lead lives that fulfil His purposes for us. They are to be lives dedicated to God. They are to be lives of wholehearted connection with God. We are created to be inspired and transformed, not fearful as Christ restores us in Himself to God, and we are to discover our identity in Him.*"

Legacy! – 'How Can I Be More For God?' Prayers

As you become familiar with or more focussed on these questions, you will find yourself replacing your first "How can I?" with "Am I?", "Did I?", or "Did we ... today?"

You may even state, "I will..." or, "I choose..." or, "Help me to..."

Ask these active questions at the beginning and end of every day. Over a period of time, you will find a revolution and transformation of your heart, your vision and your growth in Christ. Active questions stimulate these vital areas of your life in ways that nothing else can. In Psalm 37, David wrote this eternal truth: "Delight yourself in the LORD, and he will give you the desires of your heart." (Ps. 37:4.)

The "How Can I?" prayers are simply about alignment. God calls us to align our hearts with His own Heart, to align our vision with His Vision, and to feel for people as He Feels for them. He calls us daily to make a conscious choice of the decisive dedication of ourselves in consecration for Him. Romans ch.12, v1 AMP.

Lord, grant us the courage to choose to live the outpourings of our hearts below and in the very act of asking You these eternal questions, discovering your Holy Spirit enabling our lives for your Glory.

So my heart cries out to God:

❖ **How can I live my life so that it will echo in eternity for You, Lord?**

    ❖ How can I delight in You more, O Lord?

- ❖ How can I live a life worthy of the calling I have received?
- ❖ How can I align my heart with your Heart more today?
- ❖ How can I reflect God's character in my life more today

❖ **How can I be more focussed like Christ today?**

- ❖ How can I be more focussed on God's kingdom and its reality today as Christ was?
- ❖ How can I live more with Christ's assumptions about people today?
- ❖ How can I please you, Lord God, more today?
- ❖ How can I love you, Lord, my Creator, today more than I did yesterday?

❖ **How can I love you, Lord God, with all my heart, and with all my soul, and with all my mind, and with all my strength today?**

- ❖ How can I be more wholehearted for you today?
- ❖ How can I live more to the praise of Christ's Glory today?
- ❖ How can I gain and understand more of God's heart of wisdom for today?
- ❖ How can I seek you, Lord, more earnestly today?
- ❖ How can I join you, Lord God, to see your vision and plans for this world today?
- ❖ How can I partner with you, Lord God, in fulfilling your purposes today?

❖ **How can I fulfil your unique calling for my life today?**

- ❖ How can I decisively dedicate my life more again to You, Lord God, this day?
- ❖ How can I consciously consecrate my life more again to You, Lord God, this day?
- ❖ How can I be more disciplined for you today?

❖ **How can I fulfil your purpose for my life today?**

- ❖ How can I come to know your will and purpose for my life today?
- ❖ How can I be more like you, Lord Jesus, in vision, thought, word and deed today?
- ❖ How can I become the person you always planned me to be?
- ❖ How can I be transformed into the likeness of your Son more today?
- ❖ How can I attain the Mindset of Christ more in my mind today?
- ❖ How can I make myself nothing and take the form of a servant more today?
- ❖ How can I stop myself from being conformed to the world around me?
- ❖ How can I be more like Christ today?

❖ **How can I "delight" more in you, Lord, such that my focus is entirely on You?**

- ❖ How can I rejoice more in you, Lord, today?
- ❖ How can I live the life you always planned and prepared me to live?
- ❖ How can I be more grateful for you today?

- ❖ How can I be more courageous for you today?
- ❖ How can I be more focussed on you today?

❖ **How can I be fearless for you today?**

- ❖ How can I be more focussed like Christ today?
- ❖ How can I be more like-minded as Christ today?
- ❖ How can I be more focussed on the things of God today?
- ❖ How can I be more focussed on your purposes today?
- ❖ How can I be more about your business today?
- ❖ How can I love more the people you have created today?
- ❖ How can I overlook the shortcomings of those around me and instead honour them by spurring them on to become the people you meant them to be?

❖ **How can I provide Inspirational Leadership for Christ as He did?**

- ❖ How can I see better the untapped possibilities and potential in the people around me?
- ❖ How can I today help people understand more that they matter and matter to you, Lord God?
- ❖ How can I grow other people more today for your glory?
- ❖ How can I grow the people in the church where you have placed me to discover their God-given potential?
- ❖ How can I love my neighbours, for Christ's sake, more today than yesterday?
- ❖ How can I reach out to my neighbours in trust and love more today than yesterday?

❖ **How can I be more conformed to the image of Christ?**

- ❖ How can I build the road as I walk on it, the road you always planned for me to take?
- ❖ How can I see a way forward for your Glory where I am?
- ❖ How can I give my life to fulfil your purposes for your Kingdom?
- ❖ How can I provide consequential leadership for you in the days in which I live?
- ❖ How can I be consequential for you with the gifts you created in me so I can make a difference?

❖ **How can I live a life of significance for Christ today?**

- ❖ How can I understand your heart more with vision today?
- ❖ How can I live more effectively and contribute significantly today to make a difference in the world for you, Lord God?
- ❖ How can I be more engaged in something bigger than myself today for you, Lord God?

- ❖ How can I connect more with you today to better understand my purpose and Destiny?
- ❖ How can I help connect others more with you today?
- ❖ How can I soar with eagles more as you intended me to?

❖ **How can I fly with you to reach your realms unknown in my heart and spirit today?**

- ❖ How can I wait upon you, Lord, today more than yesterday?
- ❖ How can I move closer to you because you promised – "You will seek me and find me when you seek me with all your heart. I will be found by you," declares the Lord!
- ❖ How can I draw nearer to you because you will draw near to me?

❖ **How can I gain more of the heart of a servant like Christ today?**

- ❖ How can I be more inspired for You today?
- ❖ How can I inspire others for Christ today?
- ❖ How can I be more authentic for You today?
- ❖ How can I release my God-given talent and creativity for You to use today?

❖ **How can I be more:**

- ➢ Wholehearted
- ➢ Authentic
- ➢ Purposeful
- ➢ Fully engaged
- ➢ Intentional
- ➢ Meaningful
- ➢ Fulfilled
- ➢ Courageous
- ➢ Compassionate
- ➢ Committed
- ➢ Empathetic
- ➢ Patient
- ➢ Humble
- ➢ Passionate
- ➢ Significant
- ➢ Consequential

For God today

❖ **How can I build and encourage in Others:**

- ➢ Love
- ➢ Respect

- ➢ Compassion
- ➢ Shared purpose
- ➢ Shared Vision
- ➢ Shared knowledge
- ➢ Mutual respect
- ➢ Inspiration?

❖ **How can I help and grow others more by:**
- ➢ Seeing their potential.
- ➢ Unlocking and Unleashing their Unique potential for God.
- ➢ Helping them discover their gifts and talents for God.
- ➢ Helping them lead lives of significance for Christ.
- ➢ Helping them make a difference for God in the days He gives them on this earth.
- ➢ Creating a living Mindset of growth and development from the inside out.
- ➢ Helping others succeed to live a life of greatness for God?
- ➢ Yet all these matters are not about me, but about others, for Your glory alone, Lord God.

So I give You these prayers, Lord Jesus Christ, for Your Glory and not mine, to truly live the life You always planned for me to live, so that it will "echo in Eternity for You," [215] Amen.

---

[215] Dr Dan Erickson, 'People Matter Ministries'.

The following comes from Dr Dan Erickson, 'People Matter Ministries'.

> *"I could and perhaps should be angry at the waste of potential in people, the squandered lives that lived as long as they could (that was their aim) and then they died. Their lives were full of themselves. Their lives and interactions with others were simply transactional. In other words they viewed others in terms of their usefulness to themselves. They carried on the relentless banality and self-centred normality of their culture. And then died.*
>
> *But God in Christ has a profoundly better plan for you and I. It is simply this: Christ came to set us free not only from the results of separation from God through sin, but to Live Your Extraordinary Best Life, the Life You are Created for, as God's Extraordinary Masterpieces, an extraordinary transformational life of growth for God, firstly for ourselves and then others, today, by unlocking and unleashing God-given unlimited potential in ourselves and others, to stretch to our fullest potential for God who has created us."*

Legacy! – Revisiting the Continuing Actions

Here are the *TRANSFORMED!* Legacy actions revisited and seeking to Inspire You to Discover God's Higher Purpose for You by Helping You understand and:

➢ **Create Your "Why?" – Your Commitment to Action 1 – The Extraordinary Awareness to Begin:**
  ➢ Create the Desire and Intentionality to Change by Challenging Assumptions – WAKE UP!
  ➢ Create the Understanding and Awareness of God's Abundance to Seek His Highest Calling – BELIEVE!
  ➢ Create the Character and Integrity to Endure, Moving from Knowing to Learning, from Using to Investing – DEVELOP!
  ➢ Create the Capacity, Commitment and Anticipation to Think Differently by Asking the Right Questions – THINK!

➢ **Create Your "How?" – Your Commitment to Action 2 – The Extraordinary Decision to Unlock:**
   ➢ Create the Courage and Decision to Start The Breakout to Your Highest Calling – BREAKOUT!
   ➢ Create the Willingness to Stretch and Reach to Your Unlimited Highest Potential and Discover God's Meaningful Purpose for You – UNLOCK!
   ➢ Create the Mindsets and Environments for Growth, Connection and Contribution – GROW!
   ➢ Create Enrolled Hearts that are Fully Engaged and Continually Renewed – ENGAGE!
➢ **Create Your "What?" – Your Commitment to Action 3 – The Extraordinary Transformation to Act:**
   ➢ Create a Compelling Vision to Inspire with Clarity to Lead to God's Higher Purpose – LEAD!
   ➢ Create Leaders with the Skills and a Sense of Urgency to Build, Develop and Equip People to Act – ACT!
   ➢ Create Leadership to Continue for God in the Service of Something Greater than Yourself – RALLY!
   ➢ Create a Legacy that is Eclipsing the Past, Transforming the Present, and Changing the Future so that You and I and Others can be TRANSFORMED! just as God Planned for Us to Be – LEGACY!
(Always Remembering it's not about You, but for Him and for Others.)

Legacy! – The End of the Beginning – Living with No Regrets

(and conclusion to *TRANSFORMED!*)

Key Thought – Eclipse the Past, Transform the Present, Invest in Others, Change the Future.

Sub-headings review:
➢ **Legacy! – The Breakout Continues**
➢ **Legacy! – How Can I Be More For God Prayers**
➢ **Legacy! – Revisiting the Continuing Actions**
➢ **Legacy! – The End of the Beginning**

If you have come this far using *TRANSFORMED!* as a practical workbook, congratulations. You see, unlike other books, which generally end with a "conclusion" or "epilogue" chapter, this chapter is not the end. It is a new beginning.

Where other writers seek to tie up loose ends and come to a sensible, comfortable conclusion, which can be very effective, there can be no end to the path you are defining by your walking. It was Sir Winston Churchill who, in a speech in London after the victory at El Alamein in North Africa in 1942, said poignantly:

> *"Now this is not the end.*
> *It is not even the beginning of the end.*
> *But it is, perhaps, the end of the beginning."*

(Above quotation cited. [216])

And so, I invite you and me, in effect, in the never-ending battle for hearts, minds and souls, to commit ourselves, together, to God Who Created Us, to His Son Jesus Christ, in Whom we Believe, Trust, and Live, Whom we honour above all else, to the beneficial and overwhelming power of the Person of His Holy Spirit, to continue.

Continue to Awake, to Unlock, to Act, all as God Created us for, to Make a Difference for Him and for Others in the days in which we Live, the days of our Extraordinary, Best Masterpiece Lives.

It is worth revisiting God's word, which in all its whole and its parts is written for our edification, understanding and action, so we can fully understand again "where we are meant to be".

Romans 12:1-2 NIV:
"Therefore, I urge you, brothers and sisters, in view of God's mercy, to offer your bodies as a living sacrifice, holy and pleasing to God – this is your true and proper worship. Do not conform to the pattern of this world, but be transformed by the renewing of your mind. Then you will be able to test and approve what God's will is – his good, pleasing and perfect will."

Psalm 37:3-9 NIV:
"Trust in the Lord and do good; dwell in the land and enjoy safe pasture. Take delight in the Lord, and he will give you the desires of your heart. Commit your way to the Lord; trust in him, and he will do this: He will make your righteous reward shine like the dawn, your vindication like the noonday sun. Be still before the Lord and wait patiently for him; do not fret when

---

[216] 'The Churchill Society London. Churchill's Speeches.' <http://www.churchill-society-london.org.uk/EndoBegn.html> [accessed 26 May 2020].

people succeed in their ways, when they carry out their wicked schemes. Refrain from anger and turn from wrath; do not fret – it leads only to evil. For those who are evil will be destroyed, but those who hope in the Lord will inherit the land."

Together, We can Choose to Live and Commit to Our Extraordinary, Best Masterpiece Life for God again Today.

We can use the "Masterpiece Commitment Living Prayer":

~~~

Lord God, my Creator, I Choose to Love You, Trust and Delight in You, and Live and Commit My Best Masterpiece Life of Contribution to You Today; I choose Living for Your Transcendent Higher Purpose.
You Chose, Designed and Created me to Live this Extraordinary Life, Fully Committed to You and Fully Connected with You for Others Today; I Choose to Live the Extraordinary Masterpiece Life, the Life of Conscious Consecration, Decisive Dedication, Wholehearted Commitment, and Connecting with Choice to You;
I Choose Trusting in You and Doing Good, Delighting in You, Focussed Intentionally on You;
I Choose Living the Life of Transformation and Growth, Intentionality, Significance, Anticipation and Abundance, Connection and Contribution that you created for me to Live for Your Glory and for Others Today.

~~~

Through faith in Christ and transformed thinking, God calls us daily to live Our Best Masterpiece Life that Jesus modelled. It is an extraordinary life focussed on loving God with all Our Hearts and Valuing and Helping Others Grow to become the People God created and always planned for them to become. This is so that we can know the truth of Paul's writing to the church in Colossians 1:10 NIV, "so that you may live a life worthy of the Lord and please him in every way: bearing fruit in every good work, growing in the knowledge of God."

We can remind Ourselves, "What makes the difference?"

These People live their Extraordinary, Best Masterpiece Life for God, Choosing Daily, Living an Intentional, Focussed, and Inspired Life of Humility, Consecration, Dedication, Commitment and Contribution through Transformation and Growth for God and for Others. These Extraordinary

347

People understand that God has Created and Called them through faith in Christ, and He has filled them with His Holy Spirit. Their Destiny is TRANSFORMED! Crucially, these people are committed to *Thinking Differently, as God Intended* to Make a Difference for Him. They *think and assess how they are thinking, and they think and evaluate how they are learning as they renew their minds*, ensuring their Transformational Growth with Commitment and Effectiveness for God:

- ❖ They have responded to their Calling by God in Christ.
- ❖ They Uniquely Live for His Glory and Lifting and Valuing Others.
- ❖ They understand and Live in the Land of God's Transcendent Higher Purpose instinctively and permanently.
- ❖ They understand the need for a Transformed Masterpiece Life and Mindset.
- ❖ They are not distracted by the tyranny of the unimportant.
- ❖ They are constantly observing, listening and learning.
- ❖ They have deliberately moved on and upwards from the normal self-absorbed problem-solving focus that limits everyone to Higher Purpose-Centred living for God and Others.
- ❖ They truly aspire to Living Ephesians 2:10 NLT: "For we are God's masterpiece. He has created us anew in Christ Jesus, so we can do the good things he planned for us long ago."
- ❖ They are actively Transforming and Growing Intentionally to Live their Extraordinary Best Masterpiece, Lives of Significance for God.
- ❖ They are Creating Opportunities for Service and Making a Difference for Others, literally becoming, thinking and actioning out in themselves for Others, the perfect human life that Christ did and modelled.
- ❖ They Live God's Core Values with deep humility and thankfulness.
- ❖ They are Transforming the Future by Committing to God's Transcendent Higher Purpose in the Present.
- ❖ They do this by being Wholeheartedly Passionate for God and Seeing only Opportunities for Transformation and Growth.

> *Daily their lives are Focussed on*
> *Eclipsing the Past,*
> *Transforming the Present,*
> *and Changing the Future*
> *for God's Transcendent Higher Purpose.*

St. Paul wrote of them in his prayers for the Ephesians 1:17 KJV: "That the God of our Lord Jesus Christ, the Father of glory, may give unto you the spirit of wisdom and revelation in the knowledge of him." Daily, through that "spirit of wisdom and revelation in the knowledge of him", they awake and recommit to God's Transcendent Higher Purpose, thus truly making a difference as they change the future by their commitment to God's Higher Purpose. In short, God's Extraordinary Masterpiece People awake Daily, completely Focussed on fulfilling the Transcendent Higher Purpose and Reaching the Higher Destiny He Created them for through His Masterpiece Thinking and Action. Daily, they are Living the 7 Intentional practices of Extraordinary Best Masterpiece Lives to:

❖ *Reconnect Daily with God Who Created Them His Masterpieces* – re-consecrating, re-dedicating, re-committing our lives to Him, for His Glory, re-focussing our hearts and minds on Him, Intentionally Stretching and Growing To Become The Extraordinary Masterpieces He Created Them To Be.

❖ *Breakout to Live their Best Masterpiece Life Mindset* – from aimless, reactive-living Mindsets and break-in to their daily renewed Best Life Living Mindset by being:

❖ *Awake to Live their Best Masterpiece Life* – to Who has Created them, to Who they are and to Where they are meant to be, Creating Opportunities and Making a Difference.

❖ *Unlock and unleash their Unlimited Potential to Live their Best Masterpiece Life* – in themselves and Others, discovering their purpose, growing the Seeds of Greatness within themselves for Others. They then, with extraordinary focus:

❖ *Act to Live their Best Masterpiece Life* – through Transformational Leadership, inspiring and leading Others, unlocking their unlimited potential to Fulfil their God-created Purpose and Destiny, and the results are they are continually:

❖ *Choosing to Live their Best Masterpiece Life* – Focussing, Contributing, Committed and Making a Difference, Living Lives of

Significance, Preparing for Opportunities to Help Others and their Communities transform themselves for God as He intended, and:

❖ *Helping Others Live their Best Masterpiece Life* – Creating Opportunities and Making a Difference by Creating New Cultures of Extraordinary Masterpiece Best Life Living, Cultures of Transformation and Growing for God and Others.

They refuse to stay in their "normal" reactive, self-centred, aimless, mediocre, low level of living life.

✓ They Choose every day to step out, step up, rise up, reach up and stretch up – to live their directed Best Life of God's Transcendent Higher Purpose;

✓ They Choose to Live God's Extraordinary Masterpiece Thinking and Focussed Living;

✓ They Choose to Live the Life Jesus promised to give us, the Life He Lived;

✓ They Choose Living a Life that Matters;

✓ They Choose Living a Life of Contribution;

✓ They Choose Living a Life Creating Opportunities;

✓ They Choose Living a Life Making a Difference;

✓ They Choose Living with the Mindsets of Intentionality, Growth and Significance to Inspire Others to find their Purpose; Unlocking and Unleashing their Unlimited Potential;

✓ They Choose just "Lifting the Lid off People".

As Jesus did, they truly are making "A Highway in the desert", creating pathways for God and for Others where none existed before, fulfilling God's purposes in their generation.

We can ask Ourselves "21 Vital Daily Questions God's Extraordinary Masterpiece People ask":

❖ **Am I, Daily, Completely Consecrated, Dedicated and Committed To Love God wholeheartedly, Today?**

  ❖ Am I Daily reading His Word to stay Focussed and Connected to God Today?

  ❖ Am I Intentionally Seeking with Anticipation to Live My Best Masterpiece Life for God and Others Today?

  ❖ Am I Intentionally Stretching with Anticipation to Live the Masterpiece Life God Created me to Live Today?

- ❖ **Am I Intentionally Seeking with Anticipation to Breakout Daily to God's Masterpiece thinking Today?**
  - ❖ Am I Intentionally Living with Anticipation the Masterpiece Life of God's Abundance and Surplus Today?
  - ❖ Am I Intentionally Living a Masterpiece Life of Anticipation and Urgency for God and Others Today?
  - ❖ Am I Intentionally Living with Anticipation a Masterpiece Life of Focus and Commitment for God and Others Today?
  - ❖ Am I Intentionally Living with Anticipation a Masterpiece Life of Action and Opportunities for God and Others Today?
- ❖ **Am I Intentionally Growing with Anticipation a Masterpiece Life for God and Others Today?**
  - ❖ Am I Intentionally Living with Anticipation an Authentic Masterpiece Life for God and Others Today?
  - ❖ Am I Intentionally Stretching with Anticipation to Fulfil my Potential For God and Others Today?
  - ❖ Am I Intentionally Seeking with Anticipation to Contribute for God and Others Today?
  - ❖ Am I Intentionally Seeking with Anticipation to Live a Masterpiece Life that Matters for God and Others Today?
- ❖ **Am I Intentionally Seeking with Anticipation to be Significant for God and Others Today?**
  - ❖ Am I Intentionally Seeking with Anticipation to Unlock and Unleash Unlimited Potential in Others Today?
  - ❖ Am I Intentionally Seeking with Anticipation to Inspire Others for God Today?
  - ❖ Am I Intentionally Seeking with Anticipation to Make a Difference for God and Others Today?
- ❖ **Am I Intentionally Seeking with Anticipation to fulfil God's Purposes Today?**
  - ❖ Am I Intentionally Preparing and Seeking with Anticipation for Opportunities to Add Value to Others Today?
  - ❖ Am I Intentionally Seeking with Anticipation to help Others Discover, Develop and Deploy their God-designed Potential Today?

They have chosen to say, "Yes! Yes! Yes!" to all 21 questions, and they live the other side of their decision. They have transformed themselves, their thinking, and their learning, unlocked their unique potential, and discovered God's purposes for them. They have then intentionally crossed over and into the land of God's committed people, the land of God's possibilities, and they will never be the same. In short, they live the life God created them for and become the people God always intended them to be and growing Others to be the same.

Absolutely not the end, but God's Daily New Beginning to Live Our Extraordinary Best Masterpiece Lives, using the runway which we could not see before, and take flight on eagle's wings to Where We are Meant To Be...

AFTERWORD

A Personal Understanding of God's inclusive worldview inviting all to enter His Presence, based on Psalm 100. This incredible psalm is fundamentally a universal call to action and a call to respond, an invitation to Opened Gates Thinking for His Glory. Or not, because the choice is yours.

Psalm 100:1-5 NIV:
Shout for joy to the Lord, all the earth.
Worship the Lord with gladness;
Come before him with joyful songs.
Know that the Lord is God.
It is he who made us, and we are his;
We are his people, the sheep of his pasture.
Enter his gates with thanksgiving and his courts with praise;
Give thanks to him and praise his name.
For the Lord is good, and his love endures forever;
His faithfulness continues through all generations.

    ✓ We are exhorted to shout for Joy to the Lord through this Psalm
    ✓ We are encouraged to be the People of His Pasture
    ✓ We are to Enter His Gates and Courts with our Praise
    ✓ We are to understand His love is to fulfil His Purpose
    ✓ We are to live in the light of His Power

We are encouraged to engage in:
    ✓ Transformation and Growth Thinking
    ✓ Transformed Mindsets
    ✓ Transformed Thinking
    ✓ Transformed Understanding
    ✓ Transformed Vision
    ✓ Transformed Decisions
    ✓ Transformed Action
    ✓ Transformed Entry
    ✓ Transformed Completeness

I felt I needed a breakthrough after the first draft of *TRANSFORMED!*, and I mentioned it to the Lord! In truth, it was more, Lord, I really need a

Breakthrough, and not just, "I need it." I am really ready/desperate/ gasping/desiring - A Real/Transforming/Next Level Thinking Breakthrough!

Perhaps because of having read and included Psalm 100 in my writing, I then awoke the next morning with Open Gates bursting in on my mind, and I realised that this was indeed next-level thinking. Pecking Turkey thinking can transform to Open Runway thinking. And Open Runway thinking can transform into Open Gates thinking. Come alongside me now as you read; imagine this is your experience, and let's do this together.

Open Gates were chosen as the inside cover graphic for *TRANSFORMED!* But my thinking back then was more about starting the transformation, and that gates were emblematic of opened to walk through, to escape and breakout. Psalm 100 has shown me that through next-level thinking (connected with the concepts of not staying "here" and needing to move "there" thinking), <u>Open Gates Give Entry</u> and that this is part of God's "Plans to Prosper and Not Harm Us" actioning.

The Open Gates are indeed OPEN! I was aware that this obvious statement was significant and that this was another moment of a rare "Barely able to breathe experience".

As I am writing this in real-time (with apologies for the first person singular at this point), I picture myself standing. Actually, I am sitting and writing on my iPad, yet in my mind looking and using the picture from the *TRANSFORMED!* cover. This is somewhere I am familiar with and drawn towards as if normal. The gates that formerly were *used to breakout* are now, wonderfully, *Gates of Entry*. I hold my breath, realising I have a choice, and I touch the handle. The gate moves, indeed, it swings open easily though it is huge and heavy wrought iron and embellished with scrolls. But wait, I tell myself. Don't rush, don't blunder "where angels fear to tread". Savour this moment rich in meaning, real meaning, meaning you have longed for, for years. Meaning and more profound understanding that God has kept for me for this moment. The Gate Opens... There is light flooding through towards me, brighter than the sun...

"Shout for joy to the Lord, all the earth. Worship the Lord with gladness; come before him with joyful songs. Know that the Lord is God. It is he who made us, and we are his; we are his people, the sheep of his pasture."

For over 50 years since coming to faith in Christ, these words have often been read but never really understood. Now, they take on an urgent meaning. I feel I have been preparing for this moment, especially since attempting to write *TRANSFORMED!* Don't rush through, I tell myself again, almost nervously, and yet with anticipation, I linger. But I refuse to look back to the past and yet I am almost unable to move forward; the cold of the wrought iron brings me out of my reverie.

"Enter his gates with thanksgiving and his courts with praise," is the welcome I have needed all my life but was never ready to accept, appreciate or initiate. I stay standing still, conscious I am on the cusp of a new discovery in the Higher Purpose Journey. There is that sense again of "hardly able to breathe anticipating". But wait....

What if I am wrong? What if I have believed in a lie and the scoffers of this world were right? What if the scriptures were untrue and the death of Christ a falsehood? What if myself and my past are to be exposed for who I have been? I'm unworthy, I'm untrustworthy, a man of sinful nature, I'm just a sham, and if others saw me as I really am, I would never even touch that handle. The questions, thoughts, Yes, and condemnations seem to come from behind me, from the past. Yet I know it is a forgiven past, and very definitely "the past" that pales into insignificance as I look through the gates towards the light streaming all around me.

"Enter his gates with thanksgiving and his courts with praise" overwhelms my mind. It is the call I have needed; it is the call God has prepared me for. I take a hesitant step forward, opening the gate wider. There is the sound of singing, but not ordinary singing; it is the singing of a vast choir who cannot help but sing, "Give thanks to him and praise his name." I step forward again, "For the Lord is good, and his love endures forever". And as I stand on the threshold, "His faithfulness continues through all generations" beckons, nay, forcefully invites and draws me. With an urgent desire and need to move forwards I step over the threshold and in and now the Open Gate is just behind me. This is indeed another place, another world, another universe, another dimension. Psalm 100 is intentionally beyond experience, beyond comprehension, deliberately other-dimensional, and yet relevant, personal and available right now.

But there is also "The Other Gate Thinking" in my heart. You see, as I passed through, fully opening the gate that was ajar, I felt the overwhelming feeling that I could and should open the other gate fully. Why? So that others who came after me could flood in unhindered as God intended. My entry was not for me alone but to occasion the entrance of a multitude.

The Lord is "The Lord Who May be known."

And the overwhelming perception is of welcome, worship, acceptance, fulfilment and completion. Everything that "normal, reactive, inward-focussed, self-centred" life can never be.

Why did it take so long to get to this point in the journey? Is it that for decades, I had been metaphorically "wandering in the desert"? I am not convinced of that metaphor. Or is there a bigger explanation that, like Joseph being sold into slavery, God had planned something better for him than he could ever have foreseen? This Psalm is about is all about the Open Gates Thinking and Mindset. A God-focussed, Joyful, Glad Worship, Singing, Heartfelt Entering His Presence.

- ✓ *Transformation and Growing Living for God*
- ✓ *Abundance and Surplus Living for God*
- ✓ *Focus and Commitment Living for God*
- ✓ *Anticipation and Urgency Living for God*
- ✓ *Significance and Meaning Living for God*
- ✓ *Intentionality and Integrity Living for God*
- ✓ *Action and Opportunity Living for God*

1-4 are the first God-focussed Mindsets to be present in our hearts.
5-7 are the Ensuing Others-focussed Mindsets that define our Living externally.

Think differently for God.

~~~

Richard's Note

Thank you for reading this book.

We plan that it should be the first in the Trilogy of:

TRANSFORMED!, CONNECTED!, and FULFILLED!

I sincerely appreciate your review, dear reader.

If you would feel able to review TRANSFORMED! it would be gold dust for me! When I finished TRANSFORMED! and sent it off to my publisher, I innocently imagined that would be it, the book would be avidly read, and sales would rocket. The reality is not at all like that. But one thing I can tell you, is that **every review written, I will read**! And if you can read to the bottom of this page, you will understand how I came to write TRANSFORMED! By making your small effort to review, you will be part of "**Unlocking Potential in Others**." Together, we can help others start their Journey along with us! As the back page reminds us:

~~~

"TRANSFORMED!: 12 Simple Self Help Steps to say "Goodbye" to your feeling "T*here must be more to Life than this*"**

Discover Growing to Become the Extraordinary Masterpiece God Created You to Be!

Start Your Journey of Personal Growth and Transformation to "**Where you are meant to Be**" by Unlocking your Potential, Discovering God's Purposes for your Life, and making the Choice to Start.

~~~

The self-publishing publishing reality means that we are one amongst some many 1000s of books that get to be uploaded and available through digital book sales providers EVERY DAY! The only real way, apart from advertising to get to best-seller status (and that would be a dream come true for me), is that the reviews left by readers who have purchased the book actually help build the sales ranking and therefore the visibility of that book. And when others key in their search terms for whatever book they are looking for, the best sellers are presented to them. Apparently, some 52,000 people search on Amazon every month for "Best Books for Personal Growth"!

My Journey to the freedom of finding meaning and purpose in my life from low self-esteem, and the pain of rejection by others started through a breakout to writing TRANSFORMED! It really began on an October evening 2014, in Bristol, UK when I attended a Willow Creek, Global Leadership Summit video rerun at a local church. Amongst others there speaking were Don Flow, Joseph Grenny, Ivan Satyavrata, Louie Giglio, Erica Ariel Fox, amongst many, and last but not least, Carly Fiorina. Carly was for six years the world-wide CEO of Hewlett Packard. When she speaks, people sit up!

I can clearly credit Carly for kickstarting my Journey. As I sat there watching the huge screen with around 25 others from my church (I had rounded them up and cajoled them into coming with along for the two day event!) *something came alive within me.* Carly was speaking on Personal Potential being "the only truly unlimited resource on this planet". It was one of the few times in my life that I was "barely able to breathe". Such was the impact and effect of realising for the first time in my life, EVER, that I had POTENTIAL, (and you the reader are equally full of Untapped Potential) and realising I had potential that could be Released to the World, that I knew there and then that *Unlocking Potential in Others*, was to be my Mission and Calling from God. I truly believe that "Something will come Alive in You!"

Thank you, Carly, from the bottom of my heart.

These books are the direct result of that evening, when my world changed, and I discovered my Purpose, to seek to change the World, one individual at a time, for the better. Thank you for reading this page as well.

Foot Notes

PREFACE

1.   Immanent is the "indwelling" of God in ourselves.

INTRODUCTION

2.   Stephen R. Covey, *The 8th Habit: From Effectiveness to Greatness* (New York: Free Press, 2004), p. 26.
3.   Joel Osteen, *Next Level Thinking: 10 Powerful Thoughts for a Successful and Abundant Life*, First edition (New York: FaithWords, 2018), p. 37.
4.   Covey, pp. 27–28.
5.   Erwin Raphael McManus, *Seizing Your Divine Moment: Dare to Live a Life of Adventure* (Nashville, Tenn: Thomas Nelson Publishers, 2002), pt. 3193.
6.   Carol S Dweck, *Mindset: Changing the Way You Think to Fulfil Your Potential*, 2017, p. 80.
7.   Dweck, pp. 6–7.
8.   Ryan Quinn and Robert Quinn, *Lift, 2nd Edition*, 2015.
9.   Robert E Quinn and Anjan V Thakor, *The Economics of Higher Purpose: Eight Counterintuitive Steps for Creating a Purpose-Driven Organization*, 2019, pt. 633.
10.   'Merriam-Webster.Com', *Merriam-Webster* <https://www.merriam-webster.com/dictionary/dynamic.>.

LEVEL 1 – BE INSPIRED TO AWAKE!

Step 1. Awaken! To Your Best Life

11.   Rick Warren, *The Purpose Driven Life: What on Earth Am I Here For?*: Zondervan, 2012), p. 22.
12.   Warren, *The Purpose Driven Life*, p.34.
13.   Warren, *The Purpose Driven Life*, p. 36.
14.   Kurt Wright, *Breaking The Rules: Accessing Your Inner Wisdom*, 3rd printing 2015, pt. 645.
15.   Robert E Quinn and Thakor, pt. 1360.

Step 2. To Awareness! Of Your Best Life

16.   Nick Vujicic, *Life without Limits: Inspiration for a Ridiculously Good Life* (New York: Doubleday, 2010), pp. 175–76 <http://ebook.yourcloudlibrary.com/library/BCPL-document_id-f1yg9> [accessed 22 May 2020].
17.   John C. Maxwell, *No Limits: Blow the Cap off Your Capacity*, First Edition (New York: Center Street, 2017), Anais Nin quoted, p. 263.
18.   John C. Maxwell, *No Limits*, pp. 307–8.
19.   John C. Maxwell, *Intentional Living: Choosing a Life That Matters*, First edition (New York: Center Street, 2015), p. 3.
20.   John C. Maxwell, *No Limits*, p. 264.
21.   'G.K. Chesterton Quotes (Author of Orthodoxy) (Page 2 of 96)' <https://www.goodreads.com/author/quotes/7014283.G_K_Chesterton?page=2> [accessed 29 May 2020].

22.   'When Does Future Determine the Present?', *Robert E. Quinn*
      <https://robertequinn.com/uncategorized/when-does-future-determine-the-present/> [accessed 21 May 2020].

23.   'When Does Future Determine the Present?', *Robert E. Quinn*
      <https://robertequinn.com/uncategorized/when-does-future-determine-the-present/> [accessed 21 May 2020].

24.   Covey, p. 28.

25.   Robert E Quinn and Thakor, pt. 635.

26.   Robert E Quinn and Thakor, pt. 662.

27.   Warren, *The Purpose Driven Life*, p. 22.

28.   Warren, *The Purpose Driven Life*, p. 316.

29.   Warren, *The Purpose Driven Life*, p. 191.

30.   'Reference Request - Source of a Russell Quote about Purpose and Meaninglessness', *Philosophy Stack Exchange*
      <https://philosophy.stackexchange.com/questions/64916/source-of-a-russell-quote-about-purpose-and-meaninglessness> [accessed 21 May 2020].

31.   John C. Maxwell, *Intentional Living*, p. 2.

32.   Erwin Raphael McManus, *The Last Arrow: Save Nothing for the next Life*, First Edition (New York: WaterBrook, 2017), p. 178.

33.   Susan G. Smith, *Vision, Inspiration, Purpose, Power - Take Action And Discover Your Personal Keys To Success*, Kindle (HubCap Media; 1 edition (15 April 2013)), pt. 92.

Step 3. To Develop! Your Best Life

34.   Brené Brown, *Daring Greatly: How the Courage to Be Vulnerable Transforms the Way We Live, Love, Parent and Lead*, 2013, p. 177.

35.   Brown, *Daring Greatly*, p. 177.

36.   John C. Maxwell, *No Limits*, p. 36.

37.   John C. Maxwell, *No Limits*, pp. 281–89.

38.   Richard Leider, 'Is Leading Your Calling?', *Leader to Leader*, 2004.31 (2004), 36–40.

39.   John C. Maxwell, *Intentional Living*, p. 2.

40.   Warren, *The Purpose Driven Life*, p. 34.

41.   John C. Maxwell, *Intentional Living*, pp. 92–98.

42.   John C. Maxwell, *Intentional Living*. p. 101

43.   John C. Maxwell, *Intentional Living*, p. 265.

44.   John C. Maxwell, *Intentional Living*, p. 266.

45.   John C. Maxwell, *Intentional Living*, p. 182.

46.   John C. Maxwell, *Intentional Living*, p. 234.

47.   'Contributive Vision', *Robert E. Quinn*
      <https://robertequinn.com/uncategorized/contributive-vision/> [accessed 21 May 2020].

48.   'Contributive Vision'.

49.   Quinn and Quinn.

50.   John C. Maxwell, *Intentional Living*, p. 34.

51.   John C. Maxwell, *Intentional Living*, p. 217.

52.   John C. Maxwell, *Intentional Living*, pp. 4 & 29.

53.   John C Maxwell, *How Successful People Grow: 15 Ways to Get Ahead in Life*, (New York: Center Street, 2012), p. 42

54.   John C. Maxwell, *The 15 Invaluable Laws of Growth: Live Them and Reach Your Potential* (New York: Center Street, 2012), p. 156.

55.   John C. Maxwell, *The 15 Invaluable Laws of Growth*, p. 13.

56. 'Ambrose Redmoon Quotes'
    <https://www.goodreads.com/author/quotes/14958727.Ambrose_Redmoon>
    [accessed 29 May 2020].
57. Quinn and Quinn.
58. Robert E Quinn and Thakor, pt. 662.

Step 4. To Think! About Your Best Life

59. Covey, p. 26.
60. 'Declaration of Independence: A Transcription', *National Archives*, 2015
    <https://www.archives.gov/founding-docs/declaration-transcript> [accessed 30
    July 2020].
61. John C. Maxwell, *Thinking for a Change: 11 Ways Highly Successful People Approach
    Life and Work* (New York: Warner Books, 2003), p. 254.
62. 'The Greatest Obstacle to Discovery Is Not Ignorance—It Is the Illusion of
    Knowledge – Quote Investigator'
    <https://quoteinvestigator.com/2016/07/20/knowledge/> [accessed 2 June
    2020].
63. 'A Quote by John Wooden' <https://www.goodreads.com/quotes/8337239-
    when-opportunity-comes-it-s-too-late-to-prepare> [accessed 29 May 2020].
64. *The Outward Mindset: Seeing beyond Ourselves : How to Change Lives & Transform
    Organizations*, 2016.
65. *The Outward Mindset*, pt. 803.
66. Wright.
67. Wright, pt. 629.
68. Wright, pt. 814.
69. Wright, pt. 818.
70. Wright, pt. 846.
71. Wright, pt. 846.
72. Wright, pt. 850.
73. Quinn and Quinn, p. 202.
74. Mark Goulston and John B. Ullmen, *Real Influence: Persuade without Pushing and
    Gain without Giving In* (New York: American Management Association, 2013), p. 11.
75. Goulston and Ullmen, p. 12.
76. Goulston and Ullmen, p. 14.
77. Goulston and Ullmen, p. 14.
78. Goulston and Ullmen, pp. 34–35.
79. Goulston and Ullmen, pp. 37–38.
80. Goulston and Ullmen, pp. 121–24.
81. Goulston and Ullmen, p. 171.
82. Goulston and Ullmen, pp. 172–78.
83. Goulston and Ullmen, pp. 183–84.

LEVEL 2 – BE INSPIRED TO UNLOCK!

Step 5. Unlock! Your Best Life

84. Robert E. Quinn, *Building the Bridge as You Walk on It: A Guide for Leading Change*,
    1st ed (San Francisco: Jossey-Bass, 2004).
85. Richard Leider, *The Power of Purpose: Find Meaning, Live Longer, Better*, Third
    Edition, Revised&Expanded (San Francisco: Berrett-Koehler Publishers, Inc,
    2015), p. 1.

86. '2014 Global Leadership Summit Session 2: Carly Fiorina #GLS14', *Live Intentionally* <http://www.liveintentionally.org/2014/08/14/2014-global-leadership-summit-session-2-carly-fiorina-gls14/> [accessed 21 May 2020].
87. Dweck, p. 6.
88. Dweck, p. 16.
89. 'Ernest Rutherford Quotes (Author of Radioactive Transformations)' <https://www.goodreads.com/author/quotes/437411.Ernest_Rutherford> [accessed 21 May 2020].
90. 'A Quote by George Eliot' <https://www.goodreads.com/quotes/619-it-is-never-too-late-to-be-what-you-might> [accessed 21 May 2020].
91. '2014 Global Leadership Summit Session 2'.
92. '2014 Global Leadership Summit Session 2'.
93. John C Maxwell, *The Power of Significance: How Purpose Changes Your Life*, 2017, pt. 113.
94. John C. Maxwell, *Intentional Living*, p. 142.
95. Covey, pp. 41–43.
96. 'How Culture Conspires to Prevent the Emergence of Leadership', *Robert E. Quinn* <https://robertequinn.com/uncategorized/how-culture-conspires-to-prevent-the-emergence-of-leadership/> [accessed 21 May 2020].
97. 'How Culture Conspires to Prevent the Emergence of Leadership'.
98. Quinn and Quinn, p. 44.
99. Quinn and Quinn, pp. 59–60.
100. Quinn and Quinn.
101. Robert E. Quinn, *The Positive Organization: Breaking Free from Conventional Cultures, Constraints, and Beliefs*, First Edition (Oakland: Berrett-Koehler Publishers, Inc, 2015), p. 39.
102. Robert E. Quinn, *The Positive Organization*, pp. 38–43.
103. Carly Fiorina, *Find Your Way: Unleash Your Power and Highest Potential* (Carol Stream, Illinois: Tyndale House Publishers, Inc, 2019), p. 17.
104. Robert E. Quinn, *Building the Bridge as You Walk on It*.
105. '2014 Global Leadership Summit Session 2'.

Step 6. To Breakout! To Your Best Life

106. Robert E. Quinn, *Building the Bridge as You Walk on It*.
107. 'Leading on the Edge of Hope - Christine Caine', *Global Leadership Network UK & Ireland, Partial Transcript*, https://globalleadershipnetwork.org.uk/lesson/leading-on-the-edge-of-hope-christine-caine/> [accessed 22 May 2020].
108. John C Maxwell, *The Power of Significance*, pt. 1154.
109. John C Maxwell, *The Power of Significance*, pts 605–806.
110. 'Ambrose Redmoon Quotes'.
111. Covey, p. 25-26.
112. Terry Rey, *Bourdieu on Religion: Imposing Faith and Legitimacy.* (Routledge, 2014).
113. Rey, p. 130.
114. Robert E. Quinn, *The Positive Organization*, pp. 28–29.
115. Robert E. Quinn, *The Positive Organization*, p. 48.
116. Robert E. Quinn, *The Positive Organization*, pp. 26–27.
117. John C. Maxwell, *The 15 Invaluable Laws of Growth*, pp. 12–13.
118. John C. Maxwell, *Be All You Can Be: A Challenge to Stretch Your God-given Potential*, 3rd Ed (Colorado Springs, CO: David C. Cook, 2007), p. 72.
119. Covey, pp. 25–26.

120. 'I Dreamed a Dream', *Wikipedia*, 2020 <https://en.wikipedia.org/w/index.php?title=I_Dreamed_a_Dream&oldid=9673 82765> [accessed 31 July 2020].

Step 7. To Grow! Your Best Life

121. Covey, p. 71.
122. Myles Munroe, *In Charge: Finding the Leader within You*, 2008, pt. 1438.
123. 'Catherine of Siena Quotes (Author of Catherine of Siena)' <https://www.goodreads.com/author/quotes/5794057.Catherine_of_Siena> [accessed 22 May 2020].
124. John C Maxwell, *The Power of Significance*, pt. 67.
125. John C Maxwell, *The Power of Significance*, pt. 89.
126. John C Maxwell, *The Power of Significance*, pt. 20.
127. John C Maxwell, *The Power of Significance*, pt. 213.
128. John C Maxwell, *The Power of Significance*, pt. 1154.
129. 'A Quote by Abraham Lincoln' <https://www.goodreads.com/quotes/715317-without-the-assistance-of-that-divine-being-i-cannot-succeed> [accessed 22 May 2020].
130. Robert E. Quinn, *The Positive Organization*, p. 58.
131. Robert E. Quinn, *The Positive Organization*, p. 48.
132. Daniel H Pink, *Drive: The Surprising Truth about What Motivates Us* (Edinburgh: Canongate, 2010).

Step 8. To Engage! Your Best Life

133. Mark Deterding, *Leading Jesus' Way: Become the Servant Leader God Created You to Be*, 2016, p. 3.
134. John C. Maxwell, *Be All You Can Be*, p. 72.
135. John C. Maxwell, *Be All You Can Be*, p. 176.
136. John C. Maxwell, *Be All You Can Be*, pp. 177–79.
137. Isaiah Hankel, *Black Hole Focus How Intelligent People Can Create a Powerful Purpose for Their Lives* (New York, NY: John Wiley & Sons, 2014), p. 8.
138. 'Culture Creation', *Robert E. Quinn* <https://robertequinn.com/uncategorized/culture-creation/> [accessed 22 May 2020].
139. Robert E. Quinn, *The Positive Organization*, pp. 1–2.
140. John C. Maxwell, *Intentional Living*.
141. Ryan Quinn and Robert Quinn, Lift, *Second Edition*, 2015, p.2.
142. Myles Munroe, *Maximizing Your Potential: The Keys to Dying Empty*, 2008, p. 129.
143. Gordon L. Lippitt and Warren H. Schmidt, 'Crises in a Developing Organization', *Harvard Business Review*, 1 November 1967 <https://hbr.org/1967/11/crises-in-a-developing-organization> [accessed 7 August 2020].
144. Susan A David, *Emotional Agility Get Unstuck, Embrace Change, and Thrive in Work and Life*, 2017, pt. 1475.
145. 'Ready to Fly: Finding Your Greater Yes by Dr. Dan Erickson', *People Matter Ministries* <http://www.peoplematterministries.com/store/ready-to-fly-finding-your-greater-yes> [accessed 7 August 2020].
146. T. D Jakes, *Identity: Discover Who You Are and Live a Life of Purpose.* (Place of publication not identified: Destiny Image), pt. 107.

LEVEL 3 – BE INSPIRED TO ACT!

Step 9. Act! For Others For Their Best Lives

147. 'Howard Thurman Quotes (Author of Jesus and the Disinherited)'
<https://www.goodreads.com/author/quotes/56230.Howard_Thurman>
[accessed 20 May 2020].

148. Henry Cloud, *Boundaries for Leaders: Results, Relationships, and Being Ridiculously in Charge*, First Edition (New York, NY: HarperBusiness, an imprint of HarperCollins Publishers, 2013), pp. xiii–xvi.

149. 'From Silos to Collaboration: The Process of Cultural Surgery', *Robert E. Quinn*
<https://robertequinn.com/uncategorized/from-silos-to-collaboration-the-process-of-cultural-surgery/> [accessed 22 May 2020].

150. Gillian Tett, *The Silo Effect: Why Putting Everything in Its Place Isn't Such a Bright Idea.* (Little Brown Book Group, 2015), pt. 831.

151. Tett, pt. 3910.

152. Tett, pt. 3996.

153. Tett, pt. 4034.

154. 'The Source of Silo Behavior', *Robert E. Quinn*
<https://robertequinn.com/uncategorized/the-source-of-silo-behavior/>
[accessed 26 May 2020].

155. Brené Brown, *Rising Strong*, 2015, p. 4.

156. Kyle Patterson, *Transformational Leadership* (Independently published), p. 48.

157. Roy M. Oswald, *The Emotional Intelligence of Jesus: Relational Smarts for Religious Leaders* (Lanham: Rowman & Littlefield, 2015), pt. 537.

158. Frank Viola, *Reimagining Church: Pursuing the Dream of Organic Christianity.* (David C. Cook, 2012), pt. 2037.

159. Rick Warren, *The Purpose Driven Church: Growth without Compromising Your Message & Mission* (Grand Rapids, Mich.: Zondervan Pub., 1995), p. 87.

160. Warren, *The Purpose Driven Church*, p. 96.

161. Cloud, pp. 14–18.

162. '2014 GLS Highlight', *Dotsub* <https://dotsub.com/view/359fba1a-0d3f-4e05-9021-e085d5e56137> [accessed 7 August 2020].

163. Bishop Alan Wilson, 'Bishop Alan's Blog: How to Change Your Vicar (Part Two)', *Bishop Alan's Blog*, 2012 <http://bishopalan.blogspot.com/2012/09/how-to-change-your-vicar-part-two.html> [accessed 26 May 2020].

164. Robert E. Quinn, *Building the Bridge as You Walk on It*, pp. 21–25.

165. 'A Quote by Lyndon B. Johnson' <https://www.goodreads.com/quotes/3276-yesterday-is-not-ours-to-recover-but-tomorrow-is-ours> [accessed 26 May 2020].

166. 'A Quote by Douglas MacArthur'
<https://www.goodreads.com/quotes/359193-a-true-leader-has-the-confidence-to-stand-alone-the> [accessed 26 May 2020].

167. Covey, p. 4.

Step 10. To Lead! Others To Their Best Lives

168. Will Mancini and Warren Bird, *God Dreams: 12 Vision Templates for Finding and Focusing Your Church's Future* (Nashville, Tennessee: B & H Publishing Group, 2016).

169. John Blanchard and Jesse Stoner, 'The Vision Thing', *Leader to Leader, No.31 Winter 2004*, p. 2.

170. 'When Does Future Determine the Present?'

171. Munroe, *In Charge*, pt. 1502.

172. Munroe, *In Charge*, pt. 1668.

173. Munroe, *In Charge*, pt. 2176.

174. Quinn and Quinn.

175. Robert E. Quinn and Anjan V. Thakor, 'Creating a Purpose-Driven Organization', *Harvard Business Review*, 1 July 2018 <https://hbr.org/2018/07/creating-a-purpose-driven-organization> [accessed 2 June 2020].

176. Robert E Quinn, *The Best Teacher in You: How to Accelerate Learning and Change Lives*, 2014, pt. 2020.

177. Quinn and Quinn.

178. Quinn and Quinn.

179. Quinn and Quinn, p. 65.

180. Munroe, *In Charge*, pt. 477.

181. Simon Sinek, *Start with Why: How Great Leaders Inspire Everyone to Take Action* (New York; London: Portfolio/Penguin, 2011), p. 16.

182. Ronnie Floyd, '30 Leadership Lessons from 30 Years at the Same Church', *CT Pastors* <https://www.christianitytoday.com/pastors/2016/november-web-exclusives/30-leadership-lessons-from-30-years-at-same-church.html> [accessed 26 May 2020].

183. Brown, *Daring Greatly*, p. 10.

184. *The Church Should Be the Nurturer of the Human Spirit*, dir. by Erwin Mcmanus, 2011 <https://d15greoaou1b27.cloudfront.net/YR/Erwin%20McManus/FS201112/FS201112-McManus_2011_00-35-45_ChurchLeadership_HopeoftheWorld_ChasingDaylight-640x360.mp4> [accessed 29 May 2020].

185. John C. Maxwell, *Be All You Can Be*, pp. 179–80.

186. M3 Contributor, '2019 M3 Plenary Session – Don Stephens | M3 | Mobilizing Medical Missions', 2019 <https://m3missions.com/2019-m3-plenary-session-don-stephens/> [accessed 28 May 2020].

187. 'Sight Magazine - THE INTERVIEW: DON STEPHENS, CO-FOUNDER OF MERCY SHIPS' <https://www.sightmagazine.com.au/features/12647-the-interview-don-stephens-co-founder-of-mercy-ships> [accessed 28 May 2020].

188. 'A Quote by Pierre Teilhard de Chardin' <https://www.goodreads.com/quotes/38263-our-duty-as-men-and-women-is-to-proceed-as> [accessed 26 May 2020].

189. McManus, *The Last Arrow*, p. 28.

190. McManus, *The Last Arrow*, p. 34.

191. McManus, *The Last Arrow*, p. 43.

192. McManus, *The Last Arrow*, p. 22.

193. McManus, *The Last Arrow*, p. 194.

194. McManus, *The Last Arrow*, p. 194.

195. McManus, *The Last Arrow*, p. 165.

196. 'GLS18 Session Notes–Erwin McManus–The Last Arrow', *Global Leadership Network*, 2018 <https://globalleadership.org/articles/leading-yourself/gls18-session-notes-erwin-mcmanus-the-last-arrow/> [accessed 26 May 2020].

197. T. D. Jakes, *Destiny: Step into Your Purpose*, First edition (New York: Faith Words, 2015), p. 234.

198. John C. Maxwell, *Intentional Living*, p. 234.

199. Mac Pier, *Consequential Leadership: 15 Leaders Fighting for Our Cities, Our Poor, Our Youth, and Our Culture* (Downers Grove, IL: IVP Books, 2012), pt. 1700.

200. Thom S. Rainer, *Breakout Churches: Discover How to Make the Leap* (Grand Rapids, Mich: Zondervan, 2005), pt. 1946.
201. Brown, *Daring Greatly*, p. 248.
202. Leighton Ford, *Transforming Leadership: Jesus' Way of Creating Vision, Shaping Values & Empowering Change* (Downers Grove, Ill.: InterVarsity Press, 1991), pt. 88.
203. Ford, pt. 72.
204. Ford, pt. 134.
205. Ford, pt. 3154.
206. 'QI201710523', *Global Leadership Network*, 2017 <https://globalleadership.org/quote/leading-yourself/qi201710523/> [accessed 26 May 2020].
207. 'People Matter Ministries', *People Matter Ministries* <http://www.peoplematterministries.com> [accessed 26 May 2020].
208. Rainer, pt. 1138.
209. Rainer, pt. 1135.
210. Viktor E Frankl and others, *Man's Search for Meaning*, 2014, pt. 1400.

Step 11. To Rally! Others To Their Best Lives

211. Warren, *The Purpose Driven Church*, pp. 86–93.

Step 12. To Legacy! Others For Their Best Lives

212. McManus, *The Last Arrow*, p. 24,59.
213. 'People Matter Ministries'.
214. 'The Churchill Society London. Churchill's Speeches.' <http://www.churchill-society-london.org.uk/EndoBegn.html> [accessed 26 May 2020].

APPENDIX A – THE THEOLOGY OF TRANSFORMED!

215. Rey, p. 130.

APPENDIX A

THE THEOLOGY OF TRANSFORMED!

The Theology of *TRANSFORMED!*

All based on the first two chapters of Ephesians.

Ephesians 1:3-6,9-14 NIV:

[3] Praise be to the God and Father of our Lord Jesus Christ, who has blessed us in the heavenly realms with every spiritual blessing in Christ. [4] For he chose us in him before the creation of the world to be holy and blameless in his sight. In love [5] he predestined us for adoption to sonship through Jesus Christ, in accordance with his pleasure and will – [6] to the praise of his glorious grace, which he has freely given us in the One he loves. [9] he made known to us the mystery of his will according to his good pleasure, which he purposed in Christ, [10] to be put into effect when the times reach their fulfilment---to bring unity to all things in heaven and on earth under Christ. [11] In him we were also chosen, having been predestined according to the plan of him who works out everything in conformity with the purpose of his will, [12] in order that we, who were the first to put our hope in Christ, might be for the praise of his glory. [13] And you also were included in Christ when you heard the message of truth, the gospel of your salvation. When you believed, you were marked in him with a seal, the promised Holy Spirit, [14] who is a deposit guaranteeing our inheritance until the redemption of those who are God's possession – to the praise of his glory.

And Ephesians 2:1-10 NIV:

[1] As for you, you were dead in your transgressions and sins, [2] in which you used to live when you followed the ways of this world and of the ruler of the kingdom of the air, the spirit who is now at work in those who are disobedient. [3] All of us also lived among them at one time, gratifying the cravings of our flesh and following its desires and thoughts. Like the rest, we were by nature deserving of wrath. [4] But because of his great love for us, God, who is rich in mercy, [5] made us alive with Christ even when we were dead in transgressions – it is by grace you have been saved. [6] And God raised us up with Christ and seated us with him in the heavenly realms in Christ Jesus, [7] in order that in the coming ages he might show the incomparable riches of his grace, expressed in his kindness to us in Christ Jesus. [8] For it is by grace you have been saved, through faith – and this is not from yourselves, it is the gift of God – [9] not by works, so that no one can boast. [10] For we are God's handiwork, created in Christ Jesus to do good works, which God prepared in advance for us to do.

367

For those who love the nuances, complexity and intellectual rigour of theological debate, especially over Reformed Theology and the unending Calvinist/Arminian debacle, the writer of *TRANSFORMED!* "is having none of it!" None of us are "right" when it comes to understanding fully God's intentions for His creation. *Sola scriptura* has long been the bedrock of conservative protestant theologians. I fully subscribe to that view, as did Luther and our own brilliant bible text translator, William Tyndale. Calvin and Zwingli also did. But for most, if not all, the Reformers, their culture and personal histories affected their thinking and theology.

It was so much the case with Calvin and his contemporaries that although he was not personally responsible, it was a brutal act of shameful evil that allowed the execution of a man with a brilliant mind who happened to think differently from the ideas of his day, and nothing could have been worse than being burnt alive at a stake. Severus died because the authorities could not accept his different approach to faith. "It seemed a good idea at the time" is no excuse. Any religion that condones either corporal or capital punishment of those who think differently is evil simply because it injures or kills a living soul created by God in His image.

Ephesians 1-2 dramatically sweeps aside those nuances of the theologians and their ultimately self-interested correctness. Perhaps they have not noticed that being right does not equal righteousness! This brings me to the crux of the issues being discussed here. And it is simply this: for two millennia, the Church of Jesus Christ, since Rome became pre-eminent, has operated an unbiblical hierarchical management system that incorrectly pushed forward a system of <u>theological belief</u> as the basis for their religion when Jesus clearly taught that it was wrong and should be based on a <u>relationship of commitment and love for God primarily, as well as faith in Him and His completed sacrifice for sins at Calvary.</u>

It is my profoundly held view that far from effectively expanding the Church of Christ, the hierarchical Church systems, both Catholic and latterly since the Reformation, the Protestant Church as well, effectively used belief systems centred around the mass/communion and the ordination of priests to ensure that the laity could never grow to become the people God intended them to be and thus ensured their perpetual existence as children who could never mature, never grow to be the individual's God planned them to be.

Indeed, so clever were these systems of belief and practice that they induced in their congregations what Pierre Bourdieu called the "misrecognition" of the people and inevitably the collusion of the people themselves, with the ordained priesthood, in their disempowerment.

"Somewhere within all of us there thus lurks a spirit of resistance, lying for the most part dormant and 'confused' under layers upon layers of misrecognition that dupe us into submission to the social order in all of its inequalities and injustices. Until, of course, a prophet (hopefully one who has read Bourdieu!) comes along to 'reactivate' it."[217] – Terry Rea, Bourdieu on Religion.

I write, admitting my early despair and the growth of my personal "theory of educational inadequacy", which has not left me until recently, along with 20 years at the bottom of the pile in a large utility company, to simply wanting to make a difference for Others, to Matter and to "fulfil God's Purposes in my generation."

In fact, with other more recent "rejection of good ideas" issues by the local religious hierarchy, I feel as if a light has been switched on – as if God is saying, "Now do you understand, my specially created one, my Richard, why I have allowed you to experience these seemingly trivial, almost tribal nuances of interactions between individuals and groups in churches and those extremely subtle mechanisms? (where "we collude with the clergy in our own disempowerment" (R.F.)) So that I can now show you how to understand where you are, and how to create and cross the bridge from hierarchical, repetitive, power-controlling, traditional ordained clergy subjugation of congregations frozen and immobile under that clerical hierarchy, to Transformational Growth. That is what I always planned for People, and My Son Jesus exemplified."

I believe that there is significant evidence to add to the misrecognition issue, and this is primarily the inculcated inability to think or imagine truths outside the accepted belief patterns. The same underlying, essentially false misrecognition process creates the allied inability of mental and spiritual limitation on all the individuals caught up in this separate worldview bubble that keeps them enslaved and unable to move, change, grow, or break out from this cultural prison. They are locked in. Its results and implications are genuinely horrific. That is why congregations are kept like immature children, unable to grow and become adults, because the system, which is essentially symbolically abusing them spiritually and intellectually, cannot and will not allow it. The other overwhelming observation is the clergy's complete inability to contemplate or understand their culpability in this enslavement and the misrecognition of their own personal enslavement!

But the good news of *TRANSFORMED!* inherent in the New Testament work of Christ, obtaining our salvation through sins forgiven by faith in Him, is the promise of God for those who are fully and wholeheartedly committed to

---

[217] Rey, p. 130.

Him. If we mirror back to God His commitment to those who come to Him in faith and trust, by the example of the wholehearted commitment of Christ, good things will happen.

Psalm 37:3-6 NIV: "Trust in the Lord and do good; dwell in the land and enjoy safe pasture. Take delight in the Lord, and he will give you the desires of your heart. Commit your way to the Lord; trust in him, and he will do this: He will make your righteous reward shine like the dawn, your vindication like the noonday sun."

Also, in Mark 12:30-31 NIV: "Love the Lord your God with all your heart and with all your soul and with all your mind and with all your strength. The second is this: 'Love your neighbour as yourself.' There is no commandment greater than these."

In effect, *TRANSFORMED!* is the practical reality of the words of Christ in Mark ch.12:39-31. It brings out God's intended Higher Purpose and blessings for those who implement wholehearted commitment, decisive dedication and conscious consecration for Him daily. This is a practical book.

APPENDIX B – METACOG for TRANSFORMED!

God's Extraordinary Masterpiece People

Wake up - Being Awake
Switch On - Being Switched On
Unlock - Unlocking Unlimited Potential
Breakout - Preparing for Opportunities
Act - Seizing Opportunities

Valuing and Adding Value to Others

Intentionality and Integrity Living To Make A Difference

Significance and Meaning Living To Make A Difference

Action and Opportunity Living To Make A Difference

Anticipation and Urgency Living To Make A Difference

Focus and Commitment Living To Make A Difference

Abundance and Surplus Living To Make A Difference

Purpose Centred Core

We Are Here - Living Our Best Life

Internally Directed By Our Core Values

Living Our Higher Purpose
Discovering Our Higher Purpose
Unlocking Our Unlimited Potential

Our Circle Of Transformation and Growth Expanding
Our Circle Of Awareness Expanding
Our Circle Of Unlocked Potential Expanding
Our Circle Of Action And Leadership Expanding

Hope

Externally Open

OTHERS
Fulfilling God's Purposes
Where We Are Meant To Be

Others Focussed and connecting

old cultural assumptions discarded

Valuing and Adding Value to Others

Purpose Centred Core shows
The Seeds Of Greatness

Living Transformation and Growth for God
~ To Make A Difference For Others ~
Growing the Seeds Of Greatness To Maturity
~ Intentionally Living Our Best Life ~

371

BIBLIOGRAPHY

Title	Author(s)
Man: The Dwelling Place of God: What it Means to Have Christ Living in You	A. W. Tozer
Give and Take: A Revolutionary Approach to Success	Adam Grant
Originals: How Non-conformists Change the World	Adam Grant
Think Again: The Power of Knowing What You Don't Know	Adam Grant
The Power of a New Attitude	Alan E. Nelson
Bringing Out Best in People: How To Enjoy Helping Others Excel	Alan Loy Mcginnis
Teaming: How Organizations Learn, Innovate, and Compete in the Knowledge Economy	Amy C. Edmondson
The Fearless Organization: Creating Psychological Safety in the Workplace for Learning, Innovation, and Growth	Amy C. Edmondson
Peak: For Fans of Atomic Habits	Anders Ericsson, Robert Pool
The Way of a Pilgrim: Candid Tales of a Wanderer to His Spiritual Father (Penguin Classics)	Andrew Louth, Anna Zaranko
Challenge Your Assumptions, Change Your World: Introducing the Assumpt! A break through to faster, smarter business decisions	Andy Cohen
Grit: The Power of Passion and Perseverance	Angela Duckworth
Delighting in God (AW Tozer Series Book 1)	AW Tozer
Commando Mindset: Find Your Motivation, Realize Your Potential, Achieve Your Goals	Ben Williams
Take the Lead: Motivate, Inspire, and Bring Out the Best in Yourself and Everyone Around You	Betsy Myers, John David Mann
Cognitive Behavioral Therapy (CBT): Master Your Brain and Emotions to Overcome Anxiety, Depression and Negative Thoughts (CBT Self Help Book 1- Cognitive Behavioral Therapy)	Bill Andrews
The Person Called You: Why You're Here, Why You Matter & What You Should Do With Your Life	Bill Hendricks
Courageous Leadership	Bill Hybels
The Volunteer Revolution: Unleashing the Power of Everybody	Bill Hybels
Just Walk Across the Room: Simple Steps Pointing People to Faith	Bill Hybels
Holy Discontent: Fueling the Fire That Ignites Personal Vision	Bill Hybels
Axiom: Powerful Leadership Proverbs	Bill Hybels
Becoming a Contagious Christian	Bill Hybels, Mark Mittelberg
Descending Into Greatness	Bill Hybels, Rob Wilkins
Discovering Your Purpose: A Short Interview with Bill Johnson	Bill Johnson
Everybody Matters: The Extraordinary Power of Caring for Your People Like Family	Bob Chapman, Raj Sisodia
Transformation (Exponential Series)	Bob Roberts Jr.

Daring Greatly: How the Courage to Be Vulnerable Transforms the Way We Live, Love, Parent, and Lead	Brene Brown
The Gifts of Imperfection: Let Go of Who You Think You're Supposed to Be and Embrace Who You Are	Brene Brown
Rising Strong	Brene Brown
Dare to Lead: Brave Work. Tough Conversations. Whole Hearts.	Brene Brown
Deep Work: Rules for Focused Success in a Distracted World	Cal Newport
My Journey So Far	Canon White, Kate Benson
It's Your Ship: Management Techniques from the Best Damn Ship in the Navy	Captain D. Michael Abrashoff
It's Our Ship: The No-Nonsense Guide to Leadership	Captain D. Michael Abrashoff
Find Your Way: Unleash Your Power and Highest Potential	Carly Fiorina
Mindset - Updated Edition: Changing The Way You think To Fulfil Your Potential	Carol S. Dweck
Leadership: 20 Successful Tips on How to Become a True Leader Who Inspires Everyone and Creates Profound Visions That Lead to Progress	Carrie Dresden
The Power of Habit: Why We Do What We Do, and How to Change	Charles Duhigg
Smarter Faster Better: The Secrets of Being Productive	Charles Duhigg
Joel Osteen: The Man, The Message, and The Ministry - Biography of America's Most Popular Pastor (Divine Journey: Biographies of Religious Icons - The ... callings Controversies and impact)	Charles Kenny
Sully [Movie Tie-In] UK: My Search for What Really Matters	Chesley B. Sully" Sullenberger III
Made to Stick: Why some ideas take hold and others come unstuck	Chip Heath, Dan Heath
Switch: How to change things when change is hard	Chip Heath, Dan Heath
Decisive: How to make better choices in life and work	Chip Heath, Dan Heath
The Power of Moments: Why Certain Experiences Have Extraordinary Impact	Chip Heath, Dan Heath
Trapped by Assumptions: How to Break Mental Traps and Keep Your Mind Sharp (The Anchor of Our Purest Thoughts Book 6)	Chong Chen
The Circle Way: A Leader in Every Chair	Christina Baldwin, Ann Linnea
Winning the War in Your Mind: Change Your Thinking, Change Your Life	Craig Groeschel
Get Your Ship Together: How Great Leaders Inspire Ownership From The Keel Up	D. Michael Abrashoff
The Book of Joy. The Sunday Times Bestseller	Dalai Lama, Desmond Tutu
Upstream: How to solve problems before they happen	Dan Heath
Psychological Safety: The key to happy, high-performing people and teams	Dan Radecki, Leonie Hull, Jennifer McCusker, Christopher Ancona

The Culture Code: The Secrets of Highly Successful Groups	Daniel Coyle
Social Intelligence: The New Science of Human Relationships	Daniel Goleman
Leadership: The Power of Emotional Intelligence	Daniel Goleman
Focus: The Hidden Driver of Excellence	Daniel Goleman
Drive: The Surprising Truth About What Motivates Us	Daniel H. Pink
Mindsight: Transform Your Brain with the New Science of Kindness	Daniel Siegel
The Road to Character	David Brooks
Being Called: Scientific, Secular, and Sacred Perspectives (Psychology Religion and Spirituality)	David Bryce Yaden, Theo D. McCall, J. Harold Ellens
A Christian Writer's Guide to The Book Proposal (The Christian Writer's Guide to... 1)	David E. Fessenden
33 Meditations on Death: Notes from the Wrong End of Medicine	David Jarrett
The Magic of Thinking Big	David Joseph Schwartz
A Model of Servant Leadership: 140 Actionable Ideas to Build Your Heart for Servant Leadership	Deterding,Mark
Leading Jesus' Way: Become The Servant Leader God Created You To Be	Deterding,Mark
Life Together	Dietrich Bonhoeffer
WordPress for Beginners 2019: A Visual Step-by-Step Guide to Mastering WordPress (Webmaster Series Book 2)	Dr. Andy Williams
Self-Publishing on Amazon 2019: No publisher? No Agent? No Problem!	Dr. Andy Williams
Switch On Your Brain: The Key to Peak Happiness, Thinking, and Health	Dr. Caroline Leaf
The Perfect You: A Blueprint for Identity	Dr. Caroline Leaf
Think, Learn, Succeed: Understanding and Using Your Mind to Thrive at School, the Workplace, and Life	Dr. Caroline Leaf
Switch On Your Brain Every Day: 365 Readings for Peak Happiness, Thinking, and Health	Dr. Caroline Leaf
Cleaning Up Your Mental Mess: 5 Simple, Scientifically Proven Steps to Reduce Anxiety, Stress, and Toxic Thinking	Dr. Caroline Leaf
Comeback Churches	Ed Stetzer, Mike Dodson
The Power of Meaning: The true route to happiness	Emily Esfahani Smith
Great Britain and the American Civil War	Ephraim Douglass Adams
The Uprising Experience: A Personal Guide for a Revolution of the Soul, Promise Keepers Edition	Erwin Raphael McManus
Seizing Your Divine Moment: Dare to Live a Life of Adventure	Erwin Raphael McManus
The Last Arrow: Save Nothing for the Next Life	Erwin Raphael McManus
Reinventing Organizations: A Guide to Creating Organizations Inspired by the Next Stage of Human Consciousness	Frederic Laloux
Reimagining Church: Pursuing the Dream of Organic Christianity	Frank Viola
Pagan Christianity?: Exploring the Roots of Our Church Practices	Frank Viola, George Barna

Real Influence: Persuade Without Pushing and Gain Without Giving In	Mark Goulston, Dr. John Ullmen
Finding the True You: Discover Who You Were Created to Be (Discovery Series Book 1)	Mark J Musser
Becoming a Contagious Church: Increasing Your Church's Evangelistic Temperature	Mark Mittelberg
Triggers: Sparking positive change and making it last	Marshall Goldsmith, Mark Reiter
Learned Optimism: How to Change Your Mind and Your Life	Martin Seligman
Authentic Happiness: Using the New Positive Psychology to Realise your Potential for Lasting Fulfilment	Martin Seligman
Flourish: A New Understanding of Happiness and Wellbeing: The practical guide to using positive psychology to make you happier and healthier	Martin Seligman
The Hope Circuit: A Psychologist's Journey from Helplessness to Optimism	Martin Seligman
Assume Nothing, Think Again: Interrupting Assumptions in 5 Steps	Mary Stewart-Pellegrini
Black Box Thinking: The Surprising Truth About Success	Matthew Syed, Matthew Syed Consulting Ltd
Churchianity vs Christianity	Met Anthony Bloom
Unlocking Potential: 7 Coaching Skills That Transform Individuals, Teams, & Organizations	Michael K. Simpson
I Hear You: The Surprisingly Simple Skill Behind Extraordinary Relationships	Michael S. Sorensen
Flow: The Psychology of Happiness	Mihaly Csikszentmihalyi
Maximizing Your Potential Expanded Edition: The Keys to Dying Empty	Myles Munroe
Understanding Your Place in God's Kingdom: Your Original Purpose for Existence	Myles Munroe
In Charge: Finding the Leader Within You	Myles Munroe
Connect: How to Double Your Number of Volunteers	Nelson Searcy, Jennifer Dykes Henson
The Greatness Principle: Finding Significance and Joy by Serving Others	Nelson Searcy, Jennifer Dykes Henson
Fusion: Turning First-Time Guests into Fully-Engaged Members of Your Church	Nelson Searcy, Jennifer Henson
The Power of Joy: A Straight Up Guide to Lasting Freedom, Effortless Abundance, and a Limitless Life	Nick Breau
Leading from Purpose: Clarity and confidence to act when it matters	Nick Craig
Methods of Persuasion: How to Use Psychology to Influence Human Behavior	Nick Kolenda
Supercharge Your Kindle Sales: Simple Strategies to Boost Organic Traffic on Amazon, Sell More Books, and Blow Up Your Author Mailing List (Book Marketing for Authors 2)	Nick Stephenson
Life Without Limits: Inspiration for a Ridiculously Good Life	Nick Vujicic
Positive Thinking Every Day: An Inspiration For Each Day of the Year	Norman Vincent Peale

The Power Of Positive Living (Personal Development)	Norman Vincent Peale
The Power of Positive Thinking: 10 Traits for Maximum Results	Norman Vincent Peale
The Amazing Results Of Positive Thinking (Personal Development)	Norman Vincent Peale
The Positive Power of Jesus Christ: Life-Changing Adventures in Faith	Norman Vincent Peale
Smart Volunteer Management: A Volunteer Coordinator's Handbook for Engaging, Motivating and Developing Volunteers (Smart Church Management 1)	Patricia Lotich
The Four Obsessions of an Extraordinary Executive: A Leadership Fable (J-B Lencioni Series Book 31)	Patrick M. Lencioni
Instant Confidence	Paul McKenna
The Journal of John Wesley	Percy Livingstone Parker
God's Seeds of Greatness: Everybody is a Somebody with God!	Peter Wade
History Of The Christian Church (The Complete Eight Volumes In One)	Philip Schaff
No Ego - Ditch Your Ego & Find Your Dream	Phillip McKinney
The Power of Purpose: Find Meaning, Live Longer, Better	Richard J. Leider
Joy, Inc.: How We Built a Workplace People Love	Richard Sheridan
The Purpose Driven Church: Growth Without Compromising Your Message and Mission	Rick Warren
The Purpose Driven Life: What on Earth Am I Here For?	Rick Warren
Building the Bridge As You Walk On It: A Guide for Leading Change	Robert E. Quinn
The Positive Organization: Breaking Free from Conventional Cultures, Constraints, and Beliefs	Robert E. Quinn
The Economics of Higher Purpose: Eight Counterintuitive Steps for Creating a Purpose-Driven Organization	Robert E. Quinn, Anjan V. Thakor
The Best Teacher in You: How to Accelerate Learning and Change Lives	Robert E. Quinn, Katherine Heynoski, Mike Thomas, Gretchen M. Spreitzer
All About Jesus: The Single Story from Matthew, Mark, Luke, & John	Roger Quy
A. Lincoln: A Biography	Ronald C. White Jr.
The Leadership Baton: An Intentional Strategy for Developing Leaders in Your Church	Rowland Forman, Jeff Jones, Bruce B. Miller
The Emotional Intelligence of Jesus: Relational Smarts for Religious Leaders	Roy M. Oswald, Arland Jacobson
Ego is the Enemy: The Fight to Master Our Greatest Opponent (The Way, the Enemy and the Key)	Ryan Holiday
Lift: The Fundamental State of Leadership	Ryan W. Quinn, Robert E. Quinn
Kindle Direct Publishing For Absolute Beginners: A Guide to Publishing Kindle E-Books for Beginners	Sally Jenkins
Empower Your Life: The Master Achiever's Guide to Maximizing Goals, Rediscovering Purpose, Conquering Adversity and Supercharging Success	Scott Allan

Start With Why: How Great Leaders Inspire Everyone To Take Action	Simon Sinek
Leaders Eat Last: Why Some Teams Pull Together and Others Don't	Simon Sinek
The Infinite Game: From the bestselling author of Start With Why	Simon Sinek
Find Your Why: A Practical Guide for Discovering Purpose for You and Your Team	Simon Sinek, David Mead, Peter Docker
The Speed of Trust: The One Thing that Changes Everything	Stephen M. R. Covey
The 8th Habit: From Effectiveness to Greatness	Stephen R. Covey
The 7 Habits of Highly Effective People: Powerful Lessons in Personal Change	Stephen R. Covey
Out of the Darkness: From Turmoil to Transformation	Steve Taylor
The Thin Book of Appreciative Inquiry	Sue Annis Hammond
Quiet: The Power of Introverts in a World That Can't Stop Talking	Susan Cain
Emotional Agility: Get Unstuck, Embrace Change and Thrive in Work and Life	Susan David
Vision, Inspiration, Purpose, Power - Take Action And Discover Your Personal Keys To Success	Susan G. Smith
Fierce Conversations: Achieving success in work and in life, one conversation at a time	Susan Scott
INSTINCT for Graduates: The Power to Unleash Your Inborn Drive and Face Your Unlimited Future	T. D. Jakes
Destiny: Step into Your Purpose	T. D. Jakes
Identity: Discover Who You Are and Live a Life of Purpose	T. D. Jakes
Unlocked: Step into Your Next-Level Moment	T. D. Jakes
Disruptive Thinking: A Daring Strategy to Change How We Live, Lead, and Love	T. D. Jakes
Reposition Yourself: Living Life Without Limits	T.D. Jakes
Surprise: Embrace the Unpredictable and Engineer the Unexpected	Tania Luna, LeeAnn Renninger
Motivated by Passion, Held Back by Fear	Tchicaya Ellis Robertson
Bourdieu on Religion: Imposing Faith and Legitimacy (Key Thinkers in the Study of Religion)	Terry Rey
Leadership and Self-Deception: Getting Out of the Box	The Arbinger Institute
The Outward Mindset: Seeing Beyond Ourselves	The Arbinger Institute
Amplified Bible - AMP 1987 (Includes Translators' Notes)	The Lockman Foundation
Breakout Churches: Discover How to Make the Leap	Thom S. Rainer
I Am a Church Member: Discovering the Attitude that Makes the Difference	Thom S. Rainer
Autopsy of a Deceased Church: 12 Ways to Keep Yours Alive	Thom S. Rainer
Centuries of Meditations - Enhanced Version	Thomas Traherne
True Purpose: 12 Strategies for Discovering the Difference You Are Meant to Make	Tim Kelley
Blueprint for Growth: 21 TRANSFORMATIONAL STEPS TO HELP YOUR CHURCH GROW TO ITS FULL POTENTIAL	Tim King

ABOUT THE AUTHOR

Richard Flew is a practicing UK Chartered Land & Hydrographic Surveyor. He has managed a small business for 30 years, but also turned to writing in 2013.

Despite having no previous authoring experience, he started on TRANSFORMED! This came after a traumatic two year period of church management experience out of which he started to write. He quickly realized that there was not one book that he needed to write, but three.

TRANSFORMED! is the first of the trilogy, including CONNECTED! and FULFILLED!